S0-AZZ-471

Convair B-58

by Jay Miller

The famous stalky landing gear of the B-58 are particularly prominent in this front view of the prototype aircraft, 55-660, seen without an MB-1 free-fall bomb pod during the early days of the flight test program at Convair's Fort Worth, Texas facility.

AEROFAX INC.

Arlington, Texas

HUNTINGTON CITY TOWNSHIP
PUBLIC LIBRARY
255 WEST PARK DRIVE
HUNTINGTON, IN 46750

PUBLISHED BY

AeroFax INC

P.O. Box 120127
Arlington, Texas 76012

COVER PHOTO: *Convair B-58A, 59-2433, in flight over solid cloud cover. Aircraft bears standard markings for type in service with the 43rd BW based at Little Rock AFB, AR in the mid-1960s.*

Copyright © 1985 by Aerofax, Incorporated
All rights reserved.
Printed in the United States of America
Library of Congress Catalog Card Number 85-72441
Library of Congress in Publications Data
Miller, Jay N.
  Convair B-58 *Hustler*
  (Aerograph 4)
  Bibliography: P.131
  1. Convair B-58 (Bomber Aircraft)
  2. Jet Planes, Military
ISBN 0-942548-26-4 Softcover
       0-942548-27-2 Hardcover

European Trade Distribution by —

 Midland Counties Publications

24 The Hollow, Earl Shilton
LEICESTER, LE9 7NA, England
Telephone: (0455) 47256

THE CONVAIR B-58
HUSTLER
by Jay Miller

CONTENTS

USAF via Edwards AFB HO

The aesthetics of the B-58A are readily apparent in this direct side view of 55-665, the sixth B-58A built by Convair, during its Air Research and Development Command days at Edwards AFB, CA. As an early pre-production specimen, this aircraft was not equipped with a tail turret. It served as a flight test article throughout its service life, eventually ending its career on the Edwards photo test range.

Shortly after the successful completion of the XB-58's first flight on November 11, 1956, the crew poses with 55-660. They are (from l. to r.), B. A. Erickson, pilot; Charles Harrison, flight test engineer; and J. D. McEachern, flight test observer and systems specialist.

PREFACE

The story of the development and entry into operational service of the world's first supersonic bomber is one of the most unique in the annals of the United States Air Force. Conveniently for this writer, it is also one of the most perfectly capsulized. From the B-58's nebulous birth in the late 1940's, to the dismemberment of the last stored aircraft at the Military Aircraft Storage and Disposition Center at Davis-Monthan AFB, Arizona in the late 1970's, the B-58's history is one of the few that can be neatly and cleanly packaged, in total, without the nagging concerns of miscellaneous aircraft and odds and ends struggling onward for years after the guts of the program have long since been relegated to the scrapheap.

It is somewhat surprising to this writer that a detailed history of the B-58 has not made it already to the printed page. It was a truly magnificent aircraft, and even more important, it was a precedent-setting bomber that in most cases, from a performance and airframe design standpoint, has yet to be superceded. Convair (now General Dynamics) and its team of engineers, flight test department personnel, and manufacturing and support personnel are deserving of special acclaim for their work on the B-58 airframe; and General Electric is no less deserving of credit for their J79 powerplant efforts.

I hope readers will be pleased with this monographic history. It has been, for me, a labor of love. No aircraft has more directly affected my life-long interest in aviation, and I doubt seriously that any other ever will. . . .

Jay Miller
June '85

ACKNOWLEDGEMENTS

This history of the Convair B-58 is the end result of many years work and the contributions of many individuals. For as long as I can remember, the B-58 has held a particular fascination for me, much of which is unashamedly attributable to its undeniably pleasing aesthetic qualities. During the course of the many years I have spent gathering textual and photographic reference material describing the B-58, many, many people have made contributions that in one form or another, have led inevitably to the book you now are holding in your hands. My only regret is that during the course of the years that so speedily have passed, some of these contributors no longer are with us, and therefore will never see the end product of their efforts.

In particular, I would like to single out a childhood hero, Ray Tenhoff—a college classmate of my father's—who joined the Convair B-58 flight test program in 1959 as a test pilot, and a year later, was killed in the crash of the #30 aircraft, 58-1023. During a one day stint in the spring of 1960, shortly before his last flight, Ray introduced me to the B-58 at Convair's Fort Worth plant. The session included a tour of the company's mile-long production facility and a chance to touch, smell, and see an honest-to-god "Hustler"; when you're twelve years old, things like that make a strong impression, and in this case, one that has lasted for nearly a quarter of a century. I just hope that Ray, wherever he is, takes some pride in this B-58 history . . . .

There have been, of course, many others who have made significant contributions. General Dynamics' efforts on my behalf are of particular note, and I would like to make special mention of the specific company employees who helped: Fred Bettinger (Vice President and Corporate Director of Public Affairs for General Dynamics in St. Louis, who was kind enough to provide leverage whenever and wherever it was most desperately needed); Earl Guthrie; Charles Harrison; J. F. Isabel; Vince Kane; Dave Liebenson (special thanks); J. D. McEachern; Charles Reach (special thanks); Joe Thornton (director of public affairs at General Dynamics' sprawling Air Force Plant 4 facility); Phil Oestricher (present director of flight test operations for the F-16); Bob Weatherall; and Bill Williams (chief photographer for General Dynamics Fort Worth operation for over a quarter-century—his contributions to this book are simply too numerous to mention in this short credit).

Other General Dynamics folks who helped but who are now retired or working for other companies include: Churchill Boger, Jr.; Adolph Burstein (who worked with Frank Davis during the earliest days of delta wing research at Convair and who continued with the company through its B-58 period); Frank Davis (who started with the Convair—then Consolidated Vultee—delta wing program in 1945 and 1946 during the earliest engineering studies calling for a delta wing fighter and who later became president of Convair; Vincent Dolson (who directed the construction program for the first thirteen aircraft); Beryl Erickson (B-58 first flight pilot and director of the B-58 flight test program—due a very special thanks); Harry Hillaker (who was a major B-58 design contributor); Rob Mack (now with Hughes Helicopters and who, as Joe Thornton's predecessor, was kind enough to assist with the photo and information requirements of an earlier, abbreviated, B-58 effort that appeared in "Wings/Airpower" magazine); Helen Mills (who was Frank Davis' secretary during his Convair days); R. W. "Bob" Moller (who was Convair's B-58 program second-in-command for many years); Paul Ondo; Grover "Ted" Tate (a B-58 flight engineer whose insights and introductions played a key role in providing the historically significant details this book contains); Chuck Widaman (who was director of Convair's Eglin AFB B-58 flight test operations); Robert Widmer (who was program director throughout most of the B-58's days on the Convair production lines); and Charles Wilson.

Of the non-General Dynamics folks who contributed to this book, those who should not be forgotten are: the staff of the Air Force Museum, particularly Col. Richard Uppstrom and Wes Henry; the staff of "Air University Review"; David Anderton, fellow author; model manufacturer extraordinaire John Andrews of the Testor Corporation; retired Edwards AFB historian Ted Bear; Russell Blair of "Quick Check" fame; Kearney Bothwell of Hughes Aircraft Company; Tom Brewer, numbers and photo man; Ken Buchanan, unheralded photographer; Erwin J. "Pete" Bulban, long time "Aviation Week & Space Technology" bureau chief; Dave Ciocchi, hard working curator of the Southwest Aerospace Museum; George Cockle, aircraft photographer extraordinaire; Edwards AFB History Office folks, Dick Hallion, Ph.D., fellow author and information source, and Lucille Zaccardi, long time information source (now, unfortunately, retired); Robert Esposito, fellow photographer; Jeff Ethell, noted fellow author; Jim Goodall, future fellow author; Ben Gunther (special thanks for your patience); Alan Hall of "Aviation News"; R. Cargill Hall, Ph.D., fellow author and B-58 authority; Chuck Hansen, resident nuclear weapons expert; Dan Harrington, Ph.D. recently of the SAC Office of History; Marvin Krieger, lighter-than-air authority; Bill Mann, unheralded photographer; Charles Mayer, unheralded photographer; Dave Menard, numbers and photo man; Joe Mizrahi, editor of "Wings/Airpower" magazine; Rick Pavek, semi-hacker and B-58 source person; Chris Pocock, fellow author and token nitpicker; Douglas Robinson, M.D., noted fellow author and renown lighter-than-air authority; Mick Roth, researcher and photographer (special thanks); Don Spering of A.I.R.; John W. R. Taylor, editor, *Jane's All The World's Aircraft*; and Hugh Winkler and the staff of "Air Force Magazine".

Still others whose contributions and efforts remain deeply appreciated are: Don Alberts, Ph.D.; Lance Anderson; Knox Bishop; Richard Bolcer; Christopher Bowie, Ph.D.; Sidney Bremer; Alex Bremer; Olin Brown; Wayne Burr; George and Lee Bracken; Richard Campbell; Rex Carter; Patrick Cherry; Bob Clarke; Michael Clarke; Chandler Coady; Mike Crawford; George Cully; Bart Cusick, III; Don Dupre; James Eastham; E. S. Fraser; James Fruit; Dwight Weber, Charles Howe, Cliff Bushey, Joe Synar, and John Welch, Jr., C.E.O., of the General Electric Company; George Greider; Mike Habermehl; Bill Hale; "Deke" Hall; Richard Hoffman; Terry Horstead; Graham Inglis; Marty Isham; Sonny Jordan; Paul Kahl, Sr.; Craig Kaston; Richard Kierbow; Karl Kornchuk; David Levin; Bob MacDonald; Evan Mayerle; Ron McNeil; Charles Mendenhall; Stephen Miller; Mike Moffitt; Vincent Murone, Chief, Reports Branch, Directorate of Aerospace Safety; Henry Narducci, Ph.D.; S. Nicolaov (special thanks); James Niemeyer; Anthony Olheiser; Andy Perrier; William Polhemus; Lawrence Railing; Bill Reeter; William Reid; Ed Reimard; Randy Riblet; Vic Robinson; Kenneth Ryker; Walter Boyne and Nancy Shaw of the Smithsonian Institution's Naitonal Air & Space Museum; Keith Snyder; Leonard Sugarman; Dan Sweeney; James Thibodeaux, Ltc.; Edwin Turner, M.D.; Eugene Walton (our financial banker); John Williams; and Ed Yingst.

And a word of special thanks to the B-58 Hustler Association (P.O. Box 26058, Fort Worth, Texas 76116—membership dues are $15 per year). It's many loyal members are what this book is *really* all about. . . .

I would be terribly remiss if I failed also to mention several people who have played key roles in my life outside my aviation writing and publishing careers. These are Alvin and Mildred Parker, Lewis and Janet Shaw, Larry and Tehila Miller, Ori Ann Phillips, and last but far from least, the two little urchins who make it all worthwhile, Anna and Miriam Miller.

I would also like to give special thanks to my assistants Gayle Lawson and Barbara Wasson, without whose help this book would still be many months away from publication.

To Susan, the most important of them all, how about a vacation!

Finally, it should be noted that much of the pre-hardware and flight test program portion of this history was referenced from *History of the Development of the B-58 Bomber, Vols. 1 thru 6* by Richard Thomas and A1C Charles Brown (under the auspices of the Historical Division, Information Office, Aeronautical Systems Division), published in November 1965. Acquisition of this once-secret history of the B-58 program was instrumental in the author's decision to forge ahead with this project.

Jeff Ethell collection

Alexander Soldenhoft's A2 (D-1708) was one of many late 1920's German tailless aircraft configurations influencing Alexander Lippisch's interest in tailless aircraft design. Noted German aviator Gottlob Espenlaub flew this aircraft on numerous occasions. Soldenhoft obtained his first official patent for tailless aircraft in 1912.

Chapt. 1:
From Zenonia To Lippisch

The Opel-Sander Rak.1, designed with Alexander Lippisch's assistance and exploited by Fritz von Opel. The small powder rockets were mounted in tubes in the aft end of the fuselage pod. The all wood and fabric aircraft was not equipped with conventional landing gear and thus was designed to be launched from a rail and retrieved via a small ventral skid.

Jeff Ethell collection

The birth of the delta wing configuration, which was eventually to play a key role in the unique performance successes enjoyed by the Convair B-58 and other delta wing aircraft, is directly attributable to the pioneering delta wing research conducted by Dr. Alexander Lippisch of Germany both prior to and during WWII. Lippisch's work, in turn, was an extension of tailless aircraft design studies conducted by numerous aeronautical pioneers who could effectively trace the origins of their thought processes back to one of mother nature's most unusual creations, the flying seed of *Zanonia Macrocarpa*.

Found in the dense equatorial jungles of Indonesia, *Zanonia Macrocarpa*, a vine-like member of the Family *Cucurbitaceae* (which includes cucumbers, watermelons, squash, pumpkins, et.al.), has managed to survive for eons because of the unique adaptation of its seed—which in an environment shorn of even slight breezes, still manages to travel considerable distances from its place of origin.

The seed of *Zanonia Macrocarpa* is, in effect, a flying wing. The vine's propensity for climbing extant plant life, including trees with heights recorded to be in excess of 150', has positively affected its ability to survive. Once it reaches the top of its host, the vine births its kidney-shaped seeds and shortly afterwards drops them one at a time to glide, usually on modestly active thermals, for great distances.

It was this very capability that eventually attracted the attention of several pioneers in aerodynamics, including a German naturalist by the name of Dr. Fredrich Ahlborn. Two Austrian engineers, Igo Etrich and Franz Wels, who had become friends through a mutual interest in aeronautics in 1903, were introduced to *Zanonia Macrocarpa* by Ahlborn while searching for a solution to the mystery of inherent stability in aircraft. Under Ahlborn's influence, they became infatuated with the design of the seed because of the obvious simplicity of its structure and the efficiency of its aerodynamics. In particular, they acquired a fundamental understanding of the seed's swept-back, upward-twisted tips. These provided

aerodynamic washout which effectively decreased the tip angle of incidence and thus provided greatly improved longitudinal stability.

With these facts at hand, Etrich and Wels proceeded to design and develop *Zanonia Macrocarpa* seed-shaped flying scale models, and in 1906, a full-scale man-carrying glider. The latter was flown successfully on numerous occasions and eventually became the foundation for the development of a full-scale powered aircraft. This first powered machine, which followed in 1907, unfortunately did not prove to be particularly successful. After much analysis, Etrich concluded that it needed a larger engine and improved stability. Modification of the 1907 aircraft was then begun.

In 1909, because of his strong interest in Wright-inspired biplane designs, Franz Wels severed his relationship with Igo Etrich and thus dropped out of the picture to pursue other projects. Though displeased by Wels's departure, Etrich continued on his own with the assistance of a mechanic by the name of Karl Illner. Flight testing of the 1907 design, following its modification, was resumed in 1909. Further development of this same airframe, still based on the *Zanonia Macrocarpa* planform was now discontinued and in late 1909, development of a radical new design was initiated.

The new airplane proved significantly more conventional in planform than its predecessor. The seed-shaped wing was retained, but this time, a fairly conventional fuselage and associated tail feathers were attached. The end result was an aircraft that was to have a notable affect on aircraft design that would last until well past the end of WWI. Etrich's creation, later known as the *Taube* (Dove), was a small monoplane that would become one of the most important and most ubiquitous aircraft configurations of the pre-1920 era.

Dr. Alexander Martin Lippisch (b. November 2, 1894) whose introduction to aircraft occurred at Templehof Aerodrome in 1909 when Orville Wright made a public demonstration of the Wright biplane to the German military, had become an assistant aerodynamicist with the Zeppelin-Werke (later the Dornier organization) during WWI. Later, he joined the *Forschungs Institut der Rhone-Rossitten*

Gesellschaft, which was a research center dedicated to the study of glider and sailplane design. There he became technical director of the design section and began to exercise his strong interest in tailless aircraft configurations which had been successfully fueled by the Etrich and Wels studies of several years earlier. His contributions to the designs of several successful institute aircraft later led to the innovative *Lippisch-Espenlaub E 2* of 1921.

During the late 1920's, while working on his successful *Storch* tailless aircraft family (this consisting of an extensive series of sailplanes and powered aircraft under designations spanning from *Storch I* to *Storch 10*) Lippisch began exploring the possibilities of rocket propulsion by designing a series of rocket-propelled glider models. Most of these boasted wingspans of 7' or more, and some weighed in excess of 30 lbs. From these, Lippisch began development of a conventional canard type man-carrying glider and by

Jeff Ethell collection

A model of the Lippisch "Delta I" is seen in flight in 1921. Lippisch built numerous scale models to test his tailless aircraft designs.

Jeff Ethell collection

The full-scale "Delta I" glider is seen in flight in 1930. Almost all of Lippisch's tailless aircraft had vertical surfaces for directional control.

Development of the "Delta I" glider led to a version powered by a single two-cylinder 30-hp Bristol "Cherub" engine.

1929, during the course of an association with Fritz von Opel, had participated in the design, development, and flight test of several manned, rocket-propelled, tailless and canard configurations. Among the latter was the *Ente* (Duck), which became the world's first successful manned, rocket-propelled aircraft. On June 11, 1928, with Fritz Stamer in the cockpit, the *Ente* took to the air for the first time, powered by two 55 lb. thrust solid fuel rockets developed by Alexander Sander. This rudimentary experimentation would bear serious fruit less than ten years later in the form of the highest performance operational aircraft to see combat in WWII.

In the early days of Lippisch's tailless aircraft research, he had reached two important conclusions: for one, he noted that tailless aircraft configurations were not as efficient as conventional aircraft since part of the wing, of necessity, had to be used for stability rather than lift. And for another, he also concluded that the sweepback and twist usually found in tailless designs decreased their maneuverability and magnified their wing structural problems. The latter were particularly critical in high speed aircraft, as stability losses were often the consequence of modest rigidity and associated wing flex and flutter.

In order to conquer the critical problem of rigidity, Lippisch permitted evolutionary processes to dictate what soon became his first delta wing designs. Basically, the delta wing did away with the swept-wing's lack of rigidity by filling-in the space between the swept wing's trailing edge and the aircraft fuselage. In 1929, Lippisch built his first delta-shaped models and by the end of the year, was beginning to explore the possibility of full-scale man-carrying aircraft. This reached fruition in 1930 in the form of the *Delta I* glider, and was followed by a powered conversion of this same aircraft in 1931. The *Delta* configuration was further explored with the unveiling of the *Delta II*,

the *Delta III*, and various permutations of the *Delta IV*.

These early attempts at delta wing design were relatively unsophisticated first-generation studies. Accordingly, they were not pure deltas in the contemporary sense of the word, but rather could be more appropriately referred to as delta-like flying wings. With large spans, thick root sections, swept leading edges, and straight trailing edges, they were generally indistinguishable from the flying wing aircraft then being test flown by the Horten Brothers and a host of other experimenters interested in the attributes of tailless aircraft. Horten aircraft designs had, in fact, generally parallelled those of Lippisch, and in some respects were aerodynamically superior and potentially more utilitarian. The Horten-designed and Gotha-produced Ho-229 (sometimes referred to as the Ho-9) was technologically perhaps the most advanced aircraft to fly during the course of WWII and would have presented a formidable air combat opponent if Nazi Germany had been permitted the indescretion of survival.

During the course of this tumultuous decade, a significant number of Lippisch delta wing aircraft took to the air, each an improvement in one form or another over its predecessor. In January, 1937, Lippisch began design development of a new aircraft under the auspices of the DFS (*Deutsche Forschungs-Anstalt fur Segelflug*). This delta, referred to as the DFS 194, was the progenitor of the Messerschmitt Me-163 rocket-propelled interceptor series and was, in time, to become effectively the critical link between Lippisch's subsonic and transonic aircraft studies.

While exploratory work was being conducted by a series of testbed aircraft, construction of the actual DFS 194 was initiated by DFS under Lippisch's watchful eye. However, because of DFS's limited manufacturing capacity, discussions between Willy Messerschmitt and Lippisch eventu-

ly led to a transfer of personnel and hardware from the DFS establishment in Darmstadt to the Messerschmitt A.G. in Augsburg. The DFS 194 (and little-known DFS 39) went with them.

When the war broke out in September, 1939, the German government dictated that all projects that could not be completed within the space of a year be terminated in order to permit concentration on more necessary war machinery. Unfortunately for Lippisch and his small team, this dictum grossly affected funding for the DFS 194.

As originally built and test flown in 1938, the DFS 194 was powered by a small Argus piston engine that drove a propeller at the rear of the fuselage. Now, in an effort to keep the project alive, if only for a short while, Lippisch and his small team were given a contract by the RLM to convert the DFS 194 from an aerodynamic to a powerplant testbed. Accordingly, they got permission to install an experimental Walter R I-203 liquid fuel rocket engine in place of the Argus. The Walter installation caused little difficulty due to its size, and by August, 1940, test pilot Heini Dittmar was flight testing the aircraft from the famous Peenemunde-West experimental flight test facility.

In flight tests the DFS 194 proved a pleasant aircraft to fly and its performance, including a maximum level flight speed of nearly 342 mph, was exceptional. The success of the flight test program, in fact, was such that it again caught the attention of Luftwaffe commanders. Renewed emphasis was now placed on an advanced, rocket propelled development of the DFS 39/Delta IVC tentatively designated Me163, and in an unusual act of Nazi clemency, it was resurrected. Three Me-163 prototypes that had been under construction at the time of program cancellation were now moved back into the final assembly building at Augsburg, and one was soon completed and readied for flight test. This aircraft was given a variable thrust (331 lbs. to 1,653 lbs.) Walter HWK R II-203b rocket engine and, after suffering through a number of powerplant related delays, was ready to enter flight test in August, 1941.

The prototype Me-163 (V1/KE + SW) took to the air for the first time under the power of its rocket engine on October 2, 1941. With Heini Dittmar at the controls, it rose from the Peenemunde test facility at an extremely high rate of speed and after flying a circuitous route around the field and expending its available fuel supply, touched down on the grass to successfully complete the first flight of an aircraft that would soon play an important, though very short-lived, role in the history of aerial combat; its influence on aerodynamics, however, would be a decidedly different matter . . . .

The operational history of the Messerschmitt Me-163 is beyond the scope of this book to reiterate. Several excellent references exist already, however, (including Jeff Ethel's superb *Komet, The Messerschmitt 163*, Sky Books Press, 1978) and its operational record can be referenced

Jeff Ethell collection

Two views of the Lippisch DFS-194 in its rocket-propelled configuration. Though in his memoirs Lippisch denied the DFS-194 served as a prototype for the later Me-163, the type's physical similarities to the famous German rocket fighter are undeniable. Barely discernible is the jettisonable two-wheel takeoff dolly and the fixed ventral landing skid.

in detail therein. Suffice it to say that it was the first manned delta wing and rocket-propelled combat aircraft in history to achieve operational status, and it was also, until the arrival of Allied post-war high-performance research aircraft such as the Douglas D558-1 and the Bell X-1, unofficially the fastest manned aircraft in the world; on July 6, 1944, an Me-163B, piloted by Heini Dittmar, is recorded to have reached a speed of approximately 702 mph—almost certainly the first manned flight in excess of 700 mph in history, and also the first to legitimately nudge the transonic barrier.

During the course of Me-163 design and development work, Lippisch had become acutely aware of its unforgiving flight characteristics at speeds above its critical Mach number. He was well versed on compressibility phenomenon and the Mach tuck problem (caused by a rearward shift of the wing center of pressure as transonic velocities were approached) noted by several pilots who had exceeded the aircraft's Mach limitations, and he had concluded that one of the few extant solutions to conquering compressibility was the use of a slender body and highly swept wings (the latter being a concept born in the fertile mind of Adolph Busemann, another German aerodynamicist who, in 1937, during the Volta Congress on High Speed Flight held in Milan, Italy, presented a precedent-setting paper on "arrow wings" and their high speed flight attributes). Unfortunately, highly swept wings, though relatively efficient at very high speeds, were terribly inefficient, and in fact potentially unstable, at low speeds. Additionally, they suffered from complex structural design problems caused by the necessary cantilevering of the spar at an angle from the fuselage centerline.

Lippisch's solution was a slender-bodied aircraft with a delta wing that had a chord with approximately the same dimension as its span. Such chord length, he reasoned, would provide a sufficient thickness for structural members even when the thickness/chord ratio was extremely low. Lippisch would later note:

"My arguments to favour the low aspect ratio delta wing were this: our tests with aircraft with different wing sweep configurations had shown that a swept wing with angles larger than 30° sweep showed severe wing tip stall in the low speed range and was therefore quite difficult to handle during takeoff and landing. But in order to penetrate into the transonic speeds and proceed into supersonic flight it was necessary to use a higher wing sweep angle than 30°. Since the aspect ratio became insignificant in the supersonic range it would be advantageous to use a low aspect ratio which made it possible to use sections with a low thickness ratio. This was more important that the aspect ratio since the wave resistance was the major part of the supersonic drag. Subsonic wind tunnel tests with low aspect ratio delta wings at about 60° sweep back had shown that large life coefficients would be obtained without the wing tip stall since the tip vortex stabilized the flow. This observation was in agreement with the early tests of the low aspect ratio wing tested by Charles Zimmerman of the NACA. The large sweep back angle was not only necessary to delay the compressibility effects but it also prevented the large travel of the center of pressure between low speed and high speed as otherwise observed on low aspect ratio wings without sweep back. This was proved by the subsonic-supersonic test of our delta wing model. In short, these were quite basic considerations of the design philosophy of supersonic aircraft...."

Not too long after joining Messerschmitt A.G., Willy Messerschmitt and Lippisch had a disagreement which led to the latter's resignation from the company. Lippisch then moved to become chief of aeronautical research at the *Luftfahrtforschung Wien* (the Aeronautical Research Institute of Vienna), where, with the help of a small team of unpaid assistants, he continued his advanced research work pertaining to supersonic aircraft design.

It was during his tenure at the Vienna institute that Lippisch began the development of his most radical, and as it would turn out, most influential aircraft configurations, the P-12, P-13, and P-14 Projects. Justification for these aircraft had been born out of the difficulties the German military forces were now having in mass producing aircraft in quantity, and in obtaining satisfactory fuels with which to power them. In order to meet the resulting RLM (*Reichsluftfahrtministerium*) requirement, Lippisch concluded that the new aircraft should have a relatively modest high subsonic performance and exceptional fuel efficiency. In order to achieve these objectives, he elected to create an aircraft that utilized an unusually thick wing section, the center section of which conveniently would provide the chamber that would be utilized for propulsive combustion.

This initial design, which later would come to be mistakenly identified as Lippisch's ultimate WWII aircraft design study, was actually the first phase of a projected three phase research program calling for the eventual development of a legitimate supersonic aircraft. The first phase was to be an aerodynamic testbed in the form of a delta wing glider; the second was to be a version of this same glider powered by a turbojet or ramjet engine; and the third was to be a totally new advanced configuration powered by either a rocket or ramjet engine.

The first phase aircraft was designated DM-1 (also referred to as the P-13 aerodynamic testbed) and was basically a glider with the express purpose of exploring the aerodynamic and control characteristics of a pure delta configuration operating at low speeds. The DM-1, in fact, became the first pure delta wing aircraft ever to be built. The leading edge had a 60° sweep angle and the vertical tail surface was so configured as to form the pilot's cockpit and define the configuration of the windscreen. The airfoil, adapted from an NACA airfoil, had a relatively elliptical section developed by a Lippisch assistant, Dr. F. Ringleb. Miscellaneous physical characteristics of the DM-1 included a wingspan of 19'8'', a length of 20'9'' (which also was the root chord), and a height in static position of approximately 11'. The wing taper ratio was 18, there was no wing twist, and the dihedral angle was 6°. The wing trailing edge forward sweep angle was 15°, total wing area was 214 sq.', and the aspect ratio was 1.81. The original weight figures of 660 lbs. empty and 880 lbs. gross were later found to be a bit optimistic; as actually built, the aircraft weighed 825 lbs. empty and 1,012 lbs. gross (at which weight the wing loading was 4.7 lbs./sq.').

Although the wing root section was very thick, the delta platform gave a thickness/chord ratio of only 15% (with maximum thickness occurring at 40% of the chord line). Estimated performance figures included a stall speed of 44.6 mph, a minimum sinking speed of 16.5'/sec., a glide ratio of 1.7, and a terminal velocity dive speed of 347 mph. The control surfaces were true elevons combining in one surface the roll control of ailerons with the pitch control of elevators.

The DM-1 was an all-wood aircraft with conventional ribs, light stringers, a light nose spar, and a rear false spar. The manually retractable tricycle landing gear had differentially actuated brakes and torsional suspension and was extended by gravitational pull and system weight. There also was a 9.5 gallon water tank which permitted the pilot to shift the center of gravity forward or rearward by means of a hand pump. The only instruments were an airspeed indicator and an inclinometer. Though the DM-1 was not a powered aircraft in the conventional sense, a small powder rocket providing 440 to 660 lbs. thrust was mounted in the tail to permit the pilot some landing discretion and also to explore the handling characteristics of the design in a powered condition.

Construction of the DM-1 was nearing completion just as the Third Reich began its final, agonizing capitulation. By this time, a decision had been made to tow-test the new delta, and accordingly, it was being prepared for the first such flight behind a Siebel Si-204 twin-engine light transport (studies were also conducted to determine the feasibility of launching the DM-1 from a dorsal mount atop a mother aircraft) when the allies overtook the Prien facility in Vienna where it was located.

Following his capture, a briefing was given by Lippisch to Dr. Theodore von Kármán, Dr. Hugh Dryden, Maj. Gen. Donald Putt, and other US officials in Paris on May 28, 1945. Allied interest in the project was now kindled and a decision was made to ship the DM-1 to the US for testing. It was then transported by boat to the US, and when finally on American soil, was moved from Wright Field (its first destination) to the NACA facility at Langley, Virginia. There, in 1946, it was run through an abbreviated full-scale wind tunnel program.

The prototype Me-163, KE + SW, is seen immediately prior to a test flight at the famous German Pennemunde flight test facility. The small exhaust nozzle for the Walter rocket engine is visible to the right of the letter W at the base of the vertical fin.

The DM-1 wind tunnel tests, though relatively short-lived, led to a number of interesting conclusions, not the least of which was that the design, from a performance standpoint, was a disappointment. Eight relatively major modifications were incorporated to explore the configuration's full potential. Included were changes to the wing leading edges, the vertical fin, and the elevons and rudder. The initial tunnel tests had indicated a poor lift coefficient at low airspeeds, high drag throughout the envelope, poor directional stability, and other undesirable characteristics. These eventually dictated that a proposed flight test program be abandoned and that the DM-1 be shipped back to Wright-Patterson for storage. It was eventually placed on display at the Air Force Museum. Interestingly, its present whereabouts are unknown.

As mentioned earlier, the DM-1 was just the first phase in a three phase program Lippisch had conceived to explore the performance possibilities of the delta wing in high speed flight. The second phase of his project at the Aeronautical Research Institute was the design and construction of the Project P-13 aircraft to be powered by either a ramjet or turbojet (Junkers Jumo 004B) engine. This aircraft was to have been quite similar to the DM-1, but was to have had a 65° leading edge sweep, a circular, tube-like intake in the nose, a combustion chamber under the pilot (fueled, in one configuration, by coal slurry), and an intended maximum speed of between 500 and 750 mph. Wind tunnel tests of the P-13 revealed a transonic drag coefficient of only .04, scarcely greater than that of conventional aircraft traveling at relatively low subsonic speeds.

The P-13, as Lippisch would later state, was primarily a stop gap aircraft optimized for a last ditch Luftwaffe attempt to stem the tide of the war. It was an immature configuration that did not represent the end result of a conventional evolutionary process, and as a result, it was not nearly the aircraft its proposed successor, the Project P-14 was.

The P-14, or phase 3 of the original Lippisch delta wing aircraft design program, was far and away the most advanced of the three, and truly representative of Lippisch's ultimate fighter.

Though a final powerplant decision was never made, options being considered at the time of the program's demise included a Walter bi-fuel liquid rocket engine of a type similar to that found in the Me-163B, and a Lorin ramjet which Lippisch had studied in some detail.

The P-14, a beautiful blended delta configuration resembling the Douglas F4D *Skyray* of a decade later, was designed to have a maximum speed of 1,215 mph (Mach 1.85) at an altitude of 35,000'. It was indeed an exotic concept for its day, though it never progressed beyond the drawing board/wind tunnel model stage.

Under the auspices of *Operation Paper Clip* and the resultant influx of German engineering data and raw human talent into the US following WWII, Lippisch's research data was brought to the attention of many influential US government and industry representatives. This material, with heavy emphasis being placed on the attributes of the delta wing, generated significant interest in the US and led to comprehensive studies of several of his aircraft.

In particular, the arrival of a war-booty Me-163B at Freeman Field, Seymour, Indiana, on August 10, 1945, heralded the birth of an intensive program to study the possibilities presented by Lippisch tailless and delta wing configurations. The Me-163B, because facsimilies were known to be in limited production in the Soviet Union, proved of significant interest to the US military services. Accordingly, the Air Material Command's Engineering Division at Wright Field recommended complete tests of the aircraft.

Following an airframe and powerplant evaluation that consumed most of September, 1945, a flight test project was initiated on October 5th. In March, 1946, the AMC Flight Test Division called for a reduced test program due to limited instrumentation and a lack of personnel, but the aircraft was shipped to Muroc Army Air Base, California, on April 12, 1946, anyway. On April 30, AMC personnel, Lippisch, and a German test pilot by the name of L. Vogel, went to Muroc to participate in the test program. Following an inspection on May 1, both Lippisch and Vogel determined the Me-163B to be in unsatisfactory condition for powered flight test work. Unpowered flight tests, using a tow launching technique, were then conducted, these leading to the conclusion that "the Me-163B is a highly maneuverable airplane possessing unusually good stability and control characteristics, especially for a tailless design".

In the meantime, Bell Aircraft Corporation had gotten wind of the Me-163B's existence and had requested permission to analyze the aircraft at its facilities near Buffalo, New York. Following the completion of the abbreviated Muroc tests, the aircraft was transported to the Bell plant and there placed on loan under a bailment agreement. Bell's tests were completed in November, 1946, and on January 16, 1947, the Me-163B project was officially closed.

Most of Lippisch's design studies and ideas had come with him when he arrived in the US in February, 1946, under the auspices of *Operation Paperclip*. Following a year at Wright Field near Dayton, Ohio, he was transferred to the Naval Air Material Center near Philadelphia, Pennsylvania, where he stayed until 1950. After several years of government service, he entered the private sector and went to work for the Collins Radio Company near Cedar Rapids, Iowa. During his later years he continued to work as a consultant on a number of aircraft related programs, and in 1966 he founded Lippisch Research Corporation. He died on February 11, 1976, taking with him an extensive legacy of work that is now recognized as the basis for all pure delta wing design studies extant today.

Bell Aerospace Textron

This war-booty Me-163A was shipped to Wright Field immediately after its acquisition at the end of the war. From there it was loaned to Bell Aircraft Corporation of Buffalo, New York for a detailed technical examination. Though essentially flightworthy, it was flown only as a tow-launched glider.

USAF via Jeff Ethell collection

The DM-1 is seen as it appeared at Wright Field in 1946, and immediately prior to its being transferred to the NACA for full-scale wind tunnel testing. This aircraft is considered to be the first true delta wing aircraft ever to reach the full-scale hardware stage.

Chapt. 2:
Designing With Deltas

One of the earliest P-92 studies was this V-tailed configuration powered by several small rocket engines and a single ramjet. The swept wing eventually design-transitioned into a delta configuration.

The first pure delta wing aircraft actually to fly was the Convair XF-92A. Developed as an aerodynamic testbed for the stillborn XP-92 interceptor, it is seen landing at Edwards AFB in the early 1950's.

Lippisch and his German peers were not, of course, the only engineers and aircraft designers to have begun exploring the promise of the delta wing configuration. The fundamental aerodynamic requirements of operating an aircraft at speeds in the vicinity of supersonic velocities had led to an indigenous US research effort as early as 1944, and by 1947, this had blossomed into the transonic research aircraft program that gave birth to the world's first supersonic-capable manned aircraft, the Bell Aircraft Corporation Model 44—more commonly known as the X-1.

Though the science of supersonic flight was still in its infancy, the NACA, by 1947, had projected several promising solutions to the transonic drag problem: (1) thin wings with a thickness/chord ratio of between 8 and 10 percent; (2) swept wings, extending either forward or rearward from the fuselage; (3) low aspect ratio wings; and (4) high speed fuselage profiles. Each of these was assigned to a given service for exploration, with the Air Force responsible for the first and second, the Navy the second and third, and the NACA the fourth. Control, stability, structural integrity, and powerplant development were incorporated into each, with the total program oriented toward a successful solution to the question of supersonic flight.

On October 14, 1947, the myth of the "sound barrier" disappeared in the exhaust gases of the number-one Bell X-1, and the US aerospace industry began in earnest to explore the possibilities posed by the world's first manned flight at supersonic speeds. By the early 1950's, the NACA, as well as various US and foreign aircraft manufacturers, had produced voluminous data on supersonic flight and control. In general, it was concluded supersonic configurations demanded thin airfoil sections, exceptional fuselage fineness ratios (a figure derived by dividing the length of the fuselage by its diameter), and powerful engines. Each of these items served to help overcome transonic and supersonic drag.

The delta-shaped wing planform proved of particular interest as it had been discovered through research that its shape was innately suitable for reducing drag at high speed. A body, at the speed of sound, produces a conical shock wave, the

angle of which is a function of the Mach number of the body. For example, at a speed of Mach 1.2, the cone is at an angle of 55° with the axis of the body, while at Mach 2.0, the cone is at a 30° angle. Consequently, to escape the wave drag created by the intersection of the cone with the surface of the aircraft, the wings must be swept more than 35° for Mach 1.2 flight, and more than 60° for speeds of Mach 2 or more. The faster the aircraft moves, the greater the sweep must be to avoid a precipitous increase in wave drag. For angles of sweep greater than 45°, the wing trailing edge is characterized by a single notch; however, to minimize the high torsional loads placed on heavily swept wings, it was found expedient to fill in the notch permitting the use of the entire trailing edge for control surfaces. This, in turn, eliminated the need for an empennage section and its associated horizontal stability and control surfaces and concomittantly created the rationale for the delta wing planform.

The second way to alleviate wave drag—use of low aspect ratio wings—was indicated by an occurrence known as "tip relief". This showed the desirability of bringing the wingtip in towards the wing root as close as possible. When a shock wave is formed over a conventional straight wing, it moves with increasing speed toward the wing tip. This increase in velocity is due to the progressively lower thickness/chord ratio toward the tip. Since a shock wave produces compression, and since the flow around the tip from lower to upper surfaces also acts as a system which increases pressure in that particular area, the latter phenomenon tends to diminish the force of the shock. This is called "tip relief", and the bringing of the wing tips in toward the wing root results in wings of low aspect ratio. The delta wing, because of its inherently large sweep angle, provides a comparatively small span in relation to its chord, and is consequently a planform with a low aspect ratio.

The difficulties encountered with ensuring the structural integrity of low aspect ratio wings led to an increased interest in the delta wing. The delta wing, because of its inherent low aspect ratio and consequent large numerical root thickness in proportion to its span, provided ample room in

which to contain a substantial spar thickness. This attribute led to its consideration for a number of proposed supersonic aircraft projects, including that of the forthcoming B-58.

One of the foremost US proponents of the delta wing, Robert T. Jones of the NACA, had initiated studies of supersonic delta configurations mid-way through WWII. In May, 1945, he had presented several theoretical papers on the subject that included data showing that the drag acting upon a delta wing at supersonic speeds is proportional to the square of the lift coefficient. This showed that it was desirable to use a very thin profile and to operate the delta at very high speeds where the low lift coefficient could be most efficiently utilized. From that, he went on to note that the leading edge of the delta wing must be swept 15° to 20° greater than the Mach angle of the desired flight speed in order to obtain reasonable drag values (technically speaking, the lift curve slope of the delta is a function of the ratio of the tangent of the apex angle to the tangent of the Mach angle; consequently, as the apex angle approaches and becomes greater than the Mach angle, the lift coefficient of the delta wing becomes equal to that of a two-dimensional supersonic airfoil moving at the same Mach number; when a delta wing is behind the Mach cone, a large suction force is generated at the leading edge; the suction disappears when the leading edge passes through the Mach cone and the resultant force has to become normal to the plate surface).

Wind tunnel tests conducted by the NACA pointed to the desirability of using a rounded leading edge (Lippisch had made the same discovery and had incorporated it in the leading edge of the DM-1). This improved the lift coefficient of the wing which in fact peaked at 35° for a bi-convex section and at 38° for a conventional section.

One of the great unknowns of the delta wing during the early 1950's was its controllability. Though significant research had been conducted, there were still many questions, and only a few full-scale studies available for reference. One of the more critical problems concerned the delta's necessary high angle of attack to maintain lift during low speed flight. This implied serious dif-

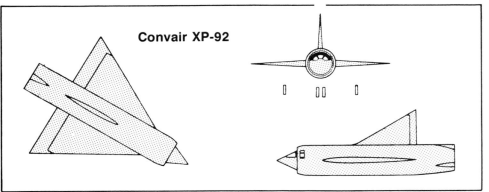

Convair XP-92

ficulties during takeoff and landing, and also problems in efficient cruise requirements. It also was known, from some of the limited full-scale research information available, that there were large variations in drag with lift which made a delta quite difficult to trim. When a delta wing was trimmed to fly at the lift coefficient corresponding to the minimum glide angle, it was found that the response to the deflection of the elevators was erratic. On a conventional aircraft, a downward deflection of the elevator on a final approach increased the glide angle, while an upward deflection decreased it. An opposite effect occurred with a delta wing aircraft. A downward deflection brought about an initial increase, but this was immediately followed by a gradual flattening of the glide angle as the aircraft approached its new trim angle. The upward deflection, on the other hand, initially resulted in a flattening of the glide angle, but in a few moments this was followed by an increase in or steepening of the glide angle.

As a result of these unique trim effects, the delta wing trimmed at a lift coefficient that was much lower than that which provided the most desirable glide angle. Furthermore, trim conditions of the delta varied widely from conventional aircraft which generally attained their minimum glide angle at near-stall angles of attack. These trim conditions were believed to be caused by an unsteady flow of air over the wing. This flow over the leading edge separated and formed two vortices which rotated downward at the center of the wing and upward from the wing tips.

The damping and roll characteristics of the delta configuration also presented a source of difficulty. The delta produced a high rate of roll due directly to its poor damping during a roll condition. The delta configuration exhibited a lateral stability just so long as the lift coefficient remained low, but when the coefficeint rose above a fairly low value, the configuration became laterally unstable.

The pitching moment remained stable when the aspect ratio was low. This showed that a 45° delta should not have an aspect ratio greater than 3.0, while a 60° delta should have an aspect ratio of about 1.0. Within such limits, the delta could be controlled longitudinally up to the stall point, but this did not hold for lateral control. Both German, and later, US research showed that a spanwise flow out from the center of a delta wing near the trailing edge increased the lift due to a lowering of the pressures in that area, consequently producing a peculiar discontinuity in the lift curve. In view of that, it could be seen that the span load distribution of a delta planform was extremely sensitive to the lift coefficient due to these flow peculiarities.

All of these problems led to the conclusion that the delta wing had some serious shortcomings. Most researchers agreed, however, that the delta had the greatest potential of any conventional wing configuration for the least drag at Mach numbers between 1.0 and 1.4. Above 1.4, it was assumed

that virtually the entire wing would be enveloped in supersonic flow and that it would not be possible to alleviate the resulting difficulties.

In August, 1945, the Army Air Force Assistant Chief of Air Staff released interim requirements calling for three types of fighter aircraft. One was for an interceptor, one was for a penetration fighter, and one was for an all-weather fighter. Of the three, the interceptor requirement proved of greatest interest to the Consolidated Vultee aircraft company (which, by now, was usually referred to as Convair) and accordingly, a design development program based on the 50,000' altitude specification (formally released on November 23, 1945) was initiated in-house.

On March 11, 1946, the Air Materiel Command (AMC) Headquarters wrote Authority for Purchase (AFP) No. 431491, requesting that Convair be issued a letter contract for Phase I studies. Numerous changes were made during the negotiations and other AFP's were eventually written. However, Contract No. W33-038-ac-14547, which was assigned as a result of the original AFP, was retained. Consolidated representatives signed this letter contract, for $5,300,000, on June 25, 1946. This agreement provided for both Phase I and Phase II studies with the latter to cover design, development, and construction of two tactical aircraft, one skeleton or static test article, one full-scale mock-up, and necessary engineering data. It was approved on June 28, 1946, by Col. H. A. Shepard, Deputy Chief of the Procurement Division. In January, 1947, the AMC prepared a definitive contract which was signed by contractor representatives subject to certain changes. Numerous revisions were subsequently made, but no satisfactory definitive contract was agreed upon. The letter contract was amended extensively. One late amendment replaced the static test article with a full-size flying model, designated by Convair as the Model 7-002.

By the time of contract signing, the proposed interceptor was to be a single-seat, land-based, rocket-propelled fighter aircraft designed to operate close to its home base as a last line of defense. To perform its mission, it would have to reach combat altitude in a very short time and would have to be directed to the vicinity of the target from the ground because of its limited endurance. In effect, the new interceptor was to be a nonexpendable, inhabited missile with a pilot guiding it to its airborne target. Since the aircraft would be inhabited, it could be returned to its base.

At Convair the main responsibility for Project MX-813, now referred to by the company as the Model 7, rested with Jack Irvine, Chief Engineer; Frank W. Davis, Assistant Chief Engineer (and later president of Convair); Ralph H. Schick, chief aerodynamicist; and Adolph Burstein, chief technical engineer (also in charge of the company's advance design and technical groups). The original response to the Air Force RFP (request for proposal) was a configuration based on

a transonic bomber being proposed by Convair to the Air Force (which evolved into the GEBO program, as we shall see). In its modified and miniaturized form as an interceptor, it incorporated a 45° swept wing, a V-tail, and a bicycle landing gear supplemented by a droppable takeoff gear. Propulsion (a relative unknown in the then still-mysterious world of supersonic flight) was to be supplied under contract W33-038-ac-20061 by the Reaction Motors Company (dated February 26, 1948 for $824,960; the date discrepancy is due to the fact that the AF Procurement Division had strong reservations about working with financially troubled Reaction Motors at the time, and in fact, delayed commitment to the contract for almost two years) and was to consist of fifteen 50 lb. thrust rocket engines (fueled by liquid oxygen and gasoline) mounted in a duct which would serve as the combustion chamber for the supersonic speed-sustaining ramjet. As a ramjet, the rocket engines would serve as flame holders. Four 1,500 lb. thrust rockets, fueled by liquid oxygen and a water-alcohol mixture, were mounted evenly around the exhaust nozzle and were to be used for takeoff and climb propulsion with the ramjet taking over as supersonic velocities and an altitude of 50,000' were reached. In addition, there also was a Westinghouse 19XB turbojet that would provide accessory system power and also propulsion for powered landings.

Later attempts to rectify and simplify problems with this propulsion system resulted in a variety of powerplant configuration studies being explored. Included was a final design consisting of three 4,000 lb. thrust rockets in place of a combination of 4,000 lb. thrust and 1,500 lbs. thrust rockets (which, in turn, had taken the place of the original concept of fifteen 50 lb. thrust and four 1,500 lb. thrust rockets). Additionally, the Westinghouse 19XB jet engine, which in the interim had been replaced by a Westinghouse 24-C jet engine, was dropped and replaced by a single reciprocating Offenhauser engine that would serve to drive all accessories and the internal rocket pump!

Several small wind tunnel models of the Model 7, (also known in-house at Convair as the Model VF-4516) which in early 1946, was officially allocated the Air Force's XP-92 designator, were built for testing at Convair's Downey, California facility under the first phase of the two phase contract. The first phase, as mentioned earlier, was to cover the research, construction, and test of the wind tunnel models, and the design, engineering data, and construction of the mock-up. The second phase was to cover the design, development, testing, static testing, and engineering data of two full-scale prototypes through initial flight test.

Construction of the full-scale mock-up got underway shortly after contract signing. Wind tunnel testing was subsequently initiated at the NACA Ames Aeronautical Laboratory, the NACA facility in Cleveland, Ohio, and the Co-op Tunnel and Guggenheim Aeronautical Laboratory at the University of California.

Following the contract award, Convair granted permission to the Air Force to wind tunnel test one of two XP-92 models that had been shipped to Wright Field prior to the final contract decision. The results of the ensuing tunnel tests were disappointing as it was immediately apparent that the design had a serious tip stall problem at angles of attack as low as 5°, and that lateral control was substandard. It was concluded that an entirely new design would have to be created to overcome these difficulties and consequently, on July 5, 1946, Davis, Schick, and Burstein, along with a number of other Convair engineers, began exploring the characteristics of other wing planform options, including a delta wing with a 60° leading edge sweep angle.

It was at this point, in the summer of 1946, that Alexander Lippisch and an associate by the name of F. Ringleb, were invited to examine Convair's proposal. Both aerodynamicists were then in residence at Wright Field near Dayton, Ohio, and it thus became necessary for a Convair representative to be sent there for consultation. Lippisch was still under tight government control at that time and his access to security related matters was kept to a minimum. Schick was chosen to make the trip to Dayton. Lippisch, in a letter to Richard Thomas dated March 26, 1963, would later recall:

"While I was in Wright Field Mr. Schick from Convair came there in the summer of 1946 to discuss the layout for a new fighter design competition of the Air Force. The people of Convair made a kind of morphological study of a large number of different layouts. They had prepared a long sheet of all these layouts with the different alternatives listed on the right hand side of the sheet and the overall drawings of the layouts on the left hand side. Mr. Schick wanted to discuss these different projects with me to get my opinion which one of those I would select as the most favorable one. Among these was a delta wing layout, and I finally succeeded in convincing Mr. Schick that this delta design did present the best chances for an advanced design. I showed him our measurements and the basic philosophy behind the low aspect ratio delta as a solution for a supersonic aircraft."

"At these discussions my assistant, Dr. F. Ringlem was also present together with Lt. Robizeck. We did not talk about the fuselage arrangements since the discussion centered about the basic layout problems: high aspect ratio against low aspect ratio, the large swept back angle, and the question of low speed and high speed flight characteristics."

Schick made a number of written and mental notes during the several meetings that were conducted over a period of several days, and shortly afterwards, returned to Downey with his information.

In October, 1946, Lippisch, Dr. Rudolph Hermann, and two other engineers traveled to the west coast to hold discussions with personnel from several of the aircraft companies located there. During the course of this trip they again met with Convair's Schick, who was accompanied by the company's primary delta wing proponent, Burstein. Unfortunately, due to the security restraints that, between Schick's trip to Dayton and Lippisch's trip to Downey, had been placed on the XP-92 project, the amount of detail Schick and Burstein could relate to Lippisch was limited.

Some recommendations that eventually proved of benefit to the XP-92 (and later, XF-92A) program were forthcoming, however, and these helped solidify Convair's stand on the delta wing planform.

Not surprisingly, the delta wing recommendation made by Lippisch during his meetings with Schick only served to underscore conclusions that already had been reached by Burstein based on his own calculations and the problems the Convair design team was having with its initial swept wing design decisions. By the fall of 1946, Convair was proceeding on its own without the assistance of any outside consultation. The XP-92 design was still evolving, however, and serious design changes were in the offing. Perhaps the most important of the latter was the result of concern over the aircraft's still-extant tail surfaces. At this point, various configurations had been studied and none had cured the various instability problems.

Interestingly, the earliest subsonic wind tunnel test had shown that the initial configuration was unstable unless the V-type tail surfaces were removed. This major revelation now proved the birthing at Convair of the delta wing. The results of the tailless delta wind tunnel tests had made sense to Burstein, who had spent many hours analyzing the NACA data. Convinced that the configuration was ideal for supersonic flight, he further concluded that the delta's inherent rigidity provided the requisite strength demanded of a high performance aircraft, and that its high maximum wing depth-to-span ratio would also lead to a lightweight structure. More importantly, however, was the fact that Burstein had also concluded that the delta wing was inherently controllable and stable if proper control surfaces were developed for it. Elevons, though not particularly new or unusual, were discovered to provide good supersonic control because of the ratio of flap to total chord. Burstein and his associates recognized that this also was a solution to control loss at high speeds.

Conveniently, the inherent rigidity of the delta wing minimized aeroelastic effects while providing a naturally strong structure. The latter made it easily adaptable to hydraulically-actuated irreversible control actuation systems—which, though new and relatively untried at this time, were considered absolutely necessary for moving the control surfaces in a high-q (high dynamic force) environment.

Best of all, the delta wing was an eminently simple structure and had a natural large internal volume permitting an exceptional fuel capacity. It involved a minimum of potentially troublesome components, and the control surfaces (elevons) were dual purpose.

In early June, 1946, once the delta wing configuration had been determined by Burstein to be the most suitable for the interceptor proposal, additional studies were undertaken to explore the various wing sweep and airfoil options. Preliminary work had fortified Burstein's belief that the delta offered excellent drag characteristics at transonic speeds, and by November, 1946, field studies prepared by the company had indicated that the peak drag coefficient for a 60° delta was only .048 compared with .072 for a delta of equal area with a sweep of only 45°. Eventually, Convair would devote more than 5,000 hours of wind tunnel time to exploring the delta wing's unique aerodynamic characteristics.

The resultant XP-92 interceptor had a wing with a 60° swept leading edge, a wing area of 425 sq.', a triangular vertical fin and rudder with a total area of 52 sq.', a length of 38'4'', a height of 17'3'', and a span of 31'3''. The NACA developed airfoil was designated 651-006.5 and had a thickness/chord ratio of 6.5%. Maximum design speed was estimated to be Mach 1.75 (approx. 1,165 mph) at 50,000' and maximum duration at that speed and altitude was expected to be 5.4 minutes. The fuel complement was normally 1,139 gals. internally and 575 gals. externally in each of two fuel tanks suspended from wing pylons. The latter were to provide fuel during the ascent stage of a mission only. Design weight was 18,850 lbs., takeoff weight was 29,050 lbs., empty weight was 10,125 lbs., combat weight was 18,850 lbs., and combat wing loading was 44.5 lbs. per sq.'

The XP-92's armament complement was to be four T-31 (M-23) 20mm cannon (213 rounds ea.) installed around the circular "shock diffuser", or intake spike, which also accommodated the pressurized cockpit and single crew member. Emergency jettison problems caused by this unusual placement were never fully overcome, but it was determined that the entire spike would be ejected during an emergency and the pilot would, in turn, extricate himself from the parachute-stabilized capsule and use a back pack, once the spike had stabilized during descent.

Among its other radical features, the XP-92 also incorporated a rather unorthodox undercarriage arrangement. Because of the wide disparity between its takeoff and landing weights (due to the planned high fuel consumption rate) and the resultant need for a hefty landing gear during takeoff

The XP-92 interceptor was an extraordinarily radical design for its day. Optimized for the point interceptor mission, it was exceptionally simple and physically, quite small. The aircraft reached the full-scale mock-up stage in 1948, prior to cancellation. Visible in the left photo are the small ports for the nose spike-mounted cannon. Note also the port on the outside of the intake to accommodate pilot vision requirements.

NASA via Dick Hallion

One of numerous wooden wind tunnel models built to permit testing of the XF-92A's low speed aerodynamic characteristics. Of particular note on this model is the flat surface windscreen, the rather unusual airfoil shape, and the rounded wing leading edge.

USAF via Dick Hallion

XF-92A publicity photo taken at Edwards AFB during the spring of 1949. The short exhaust nozzle and associated fairing are noteworthy.

but a nominal landing gear during landing, a two-component landing gear system was devised. Fully loaded the XP-92 would utilize a takeoff cart during taxi and takeoff. This unit, mounting no less than eight wheels and tires in four pairs, was designed to brake itself after the XP-92 had become airborne. For landing, the aircraft was equipped with a light, retractable tricycle gear of conventional configuration.

Work on the XP-92 design, including wind tunnel testing and the firing of six rocket-propelled ⅛th scale models, was undertaken in late 1946 and throughout 1947. Under NACA contract RA 1452, the models were launched from the NACA's Wallops Island, Virginia facility. The first such launch was consummated on November 7, 1947. A Monsanto ACL-1 rocket motor was used as a booster, and a 5'' HVAR rocket motor, shortened to 17'', was used as a sustainer. An eight-channel telemeter transmitted longitudinal, lateral, and normal acceleration, control hinge moments, control position, angle of attack, total pressure, and a reference static pressure. The elevons were actuated in flight by a compressed-air system to produce a series of abrupt pull-ups and push-downs at a frequency of one cycle in 1.2 seconds. The flight proved a failure, though it did reveal that the basic XP-92 design suffered from longitudinal instability. Modifications to the design, including extending the nose, led to success in the five following flights.

Two additional rocket-propelled model tests would also take place in 1950, one of these exploring the aerodynamics of a faired nose, and the other exploring the aerodynamics of the large, external compression nose inlet. The former was launched by a double *Deacon* booster and achieved a Mach number of 1.70; the latter was launched by a single *Deacon* booster and achieved a Mach number of 1.45.

In February, 1948 work on a full-scale XP-92 mock-up was completed and on April 20-23, Air Force and Convair teams congregated at the company facility in Downey to undertake a detailed mock-up review.

In August, 1947, the Aircraft and Weapons Board had decided that no interceptor fighter would be procured and that only experimental quantities of the XP-92 would be completed. These were to be used for research purposes. Meanwhile, it appeared that Consolidated was going to finish building the first airframe approximately ten months before the rocket powerplants would become available. It was suggested that perhaps the Reaction Motors XLR-11-RM-5, already available, might be used to power the XP-92

following minor modifications. Convair's fears of significant program cost increases eventually killed the proposal, however.

In June, 1948, the Director of Research and Development, Headquarters AMC, recommended to the Deputy Chief of Staff, Materiel, that the XP-92 project be partially terminated. The estimated cost of the project had now increased to $16,243,000 and much development work remained. The AMC recommended that the two XP-92 interceptors be cancelled but that work on the Model 7-002 be continued. On August 5, 1948, the Los Angeles Procurement Field Office was told to end the project.

Lengthy negotiations were carried out concerning the termination. A figure of $4,542,068.31 was finally settled upon as the total estimated cost of the contract, including work which was to continue. As of March 1, 1949, the revised XP-92 program included (1) a flying mock-up and the flight test program for it; (2) continued powerplant research and development program; (3) an aerodynamic research program; (4) engineering data; (5) one tactical mock-up; and (6) the portion of the tactical aircraft not terminated.

In December, 1948, the NACA had said that it did not consider the XP-92 design to be a representative supersonic configuration because the diameter of the fuselage was large compared to the wing span. Previously, during the April 1948 mock-up inspection, the AMC's Flight Test Division had concluded that ''the aircraft in its present configuration is highly impractical for any use other than a research aircraft''

XP-92A

In November, 1946, the Air Force, in an austerity move dictated by a shortage of research funds, approved construction of a single Model 7-002/XP-92A ''flying mock-up'' (in order to distinguish the Model 7-002 from the Model 7/XP-92, the Air Force had assigned the XP-92A designator to the new aircraft; three serial numbers were allocated—46-682/683/684—but only the first was used; also, it is interesting to note that, according to Convair records, 7002 was also the company accounting department's work order number for the project). The XP-92A, from a powerplant standpoint, was not representative of the actual Model 7 (XP-92) mixed-propulsion interceptor, but rather was a testbed created to explore the relatively unknown full-scale flight characteristics of a 60° delta wing. Accordingly, it was to be powered by a conventional turbojet engine and was to be simple in terms of construction technique and materials.

The XP-92A contract called for completion of the aircraft in the shortest possible time. It also called for the use of available materials and it was not required that existing specifications be met. Because of these liberal specs it was decided to use, wherever possible, extant hardware from cannibalized aircraft. Accordingly, the landing gear was obtained from a North American FJ-1; the hydraulic system and engine (Allison J33-A-21) were from a Lockheed P-80; the tailpipe and ejection seat were from a Convair XP-81; the nose landing gear was from a Bell P-63; and the control stick and master brake cylinder were from a Consolidate Vultee BT-13.

During 1947, while problems with the XP-92 interceptor continued to mount, construction of the single Model 7-002 progressed without complication. The basic design had by now been frozen and the airframe completion schedule called for a mid-summer delivery date. Length was 42'5'', wingspan was 31'3'', and height was 17'8''. Preliminary gross weight estimates established a figure of approximately 15,000 lbs. Fuel capacity was 300 gallons.

Unfortunately, during the summer of 1947, Convair's Downey operation was terminated due to company economic difficulties and all assets of the facility, including the XP-92A, were moved to San Diego. The move caused a minor delay in the completion of the airframe, but by fall, sans engine, it was ready for delivery to the NACA Ames Aeronautical Laboratory facility at Moffett Field south of San Francisco for full-scale wind tunnel tests in the Ames 40' x 80' tunnel.

By the time it was officially completed on November 4, 1947, the XP-92A, assigned AF serial number 46-682, and by this time under the engineering guidance of new project engineer Thomas Hemphill, differed significantly from its aborted rocket/ramjet interceptor sibling. Though the wing remained essentially unchanged in terms of square footage and airfoil section, all other aspects of the airframe were totally new. The vertical fin, for instance, was enlarged to provide 76 sq.' of area. Most importantly, the cockpit had become significantly more conventional and was mounted in the fuselage. This location led to bifurcation of the intake ducting several feet to the rear of the circular inlet. Additionally, a conventional canopy and windscreen were mounted over the cockpit, permitting the pilot an excellent view.

The XP-92A also incorporated the very first totally hydraulically-boosted irreversible flight control system ever flown. This unit permitted operation of the aircraft at high subsonic Mach numbers where control forces would normally be too high for a conventional manual system. Control surfaces consisted of a conventional rudder and elevons (providing both differential and symmetrical deflection).

Following departure by ship on November 4, 1947, the full-scale wind tunnel tests at NACA Ames took place between December 6 and December 24, and consisted of some 96 tunnel runs. The results were encouraging and a decision was made to return the aircraft to San Diego for engine and powerplant instrumentation installation.

The XP-92A was returned to San Diego by the Navy carrier *Boxer* on January 12, 1948, and was immediately transported to the Convair plant. Several months were consumed by the engine installation, but finally, on April 1, the aircraft was delivered to the Air Force facility at Muroc dry lake, about ninety miles northeast of Los Angeles.

Convair test pilot Ellis D. "Sam" Shannon had been chosen as chief test pilot for the XP-92A flight test program. In late May, the initial taxi trials were undertaken, and on June 9, during the fifth taxi test series, Shannon and the XP-92A became airborne for the first time. At 180 mph, an altitude of between 10' and 15' was attained over a distance of about two miles.

The two Convair test pilots assigned to the XP-92A flight test program, Shannon and William Martin, continued making the short hops back and forth across the 7-mile-long Muroc dry lake during the following two-and-a-half months. Finally, on September 18, 1948, again with Shannon at the controls, the XP-92A completed its first legitimate flight. The 18-minute mission around the Muroc facility was concluded without incident. Shannon, in fact, noted that "the control characteristics were satisfactory and that there were no discernible undesirable features".

The initial hops were followed by a decision to install a 5,200 lb. th. Allison J33-A-23 engine in place of the original -21, and along with it, a new exhaust pipe and a suitably modified tail cone. Additionally, the original clear bubble canopy was replaced by a "high speed" canopy that was structurally stronger but significantly more restrictive in terms of pilot vision.

With the demise of the XP-92 interceptor program in mid-1948, a decision was made to realign the XP-92A's test objectives in order to relieve it of development testing chores. It thus became purely a testbed for the delta wing planform and no longer a prototype for the now defunct interceptor.

Following installation of the -23 engine, the aircraft was returned to flight test status. On February 19, 1949, with Shannon once again at the con-

trols, the XP-92A took to the air over Muroc, completing a thirty minute mission without incident. Shannon's only complaint concerned a lag in the response of the hydraulic system to the stick and rudder signals. This problem would, in fact, haunt the XP-92A throughout its flight test career.

Some ten flights had been completed by year's end, including several consummated at the hands of Bill Martin. In early 1949, Convair undertook preliminary trials exploring delta flight characteristics during takeoff, climb, cruise, and landing, and at a later date, also explored the effects of cut-off elevons.

On May 20, 1949, following completion of most of the contractor's obligations under Phase I testing, the aircraft, as the XF-92A (the new designator resulting from an AF update of its designator alphabet; all "P for Pursuit" aircraft were redesignated "F for Fighter"—among other changes) officially was turned over to the Air Force.

Shannon and Martin continued to fly the aircraft following the turnover, and in August, 1949, they undertook a dive program to explore its flight characteristics at its critical Mach number. This was completed uneventfully, resulting in a maximum speed of Mach .925 being achieved without encountering any adverse control effects.

The Air Force now took over the XF-92A for Phase II testing and began exploring its stability and control characteristics out to speeds of just over Mach 1. Capt. Charles E. "Chuck" Yeager and Maj. Frank K. "Pete" Everest were assigned the task of completing the XF-92A Phase II requirements, which were initiated following a September 7th safety inspection, on October 17, 1949, with an uneventful first flight by Yeager.

Yeager and Everest officially completed Phase II flight test activity on December 28, 1949. The airplane remained active in the AF flight test stable, however, serving to introduce a number of pilots to the attributes and unique flight characteristics of delta wing aircraft. Many anomalies were noted by these pilots, not the least of which was the delta wing's rather unusual resistance to stalling. Unlike conventional aircraft, no abrupt nose pitch down was attainable with the wing in a stalled condition—only a rather rapid increase in the sink rate. Additionally, the XF-92A could not be spun. This characteristic had been noted during spin tunnel tests of models in the NACA Langley spin tunnel, but it remained no less disconcerting to pilots who tried to get the aircraft in a spin during actual flight testing. NACA Langley studies had concluded that a significant rearward c.g. shift (to 30% of the mean aerodynamic chord) would suffice to permit the XF-92A to be spun, but

unfortunately, such a change would also render the airplane longitudinally unstable and thus unfit for conventional flight.

From the beginning of the flight test program, the XF-92A had been plagued with the problem of being underpowered. Accordingly, during the course of Phase II testing, the AF released funding to Convair to retrofit the aircraft with a more powerful engine in the form of an Allison J33-A-29 with afterburner. It was calculated this retrofit, providing a net thrust increase of 3,250 lbs. over the older J33-A-23's maximum of 4,250 lbs., would permit it to explore it's full performance potential, including level flight speeds out to .98 Mach at 35,000'.

An attempt by Yeager to deliver the XF-92A by direct flight to San Diego for the J33-A-29 installation was quickly terminated by an engine failure shortly after takeoff from Edwards AFB. The power loss occurred at an altitude of only twenty feet, and though Yeager managed to walk away for the ensuing successful gear-up landing, the XF-92A was seriously damaged. This led to a slightly delayed delivery by truck in mid-May of 1950.

The XF-92A was to spend a year at Convair's San Diego facility undergoing modification and was not returned to Edwards until early July, 1951. Two weeks later, on July 20, again with Yeager at the controls, the XF-92A became airborne for the first time since modification. Further flight tests, utilizing the piloting services of Yeager and another AF pilot, Maj. Frank Abras, took place over the following six months, these quickly revealing that the additional thrust provided by the -29 engine provided little additional performance improvement. In fact, it was discovered that the aircraft was distinctly less reliable than before, thanks to the undependability of the -29 engine; and the flight test program suffered accordingly.

Late in 1951, when Convair and the Air Force were negotiating the contract leading to the construction of the first prototype F-102's, some consideration was given to rebuilding the XF-92A as a flying prototype for the new aircraft. It was later decided that rebuilding and redesigning the XF-92A for this purpose would not be economically sound due to the many major structural changes that would be required.

Problems with the -29 engine continued to plague the XF-92A into 1952, and only sporadic flights were undertaken by the AF during the course of the year. Several engine changes slowed further flight test work, and by February, 1953, when the AF concluded its powerplant demonstration program, the airplane had completed only 21 flights since modification to the J33-A-29 configuration. The maximum speed at-

Full-span elevons were installed for flight testing with significant improvements in control effectivity. Note paint and tufts on right wing.

On October 14, 1953, the XF-92A, with NACA test pilot Scott Crossfield in the cockpit, suffered a nose gear failure while landing on the dry lake bed at Edwards AFB. Following this accident, it was not repaired and it never again flew.

Jay Miller/Aerofax, Inc.

The XF-92A sat derelict at the Sewanee, TN airport for several years before being recovered by the AF Museum in 1969. It is seen at the Museum (in the Museum Annex) prior to being placed inside for long term storage and protection from the elements.

tained during these tests had been during a dive to Mach 1.1 with Chuck Yeager at the controls.

Following the AF program, the XF-92A, joined the NACA High-Speed Flight Research Station at Edwards and there was tasked with exploring all facets of delta wing performance and behavior within the limits of the aircraft's performance envelope. A. Scott Crossfield was assigned XF-92A project pilot duties.

The J-33-A-29's lack of dependability was, by now, well known to the NACA. With this in mind the agency initiated yet another XF-92A power-plant change. The new engine, an Allison J-33A-16, increased the available maximum after-burning thrust to 8,400 lbs., and conveniently, also improved total aircraft reliability.

The engine change was completed in late-March and following an abbreviated ground test program, the XF-92A was cleared for initial flight trials. Crossfield flew the XF-92A for the first time following the re-engining on April 9, 1953, and during the following several months made a number of additional test flights. During one of these, a nose pitch-up phenomenon was discovered that proved to be not only puzzling, but also of significant importance to the rapidly emerging delta wing Convair F-102 interceptor. A series of exploratory flights with the XF-92A followed this discovery, eventually revealing that wing fences would alleviate much of the pitch-up tendency and would also improve low speed controllability.

While the nose pitch-up phenomenon was explored, additional modifications were undertaken,

the most significant of these being the installation, at AF request, of a drag chute. The first flight with the drag chute in the Convair-modified tail cone took place on September 30th. Additional flights, including five to explore various facets of low speed controllability with wing fences in place, were completed during the first two weeks in October, and on the last of these, occurring on October 14th, the airplane suffered a nose gear failure which in turn, caused relatively minor damage to the right main landing gear and right wing tip.

Unfortunately, though the damage was minimal, the NACA elected not to repair the aircraft based on Convair's projected $50,000 charge and three month delay. With the exception of a proposed modification to incorporate a high-altitude (50,000') afterburner developed by Allison, most of the XF-92A's flight test program had been completed, anyway. Importantly, the NACA also was aware of the fact that the arrival of an early YF-102 (53-1785) to continue exploration of delta wing characteristics was eminent. With these facts in hand, the NACA elected to hangar the aircraft until disposition could be arranged. In April, 1954, it was returned to the Air Force.

During its active flight test career, the XF-92A completed a total of 118 flights during which 62 hours of flying time were officially logged. In general pilots had few complaints about the aircraft, other than the fact that almost all considered its flight control system to be exceptionally sensitive. Among the conclusions of the Phase II flight test program were the following:

a. Stalling Characteristics
With full elevons, the aircraft would not completely stall, but would assume a constant air speed, a very high angle of attack, and a rapid sink rate (all constant for any c.g. and weight). The airspeed indicator read 59 knots at 29% MAC and 86 knots at 25% MAC in clean configuration. A slight, easily controlled tendency to roll off was noticed at a V1 of 120 to 110 knots. At lower speeds this tendency disappeared and the aircraft was quite stable.

b. Longitudinal Stability
The aircraft longitudinal stability is very good.

c. Lateral Stability and Control
All pilots . . . . considered the roll characteristics very good and the rate of roll very fast.

d. Static Directional
The data indicated, and the pilots reported, very good side-slip characteristics.

e. Dynamic Stability
Short period dynamic oscillations were induced about all 3 axes . . . the aircraft responded rather conventionally directionally and longitudinally, but at 27.3% and 29.3% of MAC, no lateral oscillations were apparent. In all cases where a lateral-directional oscillation did occur, the time to damp to one-half amplitude and the period were satisfactory . . . . the dynamic stability characteristics about all axes were considered normal by the pilots.

f. High Speed Flight Characteristics
Dives were entered from 35,000' to a dive angle of approximately 45°. No buffeting or trim changes were encountered during the dives. The 0.91 indicated Mach number obtained in the dives corresponded to a true Mach number of 1.02 or 1.04.

g. Conclusions
(1) The overall stability of the aircraft is very satisfactory.
(2) The controls are very effective, but there is a strong tendency to over-control owing to the inability of the mechanical hydraulic control system to provide the degree of sensitivity required.
(3) The minimum drag coefficient was low (.010) but the total drag appeared to be greater than for an equivalent conventional aircraft at all speeds up to Mach 0.85 at which the drag rises occurred. The higher Mach numbers at drag rise did not appear to be as rapid as would be obtained on a more conventional configuration.

The XF-92A made significant contributions to the science of delta wing aerodynamics, and in particular, laid the groundwork for follow-on Convair delta wing configurations such as the F-102, the F2Y, the XFY, the F-106, and ultimately the awesome B-58. Its legacy did not end with the *Hustler*, however, as recent events have seen the unveiling of yet another delta wing equipped descendent, the General Dynamics F-16XL—which is now expected to enter production for the USAF in 1988 as the F-16E/F.

In the summer of 1954, following its removal from the AF inventory in March, the XF-92A's wings and fin were cut and hinged to fold for highway travel by truck. It was taken to the National Air Show at Dayton, Ohio, and from there to a series of USAF Orientation Group exhibitions. Eventually, on January 1, 1955, it appeared as a flower-covered float in the Pasadena Rose Parade. This "Promote the AF" assignment eventually died, and after apparently being abandoned, it wound up, sans engine and instrumentation, at the Franklin Country Airport at Sewanee, Tennessee. In 1969 its historical importance was brought to the AF's attention and in August, reclamation by, and shipment to the USAF Museum at Wright-Patterson AFB, Ohio, took place. Partially dismantled, it remains in storage there as of this writing.

Jay Miller/Aerofax, Inc.

Following its removal from the active inventory in 1954, the XF-92A was used as a promotional tool by the AF. In order to facilitate transportation by flatbed truck, its wings and vertical fin were cut and hinged.

Chapt. 3:
GEBO and the Parasites

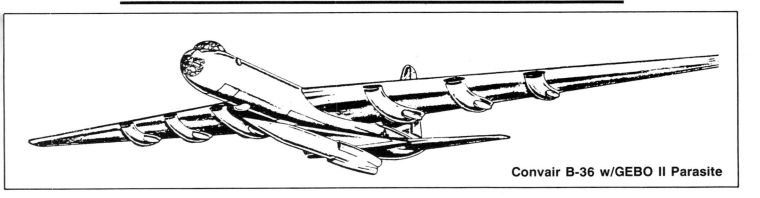

Convair B-36 w/GEBO II Parasite

GEBO I

In 1947, with WWII slowly fading into the history books, Maj. Gen. Curtis LeMay, then Deputy Chief of Air Staff for Research and Development, began the arduous task of reorienting AF priorities from a wartime footing to one of strength maintenance during peacetime. Of considerable importance to LeMay in terms of future defense needs were the medium and heavy bomber requirements that were expected to exist in the 1960's. Already, controversy had surfaced during preliminary AF discussions, and there was nothing tangible available for presentation to the new (and first) AF Chief of Staff, Gen. Carl Spaatz.

LeMay's preference, based on his estimates of strategic bombing strategy of the 1950's and 1960's, was a medium bomber. He estimated that the aircraft would have a gross weight in the vicinity of 170,000 lbs. and a cruising speed of 500 mph over a range of 5,000 miles.

In retrospect, it is now clear that what LeMay wanted was the aircraft that eventually became the Boeing B-47—and which, in fact, was well down the road toward development by the time LeMay made public his opinion. Basically, LeMay foresaw a relatively conservative configuration offering good performance at moderate cost—with the latter permitting production buys in sizeable numbers.

Conceding the conservative design approaches dictated by the economics of subsonic configurations for the near term, aerospace industry giants, such as Boeing, North American, Lockheed, Northrop, and Convair none-the-less continued extensive in-house exploration of the existing design envelope based on available materials and powerplant performance. This objective was enhanced by the immediate post-WWII arrival of voluminous German research files, and in many cases, the personnel who had actually conceived and conducted the tests, studies, and flight test work contained therein.

The War Department was well aware of the subtle industry rumblings calling for exploration of the seemingly innumerable technological and performance advances that had surfaced during the war, and coupled with an economic situation dictating the need for increases in government spending, study contracts were created and let at a rapid clip. One of these, outlining a requirement for a new medium bomber of less than 200,000 lbs. gross weight, having a 2,000 statute mile radius, a 10,000 lb. bomb load, and a complete all around defensive armament, was submitted to industry in October, 1947. Tentatively referred to as the

XB-55, it was to be a high-speed replacement for the B-29/B-50 series piston engine bombers.

Not surprisingly, Boeing Aircraft Company, of Seattle, Washington, submitted the winning proposal and a Phase I contract was initiated with fiscal year 1948 funds. Design studies were then undertaken, these attempting to devise the optimum configuration for the best speed and altitude performance. A weight reduction program was begun concurrently, the two chief considerations being equipment reduction and modification of the armament requirements.

The post-war economy had curtailed funding for all but the highest priority programs and it thus became questionable, during 1948 and 1949, as to whether there would be sufficient funding available to support the XB-55 development program during 1950 and 1951. This, coupled with the realization that development time would be longer than originally anticipated, dictated a slowdown in the proposed hardware program and a renewed emphasis on design development.

The initial design study thus became a paper testbed used to explore rapidly unfolding improvements in aerodynamics and propulsion. Consequently, the AF began an investigation of the potential of the delta wing configuration and, for the first time, began considering designs capable of supersonic speeds.

Col. George Smith, Chief of the Aircraft Projects Section in the Air Material Command's Engineering Division, noted that feasibility studies of a delta wing aircraft in the 150,000 lb. class were "extremely encouraging" and added that emphasis should be placed on the "investigation of low aspect ratio wings in general, and delta wings in particular". He also called attention to the fact that the British had selected the delta configuration for their most recent bombardment aircraft (the Avro *Vulcan*—which was, as a point of interest, strictly a subsonic configuration).

Among the initial approaches to the development of a long range supersonic bombardment aircraft was the first Generalized Bomber Study, better known as GEBO I. This began in October, 1946, and was tasked with determining the design trends that would be necessary to achieve given desired performance characteristics. The investigation was done under an AF contract with Convair (both San Diego, California, and Fort Worth, Texas offices were involved) and consisted of studies of approximately 10,000 configurations to find the effects of different wing area, aspect ratio, thickness and sweep, as well as the effects of different size, number and types of propulsion systems (turbojet and turboprop) on aircraft speed,

range, and gross weight.

By June, 1948, Convair had completed three reports in connection with GEBO I, the third of which, "Generalized Bomber Research–Turboprop Airplanes", was the first study actually prepared under the initial GEBO contract. The AF Aircraft Projects Section subsequently invited a group of contractors and government agencies to a symposium at Wright-Patterson AFB to discuss the study and related problems such as the assumptions on which the study was based (factors pertaining to buffet boundaries and structural and aerodynamic criteria), methods of systems analysis, the use and limitations of the study results, and recommendations regarding the scope of the study. The three-day symposium began on August 18, 1948, and numerous major contractors sent representatives. Among the latter was Robert Widmer of Convair who had helped direct the original work done by his company.

One major purpose of the conference had been to survey the latest developments in turbine and propeller propulsion and to determine their respective trends in terms of size, weight, and performance as they would relate to forthcoming bomber aircraft. The designs which resulted were predicated on the equipment and armament requirements then being used by bombers. From such work the concept of presenting bomber performance in terms of cruise velocity v/s range diagrams was developed. This revolutionary practice soon after became generally accepted throughout the industry.

Following the symposium, Convair completed and issued to industry and government representatives additional reports on powerplant and propeller trends including information pertaining to turboprop aircraft with a 50,000 lb. bomb load (for

One of the more unusual designs generated during the GEBO studies at Convair was this composite link aircraft assembly.

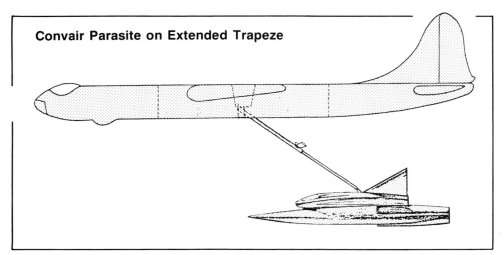

Convair Parasite on Extended Trapeze

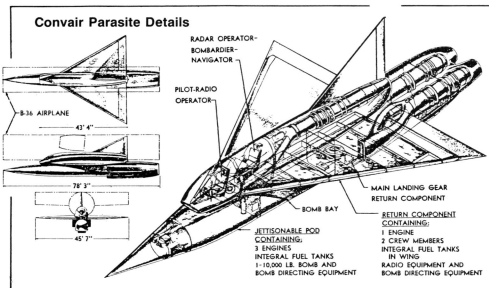

Convair Parasite Details

RADAR OPERATOR-
BOMBARDIER-
NAVIGATOR

PILOT-RADIO
OPERATOR

B-36 AIRPLANE

43' 4"

78' 3"

45' 7"

MAIN LANDING GEAR
RETURN COMPONENT

BOMB BAY

RETURN COMPONENT
CONTAINING:
1 ENGINE
2 CREW MEMBERS
INTEGRAL FUEL TANKS
IN WING
RADIO EQUIPMENT AND
BOMB DIRECTING EQUIPMENT

JETTISONABLE POD
CONTAINING:
3 ENGINES
INTEGRAL FUEL TANKS
1-10,000 LB. BOMB AND
BOMB DIRECTING EQUIPMENT

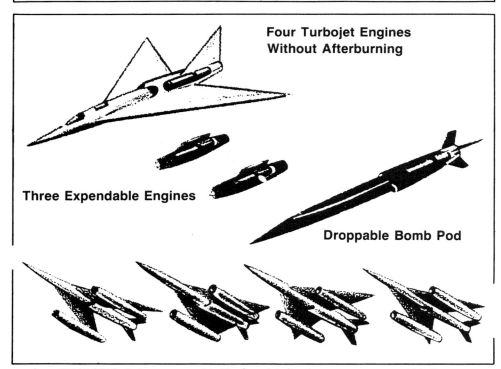

**Four Turbojet Engines
Without Afterburning**

Three Expendable Engines

Droppable Bomb Pod

Some 10,000 GEBO studies were completed by Convair before the program progressed into the more definitive configurations leading to the MX-1626, MX-1964, and finally, B-58.

gross weights of 1,000,000 to 1,200,000 lbs., and ranges of from 0 to 20,000 miles). Additional reports covering turbojet aircraft with both 0° and 35° wing sweep angles, were planned for release in December.

At the same time, a recommendation to the AF by industry representatives that the GEBO studies be continued was relayed by Col. Smith. He recommended that the studies be continued. Consideration was given to adding more funds to the GEBO study to study the effects of small changes in such characteristics as drag, specific fuel consumption, propeller efficiency, and engine weight on the aircraft shown in the study, thereby improving the usefulness of the basic aircraft data covered in the GEBO contract.

By March, 1949, Convair had released two additional GEBO reports: Report #4, Part IV, "Turbo-Prop Airplanes, 20,000 Lb. Fuselage Bomb Capacity", and Report #5, Part I, "Turbo-Jet Airplanes, 20,000 Lb. Fuselage Bomb Capacity, Zero Degrees Wing Sweep". Three months later, Parts II and III of Report #5 were released, as well as Report #6, Parts I, II, and III, "Turbo-Jet Airplanes, 20,000 Lb. Fuselage Bomb Capacity, 35 Deg. Wing Sweep". The reports ended the GEBO study on the general capabilities of the turboprop and turbojet bombers with 20,000 lb. and 50,000 lb. bomb loads.

Succumbing to industry pressure, the Air Materiel Command now agreed to initiate a new study which would be utilized to (1) explore in detail the relative performance characteristics of the high-speed bombers in the medium bomber class; (2) explore the effect of different equipment requirements; (3) incorporate many of the other useful suggestions obtained during the first GEBO symposium; and (4) to reevaluate the powerplant developments that had occurred during the succeeding two years. A nine-month time limit was placed on the new project and on June 15, 1949, it was initiated by a letter from the AMC.

GEBO II

As 1950 drew to a close, the AF had yet to approve a supersonic bomber development program for fiscal year 1951. Fortunately, the groundwork had been laid during the course of GEBO I and other government and industry studies and there was strong feeling throughout the aerospace community that the time was ripe for development to begin.

By late 1948, projected B-47 production rates had reached the point where the number of available aircraft would effectively offset the need for another subsonic medium bomber. Accordingly, on January 27, 1949, the AMC was directed to cancel the XB-55 while leaving intact the general requirement for a high-performance medium bomber.

Other projects were now reoriented or cancelled outright. Among the latter was an advanced bomber study from Fairchild which had been generated in response to GEBO I. Though of interest, it was considered too premature for further development and its cancellation was considered necessary.

Brig. Gen. Donald Putt, then Director of the Research and Development Office, Deputy Chief of Staff for Materiel, now outlined for industry and government representatives, the AMC's future tasks. Among the many, he directed the AMC to continue development of the Boeing B-52, and most importantly from the standpoint of this story, he directed that effort be applied to a newly established program item—a possible supersonic bomber. Gen. Putt further recommended that the AMC solicit the aircraft industry for a "new and possibly unconventional approach to the intercon-

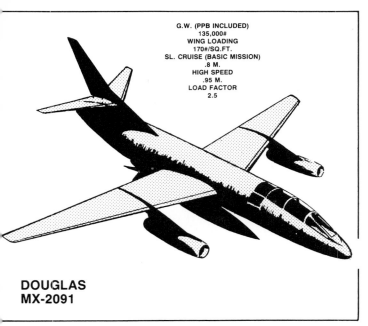

G.W. (PPB INCLUDED)
135,000#
WING LOADING
170#/SQ.FT.
SL. CRUISE (BASIC MISSION)
.8 M.
HIGH SPEED
.95 M.
LOAD FACTOR
2.5

**DOUGLAS
MX-2091**

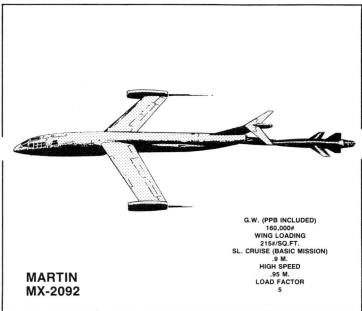

G.W. (PPB INCLUDED)
160,000#
WING LOADING
215#/SQ.FT.
SL. CRUISE (BASIC MISSION)
.9 M.
HIGH SPEED
.95 M.
LOAD FACTOR
5

**MARTIN
MX-2092**

nental bomber problem on the basis of minimum specific military requirements to be established n cooperation with this Headquarters''.

In response to Gen. Putt's direction, the AMC Bombardment Branch took steps to cope with the new task. Its chief, Lt. Col. H. E. Warden, thought the design competition would be conducted in the immediate future and consequently, he asked the Aircraft Projects Section to include $1,000,000 in its fiscal year 1950 budget for same. At the end of June, 1949, Maj. Gen. F. O. Carroll, AMC Director of Research and Development, noted that the competition had still not been placed on the program, and that it was not among the items contemplated in the event money became available as supplemental fiscal year 1949 funds. Accordingly, he asked for a clarification from AF Headquarters in Washington, D.C. with, if at all possible, a fiscal year deadline in which the AF would go to the aircraft industry with a request for proposals (RFP).

While Gen. Carroll and others were trying to clarify the AF's stand on the nebulous supersonic bomber program, a conceptual strategic bomber with supersonic performance capabilities began to emerge from the lower echelons of AF operations at Wright-Patterson AFB. On March 24, 1949, AF Headquarters had advised the AMC to expand the then-current heavy bomber program to include a reconnaissance capability. With this in mind, the Heavy Bomber Committee of the Aircraft and Weapons Board recommended that the total distance from base to target for the strategic bomber be separated into three zones which would consist of logistics, combat, and target. The objective of this zoning was to improve combat target area performance. Conferences on preliminary design intentions, which the AMC held with industry, as well as studies which the former either conducted or reviewed, now permitted the formulation of a general concept pattern which related the bomber and reconnaissance aircraft to the idea of supersonic *target zone performance.*

Among the unconventional concepts which evolved to accomplish supersonic combat and target zone capability were the use of supersonic parasites in combination with larger logistics zone carriers; an inflight-refueled medium bomber with an adequate escape radius; the use of drones; and the employment of a medium bomber with exceptionally high target zone performance.

Many of the technical studies during this period had not been able to verify that a strategic bomber

could make an unrefueled round trip and still attain supersonic performance. Other studies, however, indicated that some aircraft types could attain the desired combat zone target area performance—though at great sacrifice to weapons carrying ability and range performance. Among these were the still-viable Boeing studies being conducted under the remnants of the XB-55 contract; a Douglas proposal for using the X-3 research aircraft with an externally-mounted bomb in combination with a logistics carrier (later configurations in this project included a significantly enlarged X-3 capable of carrying five crew members and a variety of bombs and/or reconnaissance systems); a Douglas study calling for a "strip-tease" type bomber that shed various parts as it progressed to the target and which was capable of flying the entire mission at supersonic speeds; and a Douglas-designed dedicated carrier aircraft that was an outgrowth of the 1211J and 1211R strategic bomber proposal.

Convair, capitalizing on the foundation it had built during GEBO I, continued to set precedent under GEBO II which was now approved under study contract AF33(038)-2664 and financed using fiscal year 1949 funds (total cost, $109,434). GEBO II had, in fact, eventually led to a realignment of the design emphasis the company was placing on the new program, and the idea of the parasite bomber which could operate from a larger carrier aircraft was getting full attention.

Interest in carrier aircraft stemmed largely from the program funding shortage. It was assumed that a parasitic bomber would be less expensive to build than a larger, self-contained intercontinental-capable aircraft and it was also assumed that, due to the availability of the extremely large and long-ranged B-36, a parasite program could prove quite attractive. Paralleling the AF program, too, was a Navy proposal for a carrier-based composite medium range bomber. Convair was also involved in these studies, as was the Martin Company.

Prior to the redirection of interest in the potential of the parasite concept, GEBO II design parameters had been based on the reduced equipment concepts that had resulted from the development programs leading to the Northrop B-35 and the Boeing B-52. The parameters laid down at this time included a range radius of 1,200 to 2,500 miles with a 10,000 lb. bomb load, a cruise speed of more than 450 knots, a combat altitude of more

than 35,000', and a takeoff distance of less than 6,000'. These requirements would quickly be pushed aside, however, as the funding crunch took its toll and interest in unconventional approaches to strategic bombing grew.

The GEBO II study was, in fact, officially changed in April, 1950, to provide for analytical, aerodynamic, structural, and power plant studies of an aerial bombing system capable of attacking targets 3,500 to 4,500 miles from operating bases at speeds ranging from Mach 0.9 to 1.5 in the 500 to 2,000 mile deep target zone. The reoriented study was based on the concept of a composite or partially-expendable parasite bomber to be carried by a B-36. The composite features of the design were considered necessary to accomplish the mission at higher speeds; even at the speeds attainable by the non-composite aircraft, such a design resulted in substantially lower weights. Use of the B-36 as a carrier was simply one way of providing the necessary range extension, although inflight refueling, staging, or other means could have been used. As the study progressed, new concepts were continually being explored.

Convair had discussed its composite bomber proposals in a report on the potential of the B-36 program published in January, 1950, prior to the GEBO II program realignment. This report showed a four-engine, delta configured, composite design with a return component and a droppable pod containing the bomb bay, radar scanner, the three expendable engines, and fuel. The aircraft was to carry a two-man crew, but there was to be no defensive armament (due to its high speed capability).

With a launch weight of 100,000 lbs. and a landing weight of 17,900 lbs., the parasite bomber was to be capable of a maximum altitude of 48,500', a post weapon drop altitude of 41,000', a maximum speed of Mach 1.6, a to-target cruise speed of Mach 1.3, a from-target cruise speed of Mach 0.9, and a service ceiling before bomb drop of 52,000'.

Although AF interest in the parasite concept was strong, the idea had encountered some serious criticism. Brig. Gen. Howard Bunker, Chief of the AF Field Office for Atomic Energy, stated that a parasite bomber would be "much more expensive in dollars and effort than a single aircraft to accomplish the same mission''. For example, both the parasite and the carrier aircraft would require completely independent navigation systems. More importantly, Gen. Gunker raised the issue of

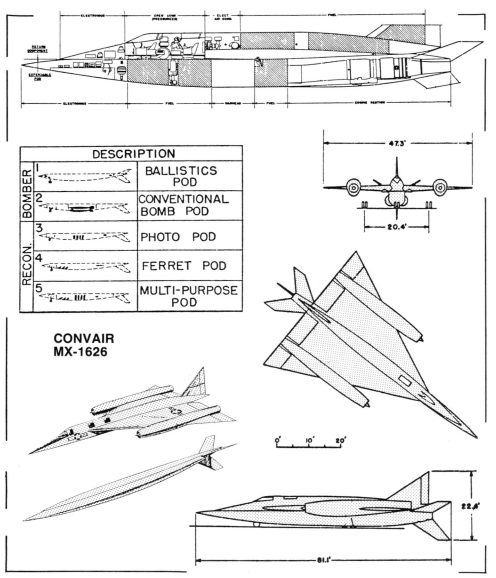

DESCRIPTION		
BOMBER 1		BALLISTICS POD
2		CONVENTIONAL BOMB POD
RECON. 3		PHOTO POD
4		FERRET POD
5		MULTI-PURPOSE POD

CONVAIR MX-1626

47.3'
20.4'

0'   10'   20'

22.4'
81.1'

whether such a system was needed to penetrate the target area since RAND Corporation Studies had indicated that high speed alone might be of less consequence than factors such as maneuverability. Also, the effects of high speed on bombing system accuracy were not known and it was pointed out that past experience indicated adverse effects; range might be compromised by the parasite's jockeying for link-up position with the carrier; the parasite might not be able to find the carrier; and once linked, the composite aircraft would almost certainly be more vulnerable to attack.

Following the reallignment of GEBO II program priorities, Convair continued to develop the parasite concept. By the fall of 1950, the contractor called for a parasite bomber or reconnaissance aircraft not unlike that which it had suggested at the beginning of the year. The aircraft, a basic configuration with an expendable pod, was to have a gross weight of 100,000 lbs., of which the pod structure, one engine, and expendable equipment would account for 18,000 lbs. Two turbojets in partially buried wing nacelles would provide power, together with an expendable turbojet engine suspended in a pod under each wing. The system had to provide for takeoff when suspended under, and partially in, the B-36 bomb bay, although the engine pods in use at that time provided for sufficient ground clearance and raised no particular concerns.

Once airborne, the B-36 was expected to carry the parasite approximately 2,000 miles toward the target, release it, and return to base. The parasite would then accelerate with its five engines to its cruise speed (an intended Mach 1.3), enter the combat zone, and continue to the target which would be approximately 2,000 miles distant. Once in the target area, the parasite would accelerate to its maximum speed of Mach 1.5, release the pod containing the atomic warhead, release one engine, and begin its homeward cruise at a speed of Mach 1.3. Once out of the combat zone, the parasite would drop its two external turbojets before continuing through the logistics zone (approximately 2,000 miles) at Mach 0.9.

Convair also planned to investigate the effects of varying the combat zone radius from 500 to 2,000 miles, and the combat zone cruise speeds from Mach 0.9 to Mach 1.5; however, the study was also to cover speeds up to Mach 2.0 and combat altitudes ranging from sea level to 60,000'.

The entire GEBO II study specified a minimum use of equipment and emphasized small crews. High speed operation demanded the most advanced bombing/navigation systems and in late 1950, Convair undertook a study of the K-1 system, the Norden radar bombing sight, and several missile guidance systems. Due to the performance problem, it was considered necessary by Convair to integrate completely the bombing systems and the bomb drop techniques. Accord-

ingly, these problems were always considered together.

The parasite aircraft was to have no active defensive armament although it was provided with an electronic countermeasures (ECM) suit. Additionally, the aircraft was expected to be reasonably maneuverable and thus capable of utilizing evasive action in combat.

Early in the GEBO II study, Convair had designed a pod with a conventional bomb bay which met the USAF volume requirements. This configuration was quickly superceded by a totally expendable warhead-equipped pod—which, the AF believed, would alleviate most of the difficulties associated with launching bombs at high speed by providing a standard droppable body with a fineness ratio and form suitable for high-speed release and fall.

In addition to a warhead, the new pod configuration also contained one engine. This was expected to compensate for pod drag, fuel tanks, and other equipment not essential for the return portion of the mission. Pod release thus relieved the aircraft of a substantial load.

To the AF and Convair, it appeared that the pod concept had the potential for undergoing a notable development evolution, depending, of course on the availability of guidance and control equipment. The pod could be released simply as a free-fall bomb, or when available, terminal guidance equipment, integrated with the pod powerplant, could be used to make it into a powered glide bomb or an air-launched missile.

In conjunction with the AMC, Convair paralleled the GEBO II performance and configuration studies with a system study, and the AF thus looked forward to seeing the results of this then-unique approach embodied in a proposal for such an aircraft. The AF anticipated that performance would be on the order of that already stated by Convair, and consequently asked the company to submit preliminary layout and profile drawings, detailed performance estimates, and cost estimates on at least three of the most promising designs to permit better correlation of the study results with other aircraft system proposals. Though the AF established a target date of February 1951 for completion of the GEBO II study, Convair concluded that it would be able to accomplish the remaining research work ahead of schedule.

By the time GEBO II came to an end, Convair had analyzed approximately 100,000 configurations embodying the parasite or partially expendable component principle. These had shown that the supersonic bomber concept was feasible when range augmentation and partially expendable component design principles were considered.

Throughout the latter half of 1950, the AF had carried the GEBO project on a high priority basis. Although essentially a generalized study, as the name implied, its purpose was to show the effects of various design parameters on bomber performance. Toward the end of 1950, Convair completed the aerodynamic, structural, and weight design criteria and, in early 1951, began feeding the raw data into computers to calculate the performance expected to be available by March, 1951. Preliminary results showed that the proposed aircraft would be capable of a 4,000 mile radius when carried by a B-36 and launched 2,500 miles out from the target. It would travel 1,500 miles at Mach 1.3 to Mach 1.6, and then return through the logistics zone a distance of 2,500 miles at Mach 0.9. Its gross weight would be approximately 100,000 lbs., it would be a parasite, and it would carry a pod, an air-to-ground missile, or a pod with engine and fuel. The course of supersonic bomber development was now projected for the future.

Boeing's Model 484 was wind tunnel tested at the NACA's Langley, VA facility, eventually evolving through many basically similar design configurations. The Model 484 was considered by the AF to be an exceptionally conservative approach to the supersonic bomber requirement. This affected its ability to compete with the more aggressive Convair design effort.

Throughout the many months Convair worked on GEBO II related proposals and design studies, its primary competitor for the still ill-defined supersonic bomber program, Boeing Aircraft Company, had quietly explored a more conservative approach to the same requirement. Boeing's long-standing reputation in the bomber design and construction business, coupled with the subtle political backing of such SAC powerbrokers as Gen. Curtis LeMay, made Boeing a formidable opponent in virtually any contract competition.

Boeing's main thrust during this period was entitled Project MX-1022, which in turn was a design study contract hold-over from the defunct XB-55 program. Prior to the cancellation of the XB-55, Boeing had worked on a series of new turbojet designs in order to compare them with its original turboprop studies. Unlike the original XB-55, the new designs had been based on the concept of minimum equipment and crew. The primary objective was, of course, to obtain higher performance.

The demise of the XB-55 in 1949 left Boeing with several partially completed conventional turbojet medium bomber configuration studies and an additional number of studies pertaining to somewhat unconventional delta wing designs. The latter were the end result of low-aspect-ratio wing configuration studies that stemmed from the AF's considerable interest in supersonic target area speeds. Boeing had performed numerous wind tunnel tests (and systems studies) in its own facilities on several highly swept and delta wing configurations in order to obtain more realistic performance estimates and a better understanding of tactical aircraft requirements.

When the XB-55 was cancelled, the door was left open for Boeing to continue the research it had begun and to carry on work directly applicable to a medium bomber capable of operating at supersonic speeds in the target zone. When these studies were completed, the company would be expected to submit preliminary drawings, reports, and specifications on an optimum design. Performance objectives included a 2,999 mile radius with a 50,000' altitude and supersonic operation in the 200 mile target zone. A bomb bay similar in size to that found in the B-47 would be mandatory.

Toward the end of 1950, Boeing published the results of its studies in Report D-10759, "Supersonic Bomber Configuration Study". High, medium, and low aspect ratio wing configurations were addressed based on an ability to cruise at high subsonic speeds in the logistics, or lightly defended enemy zones, and at Mach 1.3 in the target zone. Boeing had completed enough research by this time to show the effects of varying aspect ratio, wing sweep, thickness/chord ratio, thickness distribution, taper ratio, engine installation, and engine type. Finding the low aspect ratio designs powered by afterburning turbojet engines to exhibit superior performance, Boeing chose one such configuration to best meet the specific design objectives.

Aircraft powered by afterburning engines showed the greatest total radius when operating at supersonic speeds at distances up to 400 to 500 miles. For supersonic operation over a greater portion of the flight, it appeared desirable to provide power sufficient to permit supersonic speeds without the use of afterburners. These aircraft gave superior supersonic performance, but none,

NASA via Ben Gunther

Another Model 484 configuration study calling for two pylon-mounted nacelles housing four engines. Placement of the nacelles beyond the wing mid-point to offset the drag effects of the interference of nacelle and fuselage shock waves dictated the use of a rather large vertical tail surface.

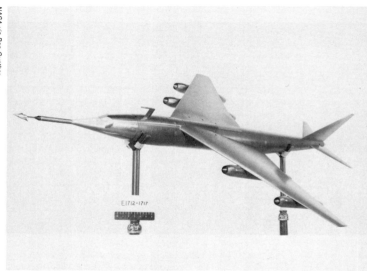

Yet another Model 484 configuration study, this one calling for the wing root mounting of the engines and dog-tooth outboard leading edge extensions. The fuselage remained essentially unchanged.

The final Boeing submission, under the MX-1712 designator had four semi-flush mounted nacelles and a rather unorthodox floating, boom-mounted canard complemented by a conventional horizontal tail surface.

in the size class which Boeing was considering, could meet the 1,700 to 2,000 mile radius objective. Accordingly, the report elucidated the possible means of range extension. By increasing the gross weight from 200,000 to 400,000 lbs., Boeing was able to increase the subsonic radius by only 10% to 20%. External tanks provided greater range increases for incremental weight increases, and extended wing tips plus wing tanks showed a 40% radius increase for a 25% increase in gross weight.

After examining the configuration studies, the AF selected the Boeing Model 484-405B as the one with the greatest potential. It had a gross weight of 200,000 lbs.; an empty weight of 83,090 lbs.; a fuel weight (16,550 gal.) of 107,520 lbs.; a military load of 13,160 lbs., a wing area of 2,190 sq.'; an aspect ratio of 3.5; a sweepback of 47° at quarter chord; a taper ratio of 0.2; a thickness/chord ratio of .095 to .055; a radius w/6,000 lb. bomb of 2,280 nm at Mach 0.9 or 1,737 nm at Mach 0.9 w/a dash of 185 nm at Mach 1.3; a cruise speed of 581 knots or 750 knots (depending on mission segment); a target altitude of 43,500' subsonic or 47,500' supersonic; a takeoff distance over a 50' obstacle of 4,300' (standard day); a landing distance over a 50' obstacle of 5,710' at design gross weight; and a landing distance using a 40' parachute of 2,790' at design empty weight.

The Model 484-405B was to be powered by four Pratt & Whitney J57-P-5 afterburning turbojet engines. To obtain supersonic speeds, the wing thickness was reduced, but in so doing, it became necessary to increase the fuselage size in order to house the fuel that could no longer be carried in the wings. Since the larger fuselage was available, the vertical tail was placed in the conventional manner and a small horizontal tail surface was added for improved trimming and increased pitch control.

The resulting configuration proved quite conventional in appearance. The engines were mounted side-by-side, two in the inboard section of each wing aft of the rear spar. The latter provided additional safety and simplified installation and maintenance. Wing leading edge inlets were provided for the engine ducts.

The fuselage was composed of a pressurized cabin housing the three-man crew and equipment, and an aft, unpressurized body which contained 90% of the fuel, the bomb bay, tandem type landing gear, and a remote control tail turret. The twin .50 calibre turret was installed primarily to occupy

space and add weight until more effective armament could be devised. The body's cross section was 180'' wide by 115'' deep, and for ease of manufacturing, the cross section remained constant from the pressurized cabin to the aft end of the bomb bay (approximately 50% of the body length). A bombing system, the K-1 type, was installed for study; it was believed that this system filled a conservative weight and space requirement which would leave room for later systems. The AF also anticipated that it would have the high speed bomb director or Norden radar bomb sight soon enough for installation in an aircraft of the Boeing type. Boeing submitted a Preliminary Model Specification, a summary report, aerodynamics, structural and weight reports, and preliminary drawings to show the layout of the basic components.

Upon reviewing the submitted reports, the AF noted a conspicuous absence of suitable Model 484-405B wind tunnel model data. Consequently, the AF elected to conduct a series of high speed tunnel tests of its own beginning on September 15, 1950, in the AMC's high speed 10' wind tunnel, on approximately fifteen wing configurations of the type used in the Boeing studies.

Once this decision had been made, the AF, knowing of the NACA's potential interest in the resulting data, informed the NACA of the impending tests. Boeing then briefed NACA Director Dr. Hugh Dryden on their preliminary findings and also placed heavy emphasis on the importance of the forthcoming conclusions—the resulting data would almost certainly be the determining factor in deciding which wing configuration was most suitable for the proposed Boeing bomber.

The program would basically encompass two separate wind tunnel studies, one sponsored by the AMC and the other by the NACA, with the objective of providing the background data necessary to design the MX-1022 aircraft; and to supply the NACA with as much data as necessary to round out its transonic research program with studies of three-dimensional wings. A comparison of the respective findings would help validate or repudiate the Boeing data, and would, at the same time, bolster the baseline wind tunnel data being generated by the NACA.

In February, 1951, the AMC was ready to transfer its data and the Boeing models to the NACA for testing which was scheduled to begin on March 5. The AF anticipated gaining data covering the entire applicable speed ranges as well as correlating the data from the Wright Field

tunnel with the data obtained from the 8' tunnel at Langley. The AF considered the entire test program a prerequisite to establishing a firm aircraft design and also considered it necessary to test engine intake ducts located in the wing or other positions. Finally, a complete tunnel program was to be undertaken on the final selection for the Phase I design competition.

When finally completed, the wind tunnel tests showed that acceptable low speed control and stability characteristics could be obtained with configurations capable of supersonic performance. The studies indicated that engines such as the J40-WE-16, the TJ-15, and the J57-PW-5 with afterburners provided the greatest supersonic radius within a total radius of approximately 1,737 miles although engines were studied in both pod and submerged configuration with afterburners. Extension of the wing span with extra fuel tanks appeared to give the greatest subsonic radius with the smallest gross weight increases. Among the many configurations studied, those with aspect ratios of 3.5, thickness/chord ratios averaging 7%, sweepback angles of 47°, and wings large enough to bring the engines aft of the rear spar and near the wing root appeared to provide the best performance capabilities.

At the conclusion of the wind tunnel test program, Boeing elected to follow conventional design criteria as much as possible and essentially projected its then current capabilities into the arena of supersonic flight. The basic design was a rather conventionally configured aircraft that could provide medium range while providing supersonic performance over a limited portion of its mission.

Under Project MX-871, Convair had synthesized its GEBO I and GEBO II data into a more radical approach to the supersonic bomber requirement. The parasite design concept remained viable, though refinements were rapidly leading to a configuration that was significantly more palatable from a logistical point of view.

The Convair airplane, by now grossing at 107,000 lbs., was in fact, as unconventional as Boeing's was conventional. The AF, at this point, leaned heavily in favor of the more radical approach and openly expressed its view that the Convair configuration, a parasite transported by a B-36 or some other large carrier aircraft, offered greater sustained supersonic flight capability (the projected combat zone was 1,500 n. miles) as well as superior suitability for long range intelligence and reconnaissance missions. Both designs,

22

though optimized for high altitude penetration, were also considered marginally suitable for low altitude weapons delivery, as well.

By the end of 1950, the Bombardment Branch of the AMC's Aircraft and Guided Missiles Section had begun preparation of the proposed military characteristics specification for both Convair and Boeing. This work reached fruition several months later and was immediately forwarded to AF Headquarters in Washington, D.C.

Based on the AMC proposal, which in turn was a combination of all the various data inputs from the Boeing and Convair design studies, requests were made for funds to be included in the 1951 supplementary defense budget and the 1952 budget, for beginning projects based on the Boeing and Convair conceptual studies. The AF then verbally directed, in December, 1950, that selected source procurement should be used wherever necessary to obligate fiscal year 1951 funds prior to January 20, 1951. It subsequently approved the over-all supersonic bomber program as part of the fiscal year 1951 research and development budget.

Contractual negotiations thus proceeded with Boeing and Convair. Many AF personnel held that the completed studies offered much promise and were aware that Boeing and Convair had produced the only substantial designs for beginning Phase I development; indeed, the two contractors were the only ones in a position to submit proposals on short notice. As for other possible contractors, estimates ranged from six to nine months for them to complete preliminary studies; preparing for a competition would require still more time.

The AF believed that the time and cost involved in relying on many contractors could be eliminated by limiting the competition to Convair and Boeing, only. Even in consideration of this, however, proposals from other contractors were not discounted. After the Boeing and Convair work had been disseminated to select members of the aircraft production community, discussions were held with Douglas, Lockheed, Martin, and North American representatives. Informal proposals from these companies were solicited with a deadline of no later than March 26, 1951. Only two companies, Douglas and Martin, responded, and evaluations quickly eliminated them from the virtually pre-ordained winners' bracket.

On January 26, 1951, Convair sent its "Proposal for Development and Manufacture of Long Range Supersonic Bomber/Reconnaissance Airplane" to the AMC which promptly assigned it the MX-1626 project designator under contract AF33(038)-21250 signed on February 17, 1951. In February, Boeing followed suit with a similar proposal and was immediately assigned the MX-1712 project designator under contract AF33(038)21388 on February 26, 1951. Boeing's contract called for Phase I development of two bomber/reconnaissance aircraft through wind tunnel testing, engineering design, and mock-up. Convair's contract called for partial Phase I development (initially less mock-up) of a bomber/reconnaissance aircraft based on GEBO II studies. The one basic difference between the projected GEBO II configuration and that which Convair was now proposing was the use of three engines instead of five; two engines would be mounted in wing nacelles, and the third would be in the droppable pod.

Projected schedules indicated that Convair would have a mock-up available in early 1952. Boeing indicated that its mock-up would be available in September. Initial flight dates for both aircraft were tentatively set for sometime in late 1954.

Both contracts placed heavy emphasis on thorough wind tunnel test programs. Following preliminary discussions between the contractors, the NACA, and the AMC, decisions were made concerning scheduling and priorities.

By the end of 1951, the wind tunnel program on the Boeing models was progressing rapidly. Supersonic tests in Langley's 4' x 4' tunnel and transonic tests in its 8' tunnel on the .025 scale model followed during the first two months of 1952. Boeing's preliminary analysis of the data indicated a longitudinal stability problem which was inherent in the particular geometric and aerodynamic combination selected for the MX-1712 configuration. Additional wind tunnel testing followed, exploring the various aerodynamic solutions available.

Parallel work was also being consummated by Convair's MX-1626 team in 1952. A requirement for transonic testing and partial supersonic testing was temporarily blocked by unavailability of tunnel time. This was quickly overcome when the AMC arranged for Convair to use the Navy tunnel at Daingerfield, Texas.

By mid-July, MX-1626 configurations were being tested in two Navy tunnels with intentions to do additional tunnel work in various NACA transonic and supersonic tunnels as they became available.

Prior to the initiation of the major MX-1626 wind tunnel program, the AF, in mid-1951, agreed to the advisability of conducting a series of MX-1626 rocket model tests to determine the general drag and stability characteristics of the proposed configurations. Particular emphasis was to be placed on the separation characteristics of the pod. With NACA assistance, a program was laid out and models were built by Convair.

The actual rocket test program, under contract RA A73L75 signed on September 17, 1951, was to last significantly longer than originally predicted. Convair representatives, in fact, had reacted adversely when first told that the program would consume nearly a year. They felt that design development was progressing so rapidly the rocket test data would prove of little value if it took longer than six months to generate.

In reality, the program eventually consumed more than four years, due in part to the fact that early rocket model program results indicated such serious design problems, it was necessary to completely reconfigure the aircraft.

For the MX-1626 program, the 1/10th-scale rocket models were 90" long and had a wingspan of about 57". The booster consisted of two *Deacon* motors side-by-side but separated by about 12". The model was placed upon the booster with the fuselage lying between. Thrust was transmitted to the model through horns extending into the lower surface of the wing, while stability of the system was provided by four small fins attached to a welded magnesium boxlike coupling at the rear of the booster assembly. Each *Deacon* had a canted nozzle designed for the thrust to pass through the cg of the entire combination at takeoff. A small divergence flap on the outboard side of each motor assured that the booster would separate downward from the model at burnout.

Because of the urgency placed on the program by Convair, the first attempted flight was made on July 8, 1952, with a complete and fully instrumented model. The results were a disaster. The rocket motor nozzles had been aligned improperly and, as described by John Palmer in the Wallops Daily Log, "apparently the twin *Deacons* fired normally, but as the model booster combination started to leave the launcher, the nose of the combination dropped rapidly and the model booster combination executed three outside loops right in front of the launching area and hit the beach on the third loop. This broke up the combination and parts went in all directions. The loops were an extremely tight maneuver, the combina-

tion probably not reaching an altitude of 50'''.

This failure was followed by a dummy model test on August 6, 1952. The dummy model benefitted from the mistakes made during the first launch and the flight was successful. Successful tests of two instrumented models now followed in rapid succession on September 11 and October 30, 1952. One model was complete, while the other had its nacelles removed. Ten-channel telemeters transmitted data on longitudinal, lateral, and normal accelerations, pod and nacelle base pressures, and total and static pressure. Six pulse rockets, providing 60 lbs. thrust for 0.10 seconds, were located in the sides of the fuselage to disturb the model in flight at times controlled by time-delay squibs. Although these pulse rockets were positioned to impart a lateral disturbance, their exhaust jets created a pressure field under the wing which caused substantial disturbances in pitch, as well. Data were obtained, therefore, on directional and longitudinal stability as well as drag.

The drag measurements of the complete model proved very upsetting to both AF and Convair representatives. The peak drag coefficient at Mach 1.02, for example, was almost twice as high as that predicted. Convair representatives at first questioned the accuracy of the rocket-model data, but after a test of one of the same models in the Langley 16' transonic tunnel showed about the same drag rise, they conceded that the rocket-model data must be correct.

An evaluation of the longitudinal area distribution of the configuration in accordance with the area rule theories of R. T. Whitcomb, along with tests of an equivalent body in the helium gun at Wallops Island, provided an explanation for the large additional drag. At about this time, independent changes were made in the full-scale aircraft design which caused the drag rise to be even higher than that shown for the original configuration. These changes, to be described in more detail later in this chapter, were tested on a 1/10th scale model test flown for the first time on March 20, 1953 on a piggyback booster. Unfortunately, a failure of the booster fins ended the flight.

NASA via Ben Gunther

The MX-1712 model was booster launched from the NACA's facility at Wallops Island, VA. Chord size of the swept wing is notable.

NASA via Ben Gunther

A 1/10th scale model of the MX-1626 (Model 2) immediately prior to a booster propelled launch from Wallops Island, VA.

Three engineers at Langley's Pilotless Aircraft Research Division (PARD), R. N. Hopko, R. O. Piland, and J. R. Hall, now set out to find what a configuration designed by the area rule, and yet fulfilling the general requirements exemplified by the MX-1964 configuration, would look like and what its drag rise would be. They started with a 3% thick, 60° delta wing, modified by a 10° swept-forward trailing edge to form a semi-diamond planform, to provide a more gradual transition in area progression. To this wing they added four separate nacelles staggered chordwise, and made the fuselage a body of revolution with an indentation to make the total area distribution of the configuration nearly identical to that of a good parabolic body. The internal volume was made 60% larger than that of the MX-1964.

A 1/15th-scale rocket model of the PARD design was constructed in the Langley shops and launched at Wallops with a single tandem *Deacon* booster on January 22, 1953. This was the first complete airplane model designed by the area rule to be flown at Wallops Island. A helium gun model was also flown. Both tests showed a drag rise coefficient of only 0.010, less than half the original value for the MX-1626.

The results of the area ruled model tests were shown to AF and Convair representatives at a joint conference at Langley. The AF insisted that Convair give some serious consideration to a complete redesign of the MX-1626 using area rule technique. Langley concommittantly agreed to test equivalent bodies of revolution in the helium gun.

The result of this was the testing of four new Convair designs. It was found that when the basic design was changed to provide a smooth area progression with minimum cross-sectional area, the drag rise was as low as that found in the PARD design. Convair, following the results of these tests, now became enthusiastic about the area rule findings and extended their analysis to various supersonic Mach numbers as well as Mach 1.

The initial area ruled MX-1626 tests were followed by several 1/15th scale model tests. Two of these, occurring in November, 1953 and October, 1954, were failures, but were followed by a successful launch on December 14, 1955. Mach 2 was achieved during this flight which was initiated using a *Nike* booster. The results indicated a drag coefficient of 0.028 at Mach 2. Not surprisingly, the rocket-model results were in good agreement with wind-tunnel results under similar conditions.

Besides airframe testing, the AF had also requested that the NACA assist in the development of the MX-1626 pod, and particularly in the development of the powered version of the pod. Accordingly, a 1/7th-scale rocket model was built under NACA contract RA A73L132, dated May 25, 1954. Two models of the pod were flown in 1954 to investigate the drag, and one model was flown in 1956 with the canard control pulsed to measure control effectiveness and stability.

One of the drag models was propelled to a Mach number of 1.5 by a double *Deacon* booster; the second drag model had a *Nike* booster to provide data to a Mach number of 2.5. The measured drag results were in good agreement with estimated values. The stability model was flown to a Mach number of 2.58 with a *Nike* booster. Extensive control and stability information was obtained.

Rocket model testing of Convair's configuration studies was paralleled in Boeing's MX-1712 project—though by the time of the rocket model tests, the MX-1712 had already lost to Convair's MX-1626. Two MX-1712 models were eventually flown, with the first ending in failure due to structural disintegration of the model immediately after separation from its booster, and the second resulting in a successful mission.

The MX-1712 model, as tested, had an 11-channel telemeter to transmit continuous measurements of accelerations, angle of attack, horizontal-tail incidence, static and total pressure, and pressures in one of the engine nacelles. The horizontal tail was pulsed between two stops during the flight, to provide longitudinal data over a range of lift conditions. A maximum Mach number of 1.75 was reached in the successful test.

The test provided an excellent set of drag data over a lift range that included maximum lift-drag ratios. Minimum drag coefficients were about 0.012 at subsonic speeds and 0.035 in the supersonic range. All data were in reasonable agreement with previous wind-tunnel tests.

While the rocket model test program was progressing intermittently at Wallops Island, Wright Air Development Center (WADC) began following, with considerable interest, the work being conducted by the NACA on what was called Recoverable Body Technique (RBT). Taking place at NACA Ames, this consisted of free-flight tests of large scale aerodynamic bodies at high subsonic and transonic speeds. To conduct the tests, models were dropped from a carrier aircraft at an altitude of 40,000' and permitted to accelerate to Mach numbers of 1.10 to 1.15. Recovery was made at 18,000'. Several MX-1626 configurations and components were tested using this method, generally verifying the results of wind tunnel and rocket model tests that were taking place concurrently.

In reviewing the fiscal year 1952 research and development program, the AF determined that it could support only one strategic bomber development program if it were to fund other urgent aircraft projects. Consequently, the fiscal year 1952 budget prepared by the Air Staff contained only funds for one of the two supersonic bomber projects funded for study programs during the previous year.

Side-stepping the issue, the Director of Research and Development for the AF and Deputy Chief of Staff/Development AF, Brig. Gen. D. N. Yates, commented that the ARDC should not terminate or accelerate the projects, or commit or obligate additional funds, but should simply support the work outlined in the contracts until AF headquarters could decide on the basic requirements for the new bomber.

ARDC headquarters eventually accepted the single line item of "Strategic Bomber/Reconnaissance Airplane", but interpreted it to mean

that the assignment of all funds to a single line did not dictate only one approach to the bomber; rather, the funds could be used to support Phase I development of several approaches to the strategic bomber/reconnaissance development.

Convair, in the meantime, worked closely with the Wright Air Development Center (WADC) in refining the criteria by which the strategic bomber/reconnaissance aircraft would be judged. This, in turn, permitted Convair the privilege of refining its own design, these providing improvements in speed while deleting the expendable pod engine and adding a three man crew, an improved bomb/navigation system, and afterburners.

Fiscal year 1951 funds included amounts of $1,100,000 for the Convair MX-1626, and $750,000 for the Boeing MX-1712 partial Phase I developments. Since AF headquarters had restricted any additional obligation of funds as of June 5, 1951, the WADC anticipated that money for the MX-1626 would be exhausted by December 1, 1951, and those for the MX-1712 would be exhausted by November 5. Col. E. N. Ljunggren, Chief of the Bombardment Branch, Aircraft Section, now appealed to the ARDC commander by stating that both contractors had successfully met their contractual obligations and had assembled program teams that were highly susceptible to funding curtailment. The colonel recommended that the ARDC sustain both programs so as not to lose the work already accomplished. He also asked that the fiscal year 1952 budget line item number 610-A-40 for the strategic bomber be used to support both the MX-1626 by $1,147,000, and the MX-1712 by $2,935,000 in order to complete Phase I development.

Although the dates on which the funds were expected to be exhausted were revised to February 15, 1952 (and later to February 28, 1952) for the MX-1626, and to January 15 for the MX-1712, the WADC had not, as of mid-December, 1951, received any further information concerning basic requirements or authorizations for the projects. Consequently, the center asked for an immediate go-ahead on the two programs and permission to use fiscal year 1952 funds to complete Phase I. WADC also called for the establishment of firm military characteristics for strategic bombers in the general performance class of the Convair and Boeing designs and tentative tactical bomber characteristics.

The estimated total cost of the MX-1712, Contract AF33(038)-21388, dated February 26, 1951, with Boeing Airplane Company, was $44,935,000 and the estimated cost of the Phase I program was $3,535,000. The scheduled mock-up inspection date was extended to December, 1952, and the first flight date, in the event that the Phase II contract received support, was December, 1954.

By March, 1952, contract AF33(038)-21250, as yet with no aircraft on order, was still supporting partial Phase I development with Convair. Engineering had proceeded under Development Directive 00034, and the AF estimated the total cost, including government furnished aircraft equipment (GFAE), contractor furnished equipment (CFE), and an air-to-surface missile, as $125,061,250, although the estimated cost of the partial Phase I program (including the missile Phase I) amounted to $5,089,790. In the event the AF ordered production of a prototype aircraft, a flight date was tentatively set for October, 1955.

In response to the WADC's mid-December, 1951, request for a defined program requirement, the AF headquarters Director of Requirements published General Operational Requirements (GOR) for Strategic Bombardment System Number SAB-51 on December 8, 1951, calling for a complete bombardment system which could deliver munitions against enemy targets in strategic warfare. The GOR was predicated upon the increasingly formidable defenses of the Soviet Union. Because of this, the strategic system's effectiveness had to improve continually by integrating new systems with superior performance.

To meet the concept of operations specified in the GOR and to cope with enemy defensive capability, the aircraft had to possess a minimum 4,000 mile radius using a two-stage concept, and a 2,300 mile radius at 50,000' from advanced and intermediate bases; perform low altitude missions at high subsonic speed, and utilize maximum supersonic dash capability; possess flexibility when performing missions with short radii; delivery munitions weighing 10,000 lbs. of a size 60'' in diameter and with longitudinal dimensions which would permit a 3-mile ballistic dispersion; and operate nearly automatically. In regard to development, the aircraft would have design priorities of minimum size and high performance (altitude and speed). It would have to be reliable, simple to operate, flexible without compromising performance, require minimum maintenance, be capable of mass production, and be economical from the point of view of national resources. The GOR further predicted that after 1957, any AF strategic system would have to be able to perform at very high subsonic to supersonic speeds, and at both low and high altitudes. Military characteristics were to follow the publication of the GOR.

Brig. Gen. J. W. Sessums, ARDC Deputy for Development, gave the program a new dimension at the end of February, 1952, by calling for a competition between Boeing and Convair, and ARDC headquarters realigned the Convair MX-1626 program as of March 10. Gen. Sessums sent to WADC the GOR's for the Strategic Bombardment System and for the Strategic Reconnaissance Systems, Number SAB-51 (December 8, 1951) and SAR-51 (February 1, 1952), respectively. Included as well were the pertinent development directives which contained operational objectives and funding information. The directive provided the WADC with the authority to begin support efforts on behalf of the operational requirements.

The GOR's were very much in agreement with the planning objectives; the requirements were stated in the broadest possible terms to allow the development command the greatest latitude in bringing forth a complete weapon system. With this in mind, the general advised that the target date of ''operational in wing strength by 1957'', established by Development Directives 00034 and 00035, represented a compromise between the projected development time and the forecast date at which the weapon system would be available for use.

The AF now placed heavy emphasis on the MX-1626 and MX-1712 programs and requested that two Phase I projects be initiated in order to support development objectives. These would engage Boeing and Convair in an official competition and, in the opinion of Gen. Sessums, would assure the most rewarding answers to the problems associated with developing a supersonic bomber.

To save time and concentrate fully upon the Boeing and Convair efforts, Gen. Sessums thought it advisable to forego additional competition along then current lines and select the contractors on the basis of experience, facilities, and the acceptability of the proposals which they had submitted. Consequently, the WADC received permission to reorient or eliminate current projects that were peripheral to the main supersonic bomber thrust. In addition, the AF use of funds and its authority to initiate or cancel projects related to the supersonic bomber program was

rescinded.

The objective in revising Project MX-1626, which by now had received a 1A priority (highest), was to develop, test, and make available for production a small, integrated, high-altitude manned strategic bomber/reconnaissance system. It was to be a two-stage aircraft for intercontinental operations and was to use inflight refueling and heavy transport for tanker support. The directives required a radius of 2,300 n. miles for advanced base operations, and 4,000 n. miles for intercontinental operations based on optimum supersonic speeds. The 4,000 mile radius was geared to a single outbound refueling at a distance no greater than 2,500 miles. The aircraft's small size was to be achieved by use of a three-man crew, techniques such as zero launch, the use of external tanks, and expendable stores or portions of the aircraft. Related techniques of high level weapon release and delivery were to be achieved as part of the over-all system, including the air-to-surface missile with a range of 50 miles, secure, non-radiating guidance systems, and a bomb weight of 10,000 lbs. with a diameter of 60'' as cited in GOR SAB-51.

The WADC decision to run two Phase I development programs was to be followed by an evaluation to determine which of the two designs was most suitable for the mission. It was well known, however, within the confines of the WADC that the Convair proposal was the front runner, and accordingly, acquisition of at least three MX-1626's (a flight test aircraft, a complete bomber, and a reconnaissance aircraft) and a prototype air-to-surface missile was being planned.

The WADC on March 12, 1952, now presented its revised program to Convair, breaking it into two Phase I sections—General and Detail. The General Phase I was devised to show all the possible trades of equipment weights for various airframe sizes. It also included a thorough investigation of aerodynamic and engine design parameters which could satisfy the size requirements. In regard to the Convair configuration, the study was to look into the integration of the air-to-surface free fall missile, as well as free fall bombs.

The AF directed both Convair and Boeing to

G.D.

discontinue all work on specific configurations and to undertake only work which fell directly in line with the General Phase I requirements. The study period was to take from six to eight months for completion with a target date of August 5, 1952. Boeing, which was investigating unconventional takeoff and landing, zero launch, and mat landing, received a definitive contract under the new MX-1965 program number to cover all work through August, 1952. Size and weight had proven something of a problem for the various Boeing studies, and accordingly, the company worked diligently on reducing these two elements to their minimums. Consequently, Boeing eventually submitted a proposal for a 180,000 lb. aircraft.

On April 14, the AF negotiated a definitive contract with Convair under the MX-1964 newly assigned program designator calling for the continuation of work on the General Phase I study which was now scheduled for completion in August. By mid-April, Convair had completed major portions of the on-going wind tunnel and aerodynamics heating programs, and had also built partial cockpit mock-ups. A general project review, to which were invited representatives of the AMC, SAC, the ARDC, and the AF, took place during the week of June 9, 1952 at Wright Field.

Both the Boeing and Convair projects were to be evaluated in February and March, 1953. In the meantime, funds were committed to cover the Convair project costs until approximately September, 1953. In June, a proposal from Convair was received calling for a new model with two engine nacelles placed under the wing, a 1/22nd scale transonic tunnel model, and a reworking of the 1/15th scale low speed model (to incorporate tips with 55° to 60° of sweep). The Procurement Division was then requested to authorize the purchase of the models. In the configuration studies, Convair also investigated increased wing area and a decrease in leading edge sweep from 60° to 65°—which was expected to improve altitude and range performance. The engines called for in the configuration studies included use of either two J75-P-1's, two J67-W-1's, four J57-P-7's, four J73's, or two J77's.

Immediately prior to the completion of the MX-1965 and MX-1964 General Phase I develop-

Numerous wind tunnel models of the MX-1626 configuration were built by Convair during 1950 and 1951. This wooden 1/10th-scale study illustrates the lower pod with its V-shaped tail fins and the mounting of the engine nacelles past the wing mid-span point.

NASA via Ben Gunther

NASA via Ben Gunther

MX-1626 transonic wind tunnel studies were conducted at the NACA's Langley, VA, facility. Two different engine nacelle studies are shown. Note that the fuselage has yet to be modified to incorporate area ruling. Tunnel tests of this configuration proved disappointing at supersonic speeds.

ments, the WADC planned preliminary configuration selection conferences with Convair for August, 1952, and with Boeing for September. The conferences were planned to enable the contractors to review program progress and recommend specific configurations and development programs.

By mid-April, Convair had completed the General Phase I studies and major portions of the wind tunnel tests, the aerodynamic heating tests, and the partial cockpit mock-ups. The August conference followed with presentations by Convair on the 19th and 20th. During the following month this data, along with that generated by Boeing on the MX-1965, was analyzed by the WADC. The results of the Convair studies were contained in Convair reports FZP-4-005 and FZP-4-007 (dated August 18, 1952). The studies indicated that a weapon system in the 150,000 lbs. category could be developed to meet the requirements of DD 00034. The WADC then prepared a Detail Phase I recommendation that was forwarded to the ARDC on October 9, 1952. This included the WADC proposed military characteristics and most importantly, a recommendation that the AF select the Convair approach to the new system.

By October, 1952, the development program required selection of more detailed characteristics and the most suitable Detail Phase I programs for the integrated aircraft weapon system, the powerplant, and the electronic and control system. WADC analyses of both the MX-1964 and MX-1965 data (on the basis of the contractor's estimates) showed that both designs met performance and size requirements and that the subsonic performance estimates were reasonable

given assured use of the General Electric X24A engine and the presumed equipment weights. However, WADC evaluators considered the Convair supersonic drag estimates to be 10% to 15% optimistic, as were the weights of both contractors, although the WADC still concluded that the GOR and size requirements could be met. To do so would require extensive monitoring of military equipment load increases.

With funding and time constraints now bearing pressure on the supersonic bomber program, a recommendation was made calling for the elimination of one of the two competing designs. This would take advantage of eliminating the need to develop electronic and control systems for two dissimilar aircraft, make possible a more extensive development of the one system through concentration of funds (expected to be $15,000,000 in 1953), save time necessary for contractor selection following the mock-up, and make it possible to transfer contractor teams to other necessary developments.

While both configurations met the GOR's, there were great differences between the characteristics and capabilities of the respective designs. On the basis of the WADC evaluation of the contractor's work, the WADC concluded that Convair's approach best satisfied the "spirit of the DPO" and provided the most promising means of achieving a supersonic capability with a weapon of minimum size. The WADC thought that the Boeing design would yield either an aircraft of small size with poor supersonic capabilities, or one so large it would not achieve reasonable supersonic performance. In short, the WADC did not believe that the Boeing design would satisfy the development objec-

tive. Accordingly, it recommended that Convair, but not Boeing, be given a Phase I development contract.

At the time, Convair appeared to be four to six months ahead of Boeing in detail and integrated design; thus, it was recommended that Boeing be eliminated from the program. Nevertheless, the WADC did not yet consider the Convair design a totally satisfactory weapon for delivery of thermonuclear warheads and suggested that a study of an optimized thermonuclear system be substituted for the Boeing MX-1965. WADC administrators again proposed the use of the weapon system concept, and that Convair be chosen for a full-scale, Phase I development program with the responsibility for integrating all aspects of the system. In summary, the WADC recommended:

(1) Adoption of the proposed military characteristics as the basis for a Detailed Phase I program.

(2) Selection of the MX-1964 approach.

(3) Beginning of a full-scale, Phase development program with Convair.

(4) Taking action to program the system into the AF inventory; to begin pre-production planning; and to prepare for production go-ahead upon the conclusion of the mock-up inspection.

(5) Placing the system integration responsibility on Convair.

(6) Placing the development responsibility for selected contractor furnished equipment (CFE) on Convair (i.e. making this the first true weapon system approach to acquisition by making Convair responsible for all aspects of program acquisition and control).

(7) Beginning the development of the X24A engine immediately as government furnished aircraft equipment and programming it into production.

The ARDC reviewed the WADC proposals and Lt. Gen. E. E. Partridge notified AF headquarters of the completion of the review in late October, 1952. After reiterating and amplifying the WADC's position, Gen. Partridge noted, "As a result of our studies and careful analysis of both contractor's proposals, this Command has determined that Convair's MX-1964 approach to the problem best fulfills the spirit and intent of the Strategic DPO and best satisfies the GOR's SAB-51 and SAR-51. It is believed that the supersonic drag figures used by the contractor are 10% to 15% optimistic; however, because of their unconventional design concepts, it is believed that the MX-1964 represents the best balances between performance capabilities, military features, size, and timing for this weapon. This command considers that it provides the most promising means of achieving a useable supersonic capability with a minimum size weapon.

"In light of the foregoing information, it is desired [that] the competition between Boeing's MX-1965 and Convair's MX-1964 be stopped immediately and one company be chosen as the prime contractor for the High Altitude Strategic Bomber/Reconnaissance System.

"The MX-1964 be selected as the approach to the . . . . system requirements . . . . and that Convair be named the prime contractor for this system.

"Authority be granted for the immediate initiation of an all-out effort to develop the X24A engine by the earliest possible date."

Though there were some ARDC changes to the WADC recommendations, most were approved. Additionally, the operational availability date was moved from 1958 to 1959 and it was recommended that the requirements for the system be re-examined in order to take into account improvements in technology and Soviet defensive capabilities. Consequently, the WADC instructed Convair to work primarily on the construction and testing of wind tunnel models pending the receipt of further instructions from the AF.

Chapt. 5:
The B-58 is Born

Possibly the earliest full-scale mock-up study conducted by Convair for its supersonic bomber program was this cockpit model for the MX-1626. Small size is indicated by pilot.

Concern over the MX-1626's intercontinental bombing mission and its decidedly cramped cockpits led to additional mock-up studies exploring improved and roomier crew accommodations.

After learning of the ARDC's recommendation to pursue Convair's MX-1964 study in the form of hardware procurement, the Air Force confirmed its requirement for a high altitude strategic bomber/reconnaissance aircraft and reiterated the need for an operational system at the earliest possible date consistent with minimum size and supersonic capability. The Pentagon then approved the MX-1964 approach and the ARDC's selection of Convair as the prime contractor; granted authority for beginning an intensive X24A engine program; instructed the ARDC to notify Boeing that the competition between Boeing and Convair had come to an end; and reviewed the ARDC proposed military characteristics. It asked that late development of the X24A not be allowed to delay obtaining test aircraft (a readily available powerplant, such as the J57, would be utilized as an interim propulsion unit). And it requested that the ARDC supply a production schedule in view of the $15,000,000 programmed for fiscal year 1953, and the $17,000,000 programmed for fiscal year 1954.

Maj. Gen. Putt, on December 2, 1952, wrote to Convair's president to state that a contract would be negotiated "in the near future" and that the officially assigned designation for the new bomber, as of February 5, would be B-58. Gen. Putt also told Convair and the WADC that the contractor would have the full responsibility for developing and producing the aircraft under the weapon system concept (which was itself being further formulated by the ARDC). A Weapon System Project Office was, in fact, organized with six personnel from WADC and AMC in December in response to this.

Among the most pressing issues which had to be resolved before proceeding with the B-58 were the military characteristics and configuration. Convair and the NACA discussed the contractor's estimates of aerodynamic drag on several occasions during December 1952 and January 1953, and established a firm test program covering the construction and firing of the 1/15th scale models (see Chapt. 4), and for wind tunnel tests of the 1/22nd scale model in order to arrive at the estimated full scale drag values. The Wright development center also asked Convair to begin an intensive study of performance capabilities,

particularly in regard to the refueling aspects with a newly proposed tanker (Boeing's forthcoming KC-135A).

In January, 1953, the MX-1964 Project Office, which had just been separated from the New Development Section of the Bombardment Branch, conferred with Convair representatives to devise the contractual clauses and procedures which Convair and the AF would follow. The "Additional Contractual Clauses", negotiated with Convair during the week of January 12 thru 16, assigned many responsibilities to Convair but still allowed the AF to retain complete control over the program. The clauses covered the assignment of the weapon system responsibility to Convair; the

Government's responsibilities; determination of and responsibilities connected with choosing items of equipment as GFAE (Government Furnished Equipment) or CFE (Contractor Furnished Equipment); procedures for obtaining approval of performance specifications for major subsystems; procedures for obtaining approval of the weapons system model specifications; establishment of the qualification testing program; and relationships between the WADC laboratory personnel and the Convair subcontractors.

The clauses became a part of the contract on February 12, 1953 as Supplemental Agreement Number 5. As a result, Convair received a complete go-ahead to begin the Detailed Phase I Pro-

The first complete full-scale mock-up was built around the MX-1964 configuration. In the foreground can be seen the lower component and in the background, the upper, or return component. To the left, an elevated stand-mounted cockpit section was used to simulate pilot impressions during takeoff.

The MX-1964 mock-up was completed in late 1952. This was the first study to incorporate a tail turret and to permit crew interchangeability in flight. Additionally, the wing sweep angle was decreased from that of the MX-1626 to 60°.

Numerous tail turret studies were conducted by Convair in an attempt to preserve the extraordinary aerodynamic qualitites of the aircraft. Empennage section drag was considered critical to the B-58's overall performance.

The MX-1964 configuration return component had a flat fuselage undersurface once the disposable pod component was jettisoned. Nose gear requirements were also complicated by the fact that both the pod and the return component required a nose gear.

Studies were conducted during the course of the MX-1964 development effort calling for the use of the Pratt & Whitney J57 in place of the General Electric J79. Development of the latter proceeded rapidly enough to call for cancellation of the J57 option, seen in mock-up form, here.

gram on the XB-58 and XRB-58 which were, by then, approved by the Air Force. WADC commander, Maj. Gen. Albert Boyd's comment of "Good" was written across the message that Convair had signed the contract on the afternoon of February 12, 1953. To all involved, this implied a firm go-ahead for the program and a strong indication that a major milestone in the history of the world's first supersonic bomber had been reached.

Selection of the design for the B-58, though narrowed to several basic configuration concepts, was the next major step in the program. On the basis of the recommendations which the WADC and the ARDC had submitted to the AF in November, 1952, the AF had approved the Convair approach, but not a specific Convair design. Prior to March 24, 1953, Convair had continued with the refinement of its August 1952 design, making preliminary studies to determine what configuration changes were necessary to meet the proposed military characteristics of October 24, 1952. On March 24, 1953, on the basis of conference recommendations, the AF was able to select what it considered to be a firm configuration and during the first week of April, authorized Convair to proceed with work on a full-scale mock-up. The configuration was to have a 60° delta wing with the trailing edge swept forward 10°, a wing area of 1,544 sq.', an aspect ratio of 2.1, and a wing thickness ratio of 4.01: it was to have four engines with the two inboard units mounted on pylons under the wing and the outboard engines mounted on the wing upper surface. The fuselage was to have the "coke bottle" shape in accordance with the area rule theory, and a small amount of leading edge camber to reduce drag due to lift.

The "coke bottle" shape, or area ruling, as it was more commonly known, had been devised earlier by Richard T. Whitcomb of the NACA Langley Field Laboratory. This theory had predicted and explained the performance shortcomings of the Convair F-102. Whitcomb had completed his study of transonic airflow surrounding the various aerodynamic shapes in the summer of 1952 and, in July, had made his results known to the AF. Additional research performed by Robert Jones of the NACA Ames Aeronautical Laboratory in California had demonstrated that the effectiveness of fuselage indentation varied with the aircraft speed; over Mach 1.2, the critical cross section area was that intersected by a cone rather than a plane. According to Whitcomb, the aerodynamic drag of a winged body at transonic speeds depended on the ratio of total cross section area at any station to the total length of the airframe. Wind tunnel tests showed that a symmetrical semi-streamlined shaped with a total cross-section area of the combined wing and fuselage at a corresponding point induced precisely the same amount of drag. Reducing the cross section area to the dimensions of an aerodynamically streamlined shape greatly reduced the drag. In the case of the wing body combination, area reduction meant indenting the fuselage sufficiently to compensate for the cross section area of the wing. This produced the oddly shaped "coke bottle" (also sometimes referred to as "wasp waist") fuselage in which the nose and tail sections appeared to be considerably greater in diameter than the midsection. Actually, the volume of the midsection (the total of cross sectional areas, when added to the volume of the wing) equalled the volume of a symmetrical, non-indented fuselage, alone; Whitcomb's formulae defined the minimum acceptable ratios of fuselage length to cross sectional area, and these dictated the configuration of the indentation.

Not surprisingly, the early Convair design was

largely inconsistent with the Jones and Whitcomb area rule theories and wind tunnel and rocket model tests. By the summer of 1952, the WADC believed that the area rule theory would be the best guide to low transonic drag and, in some respects, to supersonic drag, and consequently had these incorporated into the B-58 design which was selected in March, 1953. This configuration did use split engine nacelles, but the AF required Convair to continue its investigation into the use of Siamese nacelles mounted underneath the wing (as on the B-47's inboard pylons). It appeared at the time that it might be necessary to shift from the split to the Siamese type in order to achieve a weight reduction of approximately 1,000 lbs. and also improve maintenance accessibility.

The split nacelles, however, with one engine above and one under each wing, were finally selected to conform to the area rule requirements—even though some studies indicated that the Siamese configuration would entail very little drag penalty.

As with previous configuration studies, the crew was to consist of a pilot, navigator/bombardier, and a defensive systems operator. A jump seat was to be added so that one of the crew could sit next to the pilot to assist in the operation of the aircraft, if necessary. The tail defense of the aircraft would consist of one 30 mm gun in a remotely controlled turret covering a 60° cone and with space for enough ammunition to permit a 30 sec. burst.

Additional wind tunnel testing by the WADC in June, 1953 caused concern in the Aircraft Laboratory about the B-58's flutter characteristics. The elevons and rudder were not inherently balanced and depended on the rigidity of their actuating systems to prevent flutter. The position of the engines and the anticipated Mach number of 2.1 similarly produced some qualms. Flutter experience with the delta wing at that time was meager, although engineers had devised time-consuming and unproven theoretical methods for predicting it. The safety factors for the aircraft were consequently questionable, and the Aircraft Laboratory recommended wind tunnel tests of a subsonic flutter model and tests of supersonic flutter models using rocket powered models, the latter being limited due to cost. Work on the initial phases of the wind tunnel program began on a priority basis in June and early July and proceeded on a greatly accelerated basis.

Throughout all of the design development work that had now consumed over half a decade, there still was no firm military characteristics specification. The characteristics originally proposed had been developed by the WADC in October, 1952, but only tentative characteristics had been released by March, 1953. It appeared to some project officers that these called for more than could be reasonably expected of the B-58. Gen. Boyd wrote to Maj. Gen. C. S. Irvine that the entire matter had been of great concern to the WADC since Convair was conducting the Detailed Phase I design on the basis of the ARDC's proposed characteristics specification. Unfortunately, though there was an attempt to clarify the matter once and for all, it was not until the end of 1953 that a firm set of specifications were formulated.

Earlier, in January, 1953, the AF had asked the WADC about its B-58 program plans. The WADC presented a schedule which called for the completion of the first production aircraft in January, 1956. The first 30 aircraft would be used for test and development; of these, the first 18 would be powered by P&W J57-P-15 engines, while those that followed would have the J79-GE-1 (known in its prototype form as the X24A). Twelve aircraft, numbers 19 through 30, would get 50 hour J79's while the remainder would receive 150 hour

An MX-1964 wind tunnel model, with cambered wings and Siamese nacelles, is seen in the 16' transonic wind tunnel at the NACA's Langley, VA, facility. The fuselage, by this time, incorporated area ruling and other refinements later found on the actual B-58.

By September, 1953, the B-58 had evolved into a virtually new design with a separate pod, Siamese nacelles, wing-mounted drop tanks, and the relocation of the search radar from the pod nose to the fuselage nose. These changes helped realize a considerable weight saving with virtually no drag penalty.

Another view of the September, 1953, B-58 configuration. Details of the still-developing tail turret arrangement, the landing gear wing fairings, and the permissible ground clearance with the aircraft in a fully rotated takeoff position are visible.

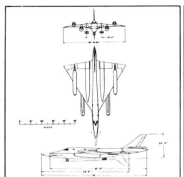
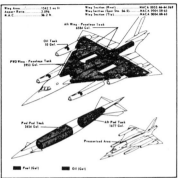
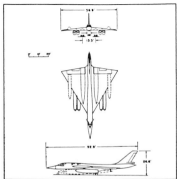
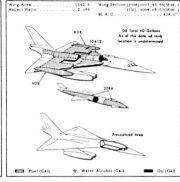
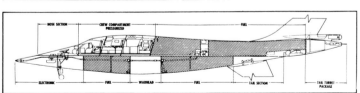
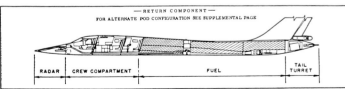

Two early MX-1964/XB-58 studies which were to reach the full-scale mock-up stage before being discarded in favor of the more suitable split nacelle configuration eventually built. The earlier study is on the left. Both configurations are shown photographically elsewhere in this chapter.

engines. An operational wing would consist of 45 aircraft and spares. The first aircraft would be delivered to SAC in January, 1958. If that schedule could be maintained, the B-58 would be operational in wing strength by early 1959.

This program eliminated the familiar prototype test articles of earlier bomber projects. Production was to move at a slow rate until the complete system had reached a suitable stage for delivery to SAC. Use of the J57 engines would hopefully insure earlier testing and evaluation of the airframe and major subsystems and eliminate the excessive maintenance associated with new engines.

In August, 1953, various AF organizations including the WADC, AF headquarters, the AMC, SAC, the Special Weapons Center, the Flight Test Center, and ARDC, sent representatives to a Development Engineering Inspection (DEI) at Convair to observe the B-58 mock-up; at that time, however, only space mock-ups for the major subsystems were available. In September, 1953, another inspection of the portions of the RB-58 which differed from the B-58 was held and again only space mock-ups were available. Out of these, a number of changes evolved.

The B-58 at this time was at a design stage called Configuration II. Basically, this consisted of a lengthy pod and an upper component which were adjacent rather than separated by a pylon. Although this configuration was adopted, both the AF and Convair continued studies in their attempt to delineate the optimum airframe and to overcome the problems imposed by the semi-integral pod. Wind tunnel testing led to alterations in the location of the fuel tanks, the landing gear arrangement, and the radar equipment. Further changes resulted in a shortening of the pod to a length of 30' and its separation from the fuselage with a pylon. Additionally, the search radar was removed from the pod and placed in the nose of the upper component; the droppable nose gear was eliminated; external fuel tanks were added to compensate for the fuel lost due to the shorter pod; and the positions of the navigator/bombardier and the defensive systems operator were reversed.

In November, 1953, the WADC finally received the official military characteristics specification for the B-58. Referred to as Number 345 (SAB-53-A1, dated September 11, 1953), the characteristics generally set greater performance standards than had the tentative ones and required the carrying of payloads in addition to the originally specified warheads.

A WADC preliminary review indicated that the B-58 configuration could probably meet the requirements of SAB-53-A1. On the basis of partial approval of the model specification, the WADC authorized Convair on December 4 to initiate construction of the B-58 front wing spar, secondary wing spars, and the chordwise bulkheads. Several weeks later, following completion of the review, the WADC forwarded formal notification of approval to Convair. With the improvements which had followed Configuration II, there appeared no reason that the newly named Configuration III would not satisfy the requirements. The formal XB and XRB-58 mock-up inspection was then set for the last week of March, 1954.

Controversy over nearly all aspects of the B-58 program intensified throughout 1954. The program objectives, the development techniques, the appearance of the airframe, the weapons system process, and many systems and subsystems were changed, rescheduled, deleted, or replaced. During February, 1954, the September 11, 1953, characteristics were formally implemented in the B-58 program. Subsequent additions to this included characteristics related only to the reconnaissance version of the B-58. The new characteristics also incorporated the requirements calling for the B-58 to carry high yield thermonuclear, biological, and chemical weapons as well as some of the more conventional high explosive bombs.

On March 3/4, 1954, the WADC and the AMC gave a presentation on the B-58 program to ARDC and AF representatives which resulted in a major shift in program emphasis. The new AF ground rules directed that primary concern be placed on research and development rather than upon production. The operational date of 1958 was no longer specified and the concentration was to be upon achieving certain successful technical developments.

No change was made in the projected 1956 date for the first test aircraft, and there was no indication of lessened urgency in the development of subsystems. However, complex equipment was to have a longer development time so that analysis of aerodynamic effectiveness could be accomplished prior to production. In short, the program was to be more flexible, and the thorough research to be performed in advance of production pointed toward a realistic rather than an arbitrary operational date.

In early March, as a result of the studies which had gone on during the first months of 1954, the WADC revised the production schedule to reflect the emphasis on development rather than an early operational date. This schedule covered the first thirty aircraft, all destined for the test program. The first nine, to be designated YB/RB-58, were still slated to receive the J57-P-15 engines, while aircraft numbers 10 through 30, designated YB/RB-58A, were to receive production J79-GE-1's. With the thirtieth test aircraft rolling out in December, 1958, the next, designated B/RB-58A, either in the same month or January, 1959, would be the first delivered to SAC.

On April 30, 1954, this schedule was presented to the Secretary of the AF. He approved a go-ahead on the YB/RB-58 program through the first 30 aircraft and directed that appropriate procure-

Gross weight takeoffs with J57s in hot weather and/or from short runways led to a RATO system requirement for the B-58 during the early mock-up study period in late 1953 and early 1954. This option was later deleted when use of the General Electric J79 became assured.

By August, 1954, the final B-58 configuration, four individually pylon-mounted engines and all fuel contained interanally and in the podded lower component, had evolved and the design was frozen.

Few major changes would transpire between the completion of the August, 1954, B-58 full-scale mock-up study and the roll-out of the actual prototype aircraft. Note various pod mock-ups to the rear of the B-58.

ment funds be released immediately.

At this time, there still existed considerable AF concern about the potential performance of the B-58. In May, Col. H. A. Boushey, Director of Air Weapon Systems, compared B-58 development with that of the F-102 and reminded Convair that the company had estimated performance for the F-102A that was not attainable due to weight, thrust losses, and lower aerodynamic performance. Col. Boushey expressed concern that "predicted performance of the B-58 also may not be attainable", and asked that the WADC be advised of management and engineering plans which Convair intended to follow to prevent a recurrence of the F-102 debacle. Information which the WADC most desired pertained to weight control, trim drag, thrust losses due to powerplant installation, and general drag estimates.

Convair's summation of the requested information arrived at the end of the month. Convair president J. T. McNarney compared the estimated performance of the B-58 and the known performance of the F-102A in terms of thrust and fuel consumption, weight, and drag. He alleged that the latter aircraft's thrust had met the predicted values in the low supersonic region (high supersonic tests had not been conducted at that time) and he therefore assumed that the company's development and testing techniques were satisfactory. An extensive test program was underway to develop the optimum entrance and exit designs for the B-58 engine/nacelle combinations. Convair, according to McNarney, had pursued an active weight reduction in all its aircraft since 1942, and the methods developed were being applied with even greater vigor in the B-58 program. In regard to drag, McNarney stated that the estimates for the B-58 were based on extensive wind tunnel tests which had not been completed. While the B-58 had made "excellent progress" in model drag improvement, its radius could not be estimated closer than 15% with the knowledge then available. McNarney indicated that increased reliance on the F-102 flight test program to provide high subsonic Mach number data at the B-58's lift coefficient, and tunnel tests of exact models of the YF-102 and the F-102A would improve the estimates for the B-58.

In the memorandum on the B-58's performance status, which accompanied McNarney's letter, the drag, weight, and fuel aspects were spelled out in detail. Convair saw the problem as one of making accurate assessments of the correctness of the original performance predictions, and of mak-

ing changes wherever necessary in the areas of aerodynamic drag, weight of the dry aircraft, expendable load and useful fuel, propulsion system thrust, and fuel consumption characteristics.

In the area of drag, the memorandum report stated that the predicted full-scale drag of the aircraft, when reduced to an equivalent skin friction coefficient, resulted in a value which appeared to be "well within reason when compared to experimental values obtained in flights on modern high-performance jet aircraft". Convair laboratory tests showed that advanced technology sandwich-type skin construction of the wings would produce surfaces which would retain their smoothness under all flight and load conditions. However, that potential improvement had not yet been applied to the full scale drag estimates then in use.

Similarly, no scale corrections had been applied to the drag-due-to-lift data for supersonic speeds, but a correction had been made in the subsonic data based on an analysis of existing data in wind tunnel and flight tests of similar low aspect ratio aircraft. The analysis predicted a decrease in the drag coefficient of .003 at the cruise lift coefficient of .25, amounting to approximately 450 n. miles radius. Trim drag predictions apparently agreed with the experimental values. The inflight control of the aircraft cg permitted the average elevon deflection to be held at 3°, a deflection within the minimum trim drag region.

Convair also contended that the drag rise critical Mach number indicated in model tests was accurate for full scale predictions, but there was then no flight test data available for aircraft designed to have a critical Mach number approaching one, and consequently no correction was justified at that time. In the area of transonic and supersonic wave drag, the data in early 1954 was quite meager although Convair believed that values obtained on the models were directly applicable to the full scale aircraft.

Weight control, the second major performance category, received the contractor's full attention throughout the entire B-58 development program, as evidenced by the delta wing, parasite, and pod principles, the original two-man crew, and the expendable engine. In-flight refueling and the replacement of the two large engines with four smaller turbojets possessing a higher thrust-to-weight ratio also meant reduced weight. Concurrently, the adoption of the area rule theory permitted an increase in gross weight along with a substantial reduction in drag and a negligible increase in empty weight. An improved pod con-

figuration, which resulted in a weight increase, was offset by a reduction of composite aircraft drag and improved pod performance. Convair thus pointed out that the weight increase of the B-58 had to be measured in terms of other factors; in particular, the ratio of gross weight to empty weight had increased during the entire development history. Items such as sandwich construction rather than plate stringers in the wing structure not only reduced weight, but provided for higher working stress levels in the basic wing bending material and precluded the need for more weight from additional fuel tank insulation. In early 1954, the weight of the aircraft configuration was below that of the model specifications, and a number of changes then under consideration were thought to be capable of producing a further 1,300 lb. empty weight reduction.

In regard to thrust and fuel consumption, Convair shared its responsibility with the General Electric Company for engine exhaust nozzle performance and had direct control of the recovery of ram pressure at the compressor inlet and extraction of power for auxiliary use. It was apparent from the beginning of the program that a variable inlet would be necessary and the company's studies soon led to the choice of a two-shock inlet consisting of a central cone within a fixed round inlet. The position of the sliding cone would be controlled automatically by sensing pressure in-

The NACA conducted a series of drag exploring booster-launched tests with the MX-1626 configuration at their Wallops Island, VA, facility.

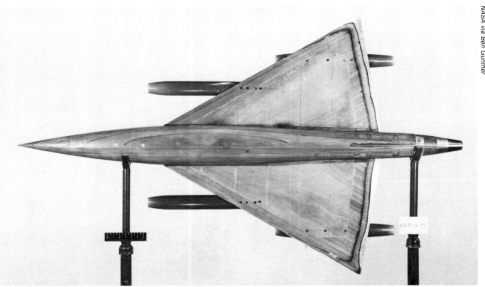

NASA via Ben Gunther

The NACA's PARD team developed this Model 5 study of the MX-1626 to serve as a a baseline for the their research into area rule work for Convair's supersonic bomber. This particular configuration was developed in June, 1953, and helped lead the way to the incorporation of area rule in the full-scale aircraft.

G.D.

By March, 1953, area rule and leading edge camber had been incorporated to create the MX-1964 configuration illustrated by this transonic wind tunnel model. These changes increased the expected gross takeoff weight to 150,000 lbs. and the inflight-refueled gross weight to 158,000 lbs.

NASA via Ben Gunther

The MX-1964, in mid-1953, still had an uncambered wing and split engine nacelles. A transonic model is seen in the 16' tunnel at the NACA's Langley, VA, facility. Top surface mounting of the outboard nacelles was an attempt to eliminate shock wave interference anomalies.

creases across the normal shock range. On the basis of its tests, Convair predicted no scale effect for inlet performance. However, a full-scale test was planned for the NACA Lewis Propulsion Science Laboratory. Auxiliary power to run aircraft and engine accessories would be a maximum of 175 input horsepower, ¼ of 1% of the total thrust horsepower needed at Mach 2 at 55,000', or 1% at Mach .95 at 35,000'. Average requirements would be lower, and it was assumed that maximum compressor bleed would never exceed ½ of 1% of the engine airflow. That amount, even though quite small, had significant effects on fuel economy and was equivalent to several hundred pounds of sized weight for a typical mission. Further fuel economy, it was noted, would result from the performance of the ejector nozzles. The early MX-1626 studies had shown that a variable convergent/divergent (C/D) exhaust nozzle would provide large gains in supersonic performance. This came partly from a fuel economy gain of up to 15%, and partly from a favorable effect on the operating level of the lift/drag ratio. G.E. therefore committed itself to the development of a variable C/D nozzle thrust coefficient of 0.975 for the J79. Tests which G.E. had performed indicated that it would be possible to meet the predicted performance.

From May 12 through 14, 1954, project managers from the WADC conducted a Development Engineering Inspection of the B/RB-58 at Convair's Fort Worth plant. Among the changes requested were several submitted by SAC: side-by-side seating for the pilot and copilot, rather than the tandem arrangement which had been projected; the addition of an ECM pod to complement the pods already programmed; and the installation of an existing bombing navigation system, suitably modified, rather than launching into a development program for a new one.

On May 5, the ARDC made the decision to use the General Electric-designed 20 mm T-171 multibarrel gun in conjunction with the new bomber's active defense system. Several units by different manufacturers, covering various bores, firing rates, and firing velocities had been considered, but the G.E. weapon had proven undeniably superior.

In early June, 1954, the WADC submitted a revised development plan to the ARDC. This was necessary to incorporate the various changes which the ARDC had requested as well as to reflect a change in the development schedule. Convair announced, on June 30, that the first flight date would be rescheduled from January, 1956, to June, 1956. This set back the production schedule by a full six months. At almost the same time, the WADC received Procurement Directive 55-10A, dated June 29, 1954, authorizing the procurement of 13 aircraft and releasing funds amounting to $191,065,100.

Warhead configuration remained an unsettled proposition during the spring of 1954. The military characteristics specified the W5 or W13 warhead, but these proved too large and too heavy, and therefore impractical for B-58 transport. Late in the spring, the ARDC deleted the W5 and W13 from the B-58 mock-up requirement and consequently asked the Special Weapons Center at Kirtland AFB to prepare a feasibility study of warheads dedicated for B-58 use. Requirements were desired for thermonuclear, or stage 2, atomic warheads. Early review of this request at Kirtland indicated that Class B, C, or D warheads could be used to accomodate the B-58's needs.

During the better part of 1954, differences of opinion between the AF and Convair grew over the B-58 configuration. Not least among these was the design of the fuselage, wing, and nacelles. Convair's estimates of drag performance were at variance with those of the AF which caused considerable discussion over basic configuration studies. Periodically, the AF and Convair advocated either split or Siamese engine nacelles and by mid-1954, the Siamese configuration was the one generally accepted by Convair. AF and NACA representatives, at this time, however, had begun to have doubts that the Siamese configuration could ever attain the performance estimated by Convair. The split nacelle, they felt, would produce less drag. Convair's decision had been to accept the increase in drag while providing maintenance and installation advantages. In late March, 1954, however, the AF B-58 project officer visited Fort Worth to discuss wind tunnel tests which had demonstrated that the Siamese nacelles would create excessive and perhaps insurmountable drag at speeds from Mach 1.6 to 1.9. While the figures could not be correlated with previous data, the B-58 project office could find no inherent error and therefore proposed that additional work be delayed while new tests were run.

Wright Field engineers and the NACA facility which had derived the new drag figures found that although the drag for the wing and fuselage corresponded with predictions for the indented fuselage, high speed drag did not decrease as expected when the Nacelles were added. When the pod was attached to the underside of the fuselage, predicted drag characteristics were further altered. Thus, Siamese nacelles were found to create greater drag on the composite aircraft (with missile or pod) than did split nacelles—although the latter had little effect upon the aircraft by itself. Without the pod, the characteristics of split and Siamese nacelles scarcely differed.

Consequently, a return to the split nacelle appeared to be in the offing. The research came to an abrupt halt at Wright Field in May when the 10' wind tunnel experienced a power failure, but the NACA Ames Laboratory continued the work during the first half of June. When on June 23, 1954, the B-58 project office received the results of the tests at Ames, use of the split nacelle became a certainty, but the changes and delays had altered the development schedule and forced the postponement of the mock-up inspection from the initially scheduled May date to September, 1954.

During July, 1954, Convair completed a series of tests which it had conducted in the NACA Ames supersonic tunnel and as a result recommended a revised configuration incorporating the split nacelles with the outboard nacelle snuggled under the wing on a short pylon. NACA advised Wright Field that this might induce buffeting in high subsonic and transonic speed ranges and urged additional tests prior to any decision, a position identical to that of engineers in the WADC aircraft laboratory. On the other hand, Convair asserted that its performance estimates indicated that this revised configuration would meet the requirements of the Military Characteristics Number 345, and the AF agreed that the altered configuration probably possessed all the known aerodynamic improvements which might increase performance. Still, the AF doubted that the configuration would attain the performance estimates established by Convair.

Consequently, the WADC decided that it would make a thorough evaluation of the aerodynamics of the B-58 as soon as it could restore the 10' tunnel. Convair, in the meantime, drew up a new set of performance estimates.

In August, the B-58's configuration was officially changed to include the individually mounted nacelles suspended on pylons below the wings. The fuselage was also revamped to agree with a modified transonic "area rule" configuration, and the use of external fuel tanks was eliminated entirely. Additionally, the vertical fin and rudder areas

were increased to a total of 160 sq'.

The numerous doubts, configuration changes, and sundry delays in beginning full-scale fabrication, caused Convair to indicate, in August, 1954, that in addition to the postponement of the mock-up, the delivery schedule would again have to be revised to reflect a slippage of seven months in the production of the first 30 aircraft.

Early in the following month, Convair formally presented the results of its most recent investigations and made performance predictions to the WADC and the NACA. The three organizations then discussed the aerodynamic aspects of the revised configuration in order to outline additional tests which would be useful in evaluating the B/RB-58A performance. The general tenor of the discussions was that Convair's performance predictions for the latest configuration were still optimistic, and Convair agreed with the WADC and the NACA that additional tests would have to be conducted before making any definitive aerodynamic evaluation. The center informed Convair—whose estimates exceeded the requirements of the military characteristics—that there was reasonable doubt that the configuration could meet any of the performance requirements. Although Convair had used the F-102 flight data to correlate the B-58 wind tunnel results, Brig. Gen. H. M. Estes considered the approach unacceptable since it involved only one set of data and the resulting figures were much higher than the WADC could substantiate. The WADC consequently withheld approval. The additional tests were then scheduled for the Wright Field 10' tunnel to obtain more F-102 and B-58 data; rocket firings of scale models were also on the agenda,

and these and the tunnel tests were to be supplemented by scale tests in the NACA transonic tunnel and by AF examination of data on other high-performance aircraft.

In a presentation to Maj. Gen. Floyd Wood on September 24, 1954, the WADC recommended that Convair continue to investigate but postpone work in certain areas until Convair and the AF could evaluate the most suggested configuration. The WADC then instructed Convair to consider three options to minimize disruption of the program. First, Convair could continue development engineering and associated testing in all areas except airframe fabrication. Second, for areas not affected by the configuration change, Convair was to go on with the developmental engineering, testing, tooling, and fabrication. Tool design and construction and fabrication of affected airframe parts would be halted. And third, the company might continue all development engineering and associated testing in all areas, but discontinue all tool design and fabrication of tools related to the production of initial B/RB-58's and, concurrently, discontinue airframe parts fabrication.

Convair engineers were to evaluate the various courses and inform the WADC of their impact on program scheduling and costs; also, the contractor was to determine the probable magnitude of the project if the changes were not approved prior to December 1, 1954. For its part, the WADC was committed to the December 1 date for making firm recommendations to the ARDC. Col. Damberg deemed it advisable to postpone the mock-up, but thought it possible to resolve the program problems before the December deadline. Gen. Estes, on the other hand, thought that the

NASA via Ben Gunther

A 1/15th scale model of the final B-58 configuration is seen just prior to booster launch from the NACA's Wallops Island, VA, facility. Speeds in excess of Mach 2 were possible using this launching technique and telemetry data was highly reliable.

tests in question would prevent any such resolutions during the remainder of the year. Consequently, the WADC withheld approval of the rocket and wind tunnel model specifications and directed Convair to continue with certain aspects of engineering and testing.

In response to Col. Damberg's directions, Convair considered the various options which it might take. A. C. Esenwein, V.P. of Convair, agreed with the project office that whatever action was in the best interest of the government and the B-58 program, must be taken, but added, "Convair believes that the configuration presented by the revised Model Specification is the best design supportable by the current state of the art and studies applicable to this particular Weapon System; the B-58 will meet the performance requirements of the applicable Military Characteristics; and it is reasonable to expect that changes to the proposed configuration within the initial design and development period will be confined to design requirements and improvements resulting from advancement of the state of the art".

Convair proceeded with its work on the B-58 in accord with the scheduled requirements except for the fact that it undertook no tooling for or manufacturing of production parts affected by the configuration change. Esenwein noted that the

reduced effort had begun to effect the July 15, 1956 first flight date (as of 9/20/54), and that the flight would be delayed on a day to day basis during the discontinuation of tooling.

Convair evaluated the three options which the WADC had suggested and then added a fourth of its own for comparing three "reduced effort" options with a proposal for fully resuming the task on October 11, 1954. According to Convair, the tooling for the basic wing structure was the controlling factor for the B-58 production schedule, and Convair's analysis showed that continuation of the restrictions on tool design and fabrication until December 1, 1954, would delay the first flight by 2½ months beyond the August 6, 1956 flight date. The other options, Esenwein stated, would cause substantial employee layoffs and reassignments, only to result in an accelerated hiring schedule upon the resumption of activities. Convair wanted the mock-up inspection held as soon as possible and a date selected whenever the AF decided upon one of the options, that is, on or before October 11, 1954.

Following an analysis of Convair's option discussion, the WADC imposed their original option and stated that Convair would maintain the manpower level and effort for tooling manufacture without change. Convair was allowed to continue

development engineering and related testing in all areas, but had to discontinue (or not begin) any fabrication of airframe parts for the initial B/RB-58. The WADC sanctioned the continuation of tool design and construction with the then-present manpower level, thereby avoiding any layoff of tooling personnel. The AF said that the restrictions would remain in effect until December 1, 1954. Cost increases of $915,000 would be absorbed by the government.

Maj. Gen. Albert Boyd, at this point, was determined to push the B-58 program ahead. Lt. Gen. Thomas Power, then commander of the ARDC, asked Gen. Boyd to express his personal opinion of the B-58 program and the best course to follow. Gen. Boyd replied that the AF should continue on its present course. He also noted that the best WADC analysis indicated that the B-58 would not meet the radius and altitude requirements of the military characteristics, but pointed out that the AF's short experience with supersonic aircraft made it difficult to assess the accuracy of the estimates. He also noted that, "The B-58 is a major advance considering that we are attempting to more than double our speed capabilites. For this reason, I believe that it has a place in the AF inventory, even if we cannot employ it in the exact manner that was intended.

The compatibility of the lower component/pod and the upper component were vigorously wind tunnel tested by Convair and the NASA before the configuration was cleared for full-scale hardware development. A transonic tunnel model of the late-1953 B-58/MX-1964 configuration and its associated rocket-propelled MA-1 pod is shown mounted upside down for photography purposes.

A 1/15th-scale transonic tunnel model of the B-58 in its final configuration. Transonic tunnel models such as this one were usually of all-steel construction to accommodate the dynamic and thermal requirements of test work at supersonic velocities. The size of the elevons on this model are noteworthy as they are considerably larger than those utilized on the actual aircraft.

"Since we are attempting such a major advance, there is very naturally a high degree of risk incurred. We do not know all the answers and will not until we have flown such an aircraft. Thus, we must accept such a risk sooner or later if we are in fact ever going to achieve a truly supersonic bomber. Failure to accept this risk now will only mean the introduction of this risk and probable resulting delays in any future program, such as the new nuclear powered strategic bomber. Deletion of the B-58 effort at this time would create a major gap in this area."

Although Gen. Boyd and others at the WADC were dissatisfied with Convair's technical management of the program, particularly in regard to duplication of test facilities and Convair's alleged tendency "to engineer the component or subsystem through detailed and restrictive specifications", he believed it was necessary to remove the restrictions which the AF had imposed and accept the risk and cost of proceeding.

In addition to the specific performance aspects of the B-58, the AF had become quite interested in the rising development costs. In November, 1954, they had asked the ARDC for its latest cost estimates and followed up with the question, "What effect would a reduction of $100,000,000 in FY 55 funds have on the B-58 program?". It was becoming clear to all concerned that SAC was re-examining its requirements for an aircraft such as the B-58 with its relatively limited range, performance, and operational time period.

In a joint presentation by the AMC and the WADC at ARDC headquarters on December 21, 1954, the WADC voiced opinions to the Master Planning Board which Gen. Boyd had already expressed to Gen. Power. By this time, the AF had

been doing business with Convair on the basis of a letter contract signed in February, 1953, and was spending a total of $4,500,000 monthly; tooling and manufacturing had been restricted to Convair's then-present facility and manpower resources, and Convair was still awaiting approval of the model specification while appearing ready for a mock-up inspection. The WADC took the position that while the B-58 had not met either its altitude or radius requirements, the configuration did contain all the aerodynamic improvements which could increase its performance. Through normal growth and possibly use of high energy fuels, the B-58 would probably meet the military characteristics or at least provide significant gains in the tactical area. The program cost, while comparing favorably with others, was such that an early decision was mandatory.

The WADC and the AMC outlined four possible courses which the ARDC might follow: one, the program could be continued as it was planned; two, the time period of the program could be stretched; three, the program could be cut back drastically; or four, it could be terminated. The WADC commander reiterated his opinion that in view of the minimal AF experience with supersonic aircraft, a risk was necessary to build a supersonic bomber. As Gen. Power had stated, the B-58 was the first opportunity to bridge the gap between subsonic and supersonic flight, a problem which demanded extensive knowledge of aerodynamic heating and aircraft materials. WADC and AMC officials concluded that even with the B-58's limitations, delay or cancellation would present far greater risks; and stretching out or cutting back the program would simply increase the cost, but

not guarantee better performance. Maj. Gen. Clarence Irvine of the AMC stated that the program was worth the money which the AF had invested if only to advance understanding of aircraft. He added that if the AF discontinued the program, it would lose $200,000,000 whereas the estimated total cost to complete it was $500,000,000. Therefore, the joint recommendation which emanated from the WADC and the AMC was that the B-58 program should be continued as planned.

Opinion was not totally harmonious, however, and Maj. Gen. John McConnell, SAC's Director of Plans, declared that his command was interested in the development of the B-58 as a future weapon system but not for the SAC inventory. SAC's lack of enthusiasm stemmed primarily from the B-58's limited range; Gen. McConnell called it a "short legged plane" and commented that "as long as Russia (and not Canada) remained the enemy, range was important". Gen. Power, who later remarked that the "B-58 is a better B-47", was more than a little concerned with SAC's position that the B-58 would not replace the B-47 as either a medium or intercontinental bomber, and he began to think in terms of orienting the new bomber toward Tactical Air Command requirements.

Among the many delaying factors in the B-58 program, two of major proportions which struck in early 1955 were SAC's outright rejection of the aircraft, and the AF's dictum that the project be extensively reviewed. Dwindling enthusiasm for the B-58 had occurred primarily because the bomber probably would not meet performance requirements (SAC had become more and more insistent upon the unrefueled intercontinental mission). SAC wanted no B-58's for the operational

HUNTINGTON CITY TOWNSHIP
PUBLIC LIBRARY
255 WEST PARK DRIVE

inventory, even if the aircraft could be made to perform as envisioned, and Gen. LeMay, then SAC Commander-in-Chief, notified AF headquarters to that effect on January 4, 1955. Program costs ranged beyond the original estimates, and a major part of the research needed to support any future bomber program was concentrated on the B-58.

Pronounced uncertainty over the program had actually emerged during the summer of 1954, and it was to continue until January, 1958. The AF had first begun to doubt the performance capabilities of the aircraft in mid-1954; at about the same time, Convair was first able to analyze fully the wind tunnel tests of a model large enough to provide relatively accurate performance predictions. Configuration changes followed in the fall of 1954, and the B-58 thereby gained the split, rather than Siamese nacelles and an area-ruled fuselage for Mach 2 performance. In December, 1954, a joint AMC/ARDC presentation at the latter's headquarters indicated that the then-current B-58 contained all the known aerodynamic improvements, and on the basis of the knowledge then available, the aircraft still did not appear to meet its desired military characteristics. The disillusionment was capped by the negative SAC position and the B-58 program was then destined for a protracted period of review.

Amid all the problems that were now surrounding the B-58 program, the Secretary of the AF appointed a B-58 Review Board on February 2, 1955, to examine or revise the B-58 program and to make recommendations to the AF. Maj. Gen. Clarence Irvine was selected as the Board Chairman. Other members included Maj. Gen. Boyd, Dr. H. G. Stever, Col. Donald Hillman, and Col. George Criss, Jr. Vice Chief of Staff, Gen. Thomas White, made the actual appointments to the board on February 8, and outlined the objectives which they would have to meet by a March 1, 1955 deadline.

The three major items which the board considered were whether the B-58 program should be continued, modified, or cancelled, the scope of the program if continued, and the procedures for accomplishing whatever the board recommended. The review would determine as well as possible: (1) the performance of the B-58; (2) its value as a strategic weapon from the date of availability to phase-out; (3) its military worth for roles such as air defense, tactical missions, and research and development; (4) the commitments,

obligations, and expenditures in the program; (5) the extent of associate and subcontractor structure and impact of program modifications or cancellation; (6) fiscal implications of program modification or cancellation; (7) effect of program modification or cancellation on other research and development programs and subsystem and component developments; (8) the contractor's capability and the probability of bringing the program to conclusion; and, (9) alternative courses to meet AF objectives in the event that cancellation or modification of the B-58 program were recommended.

The B-58 Review Board first met on February 7, 1955, in Maj. Gen. Boyd's WADC office, and subsequently through the month of February heard presentations from various WADC laboratories, the NACA, Convair, Boeing, and Lockheed. Items discussed during these, and later, meetings included B-58 roles, parametric studies, performance data evaluation, long range interceptor missions, use of super-fuels, subsystems status, and relative cost studies.

On March 10, 1955, the B-58 Review Board presented the results of its study to the AF Air Council and the Secretary of the AF. The AF analysis of the Review Board's report resulted in a statement by AF Secretary Harold Talbott that "the B-58 program could be conducted if it did not cost more than $400,000,000." Thus the program was officially reoriented in June to a 13 aircraft research and development program.

This did not end the various inquiries into the program's difficulties, however, and on April 8, 1955, Gen. Irvine outlined to the president of Convair's Fort Worth division the possible courses of action which the Review Board had considered. He warned that the Secretary of the AF had not as yet made a final decision concerning the program—although he had called for "austere control of costs by Convair and by responsible AF agencies so as to reduce to the bare minimum the total program cost of manufacture and flight test of 13 B-58 aircraft equipped with J79 engines". Gen. Irvine instructed Convair to hold its expenditures to the lowest possible level prior to any official program approval.

On June 2, 1955, Secretary of the AF Talbott directed the ARDC to prepare a plan to utilize the 13 B-58 test aircraft and to present its plan for approval by June 30. Various meetings with AF and Convair personnel followed and on June 30, the WADC presented to Gen. Power and his staff its

plan for reorienting the program from its original 1952 objective of developing, testing, and producing a high-altitude, manned strategic bomber/reconnaissance weapon system to a 13 aircraft test program "to provide high-speed, high-altitude aircraft for investigating aerodynamic problems of sustained supersonic flight and for use as test vehicles in the development of sub-systems and components for future weapon systems".

At this time, heavy emphasis was now placed on cost cutting measures, and the proposed interim use of the J57 engine was eliminated entirely. The flight test program was also reoriented to investigate the problems of sustained supersonic flight and to develop components and subsystems for future weapons. The AF was slated to conduct great portions of the flight test and static test programs. The first flight date was now set for October, 1956.

Gen. Power approved the WADC plan, thereby implementing the reoriented B-58 program on June 30, 1955. The AF consequently acted to strip the B-58 of all non-essential items, and to commence with the 13 aircraft program. Since the new undertaking made no commitment for inventory production, full qualification testing was deleted as a requirement for all major subsystems, and ground support equipment was limited to the interim type. Tooling was held to an absolute minimum and work on the station-keeping and rendezvous, refueling, and long-range communication equipment and training devices was stopped.

On August 22, 1955, the reoriented B-58 program was abruptly reversed. The AF concluded that the program it had ordered consummated at the end of June "would not provide the AF with a suitable weapon system for potential integration into the inventory on a timely basis". Consequently, "necessary actions, consistent with minimum fund obligations, must be taken to insure that this program is developed as a weapon system with the objective being to have the capability to provide a wing of B-58's in the inventory by mid-1960. Restoration of essential phases of this program necessary for development of the B-58 as a weapon system will be undertaken immediately.".

The B-58 program was once again adjusted accordingly; station-keeping and rendezvous equipment programs were restored, although work on the long-range communications and refueling gear was deferred pending the final decision to place the supersonic bomber in the AF inventory.

A 1/64th-scale transonic tunnel model of the B-58 which illustrates how the MB-1 free-fall pod separation technique was explored in model form. In this particular test series, conducted at NASA Langley, VA, the lower component was tested in 43 different positions at varying equivalent speeds and altitudes.

NASA via Ben Gunther

Chapt. 6:
Controversy and Flight Test

Two views of the B-58 production line at Convair's immense Fort Worth, TX, facility. The aircraft production line was actually elevated above floor level to permit access to the undersurface areas as well as those on top. The MB-1 pods, visible in the right photo, were produced alongside the main B-58 airframe. Aircraft visible in the right photo include airframes 33, 34, and 35.

On July 28, 1955, the AF told the ARDC that the B-58 would be continued with the objective of developing a mid-range, high-altitude, supersonic bombing system. This was followed, on November 23, by Definitive Supplemental Agreement No. 26 attached to Contract No. AF33(038)-21250 which superseded the long-standing letter contract (designated Supplemental Agreement No. 6) calling for the construction of 13 Convair Model 4 aircraft and 31 pods (12 MA-1, 16 MB-1, 2 MC-1, and 1 MD-1). This Supplemental Agreement called for the aircraft, pods, spares, ground support equipment, and test support equipment, and increased the contract funds by $340,450,762.

This was, to all intents and purposes, the final step toward the hardware realization of the world's first supersonic bomber. Convair and the AF had labored long and hard toward the elusive goal of a prototype go-ahead, and with the signing of the November 23 agreement, this objective had at last been at least partially achieved.

As has already been noted in preceding chapters, the B-58 was, from its birth, a highly controversial weapon system. At the end of 1954, for instance, Gen. Curtis LeMay, Commander-in-

Chief of SAC, and his staff, had reviewed briefings and participated in conferences pertaining to the development of the aircraft. In a final conference at ARDC headquarters on December 21, 1954, LeMay noted that, "after a thorough analysis of the B-58 program, it is concluded that the B-58 can not be developed to encompass sufficient radius of action and defensive capability required for an acceptable Strategic Bombardment Weapons System" and that the aircraft "was not desired in the SAC inventory". LeMay did note that the B-58 should possibly be continued as a purely developmental program, but he emphasized that a more conventional bomber would be preferred for the SAC intercontinental bombardment role.

SAC, even in consideration of LeMay's feelings toward the aircraft, remained relatively supportive and continued to think of the B-58 in terms of being a replacement for all or part of the Boeing B-47 fleet. SAC regarded the greatest advantages of the B-58 to be its small size and its ability to operate supersonically at high bomb delivery altitudes. With one refueling 2,500 miles from its takeoff in the "zone of interior", it appeared to

have sufficient range reserve for most targets. The aircraft, SAC believed, would be dependent upon forward bases for deep penetration, but it could be operated as an intercontinental bomber on a limited basis in the event that advance bases were denied. All delivery was predicated on nuclear systems, and the B-58 would, in service, practice this at the peace-time rate of 40 flying hours monthly; and be utilized 106 hours monthly during time of war.

At Convair, preliminary hardware construction had already been started under the various previous minimally funded contracts. Accordingly, once full contract approval was granted, work on the first thirteen aircraft was initiated as rapidly as the Convair construction teams could complete jigs and assimilate materials and reference drawings. In late January, 1956, the B-58 forward fuselage work stations were completed in the Convair plant at a cost of around $25 thousand; and at the same time, work neared completion on cradles and tooling fixtures to permit B-58 work to proceed at each of the stations simultaneously.

In February, a Convair C-131B operating from Falls Church, Virginia, was added to the rapidly

Assembly Sequence

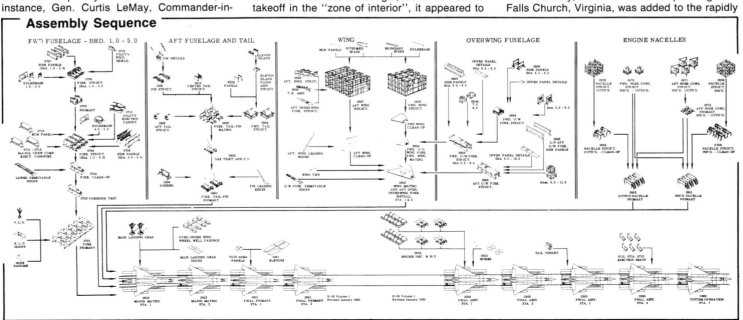

Chuck Hansen collection

The General Electric T-171 gun and associated Bendix MD-7 fire control system were initially tested while mounted in the tail gun positions of two Boeing B-47's. Two Mod IV cameras were mounted rigidly to the articulated portion of the unit to provide visual verification of tracking and aiming accuracy.

Frank Strnad collection

A single Boeing KC-97F, 51-332, was modified by Raytheon to accommodate and test the B-58's innovative doppler and search radar systems. The former unit was mounted in a special ventral fairing just to the rear of the wing section, and the latter was mounted in a simulated B-58 nose section and associated radome.

G.D.

USAF

Convair built a single ejection seat test sled for the B-58 program which was eventually utilized to test both the conventional SACseat and later, the Stanley-built encapsulated seat. This unit is now displayed at the small aerospace museum presently in the formative stages at Barkesdale AFB, LA.

growing fleet of B-58-related systems test, support, and chase aircraft. This fleet, by the end of the contractor flight test program, would include the following:

Boeing B-47, serials unknown—two aircraft were modified in mid-1956 to test the Emerson MD-7 fire control system and its associated General Electric 20mm rotary cannon; the systems tests took place at Eglin AFB to determine gunfire effects, ballistic dispersion, tracking and gun-aiming accuracy; Emerson Electric and Convair personnel worked together on the program.

Boeing KC-97F, 51-332—modified for high frequency Ku band radar and doppler radar systems tests; it incorporated a B-58 nose radome in place of the standard C-97 radome and a ventral fairing under the fuselage (for doppler system).

Convair B-36B, 44-92052—modified to test B-58 bombing and defensive systems under the auspices of the 4925th Test Group at Eglin AFB, Florida; this aircraft was equipped with an unusual nose radome to accommodate the B-58's radar bombing system and other equipment to study ballistics data of weapons dropped from high altitude; tests were conducted over Eglin AFB and the Matagorda Test Range in the Gulf of Mexico.

Convair YF-102, 53-1784—used as a chase aircraft.

Convair TF-102A—many were assigned to the program for use as delta wing trainers.

Curtiss C-46A, 42-101095—utilized to perform logistic support missions. A total of 88 B-58-related missions were flown.

Douglas C-47A, 43-30677—supported 4392nd Test Squadron and nicknamed "Hustler's Mother".

Grumman F8F-2, BuNo. unknown—used for limited variable stability tests.

Lockheed F-94B, 49-2500—this was a variable stability research aircraft developed and operated by Cornell Aeronautical Laboratory, Buffalo, New York, and utilized in the B-58 program to investigate and demonstrate the B-58's predicted stability characteristics.

Lockheed F-94C—several used for chase and test work by Convair.

Lockheed F-104A, 56-747—used as chase aircraft.

Lockheed JF-104A, 56-763—used as chase aircraft.

Lockheed T-33A—used for training.

McDonnell F-101A, 53-2424—used as chase aircraft.

McDonnell F-101A, 53-2433—used as chase aircraft.

McDonnell RF-101A, 54-1494—used as chase aircraft.

North American F-86A, NACA 135—NACA-owned variable-stability research aircraft based at Moffett Field, California, and utilized in an extensive investigation of the B-58's dynamic stability flight characteristics as related to the B-58's flight control system; many detail design confirmations and several design refinements were realized from the variable-stability F-86 program.

Northrop F-89, 51-1412—was modified to incorporate a B-58 longitudinal control system; this testbed moved the B-58 control system ahead by at least a year; it later was used for nuclear test sampling.

Expansion of the initial B-58 production program by this time was providing business for nearly 3,000 vendors, subcontractors, and suppliers. This figure would increase dramatically during the months to follow, but it was becoming very apparent that the B-58's impact on the national economy, even at this early date, was substantial.

Hardware development was continuing at this time as well. Initial full-scale testing of the SACseat, as the B-58's Convair-designed ejection seat was being called, was initiated in late February, and a first static ejection, using a 6-foot tall, 200 lb. anthropomorphic dummy, was successfully completed.

On April 19, the Air Council (a select panel of senior AF generals) recommended the release of $13,600,000 to procure long lead time items for a follow-on quantity of B-58 test aircraft, and recommended a review of the program by November, 1956, to determine the desirability of providing another $14,900,000 of pre-production funds for the follow-on 17 aircraft. Convair, just prior to this, announced the near-completion of the first B-58 wing jig fixture. One-hundred-twenty-one feet long, 54' wide, and 30' high, it was, indeed, an impressive structure. Construction, hampered by the three-thousandths of an inch tolerances required, had taken nearly eighteen months.

By July, 1956, construction of the prototype B-58, now being revealed to the public as the world's first delta wing bomber and officially assigned AF serial no. 55-660, was well along. Additionally, though not to be installed in any of the first 13 aircraft, the first complete prototype tail turret, built by the Emerson Electric Manufacturing Company and officially designated as the Active Defense System XMD-7, was delivered and made ready for static ground testing.

The name *Hustler* also was officially applied to the aircraft at this time, though somewhat surprisingly, it had been in use in-house at Convair and the AF since 1952. The name could, in fact, trace its origins back to a need by Convair engineers for a program codename. Robert Widmer, one of the chief project engineers in 1952, had discussed the problem with fellow engineer Stanton Brown. When Widmer described the new aircraft to Brown as having a bomber mission and supersonic speed, Brown's retort was, ''Sounds like it'll really be a hustler . . . . why don't we call it hustler.'' The AF later adopted *Hustler* as the program code word, and in later years, it became the aircraft's official name.

By August, the first aircraft was in final assembly and the arrival of the first four YJ79-GE-1's had permitted installation of the engines in the four suspended engine nacelles. Unfortunately, General Electric ran into J79 delivery difficulties due to a rotor blade qualification anomaly, and as a result no engines were delivered in September—leaving the second prototype B-58, 55-661, temporarily without propulsion. The engine delay was expected to prevent flight testing of this second aircraft until January, 1957.

Completion of the first prototype, 55-660, took place in late August, and on September 1, 1956, it was rolled from the north end of Convair's immense, mile-long facility on the western side of the Carswell AFB reservation in Fort Worth, Texas, for the first time. Shortly after roll-out, functional checks of all installed equipment, including the fuel system, the engines, the autopilot and power control system, the electrical system, and the communications systems were undertaken. The first engine run-up took place on October 1, and on October 29, the first taxi test was completed on the east/west taxi strip on the north end of the main Carswell AFB runway.

The fuel system, which was to prove one of the B-58's several Achille's heels early in the program, was rigorously tested prior to its first flight. A special fuel system test stand was built to provide the most realistic full scale testing of the aircraft's complicated tank, plumbing, and pump systems, and these tests were initiated in September, 1956. Controlled by hydraulic jacks and cables, the stand provided excellent insight into the difficulties of distributing nearly fifty tons of fuel in shallow wing tanks and long fuselage tanks under various flight conditions.

The prototype aircraft was optimized for its testbed role and as such had little in the way of operationally oriented equipment. Instead, test in-

The B-58's complex fuel tank and fuel transferral system was tested using this unit which was built in a test area near the main Fort Worth production facility. The entire assembly was mechanically gimballed to permit tilting and rotation in all directions.

The prototype B-58, 55-660, is seen being moved into final assembly. The aircraft was wrapped in nylon covers for protection and to keep prying eyes from seeing a proprietary configuration. At this time, the engine nacelles had not been attached and numerous subassemblies remained unincorporated.

Immediately prior to its first flight, 55-660, undergoes a final inspection and safety check. The aircraft was to be flown without a pod and with numerous redundancies and purposeful systems limitations. The red, white, and black paint scheme was distinctive and applied only to this aircraft.

Taxi tests were undertaken with FOD (foreign object damage) protector screens mounted ahead of the intakes. Slow speed taxi tests quickly transitioned into high speed runs, including several wherein the aircraft was rotated to its normal nose-high takeoff attitude.

Special markings were applied to 55-660's tires during the taxi tests so that wheel anomalies, if they occurred, could be photographically documented for detailed study. Every run was captured on film. All high speed runs were conducted on the main Carswell AFB runway.

While company employees and observers push against a temporary restraining rope, 55-660 taxis in to its bay at Convair's Fort Worth facility following the successful completion of its virtually perfect November 11, 1956, first flight.

strumentation was predominant, including monitors for powerplant performance and safety, aircraft stability and control, wing and vertical tail flutter investigation, and aircraft performance.

The second taxi test was completed on November 5 with 55-660 moving at 40 knots from north to south. This run led to a tire failure on the left main gear due to a brake anomaly. Two days later, following repairs to the brake, the third taxi test was completed, this being a high speed run at speeds of up to 92 knots. On November 8, during a night session, another high speed run was made up to 138 knots, and on November 11, a final high speed taxi run was made at a speed of 148 knots.

B. A. Erickson, a highly respected Convair test pilot who had achieved significant notoriety during his many years as chief of flight test during the lengthy course of Convair's B-36 flight test program (he was pilot during the first flight of the XB-36 on August 8, 1946—and the first flights of all subsequent B-36 models including the YB-60), had been the virtually unanimous choice among Convair's corporate hierarchy to undertake the first B-58 test mission. He was to be accompanied by similarly experienced flight test observer and systems specialist John D. McEachern in the 2nd seat, and flight test engineer Charles P. Harrison in the 3rd seat. An initial decision to go for the first flight on November 5th or 6th was rescinded when the aforementioned brake failure occurred during taxi tests, and November 11th, a Sunday (also Veteran's Day), was therefore picked as the first flight date—weather permitting. At mid-week, the flight test office notified Convair management and Air Force representatives of its decision and plan. The news media were also advised, as were the local civic and law enforcement and church organizations (the latter in consideration of the Sunday flight schedule). Carswell AFB's command also agreed to reserve the use of the main base runway exclusively for the B-58 first flight beginning at 2:00 p.m.

Flight test goals assigned to the prototype aircraft included the establishment of base line demonstrations for the B-58 performance envelope; the required clearance of structural flutter restrictions; and the confirmation of the basic acceptability of the aircraft's operating qualities including those of functional systems and aircraft stability and control.

As configured for the first flight, the prototype B-58 (officially at this time designated YB/RB-58) had been completed without a number of systems not required for flight test. In place of these, instrumentation was incorporated to obtain aircraft functional and performance data, and to permit in-flight performance monitoring of vital systems and components to assure safety of flight.

The second station, normally occupied on the tactically configured aircraft by the navigator-bombardier, was occupied by a flight test observer. A control panel was installed for monitoring flight test instrumentation. The third station, normally occupied by the Defensive Systems Operator, was occupied for flight test purposes by a flight test engineer. This crew position, similar to the second station, was also equipped with flight test instrumentation and controls.

Additionally, 55-660 had a number of temporary configuration changes incorporated to assure first flight simplicity and conservatism. Among the special modifications found only on this aircraft were:

(1) a reinforced engine inlet and spike actuation system to withstand possible inlet buzz; (2) installation of an auxiliary DC power source; (3) installation of an alternate command radio (ARC-27); (4) blocking of the aft fuel tank manifolds; (5) the auto trim was made inoperative; (6) the automatic ratio

changer was made inoperative; (7) the resolution surface actuator was replaced with a solid link; and (8) the spike controls were made inoperative.

It also was to make the first flight without a pod; it would have a gross takeoff weight during the first flight of 78,000 lbs.; only the forward fuel tank would be full (4,000 gallons)—all others, including the main tank, would be left empty; the longitudinal static margin for takeoff would be kept at approximately 6%; and the engines would have afterburner available only if needed.

The conservative test plan for the initial flight called for: a flight duration of approximately 40 minutes; no use of the afterburners during takeoff (the aircraft was being flown at only half its design gross weight); the forward fuel tank to feed all four engines throughout the flight, thus eliminating any fuel management procedures; automatic features of the aircraft flight control system not to be utilized; takeoff to be accomplished at a moderate angle of attack using an airspeed of 150 knots at liftoff; military power only to be utilized during a 250 knot climb; the landing gear to remain extended during ascent but to be retracted once the aircraft had entered a racetrack pattern over Carswell AFB at 20,000'; semi-stabilized runs at 300 knots, 250 knots, and 200 knots to be conducted for speed/power/trim and pulsed pitch and yaw data; landing gear to be extended and descent for Carswell AFB initiated; and for landing airspeeds to be 200 knots during the downwind, 180 knots during base leg, 160 knots during final approach, 150 knots at touchdown, and 120 knots for drag chute deployment.

In the mid-afternoon of Saturday, November 10, 1956, 55-660 was released for flight by the participating Convair and USAF inspection organizations. The flight test crew immediately conducted their preflight inspection and found everything in good order. The aircraft was then placed under guard in "isolation status" to await its debut the following afternoon.

Sunday morning at Carswell AFB dawned bright and clear and cool. The weather forecast for later in the day called for perfectly clear skies and 70° temperatures with a light breeze from the south. At 8:00 a.m. the flight test crew and Convair and USAF inspection team members began the final preflight inspection, while on the runway, a team of 200 Convair employees walked its length looking for debris that might cause damage to the engines or landing gear (this work would later be accomplished by a large vacuum cleaner developed by Convair and known as the JARC—Jet Aircraft Runway Cleaner). By 9:30 a.m. all of the final preflight inspection procedures and the supporting paperwork were completed and signed off.

At 10:00 a.m. the flight test crew met with key Convair engineering personnel in the flight department conference room for a final review of the initial flight test plan. This was done in consideration of the fact that engineering personnel were going to be situated in the Convair test control center during the initial flight and would be monitoring the aircraft's vital parameters by telemetry. Radio communication with the aircraft would therefore be available to provide technical staff support throughout the flight. Prior to adjournment of the meeting everyone was advised that for the first flight, the test aircraft radio communication identifier codename would be "Enterprise" instead of "660". Also, the word "routine" would be used to mean "no problem".

Present at the engineering meeting was A. S. "Doc" Witchell who, as B-58 back-up pilot, would be flying chase for the prototype in Convair YF-102 53-1784. Witchell was second only to Erickson in terms of familiarity with the B-58. He was already scheduled to become the second pilot to fly the

Posed photo of 55-660 taken less than a week after its first flight illustrates well the new bomber's pleasing lines and conservative markings. At this time, the aircraft had yet to fly while carrying a pod and all flight testing was conducted in a perfectly clean aerodynamic configuration.

In June, 1958, 55-661, successfully completed the first inflight refueling tests of the B-58 program while connecting without difficulty to a Boeing KC-135A. In later years, the B-58 gained a strong reputation for being relatively easy aircraft to inflight refuel because of its inherent stability.

Many B-58 test programs were conducted from Edwards AFB, CA. An ARDC-assigned aircraft, 55-662, is seen taxiing out on radar and related nav/bomb systems test flight without a pod. The vertical fin was orange and the fin flash was red with a white border. The placement of the serial number is unusual.

B-58 aircraft, 55-662, 55-661, and 55-660 (front to rear), are seen undergoing routine maintenance at Convair's Fort Worth facility, probably in 1958. Barely visible at the wing trailing edge root section of 55-662 is the rarely seen resolution surface which was later permanently eliminated.

A two-component pod is seen mounted under 55-663 during the TCP pod drop program conducted from Kirtland and Holloman AFB's, NM. A data link antenna is visible protruding from the aircraft's tailcone. Camera pods for photographing the pod drops are visible suspended under each outboard engine nacelle.

B-58 airframe 4A, never assigned an official AF serial number, is seen during mating to Convair B-36F, 49-2677. The B-36's inboard propellors were removed for the delivery mission, and special anti-sway assemblies were attached between the upper surfaces of the B-58's wing and the B-36's lower surfaces.

The B-36F with its hefty payload is seen taxiing out on March 12, 1957, on its one and only flight in this configuration. All four turbojets and all four piston engines were utilized throughout the mission from Carswell AFB, TX, to Wright-Patterson AFB, OH. Ground clearances were decidedly minimal.

Perhaps the best known photo of the B-36F while carrying its high priority cargo. Justification for leaving the landing gear extended throughout the flight is readily apparent, as is the rationale for removing the two inboard propellers.

Throughout most of the mission to Wright-Patterson AFB, the B-36F and its payload were accompanied by a single Fairchild C-119. This previously unpublished photo, taken from the C-119, shows the B-36 and its payload at cruising altitude and in cruise condition.

aircraft and his work as chase pilot was expected to provide valuable safeguards.

By 11:15 a.m. all preparatory work for the initial flight was complete. Accordingly, Erickson, McEachern, Harrison, and chase pilot Witchell left the plant to grab a quick lunch in nearby Ridglea. By the time of their return, large crowds had gathered all around Carswell AFB and the various Convair facilities, and special invited guests and officials had begun to congregate around the aircraft. The latter group would soon be moved to the nearby electronics building conference room where they would have an excellent panoramic view of the Carswell AFB runway. At 2:00 p.m., the three flight test crew members took leave of those around the aircraft and climbed the access stairs in order to enter their respective stations and begin preparations for flight.

Thus it was that at 2:41 p.m. on November 11, 1956, YB/RB-58 55-660, with Erickson in the front cockpit and McEachern and Harrison in the second and third stations, respectively, became airborne from Carswell AFB's Runway 17 heading south (dictated by wind direction) out of Fort Worth with "Doc" Witchell and the Convair YF-102 in fast chase. A third aircraft, a Lockheed F-94C, was also involved as photo chase.

The initial flight continued to completion entirely as planned. All scheduled flight test events were executed rapidly and with ease. And like the takeoff, the landing proved uneventful and problem free. The duration of the initial flight proved some 2 minutes less than anticipated because several flight test events had moved along a little more rapidly than predicted. Underscoring the initial crew impressions of the aircraft were the flight test data tapes which, when analyzed during the hours immediately following the mission, revealed that all mechanical and structural aspects of 55-660 had functioned as designed. As the final post-flight debriefing reports were written and delivered, 55-660 was tethered in its work station and made ready for its second flight.

Interestingly, in addition to being the first flight of the B-58, the November 11 event also proved the *Hustler's* first public unveiling. Previously, little had been released concerning the major technological advances it represented. Security had been kept tight in order to preserve its major design innovations and performance breakthroughs and the fact that it was a strategic weapon designed to carry thermonuclear devices. And though little concerning the aircraft and its capabilities was revealed following the first flight, Convair and the Air Force acknowledged that the B-58 was designed to fly at supersonic speeds over intercontinental ranges. It was obvious by the coverage given in newspapers around the world that the press was sufficiently astounded by the aircraft's undeniably unique design, and absolutely alluring aesthetics.

Following the first flight, on November 13, Letter Contract AF33(600)-32841 was amended to implement Schedule WA56-2 Extended (dated August 27, 1956). This revised the earlier delivery schedule and consequently changed the potential B-58 operational date from March 1960 to October.

On November 14, the first B-58 made its second podless flight. A maximum Mach number of .94 was achieved at an altitude of 35,000'. With Erickson at the controls, the aircraft remained airborne for one hour.

On December 31, the first MB-1 pod was delivered to flight test from Convair's production facility and preparations were made to make the pod ready for a first flight in early February. The MB-1, a free-fall configuration, had been chosen as the first pod type to be completed due primarily to its simplicity.

The seventh and eighth flights marked the first time the aircraft was flown supersonically. On flight seven, occurring on December 30, 1956, 55-660 was airborne for 1 hour and 5 minutes and achieved a maximum speed of Mach 1.17 at 35,000' (total time at supersonic speed was 9 min.). Flight number eight occurred on the same day, this leading to a maximum Mach number of 1.31 at 35,000' (total time at supersonic speed was 15 min.).

December also saw the initiation of pilot training at Convair when the first class of 10 pilots and observers was accepted. These crews, made up of AF personnel from Edwards AFB, were scheduled to participate in the forthcoming Category II test program.

The USAF Chief of Staff now approved a slow rate of production for the initial quantities of the B-58, emphasizing the development and testing of many aircraft over production capability. Eventually, no less than 30 aircraft would be dedicated to the flight test and development program—far and away a record number for a program of such large and expensive proportions.

In early 1957, Maj. Gen. R. E. Terrill, SAC Director of Operations, acknowledged that his command necessarily found itself becoming more and more involved in the B-58 program. At this time, SAC was preparing to activate the 3958th Operational, Test, and Evaluation (OT&E) squadron at Carswell AFB. This event did, in fact, take place on March 1, 1958, thus making SAC's B-58 test program involvement official. Maj. Gen. Albert Boyd, Commander for Weapon Systems, ARDC, acknowledged at this time that SAC maintained strong reservations concerning the B-58, but that due to problems with the WS 110A program (North American B-70) and possible forthcoming B-58 model improvements (i.e., the B-58B), SAC interest in the B-58 remained strong.

Studies comparing the B-52G to the B-58A were conducted amid all this controversy and the conclusions, thought by some to have been heavily influenced by Gen. LeMay, indicated that the B-52G was a superior and more viable bombing platform. Headquarters USAF bluntly disagreed with the studies' conclusions, and Maj. Gen. Jacob Smart, Assistant Vice Chief of Staff, wrote that the addition of a supersonic bomber to the SAC force at an early date was ''most desirable''.

Bolstering B-58 supporters who favored a major production program was the fact that the Air Force had already invested $750-million and there was little chance that the B-70 would be available in time to fill the already large gap between the old generation and forthcoming new generation bombers. Though the controversy within SAC raged, by the beginning of 1958, it was becoming apparent that the B-58's introduction into the operational SAC inventory was all but inevitable.

By this time, SAC's major reservations concerning the new bomber had been narrowed to its range performance. With one refueling, the B-58 had a radius of action of 3,800 n. miles; without refueling, this distance dropped to a radius of 2,300 miles. These range performances were only marginally acceptable to SAC, and they would remain highly controversial throughout the aircraft's operational career.

SAC was not the only organization to show concern over the B-58. For a week, beginning on February 3, 1958, an 85-man team from the ARDC, the AMC, and SAC conferred with Convair representatives in Fort Worth to develop in detail the final B-58 operational configuration. Their studies and conclusions were consolidated and presented to the Air Council on February 21. Following the report, Headquarters USAF approved eight of the changes which the team had recommended, including the development of a

USAF via AF Museum

Following its arrival at Wright-Patterson AFB, B-58 airframe 4A was placed in the special structural test facility located on the Wright side of the Wright-Patterson AFB complex and there, stress tested to destruction over a period of several years.

Seven Convair flight test crews pose with the ill-fated 55-664. Unfortunately, several of these crews would lose their lives during the course of the B-58 flight test program...serving as a grim reminder that the B-58 was no ordinary high performance aircraft.

Another view of 55-664 as it is prepared to up-load a test MB-1 free-fall bomb pod. This aircraft would later be involved in a spectacular accident that would kill its two crew members and lead to several major design changes affecting the entire extant B-58 fleet and all aircraft then under construction.

G.D.

Several of the initial pre-production B-58's, such as 55-661, shown, had their inflight refueling receptacles mounted further forward on the nose than succeeding production aircraft. As noted in the main text, the B-58 was considered an exceptionally stable inflight refueling receiver aircraft.

USAF via Douglas Robinson

One of the longest lived and most-used B-58's, 55-665 was the first test aircraft to be turned over to the AF. It was immediately assigned to the 6592nd Test Squadron at Carswell AFB, and eventually became ARDC property. Its participation in various little-known flight test programs is noted elsewhere in this book.

two-component pod (later known as a TCP); the use of a single-side band/high-frequency (SSB/HF) radio; the use of an emergency ultra-high frequency radio; the development and use of encapsulated ejection seats (in response to several B-58 accidents which should have been survivable using ejection); the use of TACAN; the incorporation of a deadman switch; and the deletion of the ALD-4 ferret system requirement.

The controversy surrounding the various problems and changes also, at this time, negatively affected the money budgeted for B-58 procurement. As the fiscal year 1959 program was outlined, it reflected forty-seven B-58's to be produced at a cost of $669.6 million. Changes recommended by the ARDC/AMC/SAC board that had met at Convair in February, 1958, added another $316.4 million to this figure, thus exceeding the budgeted figure. In order to stay within budget limitations, it was therefore recommended that several pods be deleted or deferred; that tooling for four, rather than six, aircraft monthly be procured; that contractor reductions be negotiated; and that thirteen aircraft be deleted from the 1959 budget.

The controversy concerning excessive costs raged for several months following the Strategic Committee report concerning options, and eventually a decision was made by Generals White and Power to moderately reduce the program in order to fund the cost increases and the more important improvements. By June 1958, SAC had authorized a buy of 77 B-58's of which 30 were to be utilized for test, and 47 for inventory. The latter quantity had been contemplated in Letter Contract AF 33(600)-36200, dated November 1, 1957, but they had not been placed on contract. The 47 aircraft were eventually reduced to 36 as a result of the aforementioned funding problems.

During this period, in order to provide shot for their cannon, Convair revealed to the AF its plan for an advanced B-58 configuration referred to as the B-58B (also known earlier as the B-58 MI—"Model Improved"). This aircraft, to have been powered by the more powerful J79-GE-9 and having a gross weight of 186,000 lbs., differed only slightly from the B-58A, but did offer increased fuel capacity in the form of more commodious tanks, an enlarged pod fuel tank system, and numerous systems modifications. The increased fuel tankage gave the aircraft significant range improvements (on paper, at least), and thus made it somewhat more enticing from a SAC standpoint.

The B-58B, interestingly enough, did not prove out on paper any better than its stablemate, the B-58A, when compared to the B-52G. Though its range and payload capacities were modestly improved, it still could not compete in the countermeasures and defensive systems department, and its speed advantage was, accordingly, offset. Though, SAC's initial reaction to the proposed aircraft—with its multiple free-fall bomb pods, its extra fuel tanks, and its air-to-surface missile capability—was favorable, it killed the B-58B proposal on July 7, 1959, due in part to the difficulties it was still having with the B-58A, and the fact that it would obviously syphon money away from the sacred North American B-70.

Prior to the demise of the B-58B, support for production funding for the B-58 reached its peak when, on June 11, 1959, the Air Force announced its plan to purchase a total of 290 aircraft (including the 30 pre-production and test aircraft). These would be used to equip a five wing force. Requirements called for permanent assignment of 19 aircraft to the test and test support units and for the equipping of the SAC force. Slippages in production scheduling had, by this time, made it necessary to reschedule the first delivery of tactical aircraft to February, 1960, this indicating that the first tactical wing would not be ready until November 1960. The first 30 aircraft were to roll out of production at the rate of one per month through September, 1959.

During January, 1957, 55-660 completed flights 9 through 13 and was used for the first flight by an AF pilot (on January 22, Lt. Gen. Al Boyd). Exploration of the B-58's control and performance envelope continued and a maximum Mach number of 1.35 was attained. The same month also saw the finishing touches put on a new 40-ton autoclave to be used for baking large B-58 composite structures at Convair.

On February 16, 55-661 made its first flight and during the month, the first supersonic flight (to Mach 1.15) while carrying a free-fall pod. On February 16, it was officially delivered to the AF just as the last B-36 was completed and rolled out the Convair plant doors.

On February 28, the 50 hour Preliminary Flight Rating Test (PFRT) was completed on the General Electric YJ79-GE-5. During this period a number of powerplant problems occurred which seriously effected the progress of the flight test program. Major delaying factors, all stemming from the YJ79-GE-1 engine anomalies, included oil leaks, afterburner lighting failures, a retrofit program for the No. 2 bearing seals, and malfunctioning fuel controls.

In late February, 1957, a single B-58 airframe, never allocated a serial number but designated airframe #4A, was pulled from the Convair production line and modified for a very necessary airframe fatigue test program that was scheduled to be undertaken at the Wright Development Center Structures Test Laboratory at Wright-Patterson AFB, Ohio. In order to expedite delivery of this testbed to the fatigue test facility, and also to provide the most complete airframe possible without jeopardizing its structural integrity, a decision was made to have the partially completed aircraft delivered to the test facility using a B-36F (airframe #152, 49-2677) as transport. In order to accomplish the mission, the B-36's inboard propellers were removed and anti-sway bars were attached to the wing root sections on each side of the fuselage. A temporary shackle system, attached to the bomb hoist mechanisms, was modified to permit snug attachment of the 40,000 lb. fatigue test specimen. The armament system, bomb bay doors, and several compartment bulkheads were removed from the B-36, and 12' of nose and the entire vertical fin were removed from the B-58. Ground clearance for the B-58 test specimen was 22''.

With Jack Baldridge and Earl Guthrie, company pilot and co-pilot respectively, at the B-36's controls, the mission was successfully completed on March 12, 1957, using four of the B-36's six R4360-PW-53 piston engines and all four of its J47-GE-19 jet engines for propulsion. The entire 5 hour flight (average speed, 210 mph) was flown with the B-36's landing gear extended and a Fairchild C-119 in chase.

The ASD-sponsored stress test program at Wright-Patterson AFB, at the time one of the most extensive ever undertaken, was originally scheduled to take some eighteen months to complete and to begin in May 1957. It began on schedule, but did not end until February 1962 after attaining 135% of the aircraft design load. The special airframe had been built to accommodate the connectors for the stress frame assembly and though it was delivered without engine pods or a vertical fin, these were later added to provide a more realistic test airframe. Seventy-five Convair employees were eventually involved in the Wright-Field project under the direction of project administrator W. H. Flickinger.

Another B-58 would also be absorbed by struc-

Shortly after its arrival at Edwards AFB, CA, in 1958, 55-665 is seen being admired by base locals. The B-58's standard polished aluminum skin and black nose radome presented a striking appearance from almost any angle.

Following its assignment to the ARDC, 55-665 is seen during a routine inspection inside one of several large hangars at Edwards AFB, CA. This aircraft is still located at Edwards AFB, though it is now a derelict resident of the Edwards photo test range.

B-58 flight test stable aircraft underwent periodic inspections on a very frequent basis. Two test program aircraft, 55-666 and 55-665, are seen inside Convair's maintenance facility following a routine inspection and shortly before resumption of their respective flight test programs.

Another view of 55-666, following its assignment to the ARDC and Edwards AFB, CA. Like most pre-production aircraft, 55-666 was not equipped with a tail gun and associated turret, and other combat-related systems.

45

G.D

B-58, 55-670, is seen being moved into the USAF Climatic Laboratory hangar at Eglin AFB, FL, on July 8, 1958, prior to the initiation of cold weather tests therein. This aircraft was tactically configured with a tail gun and other combat related subsystems.

tural testing requirements in 1958. Approval was granted on October 8 for the reallocation of 58-1022 from the 6592nd TS to the WADC's structural laboratory for cyclic loads tests. At the time, this aircraft was still new and in fact was operating from Convair's facility at Carswell AFB. On July 8, 1959, the decision to conduct the tests at Wright-Patterson was rescinded and the aircraft was retained at Convair. In October, 1959, 58-1022 was moved into the cyclic loads test facility at Convair and for the next five years slowly tested to destruction.

In the meantime, flight testing of the small, but rapidly growing stable of B-58 test aircraft continued. As part of the weapon system program, it had been decided that the flight test program would be broken down into three major phases and at least four major categories. Phase I, to be accomplished by the company, would accomodate sub-system development test and evaluation and also explore the basic flying characteristics of the aircraft; Phase II, to be initiated by the company and then taken over by the AF, would accommodate systems development tests and evaluation; and Phase III, to be initiated and sustained by the Air Force, would accommodate the development of techniques and procedures for using the B-58 as a weapon. On paper, the program looked decidedly workable; in practice, it proved extraordinarily difficult to execute.

Convair's side of the flight test program, at this point at least, was progressing smoothly. Flight number twenty-four for aircraft 55-660, taking place on June 29, 1957, became the first in which the aircraft design speed was reached. While carrying a dry MB-1 pod, and with B. A. Erickson at the controls, 55-660 reached Mach 2.03 at 43,250'. The flight lasted 1 hour and 55 minutes.

Interestingly, considerable delay had occurred in the flight test program in reaching Mach 2 because of design deficiencies in the B-58's fuel management system. Beginning on April 5, 1957, 55-660 had undergone extensive fuel system modifications (consisting of incorporation of additional fuel warning lights and an inclinometer; segregation of the rear fuselage fuel tank with provisions for pumping directly to the main fuel

manifold during deceleration from high supersonic speeds; and isolation of fuel in an extreme forward area plus automatic fuel transfer to maintain the desired center of gravity) to assure engine fuel feed and accurate fuel quantity gauging during supersonic acceleration and deceleration. These assurances were considered imperative for safeguarding powerplant functions and in providing adequate center of gravity determinations as related to longitudinal static margin control.

The pod drop program, scheduled to begin during the late summer of 1957, entailed many considerations that had not been previously required by more conventional weapon carrying aircraft. Because of the B-58's size, rapid acceleration, and pod location, it was decided by Convair and the Air Force to provide a rather unusual arresting gear arrangement in case rapid deceleration of the aircraft was required during either takeoff or landing. The design of this arresting gear was simple, but unquestionably effective. Lengths of chain, acquired from the Navy and normally used as anchor chain on large boats, was laid along each side of the Carswell AFB runway and connected at parallel ends by a steel cable. The latter would serve as the actual arresting gear (landing gear) connecting point, and would be stretched across the runway and manually elevated in an emergency. It was assumed that the 400 tons of anchor chain would suffice to slow down the aircraft as it played out....

The pod drop program was to be conducted in several phases and numerous steps, and was to be undertaken at Kirtland AFB and Holloman AFB, New Mexico and utilize the services of at least two, and possibly as many as three B-58's. To accommodate the pod consumption requirements, pods were shipped by truck from Convair to Kirtland on a fixed schedule. Many of the pods were heavily instrumented and equipped with radios for data transmission.

The first B-58 to operate from Kirtland arrived on November 26, 1957, and was preceded to the base by the first test pod, which had arrived on the 15th. The pilot for the delivery flight was B. A. Erickson, and his crew consisted of Grover Tate, Jr. and C. T. Jones.

On May 10, 1957, the Air Force announced that the MA-1 bomb pod would be terminated. This unit, a powered, guided pod of significant complexity and cost, had moved along slowly in development and had been the source of some controversy. It was now rationalized that the free falling MB-1 pod could be absorbed into the operational inventory more easily and economically. Shortly afterward, on June 5, the first MB-1 was successfully dropped from 55-662 over the Holloman AFB test range while the aircraft was flying at Mach .9 at 40,000'. A supersonic drop, from 55-663, followed on September 30, this taking place at a speed of Mach 1.4 and an altitude of 40,000'. In October, a drop at Mach 1.6 was successfully demonstrated; and in November, a pod was dropped at Mach 1.8. Finally, on December 20, 55-663, with "Doc" Withcell, Jr., Grover Tate, Jr., and C. T. Jones as crew, completed the first design speed (Mach 2) pod drop. This mission also involved the first operation of the B-58 above 60,000'.

In an attempt to partially demonstrate the real tactical capabilities of the B-58, 55-660 was flown by a Convair crew, on July 24, 1957, from Fort Worth to Wright-Patterson AFB. The total time from takeoff to landing was 66 minutes and the average ground speed was approximately 705 knots. The true airspeed varied from Mach 1.4 to Mach 1.56 at an altitude of 43,000'. The total time at supersonic speeds was 46 minutes. The takeoff weight was the highest to date—131,000 lbs.

In August, 1957, as flight test work continued and additional aircraft continued to be added to the flight test fleet, the first hangar buildings for the B-58 were completed at Convair. These were wing docks left over from the old B-36 program which—though involving a rather minor conversion program—proved ideal for B-58 hangar space. In October, a number of alternate emergency landing fields were officially chosen, these including Tinker AFB, OK; Hensley Field, TX; Kelly AFB, TX; Dyess AFB, TX; and Walker AFB, NM.

On September 27, the first two YJ79-GE-5 engines were delivered to Convair and prepared for installation and flight test aboard 55-667. The -5 engine was scheduled to become the standard production powerplant for the B-58 and would be used to replace the -1 engines found on the first eight preproduction aircraft. The first flight of 55-667, with the new engines, took place the following April.

Consequent to the rapidly increasing flight test activity and the AF's apparent commitment to at least a small production program, ground handling classes were initiated at Convair and 300 personnel were scheduled for processing during the first year. Additionally, Phase IV testing was now being scheduled under the new weapon system plan, and operational parameters for the B-58 were being rapidly developed.

During January 1958, the AF established a joint AFSC/SAC B-58 Test Force, the 6592nd Test Squadron, at Carswell AFB. This unit would be tasked with conducting Category II and III evaluation of the aircraft. On February 15, 55-665 became the first test B-58A to be turned over to the AF.

B-58, 55-660 remained one of the most active flight test aircraft during this period and on February 4, 1958, began a ten day program to determine sortie rate capabilities and pre-flight and post-flight maintenance procedures. During the ten day period, the aircraft made eleven flights for a total of 37 flying hours. On one flight, three 360° rolls were accomplished at Mach .93 at 25,000'. On another flight, supersonic speeds of Mach 1.2 were maintained for 1 hour and 31 minutes.

Pod studies had led Convair in several different directions during the course of the design development program that continued well into pre-production testing. Among the most important fallouts from these studies, however, was the February, 1958, decision to reprogram the pod configuration to a two component (TCP) unit. This configuration would effectively increase the range of the aircraft, even in consideration of the TCP's extra weight. This was made possible by the fact that the lower component (a fuel tank), would be jettisoned part-way through a mission, thus considerably lightening the aircraft and lowering its drag coefficient. A mock-up, consisting of one upper component and two lower components, with pylons, was completed at Convair on May 7, 1959.

As mentioned earlier, the B-58's major tactical failing, at least in the eyes of SAC, was its limited range. Accordingly, inflight refueling capability was essential to its success as an intercontinental bomber. Inflight refueling tests were initiated on June 11, 1958, when B-58, 55-661, with B. A. Erickson, J. A. Rogerson, and O. D. Lively as crew, was refueled by a Boeing KC-135A (55-3118, piloted, on this occasion, by Capt. Lawrence Snowden; the boom operator was MSgt. Charlie Lambert) for the first time. The flight took place at 33,000'; 10,000 lbs. of JP-4 were successfully transferred. These tests were followed by another series on July 23, when the B-58 was refueled from a KC-135A at an altitude of 30,000' and a gross weight of 156,000 lbs. The refueling trials were considered very successful and it was determined that the B-58 was totally compatible with the KC-135A. A final test on August 8 involved a 3 hour 5 minute mission (45 minutes being at supersonic speeds) in which the B-58 was refueled a total of 4 times (during six connections) and received some 62,000 lbs. of fuel.

Additional systems tests continued during this period at Convair. Among the most important were those involving the interfacing of the J79 engine with its nacelle. In December, 1958, Convair completed its engine test cell units and powerplant performance tests were immediately begun. Tests to determine powerplant absolute thrusts were conducted during 2 and 3 hour sessions, at simulated altitudes of up to 27,000'.

Environmental testing of the B-58 got underway on July 8, 1958, when 55-670 was flown to Eglin AFB, FL and there placed in the AF's climatic hangar for cold weather testing. The tests ran for two months and cleared the way for actual service testing of the aircraft under natural extreme environmental conditions (as part of "Operation Raw Deal" at Eilson AFB, AK). At the same time, the first mission profiles, duplicating those that would be used by the B-58 in an operational environment, were flown during a series of tests conducted between June 27, 1958, and March 17, 1959. These tests utilized 55-666 and a crew consisting of Ray Fitzgerald, J. D. Taylor, and B. D. Miller.

Concern over a developing Soviet surface-to-air missile threat, in late 1958, caused SAC to inform the AMC/ARDC that the B-58 would have a capability of operating at 200' altitude or less and that all equipment would be able to perform at 50'. The low level penetration speed specified was 630 knots for up to 1,200 n. miles. This capability was verified on September 18, 1959, when 58-1015, crewed by B. A. Erickson, J. A. Rogerson, and A. G. Mitchell flew a 1,220 n. mile mission at an average speed of 610 knots at a sustained altitude of 500' or less.

In January, 1960, following the successful completion of Eglin AFB and Eilson AFB environmental tests, operational cold weather testing of the B-58 was initiated at Ellsworth AFB, ND, under the auspices of "Operation Raw Deal". This project was designed to verify the integrity of the aircraft and its systems in a typical cold weather environ-

ment. The Ellsworth tests, using 59-2428 crewed by Maj. K. K. Lewis, pilot; Maj. Jim Zwayer, navigator; and Capt. Raymond Wagener, DSO, were decidedly successful.

In March, 1959, as production began to accelerate in order to accommodate AF orders, Convair completed assembly of an elevated assembly line. This unit, which permitted workers to function comfortably some 9' above the factory floor, also permitted the nose and tail work stands to move with the aircraft as it advanced down the production line. This saved considerable time and effort, and expedited the resolution of production problems that had slowed movement of the aircraft through the assembly process.

Problems with the Sperry AN/ASG-42 bomb/navigation system caused it to be nearly four months behind schedule and thus directly affected the completion of Category I and II testing of the system. This, in turn, affected scheduled changes and the incorporation of the system into the first operationally configured aircraft. When coupled with a five month lag following final delivery of the systems, these difficulties were now expected to lead initially to questionable operational capability, reliability, and maintainability of the entire operational B-58 fleet and to adversely affect the completion of Category III tests. It thus was considered advisable that the Air Force not accept any aircraft until they had been shown to possess a complete and supportable operational systems capability and that the plans for operational use be adjusted accordingly.

Two commanding AF Generals now held a short meeting wherein it was agreed that reliability and maintainability would make the Category III testing more difficult. It was also noted, however, that SAC could determine the tactical B-58's capability—one objective of Category III—only by using the system and evaluating it as soon as possible. All three of the commands—SAC, AMC, and ARDC—recognized that the Category I and II testing was behind schedule, and in March, 1959, SAC agreed to delay assumption of its responsibility from October, 1959, until February, 1960. That was to be the beginning of the SAC Category III effort, which would conclude in October, 1960,

following "High Try", a thirty day accelerated test program in squadron strength. The SAC operations directorate held that the latest configuration aircraft should be assigned to the test, at which time a total of twenty-four aircraft would have been produced (the first seven tactical aircraft would not be utilized).

SAC had long recognized that late delivery of tactical equipment was a major problem in the integration of the B-58 into the SAC inventory. SAC planned to retain the first tactical squadron at Carswell AFB through the greater part of 1960 due to the various shortages. The date for the full periodic inspection capability of the B-58 bombing system was set for April, 1960, or some two months after the SAC assumption of responsibility and coincident with the production of the ninth tactical aircraft.

SAC continued its opposition to any decision to cut back the planned B-58 force since it held that the new bomber was a marked improvement over the obsolescent B-47. The B-58's speed and flexibility would complicate the Soviet defense problem as well as offer a counterforce threat. Consequently, SAC wanted to modernize its bomber force and the B-58 was the only aircraft readily available; still, SAC developed alternative plans for a two wing force of B-58A's, with each wing consisting of 44 aircraft.

With the first full-up production aircraft (B-58 #31, 59-2428) nearing completion, the AF, in March, 1959, selected its first acceptance crew. Maj. J. B. Thompson was to be the pilot; Capt. A. Z. Doka was to be the navigator; and Capt. Robert Ballard was to be the DSO. Their responsibility would be to inspect the aircraft for anomolies during the AF acceptance process. Problems would have to be corrected before the aircraft could be officially taken over by SAC.

The forthcoming arrival of the first production aircraft also led to an increase in ground and flight crew training. Nine training classes were initiated at Convair during the first few months of 1959, and this was followed by the signing of a contract with the AF calling for Convair to develop flight simulators, navigation trainers, and defensive system operator trainers.

Wearing the nickname "Mary Ann" on its nose, 55-671 is seen flying formation with F-106A, 59-075, and Convair 880 prototype N-803TW. In 1960, when the photo was taken, these were the three fastest aircraft in the world in their respective categories (transport, bomber, and fighter, respectively).

G.D.

The fourteenth B-58A completed, 58-1007, nicknamed "Super Sue" taxies out on a test flight from Convair's Fort Worth facility. This aircraft was used by Convair as a nav/bomb system testbed. It was eventually converted to the TB-58A configuration and as such, served operationally with the 43rd BW.

Unfortunately, at this time, the B-58 program was once again in jeopardy. On July 14, 1959, Gen. Power wired USAF headquarters summarizing SAC's B-58 need. The Pentagon replied that funds were inadequate and that budgetary considerations were sometimes overriding.

As of the date of Gen. Power's letter, some 290 B-58's (both A's and B's) were scheduled for production at a peak rate of six aircraft per month. By the end of August, the fiscal year 1960 quota had been reduced to 32 aircraft. USAF headquarters directed SAC to plan accordingly, though the program was still under review and no firm decision had been made.

By December, 1959, SAC had committed to a buy of only 148 aircraft, including test and support configurations. Consequently, the number of aircraft to be procured with fiscal year 1960 funds dropped from 32 to 20 while production was to run at a rate of one per month through July, 1960, and two per month through December, 1961.

In July, 1959, Gen. Ryan noted that the current progress of B-58 development was unsatisfactory to meet major testing and operational dates that were then established. Many unsolved maintenance and engineering problems hampered the work of the test force; in addition, handbooks on the navigation/bomb subsystem had not been purchased, fiscal year 1959 funds for the procurement of spare parts were lacking, technical data for the Air Training Command (ATC) was unavailable, and equipment availability dates for the ATC's training courses had slipped.

The difficulties in the B-58 program only served to emphasize the controversy in regard to the role the bomber was to play in SAC. By 1960, it was still the only new bomber in the hardware stage and Gen. Power felt strongly that it should be used to replace the B-47. Sec. of Defense Thomas Gates said the decision to carry it forward was based on the simple fact that it was immediately available. Already the program had undergone a number of changes. The air-to-surface missile (i.e., MA-1 pod) had been cancelled after $66.4 million had been spent; the MC-1 and MD-1 reconnaissance systems had been cancelled in 1958 following an expenditure of $40 millipn; and the B-58B had been deleted at a cost of $2 million. And finally, the cost of the 118 aircraft now scheduled through fiscal year 1961 was estimated at approximately $3 billion—a staggering figure at that time and one which some news reports claimed (accurately) made the B-58 worth more than its weight in gold (which at the time was valued at some $35 per Troy ounce).

In addition to the problems raised by the bomber itself, many others stemmed from the competition of the B-58 with other systems, differences of opinion in the legislative and executive branches of the US Government, and strict budget levels. Together, these items added up to fact that the first operational squadron was now delayed from June to December, 1960, for activation. The first wing of 36, rather than 45 aircraft, was to be ready in August, 1961, while the reduced production schedule was delaying the combat ready status of the projected third wing until June, 1963. The B-58 was thus placed in a role less than that originally envisioned even though it was still the only aircraft able to satisfy SAC's operational requirements.

As time drew near for the aircraft to enter the operational inventory, it was acknowledged that the aircraft was entering the inventory with "significant unresolved problems". Many of these were due primarily to program instability that had hampered an orderly and economical development, production, and operational program. These problems were caused by an out-of-phase availability of essential elements of the weapon system to meet user command requirements.

The program's instability and the delay in designating a user command had adversely affected it. Numerous specific problems remained, not the least of which was the AN/ASQ-42 bomb/navigation system that had yet to attain sufficient reliability, and the AN/ALQ-16 portion of the electronic countermeasures system which was not operationally effective. Additionally, it was noted that low level operations, necessitated by the great effectiveness of Soviet high altitude defense, were decidedly limited, and it was estimated that the B-58 would be limited to high altitude operations for two years after its operational debut because the required BLU-2B (MB-1) pod and TX-53 warhead were still under development and not due for delivery until February, 1962. Additionally, because of performance envelope restrictions resulting from the inflight disintegration of one aircraft (55-664 on November 7, 1959) concerns over the B-58's ability to deliver weapons at supersonic speeds remained; the supersonic pod drop program had been placed on hold until the restrictions were lifted.

The ejection seat program was now renewed with the realization that the conventional SACseat as developed by Convair was not sufficient to protect the crew throughout the B-58's performance envelope (up to 600 knots EAS and/or altitudes in excess of 50,000'). Several accidents had led to serious injuries due to marginal crew protection and it had become apparent relatively early in the flight test program that a new seat was desperately needed. Subsequent studies, including a series of tests with the pilot's canopy removed (B. A. Erickson, during these tests noted, "the noise was not negligible. . . .in fact, you could safely say it was deafening.") led to the conclusion that an encapsulated seat would provide the necessary crew protection.

Accordingly, an encapsulated seat development program was approved in February, 1958, and Stanley Aviation Corporation, of Denver, CO was picked by the B-58 WSPO to design (with Convair's assistance), develop and produce it. Known initially as the "Model B" seat, it would be pressurized (via a 3,000 psi compressed air bottle that could maintain an internal cabin pressure of 2.5 psi), water tight, and totally self contained. It was expected that initial production costs would result in an expenditure of $10.7 million for enough units to equip 36 aircraft.

One year later, on February 12, 1959, transonic tests were completed on an escape capsule model at Cornell University, and supersonic tests were then scheduled for the following week at MIT. During the spring of 1959 work on the design of the encapsulated seat had progressed to the point where plans calling for full-scale hardware tests using the AF's 12,000' long Supersonic Military Air Research Track at Hurricane Mesa, AZ, were consummated. These, in fact, led to the first full-scale tests of the seat during sled runs the following May which achieved speeds of 204' per second. The following January, the capsule was tested for survivability when it was given a 72 hour cold water flotation test with a human occupant.

At the beginning of the encapsulated ejection seat program, some 16 test capsules had been built of sheet steel in order to expedite full-scale aerodynamic testing of the capsule and its stabilization sytems. These test capsules were fired from a rocket sled which initially was configured to travel at relatively modest speeds. Incremental speed increases soon placed the test capsule in a speed regime where stability became a problem and several years were then spent trying to correct this. The instability of the capsule was inherent with its basic design, which in turn, was the end product of the size constraints placed upon it by the B-58's crew cabins. Additionally, the location of the crew seats was different for the pilot and that of the navigator and the DSO, and thus the pilot's seat, because of its location and the fact that it had to accommodate a control stick, was of slightly different design. It, in fact, was eventually configured to depart the aircraft 6° off axis to compensate for the thrust alignment and related factors of the capsule rocket engine.

In-flight tests of the seat were initiated using a modified North American T-28, and eventually, no less than 27 capsule drops were conducted using this aircraft. Additionally, some 22 sled tests were run on the ground, and an additional 8 drop

Problems with blown tires and related landing gear difficulties were common-place throughout the B-58's history. B-58A, 58-1015 is seen following a blown tire-related emergency at Edwards AFB in 1959.

A striking head-on view of 58-1007 immediately following a test mission from Carswell AFB. Stalk-like landing gear caused few problems for the aircraft, though tire anomalies were commonplace.

tests occurred from a modified Boeing B-47. Out of all these tests, 55 were considered successful (i.e., survivable), and 2 were not.

B-58 testing continued under the auspices of Convair throughout the winter and spring of 1959. On January 18, 55-666, made a flight to check acceleration performance. Beginning at 30,000' altitude, at a weight of 130,000 lbs., acceleration was made to Mach 2 and 36,000' in seven and one-half minutes.

Work on the TCP pod and its associated warhead also continued, and on February 8, Convair was authorized to design the pod around the XW-53 FUFO (Full Fuzing Option) warhead rather than the less versatile MX-39.

As of May, the B-58 flight test program was now well developed. Although late delivery of aircraft had hampered various efforts, the test force had in its inventory a total of eight B-58's. By the end of May, this program had generated the following data: on a classic SAC strike mission, the B-58A could strike 87% of the targets in the Soviet Union; the B-58 and KC-135A were totally compatible from an inflight refueling standpoint; the B-58 had demonstrated its ability to fire air-launched ballistic missiles (see Chapt. 8); the B-58 had successfully penetrated US air defenses three times without using its onboard ECM capability; the aircraft had

demonstrated confusion and track-breaking ECM; the navigation/bomb system had become more reliable and maintainable, and had demonstrated specified performance; the aircraft had demonstrated its ability to carry multiple stores, the aircraft had flown low altitude dash missions at Mach .9; the aircraft had flown supersonically at Mach 2; and there was every indication that the aircraft would enter the inventory in October, 1959. Unfortunately, the latter date would soon prove overly optimistic, due to a continuation of the various problems that had plagued the program almost from its very beginning.

The advent of the B-58 and several other supersonic combat aircraft had, by the late 1950's, given rise to yet another problem that heretofore, had not been of particular concern to the AF or other agencies. The effect of sonic booms on the general populace had gone generally unacknowledged until 1958 and 1959, as complaints had been rare and the severity of the damage wrought had been negligible. The B-58, due to its size and ability to operate for prolonged periods at supersonic speeds, helped change this attitude, significantly, and accordingly, in July, 1959, 55-660 was utilized in an extensive series of sonic boom tests at Wallops Island, Virginia. Flown by an AF crew, it was accelerated to Mach 2 and

60,000' and flown over the Wallops Island test range during two passes. It was concluded from these tests that sonic booms posed a serious problem and more extensive testing would be required. Many other sonic boom tests utilizing the B-58 and other supersonic aircraft, followed, these eventually leading to the elimination of supersonic missions over land in all but a very few restricted flight corridors.

In early 1960, orders for the B-58 stood at a tentative total of 106 aircraft. Some 4,793 vendors were now directly affected and the list continued to grow. Convair was rapidly progressing through the latter stages of the various test programs related to miscellaneous B-58 systems and its performance envelope, and this effort, coupled with operationally oriented test projects under the auspices of the AF, kept activity at Carswell AFB and the co-located Convair facility, at a extremely high level.

In May, 1960, the first MB-1 pod drop with an actual TX-53 warhead (in inert form) was completed at the Holloman AFB test range. The TX-53, the first of several warheads designed by Kirtland AFB's Sandia Corporation for the B-58 weapon pod, was shaped like a large beer barrel and designed to be accommodated in the pod weapon bay.

Another view of 58-1007 as it taxies out from Convair's Ft. Worth facility on a test mission. This aircraft would have a long service career and would eventually be scrapped for metal value at Davis-Monthan AFB, AZ.

USAF

Nicknamed "Ginger", 58-1015 was another of the several B-58A's assigned to the ARDC and flown out of Edwards AFB, CA. In this photo, taken on April 10, 1961, during on-going pod drop tests, the aircraft is carrying only the upper component of the TCP.

G.D.

B-58A, 58-1023, was the first fully tactically configured aircraft to undergo flight test. Unfortunately, its contributions to the B-58 nav/bomb system test program were to be short-lived as it was destroyed on April 22, 1960.

G.D.

Aft view of 58-1023, illustrating the aircraft's abnormally tall stance on its stalky landing gear. Apparent complexity of gear supporting structure was somewhat misleading as gear retraction and extension failures were exceptionally rare.

September, 1959, proved to be a particularly significant month in the history of the B-58, for it was then that the first flight of the first production aircraft, 58-1023, took place. Parallelling this was the move from squadron (as part of the 3958th Operational Test and Evaluation Squadron) to group status of the B-58 test force at Carswell. This made room for SAC's B-58 operational training program calling for full-scale instruction of ground and air crews. The following month, the second production B-58, 59-2428, was cleared for flight test following an AF "262" inspection.

With various phases of the flight test program now either completed or nearing completion, Convair and the AF tackled the problem of what to do with test aircraft that were becoming redundant to flight test needs. These aircraft, almost all of which were specially modified or configured for a given test project while serving with the 3958th, were relatively low time airframes and thus still viable from a useful life standpoint. On June 20, 1958, the B-58 project office made a presentation to the Air Force which stated that the first 17 aircraft were suitable only for test work. These aircraft were limited by structure to a 147,000 lb. gross weight and were not convertible to a tactical configuration without major modification. Aircraft 18 thru 30, however, were built to a 153,000 lb. gross weight requirement and these aircraft, if the landing gear were replaced, could have a 163,000 lb. (normal) capability.

It was therefore decided that these latter aircraft, wherever possible, would be updated and configured for operational service. The first such aircraft, 58-1013 (out of an initial batch of five that also included 55-671, 58-1014, 58-1019, and 58-1020), was scheduled for the initial phase of *Junior Flash-Up* in early February, 1960, and shortly afterwards delivered to Convair. It was expected that these aircraft would be run through the program in ten day cycles with no aircraft being in the program for more than ten working days.

The problem of what to do with the other low airframe time pre-production aircraft was finally and formally resolved on March 8, 1959. A firm program, again under the *Junior Flash-Up* banner was established on that date for the production conversion of 15 pre-production B-58's to a tactical configuration for SAC. An initial amount of $12 million was authorized and five modified aircraft were scheduled to be delivered by October, 1961. The first aircraft to enter this program was 58-1021. Eventually, eleven of the 17 test aircraft under the second B-58 contract were updated to include changes which had been incorporated during the full production phase (many of which were in response to the loss of 55-664 on November 7, 1959).

Prior to the decision to bring up to tactical standards several of the pre-production series aircraft, Convair and the AF conducted the first of three scheduled range demonstration missions under *Operation Seven-Up.* Taking place on June 27, 1958, and utilizing 55-666 equipped with YJ79-5 engines, the mission was flown at subsonic speeds over a route that carried it on an outbound leg of 2,320 miles and an inbound leg of 2,372 miles, with a pod drop on the Holloman AFB test range in between. The total flight time was 8 hours 55 minutes and the cruise speed varied between Mach .92 and Mach .93. The takeoff weight for the mission was 161,000 lbs.

This was followed, on October 15, 1959, by the first sustained Mach 2 flight. Aircraft 58-1015, with Ray Fitzgerald, J. A. Rogerson, and B. D. Miller as crew members, flew from Seattle, Washington, to Carswell in 70 minutes at an average speed of nearly 1,320 mph.

The need for a trainer version of the B-58 had been apparent almost from the birth of the pro-

Superb side view of 58-1023 illustrates well the extraordinarily clean lines of the "Hustler" and its naturally aggressive profile. Of particular interest is the fact that this aircraft apparently has been flown without national insigne on the fuselage sides. Black mask outlining the cockpit windscreen is also somewhat unusual, though it was seen on occasion on other select B-58's.

gram. The aircraft's unusual—for a bomber—single pilot configuration, its extraordinary performance, its unusual flight characteristics, its unusual landing and takeoff characteristics, and even its gangly landing gear configuration, all dictated that special crew instruction be required. Accordingly, in early 1959, SAC agreed to fund the development of a trainer version under the TB-58A designator. This project, like *Junior Flash-Up*, involved select airframes from the original test batch, specifically, 55-669 (this aircraft was never converted due to an accident which occurred on October 27, 1959), 55-670, 55-671, and 55-672. The TB-58A program was officially approved on September 15, and the first aircraft was expected to be available on May 11, 1960. The fourth aircraft would be delivered no later than January 1, 1961, and follow-on orders for at least four more TB-58 conversions could be expected. The latter did, in fact, occur on October 5, when SAC requested that four additional TB-58A conversions be undertaken using 55-661, 55-662, 55-663, and 55-668. The last of these aircraft, 55-668, would be delivered to the Air Force on April 13, 1964.

B-58A, 55-670, on October 4, became the first aircraft to enter the TB-58A conversion program under Contract AF33(600)-36200. Prior to modification, it was removed from flight test and prepared for conversion. Thus by early 1960, plans to forge ahead with the TB-58 configuration had progressed to the point where it was expected Convair now would be delivering the first aircraft in June.

Following entry into the modification program on October 5, 1959, 55-670, was, in fact, completed in February and during the last few weeks of April, utilized for the TB-58A taxi test program. On May 10, this aircraft, with company crew Val Prahl, pilot; Earl Guthrie, second pilot; and Grover "Ted" Tate, flight test engineer, took to the air for the first time, flying from the main runway at Carswell AFB. The mission lasted 1 hour 40 minutes. A maximum altitude of 44,000' was reached on the flight and control of the aircraft was passed back and forth between the "instructor" and "student" on several occasions.

With the winding down, at this point, of the B-58 flight test program and the conversion of many of the flight test aircraft to either tactical or training configuration, the useful life of the 3958th OETG was at an end. Accordingly, during March, 1960, it was deactivated and its personnel and equipment were assigned to the 43rd BW at Carswell AFB.

In a highly successful effort to demonstrate the B-58's low altitude performance in a combat situation, 58-1015, on September 18, was flown from Fort Worth via El Paso and Phoenix, to

Rare photo of the TB-58A forward fuselage cardboard mock-up. An inflight refueling boom is seen protruding from the nose-mounted refueling receptacle. This mock-up served as a proof-of-concept article for the actual hardware modification which was initiated in October, 1959, using B-58A, 55-670.

Following modification to trainer configuration, the forward fuselage component of 55-670 is seen being mated to its original wing and aft fuselage section inside Convair's Fort Worth facility in February, 1960. As the first TB-58A, it would be rolled out and prepared for its first flight less than two months later.

G.D.

Another view of 55-670 prior to forward fuselage demating and conversion to the TB-58A configuration. This aircraft was the first of eight TB-58A's eventually created from select members of the initial batch of thirty non-tactically-configured pre-production B-58A's.

Bakersfield, California at altitudes varying from 100' to 500' and at speeds above 600 knots. The crew later reported that the aircraft demonstrated a smooth ride, excellent flying qualities, and excellent visual flight capabilities.

In the meantime, the ARDC, SAC, and other AF elements had to contend with the peculiar problems of the new supersonic weapon system. The accident rate in 1959 and 1960 was a large factor in SAC's postponing acceptance of executive responsibility for the B-58. The first crash had taken place on December 16, 1958, near Cannon AFB, NM, and was attributed to the probability that the autotrim and ratio changer had become inoperative because of an electrical malfunction or accidental tripping of the master power switch.

On May 14, 1959, another B-58 burned at Carswell AFB during a fuel transfer operation, and, on September 16, another aircraft crashed on takeoff from Carswell AFB due to tire failure. Pilot error dropped yet another aircraft on October 27.

The most perplexing problems had appeared during a November 7, 1959, test flight from Carswell involving 55-664. This aircraft, which had been tasked with the collection of vertical fin side loads data, had only two crew stations (the 3rd was filled with instrumentation) and was the airloads data test aircraft for the B-58 program. As such it was equipped with several thousand static/dynamic transducers and many strain gauges.

During the November 7 flight and while steady state at Mach 2.0 and 38,000', Convair test pilot, Ray Fitzgerald had purposefully flipped a special switch that activated an hydro-mechanical valve in the main fuel line to the starboard outboard engine. The engine power had decayed almost instantaneously and when it did, the aircraft immediately yawed the predicted 3° to the right. Mysteriously, however, following a short pause, the yaw was later determined to have suddenly increased to 15°.

As the 15° point was reached, the aircraft disintegrated. While the primary cause of the accident remained undetermined, it was apparent to all concerned that there were limitations to the aircraft flight control system and the integrity of the vertical fin structure. Some reports also alluded to concern about the forward fuselage structure. There were also questions remaining as to why the #3 engine had lost thrust within seconds of the near-instantaneous decay of #4.

Tire failure which was to become an increasingly serious problem for the B-58 throughout its career, caused another accident on April 13, 1960, at Edwards AFB; and materiel failure causing the Mach/airspeed/airdata system to malfunction was the primary cause of an accident near Hill AFB, UT, on April 22, 1960. Pilot error brought down yet another aircraft on June 4, near Lubbock, Texas.

While the number of accidents made SAC apprehensive about the reliability of the aircraft and led to postponement of Category III testing, it was the Fitzgerald accident of November 7, 1959, which raised questions of design deficiency. Because of the accident, B-58's were restricted to operation at subsonic speeds for nearly a year. A control system and tail structure modification program (part of *Flash-up* and *Junior Flash-Up*), affecting all completed aircraft and those that were either under construction or planned, followed.

Although the accident findings by June, 1960, did not indicate any consistency in the causes, the fact that eleven persons had died and several others had been badly injured, plus the loss of aircraft, was too much to dismiss. SAC acceptance was predicated upon the construction of a safe aircraft, and to achieve that, many modifications were eventually approved.

Following the June 4 crash an ad hoc committee under Col. John Smith was formed to complement the efforts of the already active AF/industry

G.D.

In early May, 1960, 55-670, as the first TB-58A, undertook preliminary taxi tests. A FOD screen was placed over the intake of each engine for protection. This aircraft also wore a distinctive paint scheme consisting of black trim with red and white nose and tail flashes and a red forward fuselage crown. A similar flash theme was executed on each engine nacelle and the pod was also painted red and white.

accident board. Both teams were tasked with examining the B-58's flight control system and subsystems, and its aerodynamic characteristics. While the teams were undertaking their examinations, the B-58 was placed under severe flight restrictions. Additionally, SAC expressed the opinion that the official B-58 takeover date of August 1, 1960, would again have to be slipped.

An interim report was released within a few weeks of the initiation of the accident investigation and consequently, B-58 flight restrictions were lifted, with the exception of several minor recommendations. Among the latter it was suggested that the roll damper authority be reduced from 5° to 3°, that the pitot-static lines be rerouted to the air data computer to eliminate bends and moisture traps, and that tactical Mach meters and fuel gauges be installed in test aircraft for more accurate operation of the automatic center-of-gravity control system. Also recommended was the publication of several safety-of-flight supplements which emphasized the preparation and use of flight plans, the limits in subsonic and transonic regions for operation at or near the maximum aft center-of-gravity, and the basic concepts of fuel system management and center of gravity control.

In general, it was concluded that there were no major design deficiencies in either the aircraft or the flight control system, and that when all functioned, the systems met the specifications. Though a recommendation that the age limit for pilots be lowered was rejected, additional Convair TF-102A's were added to the B-58 training fleet and more emphasis was placed on recruiting maintenance people with higher skill levels.

Thanks to a scarcity of firm decisions and the numerous problems affecting flight test and operational introduction, the B-58's usefulness to the AF appeared to be decreasing just as its introduction into the active inventory appeared eminent. It was now revealed that a final decision concerning the number of B-58 wings had been made, and that the total was one less than SAC had anticipated. This meant that the purchase of 32 aircraft in fiscal year 1962 would be dropped and the B-58 program would come to an end in spite of SAC programming for three wings. A wing of B-47's would have to be retained to offset the reduction.

The B-58 had been caught in the middle of a power struggle whose central issue was money. The B-70 was considered to be the next step in the bomber arsenal, and the B-58, because of the numerous delays in its introduction into operational service, was suddenly in direct competition with it for funding. The December, 1960, program guidance document (PG-63-7) reflected two B-58 wings and a total purchase in fiscal year 1961 of 24 rather than 30 aircraft. Unit cost had jumped from $12.5 million to $14 million, making the B-58, at the time, the most expensive production aircraft in the world, and almost three times as expensive as a production Boeing B-52G. By January 1, 1960, the B-58's production fate had been sealed—31 aircraft had been accepted and the AF looked forward to acquiring a total of 116. Funding had come in increments for 13 aircraft in fiscal year 1955, 17 in 1956, 36 in 1959, 20 in 1960, and 30 in 1961. Total program cost had been $3,209,600,000.

In July, 1958, the on-going pod drop program at Kirtland AFB had begun to transition from dropping single component pods to dropping the new two-component pod. Aircraft 55-663 and 59-2435 were assigned to this project which was tasked with verification of the usefulness and effectiveness of the two component pod system. The drops, which actually got underway in October, took place over the White Sands, NM and Tonopah, NV test ranges.

TB-58A, 55-670, is seen heading south from the main Carswell AFB runway, shortly after liftoff on its May 10, 1960, first flight. The flight proved uneventful and the aircraft was flown from both the instructor and pilot stations.

Work with the single component pod continued through early 1960 when, on February 12, 58-1011 became the first aircraft to drop a pod using the aircraft's AN/ASQ-42 navigation/bomb system. The Convair crew consisted of Jack Baldridge, Fred Hewes, and D. C. Ford.

The following April, the pod drop program undertook separation and accuracy tests at supersonic speeds. Nine runs at Mach 1.3 to 1.68 brought misses ranging from 1,100' to 78,250'.

On May 24, 1960, the first drop of a two component pod lower portion was made. This was followed, on November 19, by the first low level upper TCP component drop. The first supersonic drop of the upper TCP component took place on December 11, also using 55-663. Almost all the TCP drop tests to this point had been conducted by a Convair crew consisting of Earl Guthrie, Grover Tate, Jr., and O. D. Lively. On February 10, 1961, however, 58-2435, with Convair's F. J. Voorhies, F. A. Hewes, and Kenneth Timpson as crew members, completed the first Mach 2 drop of an upper component. Other test drops (including, on April 31, the first drop of both components) to verify center of gravity and drag anomalies experienced during the first Mach 2 drop followed, delaying the execution of the first Mach 2 lower component drop until August 8.

SAC assumption of executive management responsibility had been a long time in coming due to the various problems associated with the complex bomber. Finally, however, on August 1, 1960, SAC did take over B-58 operations responsibility and on the same date, initiated Category III testing. B-58, 59-2436, the first aircraft to be completely equipped with all tactical systems, was delivered to the 43rd, also on August 1. Less than two weeks later, on August 13, the first TB-58A, 55-670, was delivered to Carswell AFB.

Due to the lags and spurts in the B-58 production program, and the great technological leaps forward represented by the airframe, its systems, and the powerplants, there was a great variation in the equipment, systems updates, maintenance requirements, and capabilities among the various aircraft that had by now been accepted by SAC. Accordingly, the AF initiated the *Senior Flash-Up* program, to update and normalize as many of the

aircraft in the inventory as possible. It was hoped that a commonality factor could be brought into play permitting more leeway in terms of spare parts stocks, systems integration, and mission objectives. The first aircraft to go through *Senior Flash-Up*, was delivered to SAC on November 7, 1960. Some of the changes that had been incorporated during the cycle were anti-icing devises, electronic countermeasures systems, an improved canopy, R.V. and P.I. beacons, HACON and TACAN installations and a structurally improved vertical fin and fuselage empennage section.

By March, 1961, the active vendor list of those companies selling products to Convair for the B-58 program totalled at 4,926 in 44 states. This represented the peak vendor figure for the program, and also was an indicator of how far reaching the B-58 contract had become in terms of its national economic impact.

Capsule development continued at both Convair and Stanley Aviation in Colorado, and in early March, the first static ground ejections were conducted from 55-661 while parked on a ramp at Convair.

Pod drop tests continued using the two-component pod systems, and in August, 1961, an AF crew, consisting of Lt. Col. Joe Cotton, Maj. Jim Zwayer, and TSgt. Bobby Ryan, made the first AF low level two-component pod drop over the Tonopah, NV test range.

Encapsulated ejection seat tests also continued during October, with a B-58 (55-661) ejecting a test seat while traveling down a runway at 115 mph at Edwards AFB. The capsule traveled 1,200' and landed 15' to the left of the aircraft path. This was followed, later in the month, by the first inflight ejection of the capsule. Using 55-661 again, and while flying at 431 mph and 20,000' over Edwards AFB, the seat was successfully ejected from the middle compartment by the aft compartment crew member (only two were aboard at the time). These tests, in turn, were followed by the ejection of two capsules in December, and the ejection of a live chimpanzee during a run at 630 mph at 20,000' about a month later. On February 28, 1962, the first test ejection using a man took place while the B-58 was flying at 565 mph at 20,000' over Edwards. In March, a small bear was ejected at Mach

G.D

B-58A, 55-672, became the second TB-58A modification. The TB-58A's distinctive extended side window panels are readily apparent in this view of 55-672 during takeoff rotation. It eventually was assigned to the 43rd BW and would survive long enough to be scrapped at Davis-Monthan AFB in August, 1977.

1.3 and 35,000'.

The bear ejection was a major milestone in the history of the podded ejection seat system, as it was the first successful supersonic ejection of the seat with a viable payload. The bear took 7 minutes 49 seconds to descend. The pilot was Maj. John Allmie and the third station crew member was Robert Sudderth. Further tests in this flight regime continued into April, 1962, at which time the bear was again ejected, though at Mach 1.6 at 45,000'. Another successful ejection at Mach 1.6 and 45,000', using a chimpanzee, was also conducted about two months after the bear test.

In a modestly successful attempt to broaden the B-58's weapon carrying capability, aircraft 59-2435, 59-2439 and 59-2456, in late 1961, were assigned the task of validating the aircraft's ability to carry multiple weapons on pylons installed under the wing root section. This assignment had been prompted by a September 27, 1960 WSPO

and SAC review that explored the feasibility of, and the requirement for, providing the B-58 with a multiple weapon capability of four Class D weapons. On December 16, SAC confirmed the multiple weapons requirement and recommended that a Phase I study be conducted. This was followed by the bailment, on February 6, 1961, of 59-2456 to Convair for hardware tests of the multiple weapons system. Following preliminary successful tests with this aircraft, the WADD approved, on March 10, the design of the primary structural provision for the multiple weapons capability and it was agreed that all aircraft from number 87 (61-2051 on), would be fitted. In August, 1961, the ASD requested that retrofit kits for the multiple weapons system be procured using available production funds. In January, 1962, Phase II of the multi-weapons program began with air loads testing, multi-weapons drops, and flight tests for stability. On February 7, 58-2435, with a Convair crew consisting of F. J. Voorhies, F. A. Hewes, and O. D. Lively, made the first multi-

weapon drop. On March 12, the system was given a final stamp of approval by the AFSC and cleared for retrofitting to all tactically configured B-58's. On June 19, 58-2435 made the first supersonic multi-weapon drop and on August 2, the first Mach 2 multi-weapon drop.

Until the decision to equip the B-58 with the multiple weapon capability, the B-58's weapon payload had been limited to whatever it could carry in its pod. In the new configuration, smaller weapons, such as the Mk.43 and Mk.61 nuclear devises and different types of conventional iron bombs could be carried and released on several targets rather than just one. The tests proved successful and the configuration, which required depot level installation, was incorporated on all tactically configured B-58's during the following two years.

The completion of flight test work, on April 25, 1959, of the first of the thirty test aircraft in the flight test program, 55-662, also signaled the beginning of the end for the contractor (Convair) flight test effort. Contractor work had gone on non-stop almost from the day of the first flight in 1956, and it was now time for the balance of this responsibility to be turned over to the AF. Several important contractor projects remained, including the first flight test of the production podded ejection seat configuration (which took place using aircraft 61-2062 on March 2, 1962), but the majority of the major contractor obligations had now been met.

A final salute came on October 23, 1962, when the last production aircraft test flight, required for AF acceptance of 61-2080, with Val Prahl, W. E. Denton, and M. F. Keller as crew, was completed by the company. On October 25, 61-2078 and 61-2079 were accepted by the AF and were delivered, along with 61-2080, on October 26. On that date, B-58A, 61-2080, the last of 116 B-58 aircraft ordered, was officially turned over to the AF and flown to Bunker Hill AFB, IN.

The end of Convair's involvement in B-58 flight test work officially occurred on May 28, 1963, when 59-2435 and 59-2439, the last two aircraft to have been bailed to the company, were prepared for entry into the *Hustle-Up* refurbishment program. It was a grand finale to what had been an exciting, though sometimes rocky, contractor flight test program.

USAF via Douglas Robinson

TB-58A, 58-1007, is seen carrying the upper component of a TCP (with ventral fin retracted). The TB-58A rarely carried the TCP and flew most of its operational missions with a conventional MB-1 pod in the centerline position. Note engine exhaust patterns on wing undersurfaces.

B-58A, 61-2058, assigned to the 305th BW, is seen during a transient stopover at Forbes AFB, KS, in September, 1969. It is carrying a conventional TCP and is equipped with four underwing pylons for Mk.43 thermonuclear weapons transport.

In mid-1960 a lack of funds, competition from other weapon systems, and a variety of complex, and at times biased, political and technological decisions in high echelons had all combined to cause delays in the B-58's operational deployment. Consequently, although the aircraft had been scheduled to become operational in June, not a single wing was activated and it appeared that none would be until at least January, 1961. SAC emphasized that the B-58, when combined with the capabilities of the Boeing B-52, would provide the necessary variety of tactics to make for a viable bomber deterrent.

SAC continued to base its planning on a "small force" of three B-58 wings. According to Maj. Gen. Compton, "the worth of any force less than this is seriously questioned." SAC had come to the conclusion that a small, fully operational B-58 force would greatly enhance US strategic posture by forcing the Soviet Union to provide a Mach 2 defense for all possible targets or accept the destruction which a three wing force could inflict. Planning consequently ran into the economic aspect of the Soviet defense problem, and SAC assumed that the cost of a Soviet Mach 2 defense was far out of proportion to the expense of three B-58 wings.

In regard to its ability to reach targets, SAC held that the B-58 had demonstrated sufficient range to cover far more targets than there were aircraft programmed for production, and that most of the major targets west of the Ural Mountains would be vulnerable to a single refueled B-58 attack. Its electronic countermeasures capability would counter airborne interceptions and Soviet SAM radars while the B-52 and B-47 fleets would provide mutual support for penetration of Soviet early warning and defense nets. The B-58's navigation/bomb system accuracy was expected to be comparable to that of other manned systems and was adequate for hard, point targets. With Mach 2 high altitude or Mach .95 low altitude penetration capability, the B-58 did, according to SAC, greatly improve the over-all strategic offensive capability.

In spite of SAC desires, the number of wings to be produced for the AF remained unstated, and accordingly, SAC continued to predicate its opera-

tional planning on the assumption that a three wing fleet would be funded. While it had already been decided that the first and second wings would reside at Carswell AFB and Bunker Hill AFB respectively, there was much SAC discussion as to where the third wing would be located. Gen. Power, Lt. Gen. J. P. McConnell, and other SAC officers contended that Little Rock AFB, AR would provide superior wing facilities. Gen. Power therefore asked his staff to program the aircraft, along with a fleet of Boeing KC-135 tankers, for this base.

On the basis of these plans, SAC notified the USAF of its desire to program the B-58's and KC-135's to Little Rock AFB with all the concurrent shifts of personnel and support facilities. USAF headquarters, however, could not make the decision since it was still studying its final organization and force strengths. The USAF also was considering a two wing proposal which would limit the B-58 to Carswell AFB and Bunker Hill AFB. Little Rock AFB remained up in the air, though there were no changes from the then-extant AF decision to acquire a 148 aircraft, three wing B-58 force.

In January, 1960, the AF announced its decision to activate its first B-58 Wing. This was to be the 43rd Bomb Wing which, at that time, was still located at Davis-Monthan AFB, AZ. The AF's intention was to move the 43rd from Davis-Monthan

to Carswell starting March 1. All 3958th Operational, Test and Evaluation personnel (then functioning as an integral unit at Carswell) would be transferred to the 43rd upon its arrival.

With the forthcoming activation of the 43rd Bomb Wing at Carswell as the first operational B-58 unit, the AF began actively to recruit crew members. Requirements, due to the aircraft's unique performance characteristics and maintenance needs, were among the highest for any aircraft in the AF inventory. Additionally, due to the dimensional limitations of the crew accommodations (which were later compounded by the addition of the encapsulated ejection seats) there were strict physical limitations on crew member height and weight. Ground crews tended to be hand picked, and per the recommendation of the June, 1960, accident committee (see Chapt. 6), they usually represented personnel with exceptionally high skill levels and lengthy service careers.

Approximately 1,500 personnel were eventually assigned to the maintenance activities of each of the two B-58 wings (43rd and 305th). Because of the unique structural aspects of the B-58, field maintenance required a high percentage of fully qualified personnel. Three maintenance men were assigned to each aircraft. The special problems emerging from the aircraft's unique fuel and weapons pod were assigned to a separate Muni-

Bob Esposito

B-58A, 58-1014, was delivered to the 43rd BW from Convair and served with that unit until its delivery to Davis-Monthan AFB in 1970. Markings were standard for type with the unit badge on the right side of the nose. Most MA-1 pods and TCPs were painted silver.

USAF via Douglas Robinson

B-58A, 59-2492, one of the first operational B-58's, is seen during the SAC bombing competition at Bergstrom AFB, TX, in 1960. This aircraft and 59-2430 were the only B-58's entered; their performance was considered exceptional.

George Bracken

"The Pulaski Hustler" is barely discernible on the fuselage side of 59-2429, seen at Little Rock, AFB, AR, in the late 1960's. This was the second aircraft to have this nickname. It survived long enough to be placed in storage at Davis-Monthan AFB in 1969.

Pete Bulban

B-58A, 59-2430, was the second aircraft entered in the 1960 SAC bombing competition at Bergstrom AFB, TX. Markings for this aircraft were standard for type, unlike those seen on 59-2429 at the same time. The crew entry ladder was a standard ground support unit developed specifically for the B-58.

USAF via Douglas Robinson

B-58A, 59-2430, is seen during a landing roll-out, with drag chute deployed. A high angle of attack was maintained for as long as possible in order to utilize aerodynamic drag for braking. In this view, a red flash is visible on '2430's vertical fin.

Bill Balogh via Dave Menard

Bearing early operational markings, B-58A, 59-2431, sits statically at an unidentified east coast air show in the early 1960's. Black mask around windscreen was distinctive and not often seen after the first few years of B-58 operational service.

tion Maintenance Squadron. The complex sub-systems and unusual configuration of the B-58 called for a variety of special ground support equipment.

Maintenance of the B-58's armament and electronics was especially critical because of the fine tolerances required for proper operation of its Doppler-inertial navigation and guidance systems and advanced bombing systems.

On March 15, 1960, the 43rd Bomb Wing, which had begun shifting equipment and personnel from Davis-Monthan AFB to Carswell AFB on March 1, received its first B-58. This aircraft, which departed Carswell on a short test hop just prior to the delivery ceremony, was piloted by Col. James K. Johnson who then was serving as the 43rd's commander.

On March 23, a test unit B-58A, 55-671, crewed by Lt. Col. Leonard Legge, Capt. Andrew Rose, Jr., and Capt. Raymond Wagener, remained airborne for 18 hours 10 minutes while averaging an airspeed of 620 mph over 11,000 miles. This was, and apparently still is, the longest single flight ever by a B-58.

On August 1, 1960, SAC assumed executive control of the B-58 program; consequently the Category III Test Phase of the B-58 program was begun. Category III testing terminated on July 31, 1961 (thus changing the mission on August 1 to conduct a combat crew training program and to support the B-58 Test Program) and on August 1, 1961, the B-58 OES (Operational Engineering Section) assumed the responsibility for all future B-58 evaluations. The B-58 OES, in turn, was officially terminated on June 1, 1962.

The 43rd received deliveries beginning in December, 1960. A total of forty B-58's were assigned to the wing, these consisting of eleven "conversion" units (see *Flash-Up* program in Chapt. 6) and twenty-nine new production units (numbers 31 thru 59).

Five months after receiving its first aircraft, the 43rd entered its first bombing competition. On September 11, two B-58A's, 59-2429 and 59-2430, departed Carswell AFB and flew to Bergstrom AFB, TX. The crews selected by Col. Johnson for the competition consisted of (in 59-2429) Maj. Harold Confer, pilot; Maj. Richard Weir, nav/bombardier; and Capt. Howard Bialas, DSO. The second crew (in 59-2430) consisted of Maj. Henry Deutschendorf, pilot; Capt. William Polhemus, navigator; and Capt. Raymond Wagener, DSO. Both crews would fly only 59-2429 in the competition.

Held annually, the bomb meet was scored using a point system based on accuracy, timing, and a number of miscellaneous parameters. The events consisted of high and low level runs (100 points ea.); bombing accuracy (100 points); a high level Mach 1.5 run (100 points—specifically for the B-58); a low level mission (200 points); rendezvous and inflight refueling coupling (100 points for accuracy and completion); and defense (100 points).

The Bergstrom meet, taking place between September 13 and 16, 1960, was a highly competitive event featuring some of the very best bomber crews in the USAF. Somewhat miraculously, the B-58's performance proved extraordinary—particularly in consideration of the fact that it had been assigned to the 43rd for less than six months and had been operational for a total of only six weeks. Six B-47 crews and six B-52 crews, representing the two top wings from the 2nd, 8th, and 15th AFs and determined to be the best in the AF through previous unit "pre-competitions", gathered at Bergstrom AFB for the event.

The aircraft and its crews (the ground crew members wore special blue coveralls with gold lettering) eventually logged the best pair of radar bombing scores and the top individual high-level navigation run to accumulate a total of 1,046 points and place fifth overall (137 points behind the first place B-52 team). Two minor mechanical malfunctions, a broken spring in the tracking control lever and a jammed film magazine in the radar photo recorder, apparently kept the aircraft from winning the competition outright.

It is interesting to note that one of the two B-58 teams in contention also set a "scramble" record that may not have been superceded to this very day . . . . the B-58 was "rolling" in 2 minutes 10 seconds—almost half the time required for the rest of the competition aircraft.

With the fulfillment of equipment and personnel requirements at the 43rd, including the arrival of the first TB-58A, 55-670, in August, 1960, the second (and as it would turn out, last) bomb wing to receive the B-58 became the 305th at Bunker Hill AFB, IN. Equipping the 305th BW had been initiated in December, 1960. Following official instigation of the reorganization of the unit on January 9, 1961, and its attainment of wing status on February 1, the first aircraft, 59-2461, nicknamed *Hoosier Hustler* was flown to Bunker Hill AFB on May 11 by Col. Frank O'Brien, 305th commander, Lt. Col. George Cohlmia, and Maj. Bill Williams. Two months later, the first 305th-assigned TB-58A, 55-664, arrived. In August, 1962, the wing was declared combat ready and in September, it went on alert for the first time.

On December 27, 1960, USAF Headquarters advised the AMC that each B-58 wing would have 40, rather than 36 aircraft. Accordingly, each squadron would be assigned 12 B-58's. At that time, and throughout the forthcoming operational years of the B-58 in AF service, the assigned B-58 squadrons would consist of the 63rd (Medium), 64th (Medium), and the 65th (Medium) for the 43rd BW, and the 364th (Medium), 365th (Medium), and the 366th (Medium) for the 305th BW.

Eventually, each wing would have 70 crews certified as combat ready. A normal duty assignment for a crew was between three and five years. Accordingly, the wing training program was designed to add three combat-ready crews to the wing each six-month period.

Technical difficulties, as outlined in Chapt. 6, continued to plague the B-58 even following its entry into the AF inventory. SAC, on March 10, 1961, announced that it had decided to set back the operational readiness date of the 43rd BW because the aircraft had not yet generated the required sortie level, and because of the effect of Category III testing and training missions on combat readiness.

SAC and the AF, in what was to become a highly successful effort to publicize the extraordinary performance capabilities of the B-58, in late 1960, elected to fund attempts to recapture a lengthy series of world absolute records then held by the Soviet Union and older US aircraft.

B-58A, 59-2432, at Little Rock AFB, AR, during the late 1960's. In static position, the elevons drooped to their maximum trailing-edge-down deflection angle. Visible under the wing root sections are the four Mk.43 thermonuclear weapons pylons.

Two practice Mk.43 thermonuclear weapons shapes and a TCP upper component are seen suspended from B-58A 59-2435 during weapons trials out of Kirtland AFB, NM. This aircraft was equipped with a tail cone-mounted data link antenna and two outboard engine nacelle-mounted camera pods.

B-58A, 59-2436, during landing roll-out at Carswell AFB, TX. Markings, including the SAC badge and sash on the left forward fuselage side, were standard for type. Note black painted wheels. The wheels were painted either silver or black.

No less than six B-58A's, including 58-1019 ("Beech-Nut Kid), are seen during a practice scramble at Little Rock AFB, AR. Many of these sessions also included MITO takeoffs wherein aircraft were launched at 15 second intervals in an attempt to get as many airborne in as short a time period as possible.

Richard Bolcer

B-58A, 59-2437, of the 43rd BW was seriously damaged following a landing accident in 1968 at Little Rock AFB, AR. Its carcass was moved to the main base facility and there used as a maintenance training aid. The weight seen hanging from the nose was a dummy W39Y nuclear warhead used in the MB-1 pod.

Bill Mann

B-58A, 59-2439, of the 43rd BW is seen during takeoff from Little Rock AFB. Nose high attitude was mandated by aerodynamic characteristics of the delta wing. This aircraft was equipped with the inboard Mk.43 thermonuclear weapons pylons, but they were not attached at the time this photo was taken.

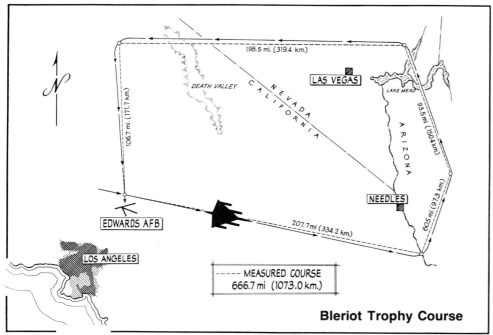

Bleriot Trophy Course

The first of these attempts, as the first segment of a three-day effort under the project name of *Quick Step I*, was conducted from Edwards AFB, CA, on January 12, 1961, when 59-2442, nicknamed *Untouchable*, of the 43rd BW, with Maj. Henry Deutschendorf, Jr., Capt. William Polhemus, and Capt. R. R. Wagener as crew, set three new international speed-with-payload (0, 1,000 and 2,000 kilogram payload weights) records for class by flying 1,061.80 mph over a closed circuit 2,000 kilometer (about 1,242 miles) course. The 0 kilogram record had previously been held by a McDonnell F-101A (700.47 mph) and the 1,000 and 2,000 kilogram records had been held by a Tupolev Tu-104A (639.18 mph). On the same flight, this crew also set a 1,000 kilometer record by flying at an average speed of 1,200.19 mph (interestingly, the closed circuit and 2,000 kg. records still stand as of this writing).

Two days later, 59-2441, nicknamed *Road Runner*, also of the 43rd BW, with Lt. Col. Harold Confer, Lt. Col. Richard Weir, and Maj. Howard Bialas as crew, was flown from Edwards AFB and used to set three more international speed-with-payload (0, 1,000 and 2,000 kilogram payload weights) records for class by flying 1,284.73 mph over a 1,000-kilometer closed circuit course. The previous records had been held by a Tupolev Tu-104A (596.7 mph).

The records set by 59-2441 led to its crew receiving the 1961 Thompson Trophy. This was the first time in the trophy's 33 year history that it had been presented to a bomber crew. Interestingly, this was the same crew that won first place honors in the 1960 SAC bombing competition at Bergstrom AFB.

Four months after the January records, on May 10, 1961, 59-2451 of the 43rd BW, crewed by Maj. Elmer Murphy, Maj. Eugene Moses, and Lt. David Dickerson, after departing Edwards AFB, flew a 669.4 mile (1,073 kilometer) closed course (the course was somewhat rectangular with corners near Needles, CA; Kingman, AZ; Mormon Mesa, NV; and Lone Pine, CA) at an average speed of 1,302.07 mph for more than 30 minutes (the actual record setting time for the circuit was 30 minutes 43 seconds), thus winning outright the prestigious Bleriot Trophy. Regulations governing the permanent award of the Bleriot Trophy required an aircraft to be flown at least one-half hour at an average speed of 2,000 kilometers per hour (1,242.74 mph). The international competition for the Trophy was originally created in 1930 by Monsieur Louis Bleriot (1872-1936) who was a noted French pioneer aviator and aircraft builder.

Some two weeks later on May 26, 59-2451, nicknamed *The Firefly* of the 43rd BW, enroute to the 1961 Paris Airshow with Maj. William Payne, Capt. William Polhemus, and Capt. Raymond Wagener as crew, set a New York-to-Paris speed record, covering the 3,626.46 statute miles in 3 hours 19 minutes and 58 seconds (average speed was approximately 1,089.36 mph). This flight also established a Washington, D.C.-to-Paris (3,833.4 statute miles) speed record of 3 hours 39 minutes and 49 seconds (average speed was 1,048.68 mph). This bettered an unofficial previous record of 5 hours 45 minutes set by a commercial airline-operated Boeing 707. The route, from Carswell AFB, TX, to Washington, D.C., to New York, and then to Paris, took just under six hours. Total distance flown was 5,150 statute miles at an altitude of between 25,000' and 50,000'. Greeting the crew upon arrival was Monsieur Louis Mills, a noted French journalist—who had also greeted Charles Lindbergh upon his arrival at Le Bourget airport some 34 years earlier. The crew was later awarded the prestigious Mackay and Harmon Trophies for this flight. Sadly, the return flight crew, consisting of Maj. Elmer Murphy, Maj.

Eugene Moses, and Lt. David Dickerson, the same crew that had won the Bleriot Trophy some two weeks earlier, crashed in 59-2451 on June 3, following departure from Le Bourget.

On June 8, 1961, a B-58 from the 43rd BW accomplished a succesful simulated profile mission dropping an MB-1 pod on the Edwards AFB range. The CEP (Circular Error Probable) was within specification and the mission was considered successful.

On September 6, SAC officially stated its desire to establish a B-58 reflex capability in an overseas area during the 1963-1970 period. SAC requested AF approval of the operational concept and requirements. Approval was granted on September 27, and the AFLC was then asked to appraise the support aspects and to begin the preliminary planning action. This, in turn, was followed by a USAF authorization of a B-58 Reflex Capability at Zaragoza, Spain to be established and functional by July 1, 1963.

Later, SAC would expand the B-58's Reflex Capability to include England, Guam, and Okinawa. The two wings would alternate participation in these forward-base training missions. Such deployments dispersed the B-58 force, gave SAC a limited forward B-58 capability, and gave base support personnel training in aircraft and weapons handling.

Continuing difficulties with the B-58 and a desire to bring all aircraft up to the same operational configuration standards, gave birth, on July 23, 1961, to the first of several *Project Hustle* conferences at Convair's Fort Worth, facility. Representatives from SAC, the AFSC, the AFLC, and their various elements, during the first meeting, agreed upon a firm plan for the *Project Hustle* modifications. Final approval for the modification and update program, as *Project Hustle-Up*, occurred on October 2, 1962, and a funding ceiling on the work of $45.8 million was imposed. On October 5, engineering and pre-production work was authorized and on October 12, the B-58 program office authorized Convair to proceed with the manufacture of *Project Hustle-Up* modifications kits. Many modifications and systems changes were incorporated during the various phases of *Hustle-Up* work, but one of the most important was the retrofit of all tactically configured aircraft with the multi-weapon carrying capability. The AFLC was tasked with the installation process from its SAAMA facility at Kelly AFB, TX, though actual installation took place at Convair.

On October 30, 59-2449 became the first B-58 to enter the *Project Hustle-Up* program. This aircraft had arrived at the Convair plant on October 24 for repair of a nose wheel anomaly. The first aircraft to be processed through *Hustle-Up* was 59-2428, which was accepted and delivered to the 43rd BW three days ahead of schedule on January 18, 1963. This aircraft would, on August 14, become the first B-58 to enter Phase II (which simply continued with the installation of modification kits missed during Phase I) of *Hustle-Up*, just as the last aircraft from *Hustle-Up* Phase I, 59-2456, was delivered. The last aircraft out of *Hustle-Up* Phase II was delivered to Carswell AFB on December 28, 1963, two days ahead of schedule.

Further B-58 records were set when on March 5, 1962, 59-2458 of the 43rd BW with Capt. Robert Sowers, Capt. Robert MacDonald, and Capt. John Walton as crew set a transcontinental speed record by flying non-stop from Los Angeles-to-New York and back again. The first leg, from Los Angeles to New York, was completed in 2 hours 0 minutes and 56.8 minutes (the old record was 2 hours 47 minutes set by a McDonnell F4H-1) at an average speed of 1,214.71 mph. The return leg, from New York to Los Angeles (referred to as the

B-58A, 59-2440, of the 43rd BW is seen without pod. When the pod was removed, the "Hustler's" c.g. was critical and in order to prevent accidental rotation onto its tail, a special weight was attached to the nose. As can be seen in this photo, the weight was suspended from the nose gear well by a special bridle.

B-58A, 59-2441, of the 43rd BW, is seen at Edwards AFB, CA, prior to participation in "Operation Quick Step" in January, 1961, wherein along with 59-2442, it was used to set several world speed records for class. The crew later received the Thompson Trophy for their efforts.

B-58A, 59-2449, of the 43rd BW, is seen inside the main Convair production facility at Ft. Worth, TX, following its delivery as the first aircraft to enter the "Hustle-Up" update program. In photo, the nose landing gear has been retracted and the aircraft is suspended by a bridle.

B-58A, 59-2450, of the 43rd BW, is seen at Little Rock AFB carrying only the upper component of the TCP. Markings are standard for type. This aircraft was eventually delivered to Davis-Monthan AFB, AZ, for disposition in 1970.

59

Bart Cusick

B-58A, 59-2442, of the 43rd BW, in flight near Little Rock AFB, AR, on June 29, 1967. Though not readily visible in photo, this aircraft was equipped with an LA-1 reconnaissance pod. It also was one of two B-58's to participate in the "Operation Quick Step" record-setting flights at Edwards AFB in 1961.

"beat the sun" flight—it became the first transcontinental flight in history that moved across the country faster than the rotational speed of the earth), was completed in 2 hours 15 minutes 48.6 seconds (the old record was 3 hours 36 minutes set by a McDonnell RF-101C) for an average speed of 1,081.77 mph. The total round trip time was 4 hours 41 minutes 11.3 seconds (the old record was 6 hours 46 minutes set by a McDonnell RF-101C) and the round trip average speed was 1,044.96 mph at a cruising altitude of approximately 50,000'. This record-setting flight won for its crew both the Bendix Trophy and the Mackay Trophy.

The 43rd BW, which had been prevented from being declared combat ready by the B-58's teething problems, was finally declared as such in August, 1962. Finally, in September, the wing ,was placed on alert.

Shortly after this, on September 18, 1962, 59-2456 with a crew consisting of Maj. Fitzhugh Fulton, Capt. W. R. Payne, and civilian flight test engineer C. R. Haines, was used to set two more world records. During a zoom profile flight over Edwards AFB, CA, the aircraft reached 85,360.84' while carrying a payload of 5,000 kg (11,023 lbs.). This broke two previously Soviet-held records and also brought the crew the 1962 Harmon Trophy

(this record still stands as of this writing).

A final record setting flight was conducted on October 16, 1963, when 61-2059, assigned to the 305th BW and with Maj. Sidney Kubesch, Maj. John Barrett, and Capt. Gerard Williamson as crew, flew supersonically from Tokyo to London during operation "Greased Lightning".

The Tokyo to London mission was chosen for a record attempt for several reasons, not the least of which was that the total route, for the most part, was identical with two regular training routes called *Glass Brick* (a regular practice mission to the Far East) and *Alarm Bell* (a similar practice mission to Spain). It also was picked because there would be no problem in obtaining tankers due to the proximity of tanker bases, and the Tokyo to London mission, because of its length, would ably demonstrate the B-58's legitimate strategic mission capabilities.

The mission had begun as part of a four ship formation that departed Bunker Hill AFB on October 9, 1963. An initial stopover at Anderson AFB, Guam, followed some 14 hours 10 minutes later, and a day after this, 61-2059 and its crew headed for Kadena AFB, Okinawa. Four days were spent at Kadena preparing for the flight, and on October 16th, the mission was cleared for takeoff. The route included inflight refuelings between

Tokyo (at which point the aircraft would accelerate to supersonic speeds) and the Aleutian Islands; over Shemya; over Anchorage, AK; near Thule, Greenland; and off the southeastern coast of Greenland.

An FAI observer in a KC-135A logged the Tokyo departure at 0459Z, and a few minutes later, *Greased Lightning* (as the aircraft was nicknamed) and its crew were supersonic over the Sea of Japan. The cruising altitude at this time was 53,000' and the ground speed was 1,230 knots. Following two inflight refueling slow-downs, the timers over Anchorage calculated an average ground speed of 950 knots up to that point in the mission.

The following inflight refueling session unfortunately did not go well due to weather anomalies and the northern lights phenomenon, but time lost was partially made up during the succeeding steady state cruise period. The fourth refueling went as planned, as did the fifth, but when the session was over, the afterburner of the number three engine would not ignite and this promptly limited the aircraft to a maximum speed of Mach 1.4. Sadly, fuel consumption levels at Mach 1.4 were almost the same as those at Mach 2, and it thus became necessary for the aircraft to decelerate to a subsonic speed shortly before crossing the coast of Scotland. The afterburner failure resulted in 1 hour 5 minutes being added to the total flight time, and also resulted in a final average ground speed of "only" 812 knots.

The aircraft passed over London at 1334Z, and after a short picture-taking session with another KC-135A, *Greased Lightning* landed at Greenham Common RAF Station (about 40 miles west of London) without further incident. The 5 hours spent at supersonic speed made this mission the longest supersonic flight in history at the time (the Lockheed A-12 would later undertake longer supersonic missions, but at the time, it was still undergoing flight test at Groom Lake) and gave to the US a record previously held by the British (17 hours 42 minutes). Additionally, the flight set five more world's absolute records, bringing to

Michel Marand via S. Nicolaev

Ill-fated B-58A, 59-2451, during its short visit to the Paris Airshow in 1961. This record-setting aircraft was destroyed as it departed Le Bourget airport on June 3, 1961, killing all three crew members. The two vertical fin stripes, painted for the trans-Atlantic speed record attempt to Paris, were red.

USAF

Because of the numerous brake and tire problems encountered by the B-58 throughout its operational service life, special cooling blowers and shrapnel cages were developed for its lower landing gear components. Hot landings dictated their use on a regular basis. B-58A, 59-2456, is seen at Edwards AFB on November 29, 1963, following a high gross weight landing which caused higher than normal brake temperatures.

nineteen the total the B-58 had registered officially with the Federation Aeronautique Internationale.

Additional records would be set by the B-58 before its operational career ended, but these would not be officially logged with the FAI and thus not placed on the record books. One B-58, for instance, which returned to Bunker Hill AFB from routine deployment to Okinawa, set two world speed records in the process. This aircraft covered the 2,858 miles between Anchorage and Chicago in 5 hours 23 minutes and 20 seconds at an average speed of 530.88 mph. The over-all Tokyo-to-Chicago distance of 6,371 miles was flown in 8 hours, 36 minutes and 38 seconds averaging 740.76 mph. At the time, no official records existed for flights between Tokyo and Chicago or between Anchorage and Chicago. Lt. Col. George Andrews, Maj. Joseph Guastella, and Capt. Clifford Youngblood crewed the aircraft on this little-known record breaker.

By the mid-1960's with its record-setting days behind it, operational use of the B-58 settled into a marginally routine service career that made it a functional and modestly effective weapon delivery system. By the end of 1963, AF crews had made over 10,500 flights and logged some 53,000 hours (1,150 supersonic including 375 at Mach 2). Training missions were flown on a daily scheduling basis from both Bunker Hill AFB and Little Rock AFB, and the normal routine included at least one TB-58A mission each morning and afternoon (these consisting of one two-hour and fifteen minute flight followed by a 30 minute ground refueling and another 30 minutes of flight immediately thereafter).

SAC continuously evaluated wing reliability by a stringent crew standardization/evaluation program and four no-notice exercises a year. One of these programs, the Operational Readiness Inspection, simulated an Emergency War Order (EWO) strike and was conducted by the SAC Inspector General. In *Bar None* exercises all the wing's aircraft and crews flew against an unfamiliar target according to a strict preset time schedule. The combat evaluation group also made

both scheduled evaluations of crew proficiency and no-notice spot checks several times each year.

These sorties, like all SAC training sorties, simulated as closely as possible an actual EWO mission profile. They included both high- and low-altitude navigation problems, aerial refueling, and simulated bomb drops. The accuracy of the bombing was plotted by a SAC radar bomb scoring unit mounted on a railroad train. The location of SAC's several "RBS Express" trains was changed at random every six months. If a B-58 sortie included a supersonic leg, this had to be flown over a specified corridor cleared for flight by Headquarters USAF and the Federal Aviation Administration.

One of the more spectacular elements of many ORI's was the MITO, or Minimum Interval Takeoff. Between fifteen and twenty B-58's were sometimes launched during one of these exercises wherein time requirements dictated that all aircraft involved be airborne within fifteen minutes. Deploying a gaggle of B-58's at 15-second intervals on a smoke-obscured runway was, to put it mildly, a rather testy experience—for both crew members and commanders alike. MITO operations for the B-58 had been cleared during *Open Road III* tests at Edwards AFB, CA, during a ses-

sion lasting from January 14 thru 22, 1963. Six B-58's participated, including 3 from each B-58 wing.

Pilots and crew members who aspired to fly the B-58 were required to meet very stringent experience standards. Pilots had to be recommended by their wing commander and possess a minimum of 1,000 hours total jet time (500 hours of which had to be as first pilot in multi-engine jets). Navigators were required to have 500 hours total jet time; and Defensive System Operators, 200 hours. Most importantly, crew members had to be of the physical requirements dictated by the B-58's encapsulated ejection system. Crew training normally took between six and eight months before a crew was considered combat ready.

Initially, B-58 training was conducted by the 43rd Combat Crew Training School. From 1960 thru 1964, this unit fulfilled the requirements of both its parent 43rd BW, and the 305th BW. In August, 1964, the 305th activated its own CCTS. During the early years of the 43rd CCTS as many as 10 complete three-man crews plus two or three extra pilots were enrolled in the upgrading program. This later slowed to three complete crews plus one or two extra pilots every three months, with two different classes being conducted continually throughout the year. Initially, the majority of the

Michel Marrand via S. Nicolaev

Photo taken just seconds before 59-2451 disappeared into a cloud bank during a roll maneuver and dove into the ground at the 1961 Paris Airshow. All three crew members were killed and parts of the aircraft were scattered for hundreds of yards around the accident site.

G.D.

B-58A, 59-2456, during tests to validate the feasibility of carrying four Mk.43 thermonuclear weapons on wing root pylons. In this photo, the aircraft is also carrying a TCP. The carriage of the four Mk.43s had a noticeable affect on the "Hustler's" marginal range performance.

USAF

Another view of B-58A, 59-2456, taken at Edwards AFB, CA, during its participation in sonic boom studies conducted there, and prior to the installation of wing bomb racks. It has an AFSC badge and "Q" on its nose, just below the cockpit anti-glare panel.

USAF via E. G. Morales

B-58A, 59-2458, of the 43rd BW is seen inside a "Hustler Hut" at Little Rock AFB, AR. Noteworthy is the three-ton weight attached to the forward pod latch to maintain the aircraft c.g. in a lightly loaded condition.

43rd CCTS's recruits were former B-47 pilots; in later years, as B-47's were removed from the inventory, more and more of the pilots came from B-52 and KC-135 units.

When first entering the B-58 program, pilots were required to spend some six weeks at Perrin AFB, TX undergoing intensive instrument flight training in the Lockheed T-33 and the Convair TF-102. Navigators were sent to Mather AFB, CA where they were placed in an eight week course covering the B-58's unique bombing/navigation system. After 1963, DSO's also were sent to Mather AFB, where they completed a six week course learning the intricacies of the B-58's radar gunnery and electronic warfare systems.

Following the crew's return to the 43rd CCTS, an additional 120 days of instruction (including 30 hours of flight simulator training) were undertaken. Covered during this period were specialized instruction conducted by the Flight Training Detachment of the Air Training Command that included for the pilot 78 hours of instruction, and for the navigator/bombardier and the DSO, 44 hours each. This was followed by seven flights in the TB-58A. Total flying time required was approximately 90 hours for the pilot and the DSO, and 70 hours for the nav/bombardier.

The comprehensive curriculum to which the students were exposed during approximately 125 hours of instruction included subjects such as aircraft performance data, flight characteristics, aircraft systems, emergency procedures, high and low level bombing and navigation, fighter intercept tactics, radar operation and inflight maintenance, nuclear weapons, tactical doctrine, mission planning, and inflight refueling.

Typical B-58 flight crew experiences have been published in a variety of military service and non-service journals, but it is generally agreed that the essay written by retired Col. Robert Hinant, appearing in the first volume of the excellent *Flying Combat Aircraft* series (edited by Robert Higham, Ph.D. and published by Iowa State University Press, Ames, Iowa, in 1975) is one of the best. It is reprinted here with permission:

"At Carswell AFB in 1960 we were afforded regular views of the B-58 supersonic bomber, then being tested at the Convair plant, which was across the runway used jointly by Convair and the Air Force. The delta-winged, coke bottle fuselage, perched on long mosquito-legged tricycle landing gear without elevators, looked weird for a four-jet-engine nuclear bomber. Having B-47 and KC-135 experience, and having been assigned B-52's on base, I found the B-58 a completely different bomber; it had a sleek, agressive look, even with its long large pod hung under the belly to carry fuel and nuclear weapons or equivalent ballast.

"It was no secret when the afterburners of the J79 engines cut in that a B-58 was being flown. Windows rattled and nerves were jangled for the 7,000 to 9,000 foot run on takeoff. I never really got used to the noise—just accepted it with earplugs or insulated earmuffs for the next nine years at three bases.

"Finally, the first aircraft went to the Air Force Test Force Group and phase testing was completed. Aircraft were assigned to the 43rd BW, were eventually declared combat ready, and went on to fly in the SAC bombing competition within three weeks—an outstanding performance considering the seasoned B-47 and B-52 crews and aircraft competing as well as the crews and planes of the RAF that participated in the competition under the same rules.

"The B-58 operations began in 1958. Later, eight aircraft were configured as trainer-bombers in which the student pilot occupied the front seat, the instructor pilot the second, and the DSO, the third (the instructor pilot's seat was installed off-center so he could peek around the pilot during takeoff and landing). Initially, a first solo flight in the B-58 was also a first flight, period. Later, when the TB-58A's entered the inventory, pilots received a few hours in the trainer before being strapped-in to a regular bomber and waved off the ramp on his own. Many times the instructor who signed him off as qualified would run beads through as he sat and sweated out the return and landing. Since the crews were hand-picked with high standards, qualification solo flights were not a problem; the weak were weeded out before this phase of training.

"Crews entered the B-58's three individual compartments from a stand that was rolled alongside the forward left side of the aircraft. In the first station was the pilot, in the second the radar navigator/bombardier, and in the third, the defensive systems operator (electronic countermeasures, remote fire control, and assistant to the pilot). The seats were open-jawed escape capsules which were extremely complicated but 100 percent reliable. After checking the proper insertion of safety pins, we took our seats in the capsules. The first amazing realization was that the B-58 had a flight control *stick*, not a control column with a wheel. Secondly, we became aware that the cockpit was completely full—engine instruments, flight instruments, buttons, switches, lights, levers, throttles, and even a rearview mirror.

"After stowing lunch, briefcase, and related papers we completed the electrical 'power off' checklist; then the ground crew connected the external power and air conditioners, and the 'before start' portion of the checklist was completed by the three crew members. A ground crew member, stationed in front of the aircraft on interphone, worked with the crew during aircraft systems checkout. When the three crew members agreed that the aircraft was satisfactorily configured for the particular mission, the aircraft commander (pilot) told the ground crew that he was ready to start engines. The 'start engine' sequence was arranged so that aircraft electrical power and hydraulic pressure output could be checked and used. The crew chief on the ramp determined that the engine air starter had properly disengaged, and the flight controls were checked visually by the ground crew in coordination with the pilot's movements of the stick and rudder. The B-58 had no fly-by-wire flight control systems or elevators. The elevons acted as aileron and elevator—a sophisticated system that gave the pilot the same feel all the time although control surface movement varied greatly during various flight conditions. When the external electrical power, air-for-start, and air conditioner were disconnected and another lengthy checklist completed by all three crew members, clearance for taxi was received from the control tower.

"The above procedures were followed for routine training flights but were altered drastically when the aircraft was 'cocked' on alert. In such a case the aircraft was configured for its specific wartime mission, normally with five atomic weapons, and a numbered crew assigned to a particular aircraft. Under these conditions the complete alert force could be launched within five minutes from ground-alert posture. Practice 'scrambles' from ground-alert posture were ordered by higher headquarters at random times and conditions, and the flight crews never knew whether or not it was the real thing until the appropriate code was given when ready for takeoff.

"Taxi-out was simple and quick with nose-wheel steering; the engines idled at about 72% rpm, gobbling fuel. Sharp turns were avoided when feasible, for the main landing gear had eight wheels each, small in size and inflated to approximately 265 psi with nitrogen (so a blown tire would not support combustion of any material). After aligning the aircraft on the runway and obtaining clearance from

Rear view of B-58A, 59-2456, at Edwards AFB. The aircraft's elevons took up much of the wing trailing edge dimension. MB-1 pod ground clearance is readily discernible in this photo.

B-58A, 59-2458, was the winner of both the prestigious Bleriot and Bendix trophies. Nicknamed the "Cowtown Hustler", it is one of eight B-58's that remain extant. It is permanently displayed at the AF Museum, Wright-Patterson AFB, OH.

B-58A, 60-1111, of the 43rd BW, during a transient stopover at McGuire AFB, NJ, in June, 1969. This aircraft was equipped with the Stanley-developed encapsulated ejection seat. Unit badge has been removed from nose, possibly in consideration of a transferral of this aircraft from the 43rd BW to the 305th BW.

B-58A, 60-1112, of the 305th BW, at Bunker Hill, AFB, IN. This aircraft was eventually delivered to Davis-Monthan AFB, AZ, for long term storage, and was finally disposed in 1977.

the control tower, the throttles were advanced, all instruments checked, then brakes released as power was advanced through afterburner cut-in.

"The aircraft seemed to lunge forward as each engine contributed over 15,000 lbs. of thrust. Computed takeoff data were used to check performance as the thousand-foot markers were passed; since takeoff airspeed, stopping distance, and three-engine performance where known, rapid decisions had to be made until you passed the point on the runway where you were committed to go regardless. By then airspeed was around 190 knots; as the computed airspeed for takeoff was attained you rotated the aircraft positively, broke ground, stomped the rudder pedals at 200' to stop wheel rotation, simultaneously moved the landing gear handle to the 'up' position, and held attitude as a definite rate of climb was indicated and airspeed increased (a 425 knot climb speed was standard). At sea level the fully loaded B-58 climbed at a rate in excess of 17,000' per minute—a rate of climb that would have been creditable for a fighter of that day. When lightly loaded the *Hustler* shot upwards at 46,000' per minute, with afterburner! When the landing gear was retracted and 'locked' indicated, airspeed was allowed to increase to climb speed; then you could listen to ground control or the bitch box and take a deep gulp of oxygen, check your flight plan, listen to the navigator or DSO, and become released from ground control.

"Now it was simple if everything went according to plan. You put the autopilot in the mode desired and followed your flight plan. If things were not operating normally, a female voice told you so (voice warning); if more than one malfunction occurred, the 'old bitch' would tell you the most important one and would keep on until you did something about it. Of course warning lights also flashed to indicate a malfunction; you could cover them up, but you couldn't stop the voice. The DSO was very helpful in reading various checklists, but the pilot took the actions or told the DSO to pull certain circuit breakers (he had hundreds in his compartment).

"The B-58 responded to control stick and rudder movement very much as did the F-102, which was used for transition training into the program because of its delta wing. When speed was increased through Mach 1 to Mach 2 or less, the center of gravity was shifted by either automatic or manual transfer of fuel into or out of the ballast tank located in the aft portion of the fuselage. This allowed

the aircraft to ride on the downhill slope of the sonic air crest. Also, as speed increased, the spikes or center cones in each engine inlet had to extend so that the sonic shock wave never entered the engine, now that the speed was limited by maximum allowable inlet air temperature and by structural factors. The aircraft was *not* power limited. Normal speed for cruise was over 525 knots (Mach .92), over 600 knots at sea level, and 1,147 knots above 40,000'. The B-58 has been flown above 85,000' with payload.

"The four engines were the J79-GE-5B General Electric axial type with afterburner. The sea level static ratings were: maximum power with afterburner—15,500 lbs. thrust at 7,734 rpm maximum continuous for 120 minutes; military power—10,300 lbs. thrust at 7,460 rpm continuous. Normal cruise was 9,700 pounds thrust continuous with a maximum allowable exhaust gas temperature of 1,105-degs. F. under all conditions.

"Air refueling for a KC-135 tanker was easy compared to other air-related receivers. The A/R receptacle was located on the nose of the aircraft, just ahead of the windscreen; when flying within the refueling 'envelope' you were below the jet wash of the KC-135, with the directional lights on the belly of the tanker right in your face. On refueling to full tanks, it was best to put the two outboard engines in afterburner, then adjust power on the inboard engines to maintain position. The dependable KC-135 tanker with proficient crew was a welcome sight, for the rendezvous was accomplished many times over midocean or polar ice cap. Range with one refueling was 7,400 miles; without refueling, 4,450 miles. The aircraft could be refueled inflight to a maximum of 176,890 pounds—which was significantly more than the maximum gross taxi weight.

"There were two types of pod carried under the belly. The MB-1 type was a single unit in which fuel and nuclear weapons/ballast were carried; some contained photo equipment. The two-component pod carried fuel in the lower section, which could be jettisoned after the fuel was used; the upper component contained the warhead. Four smaller nuclear weapons could be carried externally, two on each side, between the inboard engines and the fuselage, one behind the other. When the B-58 was configured for combat, it was loaded with five atomic weapons; thus five separate targets could be hit at either low or high level. Exit from the target area was made by a zoom to maximum altitude at Mach 2 or to low level at Mach .92. The electronic

countermeasures (ECM) equipment was superior in all respects, and the bomb/navigation equipment provided accurate delivery of high-yield weapons.

"After penetration, escape from defended areas was enhanced by the B-58's high speed, small size and minimum radar reflectivity, radar warning systems, defensive ECM systems, and tail turret. When all else failed, you could 'punch out' in the capsule with a supply of oxygen, signal for directional finders, and dispense chaff for radar tracking. Parachutes opened automatically and let you down gently; if in water, the flotation gear inflated. You had with you a full survival kit including radio, flares, gun, food, water, clothing, and even sunburn lotion and fighting gear!

"At the termination of a mission, a normal jet penetration was made from a known beacon to the airfield; usually the aircraft ground control unit would direct you for the approach to the runway, and Ground Control Approach would pick you up and complete the circuit to the runway. Both Instrument Landing System (ILS) and Tactical Air Navigation (TACAN) were installed in all aircraft and usually worked well. After computing the best approach speed, which varied with aircraft weight, you flew that speed until you bled off airspeed to the computed best flare speed for touchdown. You could not add a few knots speed for your wife and one for each chld and still stop on the runway, even though a brake chute was used. You flew the speed and rate of descent exactly, and your attitude was 16-degs. nose high. Just adding power, nose high, would not hack a decrease in descent rate. The nose had to come down to streamline the aircraft before airspeed increased and rate of descent decreased. This may sound odd to some, but the delta wing has that trait. On the runway, on the proper heading, you pulled the brake chute at 160 knots or below and raised the nose high to get aerodynamic braking with the lower wing surface. The brake chute shear pin would shear at above 160 knots—a safety feature in case a go-around was attempted after deploying the chute. At normal landing weights, a ground roll of 2,580' was required.

"After turning off the runway, completing the after-landing checklists, parking, and shutting down, you unstrapped yourself from the aircraft, installed the three ground safety pins in the capsule, and were helped to unfold and climb out onto the entrance stand. You then walked around the aircraft before going to the maintenance and operations

B-58A, 60-1119, of the 305th BW in 1965. This "Hustler" was one of the first aircraft to be modified for iron bomb tests. Unit badge is visible on nose just under windscreen.

B-58A, 60-1118, of the 305th BW. In flight, the B-58 was considered by its crew members to be exceptionally docile—as long as all systems were constantly monitored and all equipment functioned properly.

B-58A, 60-1120, of the 305th BW. Unusual cockpit access ladder is the result of landing at a field not equipped with the dedicated ingress/egress ladder required by the B-58.

B-58A, 60-1123, of the 305th BW during an airshow at Milwaukee, WI, on July 28, 1968. This aircraft was later disposed at Davis-Monthan AFB, AZ, in 1977.

B-58A, 61-2069, is seen during the course of the 1965 Paris Airshow at the beginning of a takeoff roll. This "Hustler" was a back-up aircraft to 59-2443, destroyed in a major accident during the show.

B-58A, 60-1121, undergoing "Hustle-Up" modifications in Building 361 at SAAMA during 1964. Balance weight suspended from forward pod latch assembly under fuselage, weighs 6,160 lbs.

debriefing. We were usually numb, so questions were answered with a shrug, a nod, or sometimes a recitation concerning the complete outfit with name-calling; after 45 minutes we were turned loose to make our way home to hear what really happened today—from our families.

"Overall, the B-58 handled and performed beautifully. The utmost skill was used in the application of miniaturized automatic analogue components, exotic metals, plastics, rubber, grease, and orinite to make the aircraft exceed its design specifications. It was expensive to fly (dollars per flying hour), but that's progress, I guess. The aircraft seemed to have their own personalities for some crews, especially some tail-numbered dogs or jewels. Most crew members were especially proud of the B-58. Even those in the second and third crew stations only had a 4 x 6-inch window to look through, claustrophobia never seemed to cause a problem, for you were too busy to look. The tandem seating arrangement required close crew coordination and cooperation at all times, especially during malfunction and high-speed flight. Most crews were gung ho, like that of N. R. Smith (later killed in Vietnam on his second mission in an O-2): when he came out after a weather briefing to board the aircraft, a panel was yet to be installed after a discrepancy had been discovered on preflight. He told the crew chief, 'if you want that panel to have as much flight time as the airframe, you'd better screw it on quick—I'm going'. Prior flight experience in B-47's was a real asset, as was delta-wing fighter time.

"The B-58—fast, complicated, computerized, and not power limited—ranked above the B-47 and B-52. Detailed knowledge of the aircraft systems and thorough flight planning were necessary, and takeoff time was scheduled well in advance. The two observers in the B-58 had two or three aeronautical ratings, and the aircraft commander was usually triple-rated. In the B-47 there was a copilot who could fly the aircraft, operate the tail guns, act as a radio operator, and serve coffee or water when necessary. In the B-58 the crew members were on their own in separate stalls, and everyone had his separate duties. You could stand and stretch your legs in the B-47; the B-52—with its two pilots, two or three observers, and tail gunner—gave some freedom of movement and relief from duties at odd intervals; not so in the B-58.

"Everything was not always smooth flying in the B-58. The bombing-navigation system would act up (even though there were nine modes of bombing); and there were flight control malfunctions, engine problems, and wheel and tire explosions. During the cold weather tests in Alaska an aircraft skidded sideways, and three of the four engines flamed out. The second station operator asked on interphone what was going on and where they were; there was no answer, for the pilot was giving all his attention to keeping the aircraft in the air, straightening it out, and getting some engines running again. The navigator, second station, kept asking where they were but received no response. Since the airspeed and altitude were going to pot, he decided to 'punch out'. By the time the pilot had started another engine and landed safely, a rescue helicopter had picked up the navigator and deposited him on the ramp. When the haggard pilot crawled out of the aircraft, the navigator rushed over, stuck his face within inches of the pilot's and demanded, 'Why didn't you tell me where we were? I am the navigator and I have a right to know!'

"To again illustrate the calibre of the crew and aircraft, another incident is noteworthy. A 'roll cloud' was in the vicinity of Bunker Hill AFB, and the weather was bad. The pilot was cleared for an approach, but as he was descending on the glide path he entered the roll cloud and was forced down by a draft. He applied power but was not able to avoid a high commercial power line, which sheared the control cables to the No. 3 and No. 4 engines. The landing gear snagged a chain link fence and dragged about 30 feet of it as they proceeded to the alternate and landed safely. This was a determined crew and a good aircraft...."

The B-58's more noteworthy failings were not all system related. Many were the end product of its limited production numbers (and associated high unit costs), minimal spare parts support, a questionable safety record, limited low altitude capability, and most importantly, less than nominal unrefueled range.

Ongoing modification programs and prime logistical responsibility and maintenance support of the B-58 were assigned to the San Antonio Air Materiel Area (SAAMA) on March 11, 1955. The B-58 was the first weapon system to be managed under a policy whereby the logistics support manager was granted authority to control all items peculiar to the weapon system. Establishing the SAAMA's B-58 Logistic Support Management Office on March, 26, 1958, was the forerunner of a major organization realignment whereby world-wide weapons management functions were organizationally separated from inter-depot operations.

From the start of the B-58 program, the role of the SAAMA Center in procurement of spares for this aircraft was affected by the management concept adopted. Under this concept, which was new at the time, for procuring weapons systems, the B-58 procurement program was given by the AF to Convair to manage and to subcontract to other companies; only final decisions were referred to the US Government. All legwork was done by the industrial contractor. It dealt directly with more than 4,000 sub-contractors and other suppliers who furnished all parts and equipment for the aircraft, excepting only the General Electric J79 turbojet engine and a few minor items. This was a direct reversal of the previous procedure of phasing-in a new air weapons system.

As defined by the SAAMA, Project White Horse provided for the support of the B-58 weapons system by the contractor under the jurisdiction of SAAMA Headquarters, during the initial stages of the flight test program when support items were undergoing rapid development and change. It applied, also, to the gradual phasing-in to the normal supply system of support items and support responsibility after the high probability of design change had been minimized. All field-level support requirements were received and stored at the Convair facility and supplied to test sites upon demand.

During fiscal year 1959, SAAMA began to prepare the training of personnel for maintenance of the B-58 as it came under the San Antonio Area for maintenance and modification. Because of the complexity of the many subsystems comprising the aircraft, approximately twenty skills were required, seven of which were completely new and two others of which were beyond the scope of the then-existing AF Specialty Codes. Also, it was SAAMA's responsibility to indoctrinate personnel of the single user, SAC, in supply and maintenance procedures as applying both at the base level and in the depot.

Consequently, in November, 1958, SAAMA Headquarters submitted a proposal to the Test Director, B-58 Test Force (made up of SAC and ARDC representatives) at Carswell AFB. Proposed was the augmenting of formal training programmed for shop personnel through the medium

USAF via Bart Cusick

B-58A, 61-2066, is seen during the course of Category II stability and control performance tests near Edwards AFB, CA, on April 20, 1964. This aircraft was later assigned to the 43rd BW and was eventually disposed at Davis-Monthan AFB, AZ.

of on-the-job training at the Carswell test site. San Antonio pointed out, also that its personnel would be there not merely to observe maintenance, but would also assist the Test Force in that maintenance. With the Test Directors concurrence, successive groups of ten went to Carswell AFB, received thirty days of on-the-job training, and participated as planned in the aircraft maintenance.

By this time it had been agreed that SAAMA would be the management control point for maintenance and supply, budgeting and funding, for all materiel and services peculiar to the B-58 aircraft, its sub-systems, and related ground support equipment (GSE). In addition, SAAMA Headquarters was responsible for the planning, programming, and computation of requirements for peculiar items and items common to the AF, but used in direct support of this weapon system.

During the B-58 test program, the aircraft and its components were logistically supported by Convair. However, as the weapon system passed into production for inventory use, support responsibility passed on a progressive basis from Convair to the AF. As the time arrived for a decision on the method of support of a particular component or subsystem, the most effective support at the least cost, dependent on quantity of aircraft

involved, would be the deciding factor in choosing whether contractor or AF depot support would be utilized.

Depot-level maintenance and/or repair was not planned for overseas locations, except for crash-damaged aircraft. Maintenance facilities in the continental US were to be established for overhaul and repair of all subsystems and components prior to delivery of operational aircraft. The B-58 was to be maintained under the modernization/maintenance ("Mod/Maint") concept.

By 1962, SAAMA was involved in mixed projects for field work, conversion-continuations (updates or mods) and trainer reconfigurations. In lieu of bringing certain B-58 aircraft into Kelly AFB, trained Field Teams were sent out to various SAC bases to perform varied jobs. Beginning on September 11, 1961 (with completion scheduled for November 3), four TB-58A's at Carswell AFB were modified by the Kelly Field team method. During the 1962 fiscal year, which began on July 1, 1961, Kelly Field teams performed maintenance on-site on nine B-58's at Carswell and Bunker Hill AFB's, part of two fleets of twenty-nine and twenty-two aircraft, respectively, undergoing modifications while on-site at their home bases.

As mentioned in Chapt. 6, a number of pre-production B-58's were brought up to operational

standards. This work was actually done under the auspices of SAAMA and entailed significant airframe and systems updates. In the conversions, the nose section of each aircraft was reworked and reinstalled and the tail, landing gear, engines, and control surfaces were reworked. After going through the production conversion program, these B-58's were expected to be equal in structural integrity and systems with production B-58's coming off the production line, and to have the same tactical capability. The result brought YB/RB-58A's, procured under early contracts, to the configuration of those B-58A aircraft that had been procured under later contracts.

In service, mission employment plans for the B-58 called for its maintenance and operation under the alert concept. One-third would be on alert at all times, and the crew would be in close proximity. Fifteen minutes after receipt of deployment orders were all that were allowed for starting all four engines and becoming airborne. During each month's ten-day alert, therefore, maintenance was to be minimized for the aircraft involved with that particular alert.

During 1963, as the maintenance and support programs for the B-58 continued to develop, two major efforts were launched at SAAMA that involved major reworking of various production B-58's. These were Project *Pull-Out*, and Project *Hustle Up* (the latter described earlier in this chapter).

Pull-Out was developed in 1961 by SAAMA and presented to the AFLC where approval and a high priority support were afforded under the personal aegis of Gen. William McKee. Project *Pull-Out* served to correct existing deficiencies in B-58 support, to provide immediate, short-range improvements in supply and repair support, and to provide for a high quality, long-range logistic support on a routine basis.

While the B-58 was finally beginning to attain an operational status within the confines of SAC, further decisons were playing a role in its future in terms of bases of operation. The birth of the Tactical Fighter Experimental program (TFX), which would soon give birth to the General Dynamics F-111, indirectly affected the B-58's continuing service career at Carswell AFB. General Dynamics and SAC would eventually join forces to give viability to the decision made in 1960/61 to activate B-58 operations at Little Rock AFB, AR. Accordingly, the 43rd BW, on May 14, 1964, was told by SAC (via SAC MO-1) that it was to be moved to Little Rock AFB on September 1, 1964. This event did, in fact, take place, and on August 20, the 43rd was fully operational at its new location.

Project *Main Line* for the B-58 was established on October 9, 1963, under Headquarters AMC because of a redirection of a SAC photo reconnaissance requirement. Logistics Command Headquarters assumed overall management as long as certain deficiencies had not been corrected and until a logistically supportable system was provided to SAC. Subject to this leadership the SAAMA Headquarters accepted responsibility to fund and procure aircraft and pod spares and technical data, with the proviso of receiving the sole responsibility by August, 1964.

The original proposal was changed to obtain an immediate photo reconnaissance capability utilizing a KA-56A camera system and was known as "Phase I". With contractural support from Convair (by now, becoming known as General Dynamics), successful flight testing of the first modified aircraft took place on October 25, 1963. During December, modification was completed on forty-five aircraft and ten MB-1C pods. Moving into "Phase II", SAC personnel installed "Phase II" modification kits on ten LA-331 (a re-designation

USAF via Morton Higgs

B-58A, 61-2059, of the 305th BW. This aircraft, under project "Greased Lightning" flew non-stop from Tokyo, Japan, to London, England, at an average speed of 938 mph. Markings are standard for type. SAC sash and 305th BW badge are visible on nose under windscreen.

of the MB-1C) pods and by June 30, 1964, "Phase II" modifications were incorporated into twenty-four aircraft.

The recce system capability was integrated into the B-58 multiple weapon system making it possible to substitute a specially designed photo pod for the more conventional strike pod. The photo pod was equipped with the KA-56 low-altitude panoramic camera mounted in its nose behind a V-shaped optical glass port. Ahead of this port was a small fairing that improved the drag characteristics of the modification and also helped prevent foreign object damage. The entire system was optimized to provide horizon-to-horizon coverage (with overlap) from low altitudes at high aircraft velocities. The camera had automatic exposure control and image motion compensation; it operated in an autocycle mode at from one to six exposures per second; and it was capable of producing shutter speeds of from 1/500th to 1/2000th of a second in all variations of film velocity. The control panel for the camera was mounted in the navigator/bombardier's station and was interchangeable with the weapon monitor and release panel used with the strike pod.

Operation of the recce pod system was relatively simple. During inflight checks made prior to reaching the target, the navigator/bombardier made manual inputs of altitude and speed for the image motion compensation. A scanner and scanner-converter incorporated into the photo pod took over the periodic task of corrections once the target area was reached. The scanner was an electro-optical device which passively measured speed-over-height ratios as the reconnaissance vehicle traveled over the terrain to be photographed. The converter translated the electronic signal into a DC voltage which was fed into a servo-drive unit. This unit froze the image on the film by driving it at the correct speed to synchronize with the image motion.

The 43rd BW (then at Carswell AFB) was assigned the responsibility of providing a unit to employ the modified photo pod. Major William S. Boughton, a branch chief, was selected within Wing Operations to head this unit. His previous experience in B-47 low-level recce and in B-58 low-level training proved to be immensely valuable in planning high-speed photo training sorties and coordinating the exercises with other agencies.

The designated combat crews were checked out in January, 1964, and were declared operationally ready. Routes were selected and surveyed and flight plans and maps were prepared on a reproduction bases for instant use.

The objective of these flights was high-resolution photography of an order in which tiny objects could be identified from altitudes of 500' at speeds approaching Mach 1. Any deviation from high resolution standards resulted in proportionately lower scores on each mission. Crews were evaluated on their photography scores and on their adherence to an exact course.

The navigation technique of B-58 low-level recce flying combined limited-range search radar with dead reckoning and map reading. A combination of minds, equipment, and correlation continually accomplished in seconds by the three crew members was the hallmark. The DSO generally fed information to the pilot about map reading checkpoints and headings on each leg, while the navigator verified position and headings. Corrections based on counter settings and radar fixing were given to the pilot by the navigator. Indicated altitudes were checked by all crew members and the navigator measured absolute altitude with search radar or a radar altimeter.

SAC initiated the first no-notice evaluation of the 43rd's recce crews on March 6, 1964. This exercise was directed against a familiar target,

SAAMA B-58 activity peaked in the mid-1960's with the instigation of various update programs and the need for on-going maintenance. Activity at Kelly AFB, TX, is represented by maintenance work being undertaken on three B-58's, including 61-2068 and 61-2071.

Matagorda Island Airfield, and the results were excellent. On March 17, 1964, sorties were directed against a specific tank in a tank farm near Vinton, LA. A high-speed tactic approaching Mach 1 at 500' was employed on the mission. Again, performance was excellent, despite the more difficult conditions of higher speed and unfamiliar targets.

At approximately 2130 hours Central Time on March 27, 1964, the SAC Command Post temporarily lost its wire circuits to Alaska. An immediate radio check with SAC units near Fairbanks gave the SAC controller first word of a major Alaskan earthquake.

The next morning, SAC headquarters received a wired message from Headquarters USAF that said, in part:

"Request SAC accomplish on a priority basis aerial reconnaissance of Alaskan disaster areas at Seward, Kodiak, Valdez, Whittier, Cordova, Anchorage, and highway from Gulkana to Seward. Objective is to provide damage information to Headquarters USAF and Headquarters Alaskan Air Command..."

Within two hours of notification from SAC headquarters, two B-58's departed Carswell AFB on the requested photo recce mission. During the two hours, the crews and staff had planned their flight, loaded their camera pods, and prepared their aircraft. The targets—names heretofore only vaguely known to the crew members, had been examined and reviewed in the Intelligence Branch of Wing Operations. The B-58's were assigned to do low-level reconnaissance; two WU-2A's from Davis-Monthan AFB and two RB-47K's from Forbes AFB, were to photograph from high altitude.

On this mission, the B-58's flew a total of 10 hours 20 minutes; covered a round trip distance of 5,741 miles; photographed the shattered Alaskan towns and countryside from 500' under a heavy overcast; and delivered the film to Offutt AFB, NB. Just 14 hours 38 minutes from the time the mission was given to SAC, processed photographs were available in Washington, D.C. From these photographs, immediate assessments of the devastation were available to both military and civilian authorities. The next day, two more 43rd BW B-58's flew the entire mission over again, covering all seven targets.

The twelve B-58 crew members who flew these missions in adverse weather over hazardous terrain were awarded the Air Medal for meritorious achievement and were personally decorated by Gen. Thomas Power, then Commander in Chief of SAC.

Other recce missions of similar significance

B-58A, 61-2079, of the 305th BW, at Grissom AFB, IN, on May 12, 1968. This aircraft was nicknamed "The Thumper" and was eventually disposed at Davis-Monthan AFB, AZ, in 1977.

B-58A, 61-2080, became the 116th and last B-58A manufactured by Convair. It is seen during roll-out following completion in the final assembly bay at Convair's Ft. Worth, TX, facility in October, 1962. It was delivered to the AF during the same month and following some seven years of active service, was placed in temporary storage at the Davis-Monthan AFB, AZ. It was eventually donated to the Pima County Aerospace Museum.

were flown, including one in reaction to yet another Alaskan natural disaster, a major flooding of the Cheno River at Fairbanks. A single B-58, departing Little Rock AFB, AR, flew to Fairbanks, flew its mission, and then returned to Barksdale AFB, LA with the exposed film. This was then removed from the camera pod and loaded aboard a T-33 for transport to Washington, D.C. where it was processed and delivered.

Installation of cameras in the nose fairings of the MB-1 pod of the B-58's of the 43rd BW enabled SAC to employ the B-58 in a reconnaissance capacity. Although this capability was not frequently employed, it was exercised for special cases and to maintain currency. During the first six months of 1965, the B-58's reconnaissance capability was brought into play for *Project Steve Canyon*, a no-notice evaluation which required the 43rd BW to launch two B-58's in the photo configuration against Zaragoza AB, Spain, on May 24-28, 1965. Fragmentary Order, 60-65-06-1, *Steve Canyon*, directed this semi-annual evaluation of the wing over an approved route. Two aircraft deployed to Moron AB, Spain, made the photographic reconnaissance strike at Zaragoza on a low level (500') route, and post-strike recovered at Offutt AFB, NB. The results were excellent and there were no discrepancies noted throughout the operation. An evaluation of the photographs revealed there was a 100% coverage of the designated targets with a 4'' resolution.

Between July and December of 1965, only one further exercise, *Sack Race*, utilizing the B-58's recce capabilities, was conducted. Six 43rd BW B-58's were launched between December 14-17, in cells of three each, separated by 48 hours. The route selected was the Barksdale 2-4 Poker Deck (low level). The choice of this particular route rested on the fact that it offered few visual or radar returns. The objective of the exercise was to ascertain how well the crews could perform in obtaining low level photographic coverage while operating under such limiting conditions. The results of the six sorties were as follows:

Overall mission critique
  Generation—Excellent
  Launch—As briefed
  Control Times—As briefed
Target Summary—94.4% (17/18)
Average CE—Target #1 (411')
           Target #2 (653')
           Target #3 (632')
Target Resolution—3''
Overall Results—Excellent

This was the most extensive low level test of the B-58's recce capabilities through the end of 1965.

In a little-known attempt to make the B-58 into a more flexible weapon system, tests were conducted during April, 1967, under *Operation Bullseye* to explore the B-58's use in a tactical warfare scenario. Accordingly, several 305th BW aircraft were modified at Eglin AFB, FL, to accommodate conventional, non-nuclear weapons on the wing root bomb racks that had earlier been added (under SAAMA direction) to accomodate four Mk.43 thermonuclear weapons.

Systems utilizing both MERs (Multiple Ejector Racks) and TERs (Triple Ejector Racks) were tested. In coordination with Republic F-105D's and McDonnell F-4C/D's, sorties were flown using B-58's as lead ships and pathfinders and when necessary, as independent strike aircraft. It was assumed that the B-58's excellent navigation/bomb system could be utilized in formation bombing exercises of this kind to improve the CEP's of the accompanying fighter bombers. Peripheral tests also explored any advantage that might be gained by replacing F-4 WSO's with B-58 nav/bombardiers.

Various Eglin AFB, Nellis AFB, and Matagorda Island bombing ranges were used leading to the successful dropping of iron bombs of varying weights up to 3,000 lbs. Almost all the missions were flown at low altitudes and at speeds of 600 knots. Almost all the drops were visual with the AN/ASQ-42 bomb/nav system rarely being utilized. During one twenty-seven day period, some 75 sorties were flown. And during one flight, a bomb, or fragments of a bomb, ricocheted into a B-58 following delivery. Damage was relatively minor and the aircraft landed without incident.

The iron bomb tests proved feasible and verified that the aircraft could be used for the required mission profile. The disadvantages to the formation approach included difficulty in maintaining visual contact in bad weather, susceptibility to SAM activity when flying in the required tight formation, and an only marginal improvement in bombing accuracy. A fear that the aircraft's integral wing tanks would make it vulnerable to ground fire during the required low-altitude delivery modes, coupled with the noted marginal improvements in bombing accuracy, eventually killed the program from an operational standpoint.

On May 12, 1968, Bunker Hill AFB, IN was officially renamed in memory of astronaut Virgil Grissom who had been killed along with fellow astronauts Edward White and Roger Chaffee in a tragic fire on January 27, 1967, while ground

Another view of B-58A, 61-2080, during its roll-out from Convair's main production facility in October, 1962. This aircraft would be assigned to the 305th BW at Bunker Hill AFB (later, Grissom AFB), IN.

Paul Stevens

B-58A, 61-2080, during an airshow at Grissom AFB, IN, on May 24, 1969, during the latter stages of its operational service career with the 305th BW. It first flew on October 23, 1962, and was delivered to the AF some three days later. Markings, as seen in photo, are standard for type. Panel surface coloring variations are noteworthy.

checking the *Apollo I* space capsule.

SAC concerns over the B-58's viability as a weapons delivery vehicle, fueled by the aircraft's never-completely-overcome range limitations, advances in Soviet anti-aircraft capability, and its significantly higher than anticipated production, maintenance, and support costs, continued to plague its "raison d'etre" throughout the latter half of the 1960's. Range, in fact, had been sapped by another 10% following fleet modification to multiple weapons capability, and maintenance and support costs were continuously on the rise due to the small number of aircraft in the inventory, and their relatively high utilization rates (in fifteen years the B-58 fleet logged a total of 225,000 flight hours). Additionally, because of the B-58's unique (for a bomber) high speed capabilities and the dynamics of operating a heavy aircraft in that environment, there was every indication that the B-58 would, by the end of the 1960's, begin reaching the end of its airframe fatigue life. Costs of modifying the aircraft and zero timing its airframe were considered prohibitively high—particularly in consideration of the fact that so few aircraft were available.

Less noticeable, but just as important from a supportability standpoint, was the poor safety record image the B-58 had in SAC circles. Its accident record, though during the second half of the decade becoming fairly average, still haunted it. Flight test program and early operational career accidents had been numerous and spectacular, and because of this there was more than a slight residual dislike for the aircraft among SAC and AF hierarchy.

Perhaps the most overriding negative element faced by the B-58 during the second half of what was to be its only decade of service was its unfathered birthing. As R. Cargill Hall so succinctly put it in his essay "To Acquire Strategic Bombers, The Case of the B-58 *Hustler*" (Air University Review, September/October, 1980):

"The Air Force (had) embraced, virtually without reservation, the notion that science and technology could be driven to meet operational requirements far beyond the state of the art within a short period and at an affordable cost. More to the point, its leaders seemed to believe that this process could be defined, analyzed, and planned in advance to limit technical uncertainty and then managed to control costs. If before World War II Air Corps procurement officials at

Wright Field favored quantity over quality, ARDC officials in the 1950's appeared willing, without firm cost estimates, to recommend for development paper designs that offered only a promise of superior performance. They might have avoided at least some of the difficulties if they had been more attentive to the history of the Air Corps and Army Air Forces procurement organizations. Though smaller in scale, prewar operations did reveal how different procurement procedures and organization responses produced different results in the acquisition of aircraft."

Hall, in another essay entitled, "The B-58 Bomber, Requiem for a Welterweight," (Air University Review, November/December, 1981) would also address the problem of B-58 cost:

"Costs affected the B-58 adversely, from the cradle to the grave. Not only did the projected costs of modifications preclude improvements in low level performance, the original cost to procure this bomber was much greater than that of its predecessors. The program unit cost of the B-58 was $33.5 million in constant 1967 dollars, compared to $9 million for the B-52 and $3 million for the B-47. Once aircraft entered the inventory, SAC found the cost of maintaining and operating two B-58 wings equaled that of six wings of B-52's. High costs and a flawed operational potential made the B-58 expen-

dible. When the Strategic Air Command faced a choice of activating six wings of subsonic B-52's or two wings of supersonic B-58's in the late 1960's, there was really no choice at all."

Each of these elements, coupled with a deep rooted and by now long term dislike of the aircraft by SAC (which had felt for years that the AF, through Congressional pressure, had had the aircraft forced upon it) led, on October 27, 1969, to an announcement by then-Secretary of Defense Melvin Laird that stated cutbacks in military spending would force the closing or reduction of operations at 307 military bases in the US and overseas, including Little Rock AFB and Grissom AFB. These two facilities, though remaining intact as air bases, would lose their two wings of B-58's. The aircraft would, in fact, be removed from the inventory by Janaury 31, 1970 and be scrapped, "because of improvement in our strategic deterrents resulting from the forthcoming addition of new FB-111 bombers and improved *Minuteman* and *Polaris/Poseidon* missiles." Laird continued by noting that the elimination of the B-58's along with other savings, would cut defense spending by $3-billion.

At 9:30 a.m., on November 5, 1969, 59-2446, crewed by Lt. Col. Gean Kolwalski, Maj. Richard Nellis, and Lt. Col. Paul Fritz, became airborne

Ken Buchanan

The second B-58A, 55-661, was converted to a TB-58A following its career as a test aircraft. After conversion, it was assigned to the 305th BW at Bunker Hill AFB, IN. It was eventually scrapped at Davis-Monthan AFB, in 1977.

from the Little Rock AFB runway and immediately headed west for Davis-Monthan AFB where it was scheduled to become the first SAC B-58 to be placed in storage at Davis-Monthan AFB. Just over two months later, 55-668 (TB-58A) became the last B-58 to depart Little Rock. Crewed by Lt. Col. Thomas Clodfelter, Jr., Lt. Col. Gean Kolwalski, and Capt. John Watson, it too headed west, landing at Davis-Monthan several hours after departure.

On November 7, 1969, a 43rd BW B-58, the last to receive modification and maintenance at Convair's satellite refurbishment facility at James Connally AFB, TX, departed the base at 10 a.m. for a one-way mission to Davis-Monthan AFB, AZ. This aircraft was the last to go through modification at the Waco facility, which had been activated in 1967 in order to make room for work on other General Dynamics projects in Fort Worth, and the first scheduled to go into storage at the Military Aircraft Storage and Disposition Center. The Waco operation at one time employed as many as 1,250

personnel and was primarily involved in integrating modifications required under Operation *Hustle Up.*

With the loss of its B-58's, the 43rd BW was temporarily inactivated (on April 1 it was reactivated using the assets of the 3960th Strategic Wing at Andersen AFB, Guam under SAC's Illustrious Unit Designator Program; it remains a viable wing to this day) and its personnel disbersed to other units; the 305th, following the retirement of its last two B-58's (55-662 and 61-2-78 on January 16, 1970) was converted to an inflight-refueling wing and equipped with Boeing KC-135As.

By the end of January, 1971, all surviving B-58A's and TB-58A's were in storage at Davis-Monthan AFB. Of the few that had not been placed in storage, several of the record setters had been preserved for museum display, one aircraft remained in derelict condition at Little Rock, AFB, and a single example was left for long term nonfunctional use as a photo target on the photo test range at Edwards AFB. Almost overnight the en-

tire B-58 operation had rolled quietly to a stop.

After all salvageable equipment, such as the engines, some instrumentation, and other miscellany, were removed, the 80-odd B-58's were spraylatted and placed in storage at the Military Aircraft Storage and Disposition Center (MASDC), Davis-Monthan AFB, AZ. They were initially positioned in several rows of approximately twenty aircraft each with each two row component facing into itself. This system, which saved space (not a particularly rare commodity at Davis-Monthan AFB) was changed in 1977, primarily to accommodate the requirements of the forthcoming scrap metal dealers. This was accomplished by moving and rotating the aircraft about so that all faced in the same direction. In May, June, July, and August, 1977, following over a half-decade in the Arizona desert, all but two of the MASDC B-58's were sold at auction to the Southwestern Alloys company of Tucson, AZ for disposal (see Appendix A for disposal dates). Two years later, not a single aircraft remained.

A view of just part of the B-58 storage area at Davis-Monthan AFB, AZ, taken in 1973, several years before the aircraft were auctioned for final scrapping. Over eighty B-58's met their final fate at this facility, with Southwestern Alloys of Tucson, AZ, performing the reclamation service. By the time of photo, all items that could be returned to service, such as the engines and some instrumentation, had been removed and reclaimed.

B-58A, 55-662, was eventually converted to a TB-58A following completion of its flight test program. This aircraft was assigned to the 305th BW following an active chase aircraft career at Edwards AFB during the course of the ill-fated North American XB-70A program. It is seen in storage at Davis-Monthan AFB, AZ, shortly before its disposition.

Paul Jarvis

Chuck Mayer

B-58A, 55-668, was converted to a TB-58A and as such, it became the last B-58 to be assigned to the 43rd BW. It is seen with the upper component of a TCP. The nickname visible on the nose is "Wild Child II".

Three of the four TB-58A's assigned to the 43rd BW, including 55-670, 55-672, and 58-1007, are seen in this photo taken at Little Rock AFB, in the late 1960's. The first aircraft, 55-670, was the first TB-58A conversion.

Bill Mann

Another view of TB-58A, 55-670, at Little Rock AFB, AR. The aircraft is carrying the upper component of a TCP and is bearing standard markings for type. This aircraft was eventually disposed at Davis-Monthan AFB, AZ, in 1977, following a lengthy career as both a test aircraft and an operational trainer.

Doug Olson via Doug Slowiak

TB-58A, 55-670, on March 17, 1970, shortly after its arrival at Davis-Monthan AFB. Covers over the intakes and exhaust nozzles, and tape over the canopies, indicate that an attempt was made to protect the aircraft from the affects of climate. It would remain in storage at Davis-Monthan for some seven years before Southwestern Alloys of Tucson, AZ, would convert its carcass to aluminum ingots.

USAF

Following a maintenance and update session at Kelly AFB, TX's SAAMA facility, TB-58A, 55-671, is seen being prepared for flight. The aircraft is not carrying a pod. Assigned to the 43rd BW at Little Rock AFB, AR, this was the 4th TB-58A conversion.

USAF

With a Lockheed T-33A as chase, TB-58A, 55-672, assigned to the 43rd BW, is seen in cruising flight during a training mission. This aircraft has an interesting modificaiton to the leading edge just outboard of the outboard engine nacelle that is visible as a short cuff. It is also carrying only the upper component of a TCP.

George Bracken

TB-58A, 58-1007, one of four TB-58A's assigned to the 43rd BW at Little Rock AFB, AR, is seen following a training mission. This aircraft, the third TB-58A conversion completed by Convair, is carrying a conventional MB-1 pod. Note the open drag chute doors from the preceding flight.

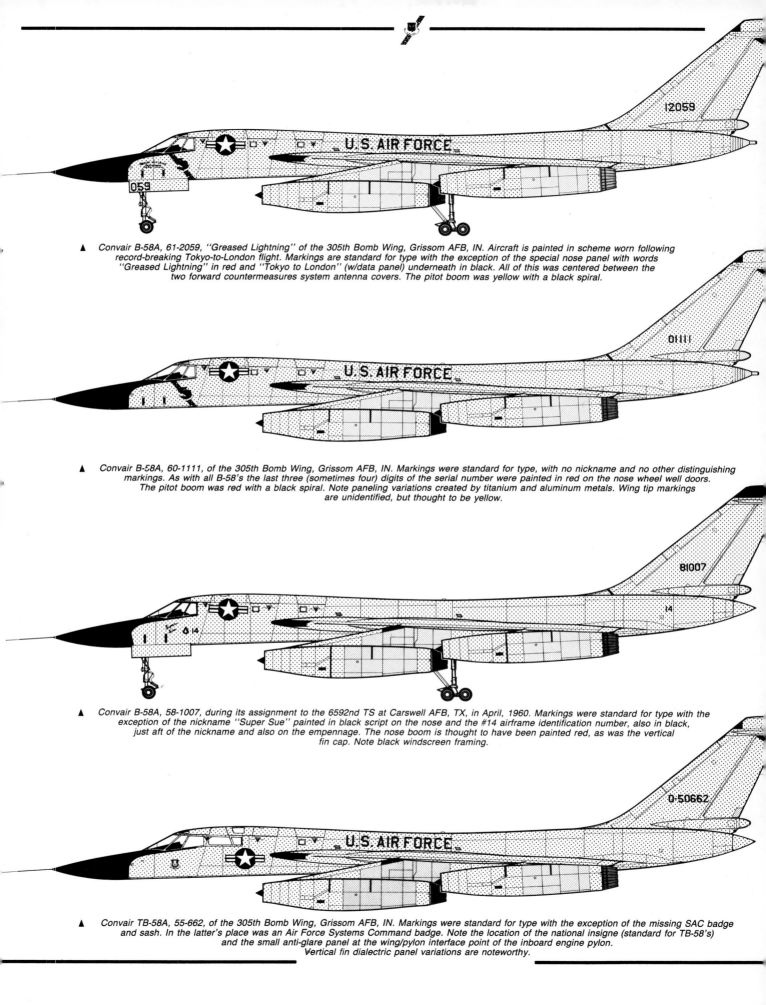

▲ Convair B-58A, 61-2059, "Greased Lightning" of the 305th Bomb Wing, Grissom AFB, IN. Aircraft is painted in scheme worn following record-breaking Tokyo-to-London flight. Markings are standard for type with the exception of the special nose panel with words "Greased Lightning" in red and "Tokyo to London" (w/data panel) underneath in black. All of this was centered between the two forward countermeasures system antenna covers. The pitot boom was yellow with a black spiral.

▲ Convair B-58A, 60-1111, of the 305th Bomb Wing, Grissom AFB, IN. Markings were standard for type, with no nickname and no other distinguishing markings. As with all B-58's the last three (sometimes four) digits of the serial number were painted in red on the nose wheel well doors. The pitot boom was red with a black spiral. Note paneling variations created by titanium and aluminum metals. Wing tip markings are unidentified, but thought to be yellow.

▲ Convair B-58A, 58-1007, during its assignment to the 6592nd TS at Carswell AFB, TX, in April, 1960. Markings were standard for type with the exception of the nickname "Super Sue" painted in black script on the nose and the #14 airframe identification number, also in black, just aft of the nickname and also on the empennage. The nose boom is thought to have been painted red, as was the vertical fin cap. Note black windscreen framing.

▲ Convair TB-58A, 55-662, of the 305th Bomb Wing, Grissom AFB, IN. Markings were standard for type with the exception of the missing SAC badge and sash. In the latter's place was an Air Force Systems Command badge. Note the location of the national insigne (standard for TB-58's) and the small anti-glare panel at the wing/pylon interface point of the inboard engine pylon. Vertical fin dialectric panel variations are noteworthy.

General Dynamics

YB-58A, 55-663, is seen shortly after takeoff from the main runway at Carswell AFB, TX. Landing gear retraction sequence has just begun. In order to photograph TCP pod release events, aircraft has camera pods mounted underneath the outboard engine nacelles. Note pod symbols painted just underneath forward windscreen. Red and white markings were typical of the first few B-58 test aircraft.

Bill Mann

B-58A, 59-2454, of the 43rd BW, is seen departing Little Rock AFB, AR in December, 1965. Nose-high attitude was typical of B-58 takeoff procedure. Markings seen were typical for the B-58. The black nose radome and nose gear door numbers were standard. Few other markings besides national insigne were applied due to maintenance difficulties related to high speed capabilities of the aircraft.

B-58A, 61-2074, of the 305th BW, is seen during a temporary stopover at MacDill AFB, FL. Markings are typical for the B-58A. Note coloring of fiberglass tail gun radar radome, barber pole pitot boom, and warning stripes on engine nacelles. Open drag chute compartment doors are also visible.

TB-58A, 55-662, seen just prior to a test flight from Kelly AFB, TX, immediately following a systems inspection and update program. Location of fuselage national insigne is noteworthy. TB-58A's were not equipped with the MD-7 tail gun system or TCP pod. This particular aircraft, following its use in a variety of test programs, was eventually assigned to the 305th BW.

SELECT MARKINGS

Scale: 1/150th
Drawn by Jay Miller

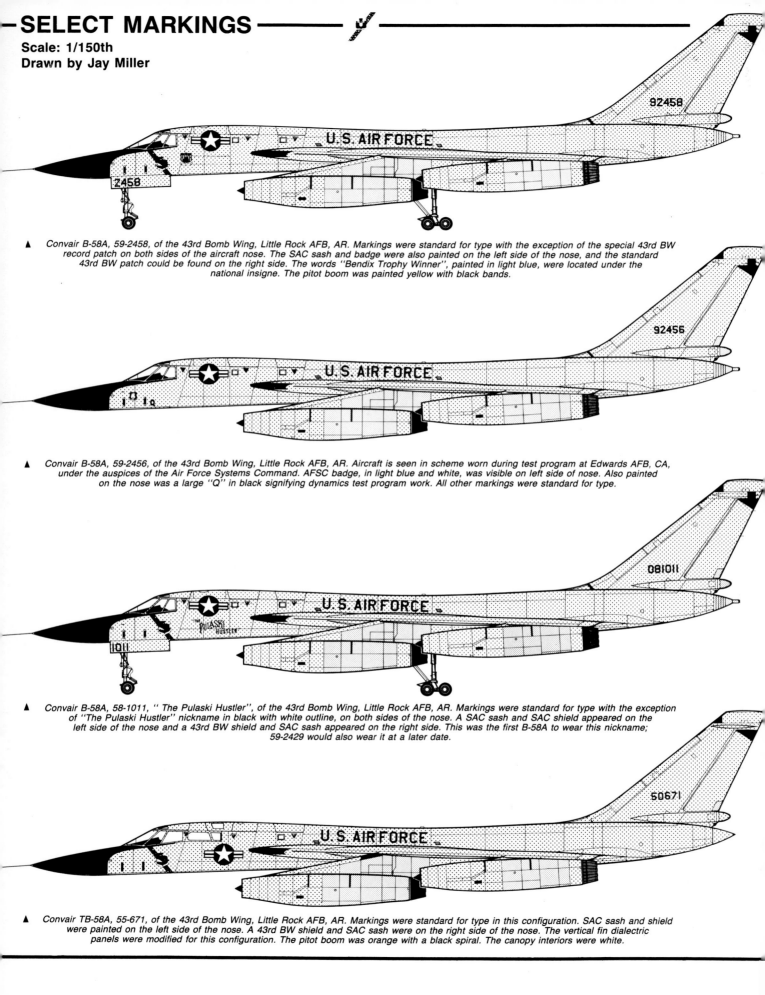

▲ *Convair B-58A, 59-2458, of the 43rd Bomb Wing, Little Rock AFB, AR. Markings were standard for type with the exception of the special 43rd BW record patch on both sides of the aircraft nose. The SAC sash and badge were also painted on the left side of the nose, and the standard 43rd BW patch could be found on the right side. The words "Bendix Trophy Winner", painted in light blue, were located under the national insigne. The pitot boom was painted yellow with black bands.*

▲ *Convair B-58A, 59-2456, of the 43rd Bomb Wing, Little Rock AFB, AR. Aircraft is seen in scheme worn during test program at Edwards AFB, CA, under the auspices of the Air Force Systems Command. AFSC badge, in light blue and white, was visible on left side of nose. Also painted on the nose was a large "Q" in black signifying dynamics test program work. All other markings were standard for type.*

▲ *Convair B-58A, 58-1011, " The Pulaski Hustler", of the 43rd Bomb Wing, Little Rock AFB, AR. Markings were standard for type with the exception of "The Pulaski Hustler" nickname in black with white outline, on both sides of the nose. A SAC sash and SAC shield appeared on the left side of the nose and a 43rd BW shield and SAC sash appeared on the right side. This was the first B-58A to wear this nickname; 59-2429 would also wear it at a later date.*

▲ *Convair TB-58A, 55-671, of the 43rd Bomb Wing, Little Rock AFB, AR. Markings were standard for type in this configuration. SAC sash and shield were painted on the left side of the nose. A 43rd BW shield and SAC sash were on the right side of the nose. The vertical fin dialectric panels were modified for this configuration. The pitot boom was orange with a black spiral. The canopy interiors were white.*

B-58A, 59-2458, winner of the prestigious Bendix Trophy, is seen at its permanent home, the USAF Museum, Wright-Patterson AFB, OH, shortly after its complete restoration in 1984. Polished aluminum finish involved many hours of hand labor. This aircraft is undoubtedly the best surviving "Hustler" specimen.

B-58A, 60-1112, of the 305th BW, is seen at Mather AFB, CA, on May 3, 1969, shortly before its delivery to Davis-Monthan AFB, AZ. De-energized elevons are seen in their maximum trailing edge-down position. Barely discernible are wing root pylons for free-falling nuclear weapons, wing root camber, and wing static discharge lines.

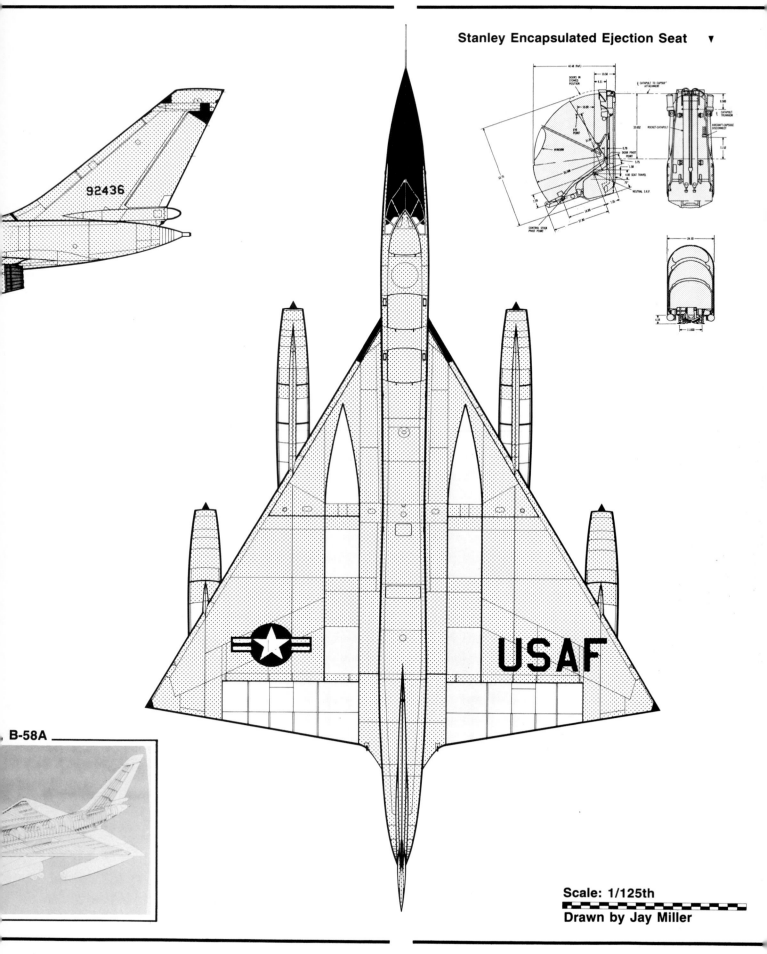

Stanley Encapsulated Ejection Seat ▼

92436

B-58A

USAF

Scale: 1/125th
Drawn by Jay Miller

CONVAIR B-58A, 59-2436

Convair B-58A, 59-2436, during its initial assignment to the 43rd Bomb Wing while the 43rd was still stationed at Carswell AFB, TX. Markings were standard for type with an over-all natural metal finish, the words U.S. Air Force in black, and the serial number in black. The standard SAC sash and shield were readily visible on the nose. The right side of the aircraft carried a 43rd BW shield and similar band. The dialectric panels on the vertical fin were dark brown, or black, depending on the panel. The nose radome and leading edge root fairings were black. The pitot boom appeared to be painted black. The intake spikes and the insides of the intake ducts were grayish white.

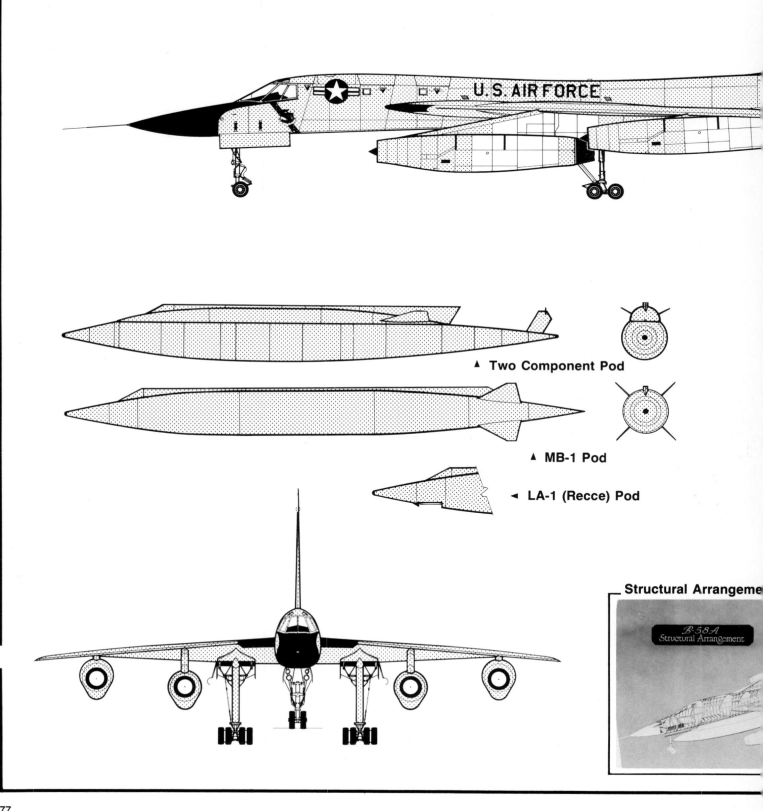

U.S. AIR FORCE

▲ Two Component Pod

▲ MB-1 Pod

◄ LA-1 (Recce) Pod

Structural Arrangeme

B-58A
Structural Arrangement

The end of the road for 61-2074, seen on p.66 during happier days. Over eighty surviving B-58's transferred to Davis-Monthan AFB, AZ, were given similar treatment during the disposition process.

Close-up detail of 59-2458, following recent USAF Museum restoration. Special markings are noteworthy. Note that TCP pod is painted in aluminum paint.

Pilot's cockpit of B-58A, 61-2080, at Pima County Aerospace Museum next to Davis-Monthan AFB, AZ. Provided for color reference only.

Pilot's cockpit left console of B-58A, 61-2080. Provided for color reference only.

Bombardier/Navigator's cockpit of B-58A, 61-2080. Provided for color reference only.

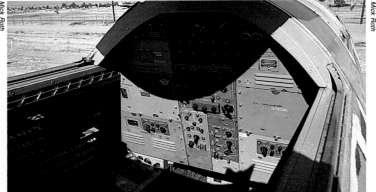

Defensive Systems Operator's cockpit of B-58A, 61-2080. Provided for color reference only.

Pilot's encapsulated ejection seat for B-58A. Provided for color reference only.

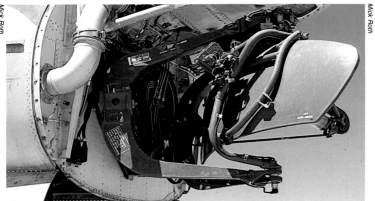

Detail of the Ku band Raytheon developed radar system as installed in the nose of a B-58A. Provided for color reference only.

Chapt. 8:
Testbeds, Experiments, and Proposals

This previously unpublished photo of B-58A, 55-665, following conversion to a testbed for the Hughes AN/ASG-18/GAR-9 air-to-air missile system reveals that the aircraft was also equipped with infra-red sensors (just to the rear of the nose radome) and special outboard nacelle-mounted camera pods. The special missile pod, of which two were built by Convair, was equipped with an avionics bay and dedicated missile support system.

As is the case with most production aircraft, the B-58 went through a long series of design studies, modifications, and configuration-changing flight test programs throughout the years it was considered a viable production element at Convair. The B-58, in particular, was highly susceptible to such changes, due in part to its amazing performance, and in part to its unique configuration. Its "system" design, requiring it to carry its payload in podded form underneath its fuselage, permitted great flexibility in pod and carrying-component design. This, in turn, permitted the B-58 to serve as a testbed for a large number of projects that otherwise would not have been undertaken due to the great cost of having to modify the entire aircraft.

Additionally, the aerodynamic qualities of the B-58 gave Convair and the AF reason to continuously explore potential advances in performance simply through a change in construction materials and the addition of more powerful engines—during development the design had been sufficiently refined to the point where reconfiguration of the aircraft would have provided only marginal performance improvements, at best.

Though for years it was rumored that B-58D and B-58E designators had been assigned to advanced versions of the B-58, the author has not been able to find proof that such designators were, in fact, officially allocated. Drawings of a variant powered by two Pratt & Whitney J58's have surfaced and are illustrated, here, but there is no *official* indication that these represent either the supposed B-58D or B-58E. The B-58B and B-58C designators were assigned, however, and eventually came to represent the B-58MI and BJ-58 configurations. Their early cancellations prior to the completion of full configuration definition terminated the use of the B-58B and B-58C designators.

Data available on the B-58C configuration included a maximum speed capability in level flight of Mach 2.4 at 68,000', a 5,200 n. mile maximum range, and a maximum single inflight refueling range of 7,500 n. miles.

What follows then is a complete chronological listing of all known modifications and design studies completed during the course of the B-58's production and operational life:

1951—Late in the year, Convair began developing preliminary proposals calling for the development of a long range interceptor and tactical variant of its proposed supersonic bomber.

1953—In the fall of the year, Convair presented a proposal to the Air Defense Command calling for the development of a long range interceptor version of its proposed supersonic bomber.

1954—During the summer, a special Tactical Air Command version of Convair's supersonic bomber project was presented.

1954—On October 25, an electronic countermeasures escort pod to counter radar-guided air-to-air and surface-to-air missiles was proposed by Convair.

1955—During the spring, a dedicated reconnaissance version of the B-58A was proposed to the AF by Convair.

1955—During the spring, the first B-58 "growth configuration" was wind tunnel tested. It had folding wing tips and supersonic wing camber.

1955—During the winter, a Tactical Air Command bomber variant was proposed and submitted to the AF. Also, a B-58 "manned interceptor" variant was wind tunnel tested and configured with a rocket-propelled pod and extended fuselage.

1956—In January, a special reconnaissance B-58 configuration was proposed calling for the development of a dedicated side-looking radar pod under the AN/APQ-69 designator. The project was officially begun in September, 1968, with scheduled completion to be at the end of June, 1960. The pod and its radar were built by Hughes Aircraft Company and delivered to Convair in February, 1959. Testing of the system kept it in isolation until October, at which time it was installed under 55-668 and fit tested on November 25. The first test flight with the pod in place took place on December 24 and additional flight trials continued through June 30, 1960. The AN/APQ-69 was a "real aperture" radar and thus required an extremely large antenna in order to accomplish its mission objectives. The antenna was, in fact, some 50' long—making it one of the largest antennas ever mounted aboard an aircraft. Some

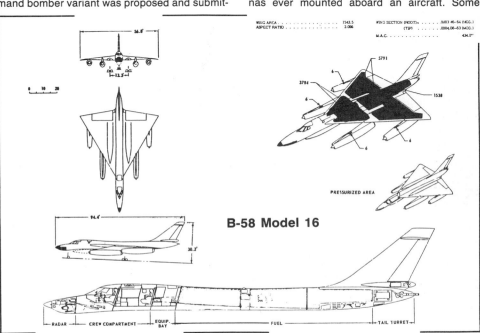

B-58 Model 16

WING AREA	1542.5	WING SECTION (ROOT)	.0003 46-64 (MOD.)
ASPECT RATIO	2.086	(TIP)	.0004.06-63 (MOD.)
		M.A.C.	434.0"

PRESSURIZED AREA

RADAR · CREW COMPARTMENT · EQUIP. BAY · FUEL · TAIL TURRET

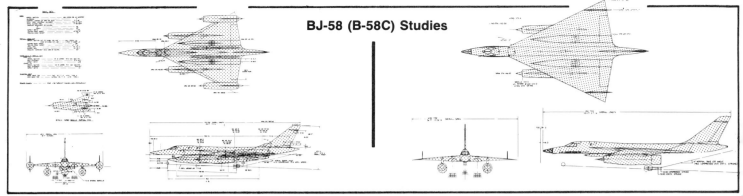

BJ-58 (B-58C) Studies

twenty-five flights were completed during the course of the program with results being considered nominally good and the range reported to be approximately 50 miles with about 10' resolution. Unlike its successor, the Goodyear AN/APX-73, the AN/APQ-69 limited the B-58's flight envelope to subsonic speeds. Because of its unusual rectangular cross section and rather blunt nose, problems occurred with nose gear retraction because of the pod bow wave. In order to retract the gear, it was necessary to do a .5 g pushover shortly after takeoff. Average mission flight time, due to fuel constraints caused by the loss of the fuel load carried by the conventional B-58 pod, was 3 hours 15 minutes.

1956—During the fall, an all-supersonic B-58 variant was proposed with General Electric X-207 engines.

1956—During the winter, a proposal was submitted by Convair calling for the B-58 to be used as a nuclear propulsion system testbed with General Electric nuclear engines.

1957—During January, NACA representatives from Edwards AFB met with Convair personnel in Fort Worth to discuss the possible use of the B-58 as a first stage launcher for the North American X-15 research aircraft. It was noted that the B-58, having been designed as a carrier for a large, externally mounted store, appeared geometrically adaptable as an X-15 launcher. X-15 dimensions, however, dictated that it be placed as far forward as possible in order to avoid interference with the B-58 landing gear. Other clearance problems included the X-15's vertical tail surfaces and

wingtips. It was also proposed that the B-58's DSO compartment be converted to accommodate the LOX top-off system. Interestingly, future astronaut Neil Armstrong did much of the study work for this project.

1957—In March, a Model Improved B-58 was proposed as a "split mission" aircraft. In this configuration, the fuselage was extended 8'; one crew station was eliminated and the two remaining crew members were placed side-by-side; the design gross weight was increased to 185,400 lbs.; maximum fuel load was increased to 116,800 lbs.; wing area was increased to 1,581 sq.'; and the wingtips were made foldable. Additionally, the aircraft was equipped with a more powerful ECM package and General Electric X-207's (advanced J79's) for propulsion. One interesting feature of the growth version was the proposed use of jettisonable outboard nacelles. This was designed to increase the B-58MI range performance. The B-58MI was eventually referred to as the B-58B (see 1958).

1957—On October 1, an air launched ballistic missile was proposed for the B-58.

1957—During the winter, Convair released to the airline industry the first information pertaining to its supersonic transport design studies.

1957—During the winter, Convair proposed a high Mach SAC intercontinental bombing system utilizing the B-58 as a recoverable booster under the project name of *Super Hustler*. This name was actually somewhat misleading as the B-58 was involved only from the standpoint of being a carrier aircraft and was not actually modified at all beyond

the minor systems changes necessary to permit transport of its unique payload.

The actual *Super Hustler* was, in fact, an extremely advanced parasitic aircraft that would have been carried to a launch point by the B-58, launched, flown to a target where it would release its weapon, and then continue on to a recovery base. The *Super Hustler's* configuration was unusual in that it called for a coupled two-component system. One component would be a powered, manned vehicle containing the crew of two (with side-by-side seating); and the other would be a powered unmanned vehicle optimized for payload transport. The latter could be either a nuclear warhead (weighing up to 3,400 lbs.), or additional fuel, depending on mission requirements. A reconnaissance version of the manned vehicle with X-band hi-resolution radar and various optical sensors installed, for instance, would dictate the use of the fuel tank version of the unmanned vehicle. Additionally, a trainer version was proposed that would have deleted propulsion from the fuel tank component.

The manned component was to be powered during cruise by a single Marquardt RJ-59 ramjet engine that had a length of 94.5'', a 38.6'' diameter nozzle, and a weight of 729 lbs. (some design studies called for as many as three ramjets of smaller, 33.5'', nozzle diameter). This unit was expected to generate 10,000 lbs. thrust at Mach 3, with a Mach 4 cruise thrust of about 5,000 lbs. using high energy fuel (HEF-3).

The manned component also was equipped with a single General Electric J85 turbojet engine

Three views illustrating the little-known Hughes AN/APQ-69 SLAR pod. This unit, with its real-aperture antenna, was possibly the largest SLAR pod ever built for transport by an aircraft. Because of its size and configuration, the B-58's performance was seriously affected. The pod also affected the aircraft's range performance because it carried no fuel.

Super Hustler

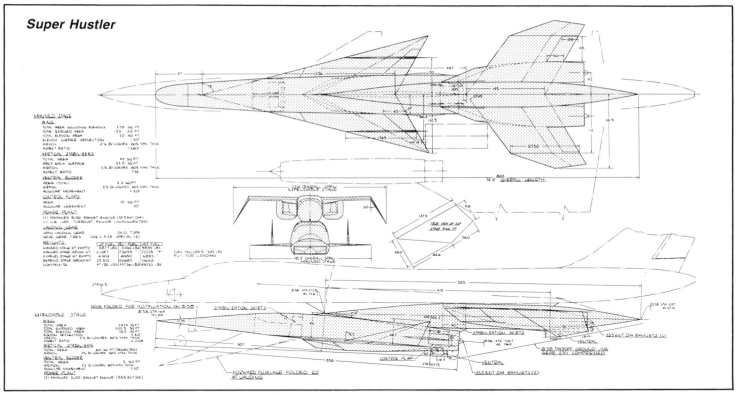

that was expected to assist during approach to landing (thus providing the crew with some margin for error at this critical point in the mission). The expendable component would have been powered by two Marquardt RJ-59's. All three ramjet engines would have been operated together during cruising flight.

Ground launching was also explored and a number of booster systems were proposed. The normal ground launch technique would have utilized the ZELL (Zero Length Launch) method with solid fuel RATO units attached to the vehicle for acceleration out to ramjet ignition speed. Launch from the B-58 would have been accomplished at a parasite mission weight of 45,903 lbs. (about 8,700 lbs. more than the weight of the B-58's standard TCP) of which 25,000 lbs. was fuel.

Launch range was expected to be approximately 2,270 n. miles. Once that point was reached, the B-58 would accelerate to Mach 2 and the Super Hustler's ramjets would be activated. Once powerplant performance stabilized, the parasite would be dropped and would immediately begin accelerating out to its cruise speed of Mach 4. This would take about four minutes, during which the aircraft would also be ascending to its initial cruise altitude of 75,000'. A gradual ascent to a maximum altitude of 91,000' would follow, this being dictated primarily by fuel burn-off and weight considerations. During this portion of the flight, the main fuselage area would reach an equilibrium temperature of about 700°F. while the nose temperature would rise to 950°F. Mission radius

was expected to be 2,920 n. miles if recovery on US soil was required. A total mission range of 8,580 n. miles was possible under normal circumstances, with a total sortie time of about 9 hours. Studies calling for the use of high-energy fuels was expected to increase the maximum radius at launch to 3,115 n. miles with a cruising speed of Mach 6. The Super Hustler was equipped with a nose tip that folded under and back during B-58 transport to accomodate the B-58's nose landing gear clearances; a forward fuselage section that "drooped" to permit crew vision during landing with the heat-protection canopy shields raised; a skid main gear and a conventional wheeled nose gear; a television system for viewing the outside world with the canopy shields lowered; and a stainless steel, pyro-ceram, and titanium structure to withstand the heat generated by cruising at speeds in excess of Mach 4.

Upon landing, the Super Hustler was expected to require at least 4,450' of runway with a touchdown speed of 162 knots. Emergency egress was via the forward fuselage section, which served as an encapsulated ejection system. The manned component had a length of 46'7'', a wingspan of 18'9'', a wing area of 278 sq.', a wing aspect ratio of 1.263, a wing thickness/chord ratio of 2%, an empty weight of 10,447 lbs., and a gross weight of 21,947 lbs. The powered expendable component had a length of 48'9'', a wingspan of 23'4'', a wing area of 242 sq', a wing aspect ratio of 2.25, a wing thickness/chord ratio of 2%, an empty weight of 10,303 lbs., and a gross weight of 25,303 lbs. The unpowered bomb/fuel tank component

had a length of 34'9'' and a diameter of 32''.

Convair estimated that the first flight of the Super Hustler could have taken place three years after contract signing, with the first production vehicle delivered two and a half years later. Development costs were expected to be $285 million with a buy of 100 manned and 400 expendable stages to run an additional $780 million.

Interestingly, Super Hustler did not die a normal death. In fact, design development of the aircraft continued at Convair into the early 1960's under several different codenames, these including Fish, and later, Kingfish. The latter projects proved to be the ultimate Super Hustler design studies, as they were optimized for surreptitious reconnaissance missions and seriously considered for production by the Central Intelligence Agency. Development of these latter configurations had, in fact, been proceded with under the auspices of the CIA in a project calling for the development of a high-speed, high-altitude reconnaissance vehicle. Convair and Lockheed were the main contenders in this competition (which also included an in-house Navy project in cooperation with Goodyear Aerospace) and during a period spanning from 1959 through late 1960, studies conducted by the two teams were carefully scrutinized by ARDC and CIA representatives.

Kingfish, which represented Convair's final submission, utilized an enlarged version of the basic Super Hustler fuselage configuration, and incorporated a totally new wing planform that was basically an ogival delta. The aircraft would takeoff and land conventionally utilizing the power pro-

Evolution of Super Hustler

1. SPLIT MISSION B-58 MI (M=2.2) EXTENDED RANGE WITH SIDE-BY-SIDE SEATING

2. ALL SUPERSONIC (M=2.0) DRY TURBOJET ENGINES

3. ALL SUPERSONIC (M=3.0) AFTERBURNER TURBOJET WITH H.E.F. IN A.B. ONLY

4. M=4.0 SPLIT MISSION WITH DUAL CYCLE ENGINE

5. M=4.0 SPLIT MISSION WITH COMBINATION OF SEPARATE RAMJET AND TURBOJET ENGINES

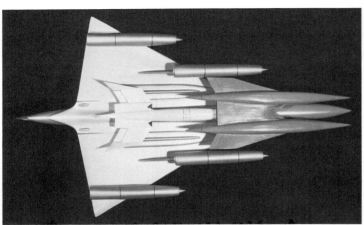

A full-scale "Super Hustler" cockpit mock-up was built by Convair to study the difficulties that might be realized through the use of periscopes for landing and inflight visual reference.

Many "Super Hustler" configuration studies were conducted in an attempt to create the most flexible airframe and propulsion system configuration. A twin-fuselage, single booster unit is shown.

vided by two retractable General Electric J85's—which also served to accelerate the aircraft out to ramjet ignition speeds. Inflight cruise propulsion was to be provided by two Marquardt RJ-59's. This aircraft was one of the first to have its radar signature consciously improved through the use of advanced design technique and the utilization of non-reflecting materials. *Kingfish* was expected to cruise at Mach 6 at an altitude of 125,000'. In late 1960, Lockheed's more conservative double delta configuration, eventually to become known as the A-12, was chosen over the Convair proposal, and the *Kingfish* project design study was placed in storage.

1958—During the spring, the Model Improved B-58 as proposed by Convair was revised and presented as the B-58B. In this configuration, the aircraft had nose mounted canards and more powerful J79-GE-19 engines.

1958—During the spring, Convair and Lockheed proposed to the AF a joint venture project calling for the development of a special air-launched ballistic missile (ALBM). This was the end result of an exploratory program initiated during the fall of 1957 by Convair which attempted to verify the usefulness of the B-58 as an ALBM transport. The conclusion was that the B-58 could accommodate such a stand-off weapon and that an ALBM could become a viable and highly versatile extension of the B-58's own abilities.

Lockheed Missiles and Space Systems Division was contacted following the completion of these studies and agreed to serve as a primary subcontractor with complete responsibility for missile design and development. In early June, 1958, a letter contract was signed by the two companies calling for the design, development, and flight test of four missiles. Referred to as Project 199C, it was given the code name of *High Virgo*. During the following several months, Convair fabricated a dedicated missile transport and launch pylon and installed it under 55-660 (the prototype B-58).

Lockheed, in the meantime, initiated construction of the missiles, utilizing, wherever possible, "off-the-shelf" components from the XQ-5, the X-17, the *Polaris*, and the *Sergeant* missile pro-

grams. Each of the first three ALBM's was 30' in length with a maximum diameter of 31''. The fourth missile, because of a reconfigured nose to accommodate a series of cameras, was slightly longer than its stablemates. An inertial guidance system was installed behind a control and telemetry unit which was, in turn, installed behind the space that would normally be occupied by a warhead (ballast only during the tests). The aerodynamic nose cone was made of reinforced plastic and had mounted behind it the warhead reentry vehicle which was of the high heat sink type. The powerplant was a Thiokol XM 20 solid fuel rocket engine, similar to that used on the Lockheed X-17, and rated at 50,000 lbs. thrust for 29 seconds. Aerodynamic directional forces were inputted by four hydraulically actuated fins mounted around the exhaust nozzle skirt. Total missile weight was just over 12,000 lbs. During the first two flights, guidance came from a programmed autopilot, and during the second two flights, from the Autonetics inertial navigation unit.

On August 6, 1958, the first missile was delivered to Eglin AFB, FL, and prepared for the initial test flight. On August 11, 55-660 also arrived at Eglin AFB with crew J. L. Baldridge, J. E. Cook, and C. T. Jones, and during the following ten days was ground tested and mated with the ALBM. On August 21, a shakedown flight serving to verify the compatibility of the missile and the aircraft was successfully completed.

The missile was now painted a bright yellow (the nose cone was black) and remated to the B-58. On September 5, 1958, the first launch was completed while 55-660 was flying at 40,500' and Mach 1 over the Cape Canaveral test range. After free-falling for six seconds, the missile's Thiokol engine ignited and the missile accelerated away. Several seconds into the powered portion of the flight, however, control system anomalies caused a series of oscillations which quickly terminated the test. Thirty-three seconds later, the missile impacted into the Atlantic Ocean.

The second missile was delivered to Convair's Fort Worth facility not long after the first missile's flight. There it was tested and preflighted, and then

delivered to Eglin AFB where it was painted bright red and mated to 55-660. On December 19, the second ALBM launch was conducted, this taking place at an altitude of 35,000' at Mach 1.6. The flight was almost completely successful and the missile reached an altitude of 250,000' and a speed of Mach 6. It impacted approximately 185 miles and 280 seconds from the launch point.

The third launch, which took place on June 4, 1959, became the first to utilize the inertial guidance system. An altitude of 32 miles was reached by this missile and total flight time was 240 seconds.

The fourth flight of the program was purposefully different from the others. Under separate contract, Lockheed modified ALBM number 4 to be significantly lighter than its predecessors and to incorporate a longer nose with a total of 13 cameras mounted therein. Nine of these would be utilized to photograph a satellite, and four would be used to photograph the missile and its functions. The objective of the last launch was to intercept and photograph the *Explorer IV* satellite and thus to verify that it was possible to intercept, and conceivably destroy, a satellite in orbit. Shortly before the scheduled launch, *Explorer IV's* orbital parameters were found to be inaccurate and a decision was made to pursue the newly launched and better known *Explorer V*.

On September 22, 1959, a final ALBM (nicknamed *King Lofus IV*) launch was conducted, again out of Eglin AFB, this time in an attempt to intercept and photograph the newly launched satellite. The launch, taking place at an altitude of 37,500' and a speed of Mach 2, went smoothly, but some 30 seconds later, all communication with the missile was lost. A search for the camera package (which was to have been returned by a Cook Research recovery unit) failed to find it, and no other remains were located. Though modestly successful, and definitely precedent setting, the Convair/Lockheed ALBM program generated no long term sustaining interest in the DoD and accordingly, it quietly faded into history.

1959—A request from the Aerial Reconnaissance Laboratories of the Wright Air Develop-

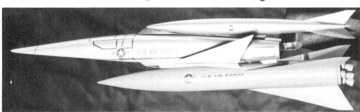

This multiple piggyback "Super Hustler" configuration was designed for a ZELL (Zero Length Launch) launch method, with the lower component dropping away after its fuel was spent.

A Convair-built model of the B-58 carrying the "Super Hustler". The folding nose and tight clearances dictated by "Hustler/Super Hustler" combinination are quite noticeable.

ment Center during June, 1958, initiated a series of proposals and studies for an "All Weather Reconnaissance and Charting Collection Subsystem on a B-58 Aircraft", under the code name of *Monticello II*. Lack of an available aircraft delayed negotiations until September 1, 1959, when renewed interest in the program resulted in a request by Convair's San Diego-based Electronics Division for Goodyear Aircraft Corporation to submit a proposal for accomplishing the program.

A letter contract, AF33(600)-40367, was accepted by Convair on November 2, 1959, and revised preliminary proposals were submitted under the code name of *Quick Check*. *Quick Check* was approved shortly afterwards and construction of the Goodyear AN/APS-73 (XH-3) X-band synthetic aperture radar (SAR) system was initiated following a design change from millimeter, to synthetic aperture. SAR, also known as synthetic array radar, was a high-resolution ground mapping technique in which advantage was taken of the forward motion of a coherent pulsed radar to synthesize the equivalent of a very long side-looking array antenna from the radar returns received over a period of up to several seconds or more. Another way of looking at SAR was that it increased the angular resolution of the radar antenna by differentiating between the radar returns received from various angles within the real antenna beam on the basis of their different doppler frequencies.

The AN/APS-73 featured simultaneous terrain mapping on each side of the aircraft at ranges up to 80 n. miles with a resolution of 50'; X-band operation assuring a virtually all-weather ability; focused doppler beam-sharpening for azimuth resolution that was greatly improved over that of conventional radars; and matched filter pulse compression (CHIRP) to reduce peak power requirements. Two back-to-back 10' long by 20" high side-looking antennas which were stabilized so as to illuminate ground targets lying normal to the ground track of the aircraft were mounted forward of the data processing unit. Ground-based film processing was provided by the AN/GSQ-28 (XH-1) coherent optical correlator which made the final radar map.

Preceding the AN/APS-73 (XH-3) into the air were the AN/APS-73 (XH-1) with two 5' antennas mounted and tested in a Boeing B-50, and the larger AN/APS-73 (XH-2) with two 9' antennas mounted and tested in a Boeing C-97.

The *Quick Check* project involved modification of the aircraft airframe as well as construction and installation of the side-looking airborne radar (SLAR) system in a highly modified MB-1-type pod. Unlike its predecessor, the Hughes AN/APQ-69 with its huge real-aperture radar antenna, the Goodyear AN/APS-73 (XH-3) SAR required significantly less pod space. This permitted the pod to be utilized conventionally for fuel transportation while accommodating the Goodyear radar.

A single B-58A, 55-668, starting in late June, 1960, was modified for the program by Convair, the major changes including a new and slightly bulged nose radome to accommodate a special Raytheon forward looking radar, a revised second station instrumentation and system control package (one of the first significant solid state systems of its kind ever), and a second station hatch mod to accommodate the revised systems associated with the special stellar tracking equipment.

As an integral part of the Goodyear-built radar, there was a Bausch and Lomb AN/GSQ-28 optical signal processor using 5" film which had been built for the University of Michigan but which had been transferred to Goodyear under government contract. This unit permitted an intensity-

Photos of the B-58/ALBM program have never previously been released for publication. The number 1 missile is shown attached to 55-660 as the latter rotates to takeoff attitude at Eglin AFB, FL.

The second Lockheed-built ALBM being mounted under 55-6670 at Eglin AFB, FL. This missile was painted red, over-all, with a black nose fairing. This missile achieved a speed of Mach 6 before impacting some 185 miles from its launch point.

The fourth Lockheed ALBM was nicknamed "King Lofus IV" and was used during an attempted intercept of the "Explorer V" satellite. This was probably the first air-launched satellite intercept ever conducted. Though its success was minimal, it proved that satellite destruction was a feasible undertaking.

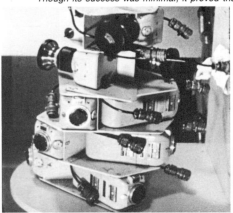
The camera package developed for "King Lofus IV". This was to have been used to photograph the "Explorer V" satellite.

Close-up of the special camera-equipped nose of the 4th ALBM, "King Lofus IV". Camera ports are readily visible.

B-58A, 55-668, with its highly modified nose, second crew station, and bulbous Goodyear AN/APS-73 SLAR pod is seen at the beginning of a test flight from Convair's Ft. Worth, TX, facility. The special nose radome housed a very powerful search radar for coverage of areas not within the SLAR's field of view.

The AN/APS-73 was a large unit with approximately the same cross-sectional area of a standard MB-1 free-fall bomb pod. The actual radar antenna was located behind the black fiberglass nose cone. Modifications to 55-668 included a special fairing for the second crew station canopy, and a bigger nose radome.

The AN/APS-73 was configured to conform to the dimensional limitations created by the standard MB-1 bomb pod. Aerodynamic limitations were minimal and the pod could be flown at supersonic speeds—though this affected the quality of the imagery generated by the synthetic aperture radar system.

The actual AN/APS-73 was mounted in the nose section of the pod with the two X-band antennas aligned to face tangentially to the flight path with one antenna on each side. Only one AN/APS-73 SLAR pod was built for the B-58 program, though several others were completed and flown aboard other aircraft.

modulated scanner to photographically record the coherent video output of the radar receiver in a two-dimensional raster format on film. Recorded concurrently were aircraft speed, location, altitude, and direction.

The *Quick Check* project reached the hardware stage in late 1960, and in May, 1961, it was delivered to Fort Worth. By early July, it was being flight tested out of Convair's Fort Worth facility. The SAR produced usable data and was found to have a range of nearly 80 miles (though there was a "dead space" for about 5 miles on each side of the aircraft).

On at least one occasion *Quick Check* was used "operationally", participating in an overflight of Cuba during the height of the Cuban missile crises. The system was functional throughout the B-58's performance envelope, though resolution was found to be highest at subsonic speeds. This program was cancelled following successful completion of the system and flight test program in August, 1962.

1958—During the fall of 1958 Convair proposed during an industry-wide competition, that the B-58 be used as a strike-reconnaissance aircraft.

1958—During the fall, Convair proposed an advanced B-58 configuration under the BJ-58 designator. This aircraft was to be powered by four non-afterburning Pratt & Whitney J58 engines and offer a Mach 2.5 cruise performance. Modifications would also include moving the outboard engines to the wingtips, the addition of two "winglets" attached to each outboard engine nacelle, improved internal fuel tankage, and an improved ECM complement. This configuration would eventually become known as the B-58C.

1959—Birth of a Central Intelligence Agency requirement for a high-speed, high-altitude reconnaissance aircraft which was to reach the hardware stage in 1962 in the form of the Lockheed A-12, indirectly led to the birth of a project wherein a single B-58, 55-665, was modified to flight test a special air-to-air radar and air-to-air missile system developed for an A-12 derivative known as the YF-12A.

The YF-12A, the first interceptor in the world capable of cruising at speeds in excess of Mach 3, had been developed in-house at Lockheed's enigmatic "Skunk Works" facility at Burbank, CA under the watchful eye and with the financial backing of the ARDC. Tasked with developing a radar and weapon system that was functional throughout the YF-12A's rather large performance envelope, Hughes Aircraft Company borrowed its still-under-development AN/ASG-18 fire control system and associated GAR-9 (AIM-47A) Mach 6 air-to-air missile from the rapidly expiring North American F-108 *Rapier* program (also a Mach 3-capable interceptor based, in part, on the technology generated by the on-going North American B-70 program).

The AN/ASG-18 system actually had been born in July, 1956 (GAR-9 missile development started a year later), when the ADC formulated specifications and characteristics that gave birth to the F-108. Hughes had subcontracted to develop the radar system for this aircraft, and when the program was killed, it joined forces with Lockheed to promote the development of an interceptor version of the A-12.

The demise of the F-108 was, in retrospect, directly attributable to the development of the amazing Lockheed "Blackbird" family as it was unquestionably an inferior design from a performance standpoint and a redundant developmental burden from one of economy. By late 1959, because of the F-108's cancellation, there was no aircraft then readily available to accommodate its capabilities. Earlier, even as the F-108 program began to crumble, Hughes and the AF had determined that development of the AN/ASG-18 should continue. It was then proposed that the system be mounted on an interim testbed aircraft for full-scale development.

On October 17, 1958, Convair received a contract from Hughes and the AF to manufacture two special purpose pods and modify one B-58 for AN/ASG-18 testbed work. The pods were completed on July 15, 1959 and shipped by Douglas C-124 to Hughes' Culver City, CA facility, and just over two weeks later, on August 2, B-58 55-665 was completed by the Convair special projects section and consequently delivered to Hughes, also. The AN/ASG-18 mounted what was, at the time, one of the largest antennas ever seen on an air-to-air combat radar system. With a diameter of 40'', it required hydraulic actuation for articulation.

The special Convair pods carried no fuel, but had a large internal bay for carriage of a single cartridge-ejected GAR-9 missile. Each pod also accommodated a freon cooling system, telemetry equipment, and tracking flares.

The rather extensive nose modification caused some serious changes in 55-660's profile, and a totally new, and rather radical looking nose radome (and associated fairing) was added that increased aircraft length by nearly seven feet. Additionally, two infra-red sensor domes (operating in the 2.5 micron range, initially) were mounted on each forward fuselage side, and internal systems changes were made in the second crew station and elsewhere to accommodate the dedicated AN/ASG-18 instrumentation and control equipment and associated panels.

Hughes Aircraft Company

The Hughes AIM-47A, also known as the GAR-9, was first launched in flight while mounted in a special pod under B-58A, 55-665. This Mach 6+ missile, designed for use with the Lockheed YF-12A, eventually served as a systems and aerodynamic testbed for the still more advanced Hughes AIM-54 ''Phoenix''.

G.D. via E. G. Morales

Shortly after its conversion to the AN/ASG-18 radar system and AIM-47A/GAR-9 system testbed, 55-665 was flown from Carswell AFB, TX on its initial test hop. The special pod designed to house and launch the AIM-47A can be seen, along with the B-58's somewhat awkward looking nose modification.

Following its arrival at Hughes, B-58A, 55-665, was further modified to incorporate an infra-red sensor system and other testbed related equipment. A large number of test flights, exploring the potential of the extremely powerful AN/ASG-18 radar system, were undertaken long before the aircraft was used as a launch platform for the AIM-47A.

The AN/ASG-18 radar system had one of the largest articulated antennas ever mounted on an aircraft at the time of its debut in the early 1960's aboard B-58A, 55-665. This unit would later be installed in Lockheed's precedent-setting YF-12A Mach 3+ capable interceptor.

Aeroflax, Inc. collection

One of the lesser known B-58 testbeds was 55-662 which was modified by Convair and General Electric to accommodate a General Electric J93-GE-3 turbojet engine rated at some 31,500 lbs. th. at sea level. This engine generated almost twice as much thrust as a stock J79-GE-5.

General Electric

Another view of 55-662 with its unusual payload. The J93 was developed to meet the propulsion requirements of the North American XB-70A and F-108A—both of which proved to be abortive undertakings. Flight tests were undertaken at Edwards AFB, CA.

Jay Miller/Aeroflax, Inc.

Several studies were generated by Convair calling for the development of supersonic transport derivatives. One of these was configured as a long-range reconnaissance system platform. Capable of cruising at Mach 2.5, it would have been powered by four non-afterburning Pratt & Whitney J58's.

G.D.

This military model of the Convair Model 58-9, sometimes referred to as the Model 62, could accommodate up to 52 passengers while cruising at speeds of Mach 2.5. It was powered by four non-afterburning Pratt & Whitney J58's and was equipped with nacelle-mounted winglets for improved directional stability.

Initial ground tests with the complete system in place included dummy GAR-9 launches into a styrofoam lined pit, and additional dummy launches while the aircraft was airborne. Hughes completed the first AN/ASG-18 system for the YF-12A in 1961, and in 1962, it was mounted on 60-6934. In August, 1961, the first GAR-9 missile was launched from the ground. By January, 1962, three unguided missile firings had been accomplished to verify the GAR-9 launching envelope. On January 15, a GAR-9 launched from the ground came within 55' of a QF-80 target drone flying at 13,500'. Four months later, on May 25, 1962, the first GAR-9 air-to-air launch was conducted from 55-665 (which had, in fact, been flight testing the AN/ASG-18 system since early 1960) while the aircraft was flying at 36,000' over the Edwards AFB test range. This resulted in a 6' near miss of a QF-80 target drone which was some 15 miles from the B-58. Striking even closer was the next air-to-air guided launch from a B-58 on August 17, 1962, during which the QF-80 target drone was grazed.

While nothing short of complete success seemed to attend the 1962 GAR-9 test firings, a sharp turn of direction occurred in early 1963. On February 21, 1963, a GAR-9 was launched at a supersonic Vought *Regulus II*, again from 55-665, but this time the missile disintegrated in flight. An investigation immediately followed in an attempt to discover the break-up cause, and concurrently, methods to increase the availability of the B-58 testbed, which had been denied the test team an inordinate number of times because of repeated groundings and numerous maintenance difficulties, were conducted. By July, 1963, certain modifications had been applied to both the GAR-9 and the B-58 and additional flight tests followed. By late 1963, the YF-12A flight test program had progressed to the point where it was possible for GAR-9 launches to be accommodated by the awesome Lockheed interceptor, and with this development, a wind-down of 55-665's contribution to the AN/ASG-18/GAR-9 program was begun. The last launches from the B-58 took place in February, 1964, and following termination of the program, 55-665 was demodded (except for the long nose radome) and eventually placed on the photo test range at Edwards AFB. It resides there to this very day.

1959—On July 1, Convair began an update and modification program utilizing B-58A 55-662 which configured it to accommodate the fuel and instrumentation requirements of a specially podded General Electric J93 turbojet engine. This powerplant, destined for use aboard the North American XB-70A *Valkyrie* and the eventually stillborn North American F-108 *Rapier*, and still somewhat of an unknown quantity in early 1959 and it was determined that a flight test program using a specially instrumented engine would benefit the North American program, greatly. The J93 was basically a single-shaft, axial-flow turbojet equipped with a variable-stator compressor, and a fully-variable convergent/divergent exhaust nozzle. It weighed approximately 6,000 lbs., had a length of 237'', and a maximum diameter of 52.7''. It was the first production-configured turbojet engine to have air-cooled titanium turbine blades and an automated thrust control system. The maximum sea level thrust rating of the engine was 31,500 lbs.

By August 24, 1959, the B-58 airframe modification effort was completed and following an official turnover to the AF, the aircraft was delivered to General Electric's Edwards AFB operation as an NB-58A. A J93-GE-3 and its special pod were then installed and preparations undertaken to clear the combination of powerplant pod and aircraft for flight test. A number of flights were eventually consummated, these involving tests to explore compressor stall anomalies, air start configurations, afterburner operation, fuel consumption, compressor/burner/afterburner temperatures, and ground handling difficulties.

On numerous occasions 55-662 and its unique five engine configuration were flown at Mach 2, though with the J93's relatively high thrust and the B-58's aerodynamically clean airframe, it was not necessary to run the four J79's at full throttle. A severe down-scaling of the B-70 and F-108 efforts during the course of this effort eventually terminated funding, and before 55-662 and its unusual test package could complete their test schedule, the program was terminated and the engine pod was removed.

1959—In the autumn, formal B-58C studies were officially begun at Convair. This version would have had extended wing tips, non-afterburning Pratt & Whitney J58's, a missile launch capability, a high-Mach cruise with Mach 3 dash, and the ability to be used as a long range interceptor in a Tactical Air Command environment. This project was cancelled in the spring of 1960.

1959—During the winter, Convair proposed that NATO acquire the B-58 to meet NATO needs.

1959—The AF initiated a study calling for the B-58 to loiter in the "standing wave" that was generated by the Sierra Madre's in California. This atmospheric phenomenon, which created a near vertical wind with steady state velocities approaching 200 mph, gave rise to proposals calling for the B-58 to sit, in a virtual hover, with engines at idle thrust, for twenty-four hours at a time while standing on alert.

1960—During the spring, the DoD and various US intelligence agencies began receiving information indicating that the Soviet Union was initiating preliminary work that had the obvious intent of developing a viable supersonic transport. Accordingly, NASA was tasked with studying supersonic transport options, including the possibility of modifying an extant aircraft, such as the Convair B-58, into a supersonic transport configuration. The B-58 was also to be utilized to develop supersonic transport parameters and to explore the difficulties that might be associated with the operation of a large aircraft in a sustained supersonic environment.

Convair's involvement, though at first tempered by the company's inability to successfully penetrate the rapidly growing subsonic jet transport market, soon became full-fledged and by late 1960, the company was proposing a three-step program aimed at developing the easiest, fastest, and cheapest way to get operational experience with an aircraft simulating a supersonic transport. These steps consisted of:

(1) Utilizing an existing B-58A to fly simulated or actual airline routes at supersonic speeds working in the range from Mach 1.5 to 2.0. This would provide insight into the difficulties controllers might have with a supersonic transport, or the logistical problems that might be encountered at airports;

(2) The development of a "people pod" with room for five passengers and test instrumentation. This would be carried by the B-58A and would be used to explore the subjective reactions of passengers in the unusual environment of supersonic cruise;

(3) The design and construction of a dedicated B-58 supersonic transport.

One of the several studies of the latter eventually proposed by Convair was designated Model 58-9 and was loosely based on the B-58C wing and powerplant configuration coupled to an almost totally new fuselage with conventional horizontal and vertical tail surfaces. Accommodations were to be available for up to 52 passengers. The cabin interior was designed to have two rows of single

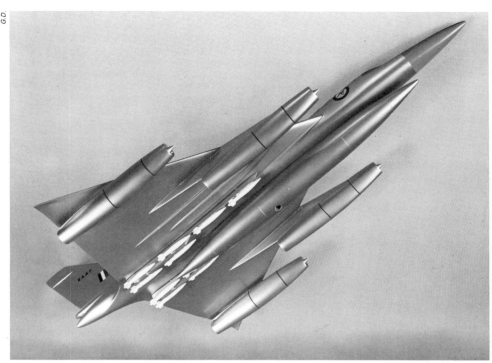

An attempt was made in 1959 and 1960 to sell stripped versions of the B-58 to the Royal Australian Air Force. Part of the sales effort was generated around the B-58's ability to carry conventional iron bombs on special wing root-mounted pylons. This Convair model illustrates the RAAF B-58 proposal.

The slightly enlarged and significantly more powerful B-58B was proposed as an iron bomb-capable transport to the USAF. This configuration, in 1967, would later be tested at Eglin AFB, FL, using stock B-58's from the 305th BW.

Because the B-58 had been designed from the outset as a high altitude bombing platform, the change to low-level penetration capability called for by SAC in the late 1950's proved difficult to accommodate. One proposed solution was the installation of a podded terrain following radar system in the wing leading edge.

seats with each seat having a 38'' pitch and an 18'' wide center aisle. A takeoff weight of 190,000 lbs. was estimated with takeoff and landing speeds being 199 knots and 148 knots, respectively. Cruise speed was estimated to be Mach 2.4 over a range of 2,525 miles.

Convair originally estimated that if the program approval had been granted in January, 1961, the first flight could have taken place in October, 1963. DoD interest in the project was also strong, though for a number of reasons outside the field of transporting passengers at a very high rate of speed. One of the many military proposals generated during this period, in fact, included a dedicated reconnaissance version of the Model 58-9 that would carry a rather large collection of optical sensors in the fuselage in place of the passengers. These would have been aimed through a series of large, rectangular ports in the fuselage side and would have been activated during high speed flights around the perimeters of unfriendly countries. Like most B-58-related ad-vanced design studies, the supersonic transport project quietly died on the vine as more advanced and more viable projects from other companies began to reach fruition.

1960—During the summer, a B-58 air-to-air missile capability was proposed by Convair to the AF.

1965—During the spring, a new navigation/bombing system was proposed with a lower electro-magnetic radiation factor.

Continued problems with limited range led Convair to explore a number of options, including the twin jettisonable fuel tank system, shown. This project apparently never reached the hardware stage.

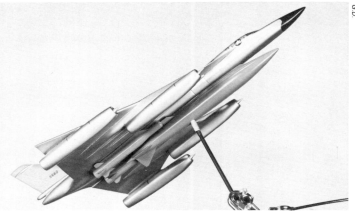

The ALBM program did not die with the demise of the Lockheed/Convair project of the late 1950's. Further development of the concept continued into the 1960's with missile proposals by companies such as Martin, Bell, and Douglas.

All B-58 test programs required photographic coverage for documentation and research purposes. Photo pods were installed in a variety of places, including the tops of engine nacelles as seen in this photo of 55-661.

As part of the ejection seat test program associated with the B-58 encapsulated ejection system and that of the XB-70A, 55-661, was modified to carry a special MB-1 pod that had its weapons bay reconfigured to accommodate experimental ejection seats. The seats, often with live occupants, were mounted in an upright position and ejected downward. Note the camera pod attached to the top of the inboard engine nacelle.

B/TB-58 Station Points

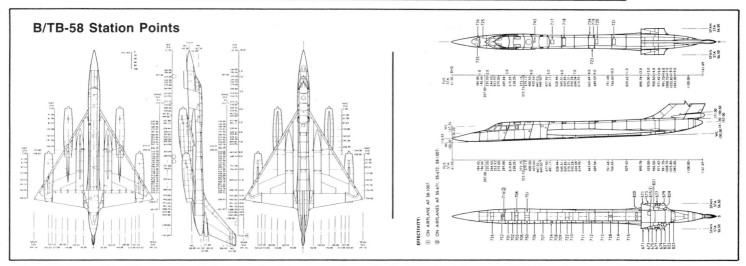

The B-58's configuration represented the culmination of an unprecedented design effort which pushed the state-of-the-art in the design of tactical aircraft to the limit in its time era. Furthermore, use of this aircraft represented a reversal of the trend toward continued increase in aircraft size for the accomplishment of a given mission.

Design requirements for the B-58 weapon system had a significant impact on its configuration. Among the most important were high performance in range, speed, and altitude; operational versatility for bombing, reconnaissance, and other designated functions; and maximum survival probability and economy. The fulfillment of these requirements resulted in an aircraft of small size (resulting in, among other things, a radar signature 1/10th to 1/30th that of a B-52 depending on the angle of view), high weight ratio (full-up weight to empty weight), and exceptional aerodynamic cleanliness. Interchangeable pods provided the desired flexibility of operation.

For previous operational bombers, the lowest ratio of structural weight over maximum gross weight had been 19.8%. For the B-58, a figure of 13.8% was achieved, even though speed was more than doubled.

Supersonic flight introduced many new factors for consideration in the structural design of the B-58's airframe. Paramount among these was aerodynamic heating and its effect on structures and construction materials. Because the B-58 was from its beginning designed to fly supersonically, the selection of materials, type of structure, development tests, specification requirements, analyses, flight tests, and aircraft static tests were aimed at the achievement and demonstration of this goal. Convair's engineering team succeeded admirably; the B-58, without modification, proved easily capable of a long service life while providing SAC with a Mach 2 capability. Additionally, though it was never utilized, the B-58 structure proved without modification to be capable of sustained speeds of Mach 2.4 at reduced gross weights.

The basic B-58 airframe and structure provided maneuver load factors of 2 g's at the takeoff gross weight of 163,000 lbs. and 3 g's at the combat gross weight of 100,000 lbs. Following completion of the fatigue certification program, total structural life was eventually determined to be 7,000 hours.

Basic structural materials consisted almost totally of aluminum alloys with steel used only in excessively high temperature areas. The wing covering structure, for instance, consisted of panels of chemically bonded 2024-T86 aluminum skins with phenolic-resin-fiberglass or aluminum cores. The fuselage had 2024-T80 beaded stiffeners filled with aluminum honeycomb and bonded to the 2024-T81 aluminum skin.

In the structural development program for the B-58, analyses and tests were based on a material temperature of 260°F., which was the calculated adiabatic wall temperature on an AF ambient hot day at 36,000'. Extensive analyses, design studies, and tests were conducted during the development program to obtain a reliable structure for high temperature service. Aluminum alloys, honeycomb sandwich cores, adhesives, plastic laminates, and other materials were screened and evaluated to assure the capability for supersonic flight. Composite structures of these elemental materials were subjected to demanding environments and tested for durability and structural integrity. The fiberglass honeycomb cores were fabricated of glass cloth impregnated with high temperature resin. When sandwiched between two sheets of aluminum, they were then cured at a pressure of 175 psi at 350° for two hours. This combination of materials retained high strength at temperatures beyond 325°F. and was not affected by prolonged exposure at this temperature.

Tests in a sonic chamber and in the presence of a J79 engine with full afterburner showed the B-58 bonded structure to be greatly superior to other types of construction. These tests were run at decibel levels as high as 170. Panel flutter was virtually eliminated by the inherent stiffness of the B-58's honeycomb sandwich in all directions. Buckling under load and/or thermal buckling was prevented by the sandwich design. The bonded skin joints also proved to be far superior to the normal riveted joints of conventional structures. Panel attachments were made through "thick" material on thick-skinned panels, giving increased fatigue life.

From the earliest formative stages of the B-58 subsystem designs, provisions were considered for integration among systems, and the duplication of subsystems elements was avoided wherever possible. Between the various major and minor subsystems in the aircraft, 155 tie-ins were created. In addition to providing matched signals between subsystems, every effort was made to proportion accuracy requirements properly, to consider alternate modes of operation for maintaining operational reliability, and to utilize such common equipment as a single power supply.

Fuselage: The semi-monocoque fuselage had

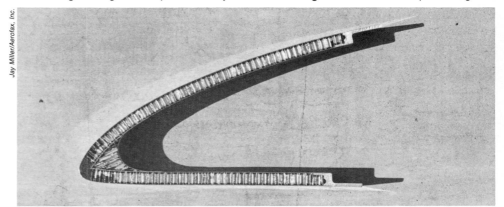

Jay Miller/Aerofax, Inc.

The B-58's wing leading edge section was rigidly formed from a brazed honeycomb structure to accommodate the tolerance and structural requirements dictated by the high temperatures and extraordinary dynamics created by flight at speeds in excess of Mach 2.

The B-58's wing was an extraordinary structure without conventional ribs. It provided exceptional strength throughout the aircraft's performance envelope. Particularly noteworthy in this photo are the compact hydraulic rams required to actuate the elevons.

E. G. Morales collection

AF Museum/Hugh Morgan via Dave Menard

The B-58's nameplate was mounted in the pilot's cockpit on the right side to the rear of the ejection seat.

B-58A General Arrangement Diagram

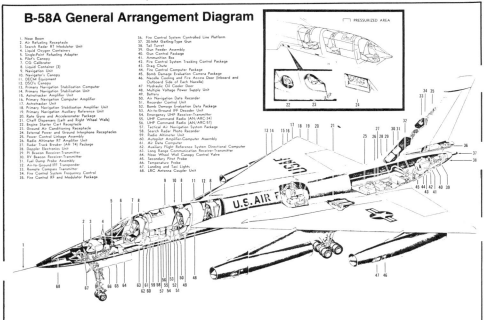

1. Nose Boom
2. Air Refueling Receptacle
3. Search Radar RT Modulator Unit
4. Liquid Oxygen Containers
5. Single-Point Refueling Adapter
6. Pilot's Canopy
7. CG Calibrator
8. Liquid Container (3)
9. Navigation Unit
10. Navigator's Canopy
11. DECM Equipment
12. DSO's Canopy
13. Primary Navigation Stabilization Computer
14. Primary Navigation Stabilization Unit
15. Astrotracker Amplifier Unit
16. Primary Navigation Computer Amplifier
17. Primary Navigation Stabilization Amplifier Unit
18. Astrotracker Unit
19. Primary Navigation Auxiliary Reference Unit
20. Rate Gyro and Accelerometer Package
21. Chaff Dispensers (Left and Right Wheel Walls)
22. Engine Starter Cart Receptacle
23. Ground Air Conditioning Receptacle
24. External Power and Ground Interphone Receptacles
25. Power Control Linkage Assembly
26. Radio Altimeter RT Amplifier Unit
27. Radar Track Breaker (Aft T4) Package
28. Doppler Electronics Unit
29. PI Beacon Receiver-Transmitter
30. RV Beacon Receiver-Transmitter
31. Fuel Dump Probe Assembly
32. Air-to-Ground IFF Transponder
33. Remote Compass Transmitter
34. Fire Control System Frequency Control
35. Fire Control RF and Modulator Package
36. Fire Control System Controlled Line Platform
37. 20-MM Gatling-Type Gun
38. Tail Turret
39. Gun Feeder Assembly
40. Gun Control Package
41. Ammunition Box
42. Fire Control System Tracking Control Package
43. Drag Chute
44. Fire Control Computer Package
45. Bomb Damage Evaluation Camera Package
46. Nacelle Cooling and Fire Access Door (Inboard and Outboard Side of Each Nacelle)
47. Hydraulic Oil Cooler Door
48. Multiple Voltage Power Supply Unit
49. Battery
50. Air Navigation Data Recorder
51. Recorder Control Unit
52. Bomb Damage Evaluation Data Package
53. Air-to-Ground UHF Decoder Unit
54. Emergency UHF Receiver-Transmitter
55. UHF Command Radio (AN/ARC-34)
56. UHF Command Radio (AN/ARC-57)
57. Tactical Air Navigation System Package
58. Search Radar Photo Recorder
59. Radio Altimeter Unit
60. Autopilot Amplifier-Computer Assembly
61. Air Data Computer
62. Auxiliary Flight Reference System Directional Computer
63. Long Range Communication Receiver-Transmitter
64. Nose Wheel Well Canopy Control Valve
65. Secondary Pitot Probe
66. Temperature Probe
67. Landing and Taxi Lights
68. LRC Antenna Coupler Unit

TB-58A General Arrangement Diagram

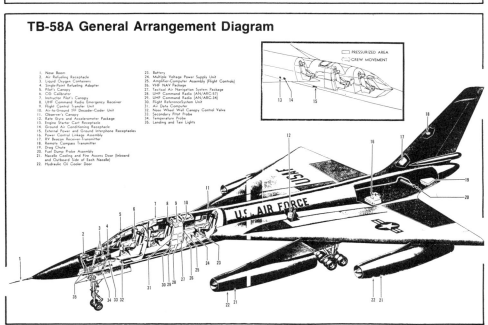

1. Nose Boom
2. Air Refueling Receptacle
3. Liquid Oxygen Containers
4. Single-Point Refueling Adapter
5. Pilot's Canopy
6. CG Calibrator
7. Instructor Pilot's Canopy
8. UHF Command Radio Emergency Receiver
9. Flight Control Transfer Unit
10. Air-to-Ground IFF Decoder-Coder Unit
11. Observer's Canopy
12. Rate Gyro and Accelerometer Package
13. Engine Starter Cart Receptacle
14. Ground Air Conditioning Receptacle
15. External Power and Ground Interphone Receptacles
16. Power Control Linkage Assembly
17. RV Beacon Receiver-Transmitter
18. Remote Compass Transmitter
19. Drag Chute
20. Fuel Dump Probe Assembly
21. Nacelle Cooling and Fire Access Door (Inboard and Outboard Side of Each Nacelle)
22. Hydraulic Oil Cooler Door
23. Battery
24. Multiple Voltage Power Supply Unit
25. Amplifier-Computer Assembly (Flight Controls)
26. VHF NAV Package
27. Tactical Air Navigation System Package
28. UHF Command Radio (AN/ARC-57)
29. UHF Command Radio (AN/ARC-34)
30. Air Data Computer
31. Flight Reference System Unit
32. Nose Wheel Well Canopy Control Valve
33. Secondary Pitot Probe
34. Temperature Probe
35. Landing and Taxi Lights

standard bulkhead, former, and longeron construction though much of the skin was of the beaded inner skin type which reduced thermal buckling and deformation. A nose package extended from the forward tip of the nose aft to bulkhead 1.0. The area between bulkheads 1.0 and 5.0 was the crew compartment. The area aft of the crew compartment to bulkhead 19.0 was devoted to fuel storage except for the navigation system stable table area between bulkheads 8.0 and 9.0. The portion of the fuselage aft of bulkhead 19 contained the deceleration parachute, the armament tail package, and electronic equipment. The fuselage underwing area between bulkheads 5.0 and 12.0 contained electrical lines, tubing, ducting, and control cables. Access to the equipment was provided by a series of removable panels.

Cockpits: The flight crew consisted of a pilot, a navigator/bombardier, and a defensive systems operator (DSO). They were situated in three separate stations or compartments arranged in tandem along the fuselage centerline (the pilot's seat was offset to the left side of the centerline). The pilot was located in the forward compartment, the navigator/bombardier in the middle compartment, and the DSO in the rear. A crawlway located between the pilot's station and second crew station on the right side of the fuselage was used for maintenance of electronic equipment only. A crawlway between the second and third crew stations was open for passage.

The pilot's instrumentation and systems monitors were fairly conventional with the exception of fuel management, cg, and autopilot systems. The navigator/bombardier's panel was equipped with bomb and pod dropping indicators, the bombing system indicators and monitors and data input devices, and the navigation equipment. The DSO's panel was perhaps the least encumbered of the three but was equipped with the passive and active defensive systems monitors and instrumentation and the majority of the circuit breakers.

Structurally, the compartments comprised a single pressurized cabin volume though the partitioning effects of structural bulkheads and equipment created compartmentalization. Each compartment was equipped with its own canopy (hinged at the rear and pneumatically opened and closed) for normal ingress and egress and for emergency egress.

Direct vision or physical contact between the crew members was not possible. Crew intercommunication required complete reliance on the in-

B-58A Pilot's Station

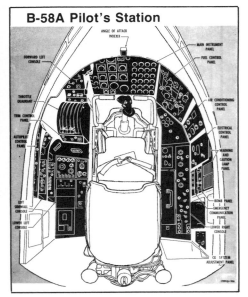

TB-58A Pilot's Station

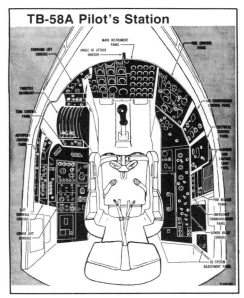

Control Stick

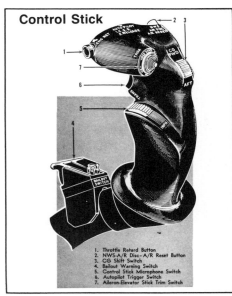

1. Throttle Retard Button
2. NWS-A/R Disc- A/R Reset Button
3. CG Shift Switch
4. Bailout Warning Switch
5. Control Stick Microphone Switch
6. Autopilot Trigger Switch
7. Aileron-Elevator Stick Trim Switch

terphone system. The crew remained seated in their ejection seats (later encapsulated) throughout flight as there was no space for movement within the compartments and insufficient head room existed for standing erect.

The original SACseat type ejection seat initially utilized in the B-58A, and later in the TB-58A, was provided with padded armrests and a cradle-type headrest. A ballistic-initiated, rocket-catapult ejection system, which operated independently of other aircraft systems, fired the seat out of the aircraft in an emergency. The backrest portion of the seat accommodated a back-type parachute and the bucket portion of the seat accommodated the seat-type survival kit. A gas-operated seat-man separator insured separation of the survival kit and crew member from the seat after ejection.

Each seat was mounted on ejection rails which were attached to each aft cabin bulkhead. Slide blocks on the back of each seat engaged the ejection rails and maintained the seat in a position such that its path of travel was parallel to the rails. The seat catapult, being mounted on bulkhead attached brackets behind the seat, supported a seat adjustment actuator which, in turn, supported the seat and the canopy actuator. An M3A1 initiator and an XM26 delay initiator was provided inside each seat armrest for initiating automatically sequenced canopy jettison and seat ejection.

Pressure type oxygen equipment or partial pressure suits were utilized as dictated by the mission (the encapsulated ejection seats later provided a "shirt sleeve environment") and protective helmets were worn on every flight. Flight crew feeding and relief provisions were minimal.

As noted in preceding chapters, problems with the SACseat initially deployed in the aircraft led to the development of an encapsulated ejection seat system. Designed by Stanley Aviation of Denver, CO, this unit protected the pilot from supersonic wind blasts, supplied oxygen and pressurization during an ejection at high altitude, accomplished an automatic recovery while maintaining manual override provisions, absorbed landing impact, and provided food, shelter, and equipment for survival on land, water, and ice. Each capsule featured a four-point hook-up (lap belt, torso restraint, oxygen hose, and intercom wire).

Each capsule was an independently operating unit and required no outside source of power for making an emergency escape. Its various functions were actuated by mechanical linkages, explosive devices, pressure bottles, thermal batteries, and other such systems.

The second and third crew station capsules

were operationally and functionally alike and they both ejected on vertical rails. The pilot's capsule was similar, but included a flight control stick. It ejected on slightly canted rails. This canting allowed the pilot to remain 3½" to the left of the aircraft centerline for optimum vision. During an emergency, the pilot's capsule could be closed (and, if required, reopened) while still in the aircraft and the aircraft could be flown while the pilot was encapsulated. A small window in the capsule clamshell door system provided a view of the aircraft instrument panel; the control stick permitted controlled flight.

The three-piece telescoping clamshell door was pivoted on each side of the seat. It was stowed above the crew member's head during normal flight. Seat actuation was accomplished by raising either or both ejection handles, thus causing the doors to rotate downward and form a pressure-tight capsule. Emergency oxygen (maintained at 1,800 psi in two 25-cubic" cylinders) and pressure were automatically actuated by door closure to maintain a safe atmosphere within the capsule during free-fall descent from maximum altitude.

After the doors were closed (in about .25 seconds) and pressurization had been achieved each crew member ejected his own capsule by squeezing one or both ejection triggers located on the ejection handles (one on each handle). This action fired the canopy jettison actuator and the rocket catapult initiator. If the canopy failed to jettison, the capsule would push the canopy off in the same manner as the earlier B-58 open seat system.

During high speed ejection, capsule stability was provided by the stabilization frame and stabilization parachute. A recovery parachute was automatically deployed at a pre-set altitude to provide a controlled descent. Landing impact was absorbed by crushable cylinders and stabilization fins, which cut through the metal flanges on the sides of the capsule. For water landings, flotation bags could be inflated with the capsule then becoming a life raft. It also could be used as a shelter from heat or cold.

The dual-unit, manifold rocket catapult used to egress the capsule produced sufficient thrust to provide a safe escape under all conditions ranging from 100 knots at zero altitude to maximum aircraft design speed and altitude.

Despite the size constraints, the crew compartments, even with the encapsulated ejection seats, were very comfortable, attractive, and functionally arranged. All systems requiring manual operation were within easy reach of the crew members even

when wearing partial pressure suits, and all displays requiring monitor were within a reasonable cone of vision.

Compartment temperatures were maintained at nominal levels for all operating conditions ranging from ground hot or cold day up to sustained limit speed. Cabin pressurization was maintained on an isobaric schedule of 8,000' altitude until a differential of 7.45 psi was attained.

The cabin area was provided with a liquid oxygen system. This unit provided breathing oxygen from a system of from one to four liquid oxygen containers which supplied their contents to a converter that in turn supplied gaseous oxygen to the regulator in each compartment. When worn, the partial pressure suits were fed from this system, also.

Cabin noise and vibration levels were unusually low. Cabin air conditioning system sonics accounted for most of the cabin noise. The quietness was attributable to the rearward mounting of the aircraft's engines and the aircraft's overall aerodynamic cleanliness.

Pilot outside vision was more than adequate for all flight conditions including takeoff, landing, formation flying, and flight refueling. The pilot was afforded some vision of the exterior of the aircraft, and the engine nacelle inlets and wing leading edges were visible by use of rear view mirrors. The navigator/bombardier and DSO also had vision provisions through small side windows.

First station glass panels consisted of six adjacent panels which formed the pilot's windshield and two panels which were installed one on each side of the canopy. The panels at this station were made up of two sheets of ¼" full-tempered glass laminated with a silicone rubber interlayer material. The panels were secured by means of metal retainers which attached to the surrounding structure with screws. The panels were sealed with room temperature vulcanizing silicone rubber sealant which was applied to the glass panel retainers and the structural frame which surrounded the retainers. The glass panels at the second and third crew stations differed from panels at the first crew station only in tht they were made up of ³/₁₆" semi-tempered plate glass. On the TB-58A, the first and second station enclosure panels were both made of ¼" full-tempered glass. Also on the TB-58A, ½" transparent thermoplastic panels were installed in the bulkheads which separated the crew stations.

The TB-58A was basically a B-58A modified to accommodate the requirements of an instructor pilot. Externally, the TB-58A differed from the full-

The pilot's main instrument panel for prototype aircraft 55-660. With the exception of the Mach meter, the instrumentation was conventional for a multi-engine aircraft.

The cockpit of operational B-58's differed only slightly from that of 55-660. This view of 59-2458's cockpit, with seat and stick removed, shows how the pilot was offset to the left side of the aircraft.

The pilot's left console accommodated the throttle quadrant and some of the communications equipment. The landing gear handle protrudes from the far right.

The pilot's right console accommodated the fuel monitoring system, the cabin environment control panel, some communications equipment, and the warning panel. The pulley and cord system was for emergency communications.

The front cockpit (left) of the first TB-58A, 55-670, while it was undergoing conversion to the trainer configuration. Robust rudder pedal support structure is particularly notable. The instructor's cockpit (right) was offset to the right side of the aircraft and was equipped with a full control system and full instrument panel. Plexiglass panels separated the instructor's cockpit from that of the student.

The navigator/bombardier's panel and related computer systems were contained in a self-contained package that could be removed and replaced at will. Part of the navigation package sat on top of this unit.

The navigator/bombardier's station was unquestionably the busiest of the three in the aircraft. Panel in photo has CRT unit removed for maintenance. Radar control handle is folded on the right.

The navigator/bombardier's left console was dedicated to communications and circuit breaker panels and like most cockpit panels in the B-58, was easily accessed from the seat.

The navigator/bombardier's right console accommodated the radar control handle (seen in its retracted position), a systems monitoring panel, and navigation reference instrumentation.

The defensive systems operator's (DSO) cockpit was somewhat less crowded than that of either the pilot or navigator/bombardier. The fire control sytem for the MD-7 tail gun was monitored from the center panel.

The DSO's station served as the control station on 55-660 during the ALBM program that was conducted with limited success at Eglin AFB, FL, during 1958 and 1959.

Nav/Bombardier's Station

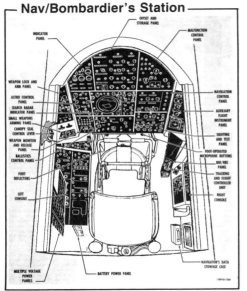

DSO's Station

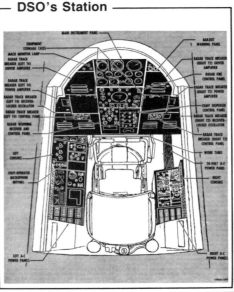

Ejection Seats (Typical)

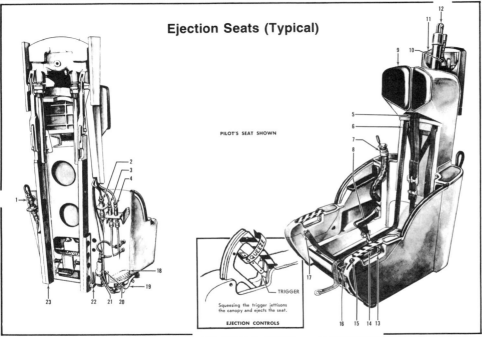

PILOT'S SEAT SHOWN

SQUEEZE

TRIGGER

Squeezing the trigger jettisons
the canopy and ejects the seat.

EJECTION CONTROLS

The SACseat was a modestly successful emergency egress system as verified by this seat which was used successfully by Convair flight engineer Michael F. Keller to emergency egress 55-669 on October 27, 1959, near Hattiesburg, MS.

History Office, Kelly AFB

up tactical aircraft in having additional transparencies in the second cockpit area (to the side and overhead) to meet the needs of the instructor pilot. Internally, all tactical systems were removed (there was no autopilot, no primary navigation system, no bombing system, no defensive electronic countermeasures system and no active defense system), the second crew station was redesigned to afford the instructor pilot all the necessary controls for inflight instruction and safety of flight. This included conventional flight controls (stick and rudder pedals) which were connected mechanically to those located in the front cockpit. The instructor pilot's seat was also offset to the starboard side of the aircraft to permit better forward vision. Both stations had an electronic control panel for the flight control systems non-mechanical requirements, and the instructor pilot's position was also equipped with a functional throttle quadrant, active rudder pedal braking, and a duplicate instrument panel. The instructor pilot could also control fuel transfer operations from the second station.

The instructor's compartment was completely sealed from that of the student (front cockpit), though a split transparency permitted forward vision. The third station was usually occupied by a pilot requiring proficiency training. During flight this pilot could change places with the instructor pilot by crawling through a passageway between the second and third crew stations.

Wings: The wings were of the full cantilever midwing, modified delta type with cambered leading edges and outboard tips, incorporating multispar construction with sandwich panel covering secured with titanium screws. The leading edges were of sandwich-type skin construction preformed to shape without any internal bracing.

The leading edge was made up of ten sections which were attached to the wing by means of hinge fittings. The internal structure of the wing consisted of multispar-type construction with bulkheads at the points of major load introduction or redistribution. The two inboard bulkheads located in the wheel well area were large channels flanged away from the wheel well to allow maximum clearance for landing gear retraction. The spars were made so that contact with the wing skin was on a curved surface to allow the wing skin to more closely approach the contour of the desired airfoil. Sweepback in the spars near the wing tip section gave greater rigidity to the wingtip (to which were attached the static discharge lines). The spars were made of corrugated aluminum for strength and were spaced 11'' to 15'' apart. There were no chordwise ribs, only chordwise members or bulkheads to serve as attachment points for the elevons, engine nacelles, and landing gear.

The typical wing sandwich panel was made up of skins (aluminum sheets), adhesives, fiberglass, and aluminum honeycomb core, and a machined aluminum grid, or slug. The wing cross section was increased at the main landing gear area to afford complete enclosure of the main landing gear when retracted.

The entire wing served as an integral fuel tank which because of its physical depth, had to be sealed from the outside during construction (since fuel-tight adhesives were used, the only joint that could leak was the seam; sealant was placed along the seam with a minimum weight penalty and maximum effectivity). Free-flow openings in other spars and bulkheads allowed fuel to flow between sections of the individual tanks for equal load distribution. Strategically located flapper check valves in some spars and bulkheads prevented fuel flow between left and right wing sections when one wing was high. The wing had an absolute minimum of bulkheads. The wing panel fiberglass cores served to insulate the fuel from the external heat and helped prevent loss of fuel from vaporization.

Wing aerodynamic smoothness was maintained by applying aerodynamic smoothing compound in the skin panel seams and by inserting soft aluminum plugs over all attaching bolts.

Engine Nacelles: The basic nacelle arrangement consisted of four minimum frontal area faired nacelles suspended on struts below the wing. The inboard location was buttock line 145.93, and the outboard location was buttock line 259.845. Each nacelle was divided into a nose cowl section (induction system), an engine accessory compartment, an afterburner section (exhaust compartment), and a strut station. Nacelle construction was semi-monocoque with longerons and circumferential frames and bulkheads of aluminum alloy and steel construction serving as load bearing members in conjunction with stressed, removable panels. The intake spike and its actuation system were an integral part of the nose cowl section (they are described more fully in Chapt. 10).

Vertical Tail: The vertical fin was a sweptback, truncated structure. Spars and ribs provided the internal framework. The leading edge and side surface panels were of sandwich-type construction with a honeycomb core and an aluminum sheet face. The leading edge was divided into two sections. Each section could be removed independently or the complete leading edge could be removed as one section. Provisions for attaching the rudder were made along the rudder support spar. The fin cap was fabricated of laminated fiberglass.

Control System and Control Surfaces: The B-58's airframe configuration resulted in a set of unique problems in terms of the design of a satisfactory flight control system. The requirement for satisfactory flying qualities at both supersonic and subsonic speeds made the application of new concepts and techniques a critical necessity in the design of this particular system.

Typical unique elements of the flight control system included three-axis damping, constant stick forces throughout the speed range of the aircraft, continuous "g" protection making it virtually impossible to manually overstress the airframe while the aircraft was in automatic flight mode, an artificial feel system, altitude and Mach number control, and coupling provisions for station keeping, approach control, landing, and flare-out.

The flight control system included an automatic trim system which had three modes of operation: (1) takeoff and landing (wherein the trim system was locked at 3° up elevator); (2) manual (wherein the trim system was locked at 3° up elevator); and (3) automatic (wherein the automatic trim system provided the elevon deflection required for 1 g flight). Automatic trim was required to provide symmetrical elevator control, to enhance elevator g limiting, and to reduce the effect of negative speed stability during cruise. The auto trim system was closely associated with the ratio changer or g protection system. The ratio changer limited elevator deflection so that full stick deflection produced a normal load factor between 100% and 150% of limit load factor.

The control surfaces consisted of a rudder, two elevons (surfaces combining the control forces of both elevators for pitch control and ailerons for roll control), and two resolution surfaces. The latter were provided inboard of the elevons to mask the effects of mechanical backlash in the longitudinal control system and were completely automatic. They were eventually found to be redundant to the primary trim system and were eliminated from all production (and later, all pre-production) aircraft.

The rudder had a full depth aluminum core which had an aluminum alloy skin bonded to it.

The pilot's SAC seat was offset to the left side of the aircraft but ejected up a pair of rails that were offset toward the aircraft centerline.

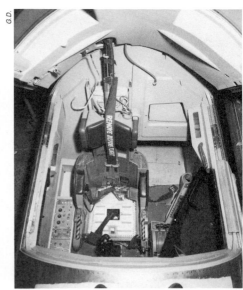

Though the instructor's seat in the TB-58A (55-670, shown) was offset to the right side of the aircraft, the seat rails were vertical.

Boilerplate encapsulated seats were built in fairly sizable numbers by Stanley Aviation and test fired in initially frustrating attempts to create an aerodynamically stable configuration.

Following the completion of preliminary static trials, the encapsulated seat was fired from high-speed sleds at several test tracks in New Mexico and Arizona. Results were initially disappointing, though performance improved as data was accumulated and analyzed.

Once it was determined that the encapsulated seat was performing consistently well when ejected from the various high-speed rocket sleds, a full-scale test program using B-58A, 55-661, was undertaken at Edwards AFB, CA. Note wingtip mounted camera pods for photographing test ejections.

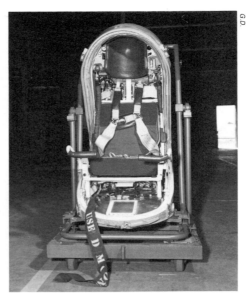

The encapsulated ejection seat was a tight fit for all three B-58 cockpits. Crew ingress and egress also was complicated by the seats.

Though the accommodations were not overly roomy, most crew members found the encapsulated seats to be extremely comfortable.

Pilot's Encapsulated Seat

NOTE
Extended red pin indicates actuator has fired rendering canopy opening and jettison inoperative.

CANOPY ACTUATOR WARNING PIN DETAIL

CAPSULE HANDGRIP — CAPSULE HANDGRIP RELEASE LEVER
CAPSULE EJECTION TRIGGER

DETAIL EJECTION CONTROLS

DETAIL DOOR RELEASE HANDLES
(Door Closed—Left Side)

Pilot's Capsule Shown

BILGE LINE ATTACHMENT

AIR OUTLET

HAND PUMP

1. Upper Shock Absorber (2)
2. Door Uplock
3. Drag Plate
*4. Canopy Actuator
5. Spoiler Band (2)
6. Stabilization Chute Mortar
7. Headrest
8. Crew Ejection Indicator Lamp
9. External Door Release Handle (2)
10. Internal Door Release Handle (2)
11. Parachute Disconnect Handle
12. Manual Parachute Deployment Handle
13. Inertia Reel Control Handle
14. Inertia Reel
*15. Shoulder Harness
16. Flashlight Holder
*17. Control Stick (P)
18. Seat Adjustment Switch
19. Ejection Handgrips
20. Leg Retraction Bar (2)
21. Pneumatic System Gauge
22. Door Down Latch (2)
*23. Handgrip Safety Pin (2)
24. Bridle Release Explosive Bolt (2)
25. Bridle Line
26. Hand Pump
27. Seat Pan Adjustment Lever
28. Hand Pump Connector (4)
29. VVS. Override Button (Interphone, Nav, DSO)
30. Hoist Point
31. Lower Flotation Boom (2)
32. Parachute Riser Link
33. Parachute Compartment
34. Hinged Impact Shear Plates (2)
35. Stabilization Fin (2)
36. Pendant
37. Recovery System Delay Initiator Safety Pins (2)
*38. Safety Belt
39. Parachute Anchor Points
40. Personal Gear Leads
*41. Door Seal
42. Aneroid Timer Gas Generator Safety Pins (2)
43. Aneroid Timer Altimeter
44. Upper Flotation Boom (2)
45. Stabilization Chute Mortar Initiator Pin (1)
*46. Capsule-Aircraft Disconnect Engagement Indicator
47. Rail Switch (2)
48. Capsule-Aircraft Disconnect (2)
49. Rocket Catapult Tube (2)
50. Stabilization Frame (2)
51. Chaff Dispenser

*Items Normally Checked on Preflight

Recovery Sequence

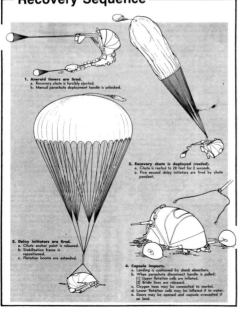

1. **Aneroid timers are fired.**
   a. Recovery chute is forcibly ejected.
   b. Manual parachute deployment handle is unlocked.

2. **Recovery chute is deployed (reefed).**
   a. Chute is reefed to 28 feet for 2 seconds.
   b. Five second delay initiators are fired by chute pendant.

3. **Delay initiators are fired.**
   a. Chute anchor point is released.
   b. Stabilization frame is repositioned.
   c. Flotation booms are extended.

4. **Capsule impacts.**
   a. Landing is cushioned by shock absorbers.
   b. When parachute disconnect handle is pulled:
      (1) Upper flotation cells are inflated.
      (2) Bridle lines are released.
   c. Oxygen hose may be connected to snorkel.
   d. Lower flotation cells may be inflated (if in water).
   e. Doors may be opened and capsule evacuated if on land.

Encapsulated Seat Cutaway
(Pre-Ejection Configuration)

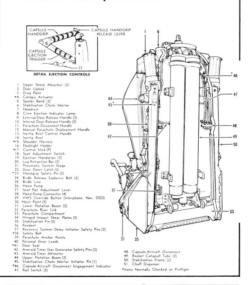

The rudder was hinged at eleven points along the front spar. The elevons were made of steel sandwich panels with a brazing alloy used as a bonding agent. The heat treat cycle of this steel was compatible with the brazing process.

The flight control surfaces were actuated by servos composed of irreversible hydraulic valves and rams with appropriate feedback linkages located adjacent to the control surfaces. Each elevon surface was positioned (at a maximum deflection angle of 20° per second) by ten actuators controlled by a dual valve. The autopilot and damper servos were integral components of the power control linkage assembly.

The aileron-rudder interconnect system served to help cancel the yawing response that was the normal result of aileron deflection due to pressure field interactions. Artificial pitch, roll, and yaw damping were supplied to minimize variation in flight characteristics and to provide satisfactory damping.

The aircraft also was equipped with a "wing heavy" control system. This was provided to sense lateral accelerations and provide corrective rudder through the rudder damper servo to prevent lateral fuel shift and subsequent wing heaviness. With the proper switch configuration, the system was activated at speeds above Mach .6, providing a maximum of 3.5° of left or right rudder.

The Eclipse Pioneer autopilot system for the B-58 was significantly different than other similar systems found on more conventional aircraft. The B-58's system provided constant Mach hold in which aircraft speed was maintained at the desired Mach number by automatic control of the elevators; constant Mach-altitude which maintained the aircraft at the desired altitude and Mach number by automatically controlling the elevators and throttles; heading control which automatically steered the aircraft along a constant track or a computer ground track, as required to fly a great-circle course or an aim-point course; beam-guidance control which provided for automatic all-weather instrument approaches and a secondary means of enroute navigation in areas where omni-directional range stations are located; and control stick steering which permitted maneuvering of the aircraft without disengaging the autopilot.

An "emergency increase elevator available" handle on the pilot's lower left console was used to manually position the elevator ratio changer to increase control available in the event of a failure in the normal system.

Landing Gear, Brakes, and Drag Chutes: Landing gear retracton and extension, which normally took approximately 10 seconds, was initiated by pilot movement of the landing gear actuation handle in the forward cockpit. The actual gear retraction sequence was accomplished by hydraulic actuators which were of the double-acting, linear, cylindrical-type (the nose gear door was equipped with an auxiliary pneumatic boost actuator which compensated for heavy airloads created in the nose wheel well during takeoff). Emergency extension of the gear could be accomplished using the actuators in a pneumatic mode. Each of the gear units was equipped with uplatch and door cinching actuators.

Maximum gear extension and retraction speed was 304 knots, maximum turning speed while taxiing was 14 knots, tire limit speed was 217 knots, and minimum aircraft turning radius was 50'. Directional control of the aircraft during taxi, takeoff, and landing rolls was provided by the steerable nose gear. An electrically controlled, hydraulically powered steering mechanism provided the steering force via pilot rudder pedal inputs. The nose gear was automatically centered during the retraction sequence. The nose gear steering system furnished dual control capability

Bottom view of pilot's encapsulated seat with the control stick removed. The bottom shell was a cast aluminum structure.

The first full-scale operational installation of the Stanley Aviation encapsulated seat was undertaken with B-58A, 61-2062. Sadly, this aircraft crashed at Bunker Hill AFB, IN, on April 18, 1968, killing all three crew members.

to allow the pilot to select 50° maximum steering control for taxiing or 10° maximum steering control for takeoff and landing.

The four-per-gear multiple disc-type braking units (with anti-skid system) were hydraulically actuated via pilot rudder pedal inputs and a series of cables, bellcranks, and linkages.

Both the main gear tires and the nose gear tires were extra high pressure (240 psi) Goodyear tubeless units weighing approximately 27 lbs. each and good for a minimum of ten takeoffs and landings each. Tire dimensions were 22 x 7.7-12. Each main gear unit consisted of a single eight-wheel bogie; the nose gear had two wheels on a single axle. After mid-1961, mounted between each pair of main gear wheels was a steel non-frangible wheel that could serve as an emergency roll-out and support wheel in case of tire blow-out (this was in response to several accidents early in the B-58 flight test program caused by tire blow-outs during takeoff and/or initial ascent).

The deceleration parachute system which was housed underneath the empennage just behind the tailgun installation, consisted of a 28' ring slot deceleration parachute assembly, a parachute stowage compartment with dual clamshell-type

doors (hinged at the outer edges), and a parachute deployment and jettisoning mechanism which was supplied with electrical and pneumatic power. The operating control for the drag chute was a T-handle mounted just aft of the throttle quadrant in the pilot's compartment. The pilot could jettison the parachute at his discretion and the chute could be deployed at up to 184 knots.

Electrical System: The electrical system consisted of three oil-cooled, 40-KVA, 111-ampere engine-driven alternators (on engines #1, #2, #3) supplying 115/200-volt, 400-cycle alternating current; a multiple-voltage power unit assembly (consisting of eight transformer-rectifiers) supplying 250-volt, +150-volt, -150-volt, and 28-volt direct current and 28-volt alternating current. The alternating current was distributed by two buses, the left main AC bus, and the right main AC bus. These buses were normally supplied by the primary alternators. The AC power supply system operated automatically provided the electrical control panel was set up in the normal configuration. Direct current was supplied by the multiple-voltage DC power units and a 24-volt nicad battery. Operation of the power units was entirely automatic. An

emergency DC power supply system was installed on early test aircraft.

Hydraulic and Pneumatic Systems: The 3,000 psi, 100 gpm, 4 pump (one on each engine) hydraulic system was of the dual parallel type consisting of utility and primary systems. The two sub-systems were completely independent with no interchange of fluid pressure. The primary system supplied hydraulic pressure solely for flight controls actuation and the utility system supplied hydraulic pressure for operation of the landing gear, nose wheel steering, wheel brake systems, nose radar, tail turret, chaff dispensers, inflight refueling system, aileron-rudder interconnect, autopilot servos, and elevator and aileron-damper servos. In addition, the utility system also supplied hydraulic pressure to assist the primary hydraulic system in the actuation of the flight control surface actuators. Normally, each system supplied one-half the hydraulic fluid pressure for the flight control system; however, the flight control system could be operated at a reduced rate with only one system operating.

Each system consisted mainly of a pressurized reservoir, two engine-driven pumps, two ram air

The TB-58A (55-670, shown) featured increased transparency areas at the second crew station to accommodate the needs of the instructor pilot. Not often noticed, but well defined in the photo on the left were the large hatch windows. TB-58A's also maintained the SACseat and were never scheduled to receive the encapsulated seat.

Control System Schematic

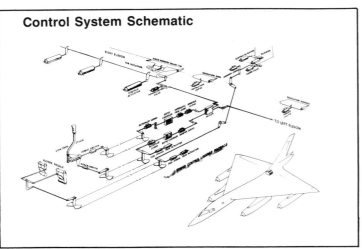

Terry Morgan via Douglas Robinson

The nose landing gear well doors were simple in design and were actuated by direct linkage to the nose gear strut. The last three or four digits of the aircraft serial number were often painted on these doors.

G.D.

View looking forward inside the nose gear well shows the robust gear struts and the various hydraulic lines associated with steering and gear retraction.

G.D.

View looking aft inside the nose gear well shows miscellaneous hydraulic lines and the gear up-lock assembly. Note articulated line attached to left gear door.

Jay Miller/Aerofax, Inc.

Jay Miller/Aerofax, Inc.

Jay Miller/Aerofax, Inc.

The nose gear was a hefty, but none-the-less complex structure that was hinged so the main strut could rotate up and back into the well while providing clearance for the MB-1 pod or TCP. Landing and taxi lights were attached to the strut assembly and most operational aircraft had a radar reflecting panel attached to the main strut for ILS requirements. The nose gear was fully steerable from the front cockpit.

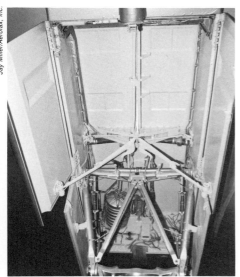

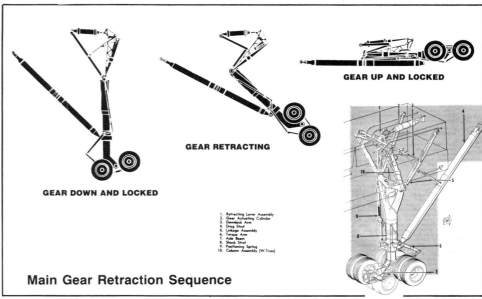

Main Gear Retraction Sequence

GEAR UP AND LOCKED

GEAR RETRACTING

GEAR DOWN AND LOCKED

1. Retracting Lever Assembly
2. Gear Actuating Cylinder
3. Downlock Arm
4. Drag Strut
5. Linkage Assembly
6. Torque Arm
7. Axle Beam
8. Shock Strut
9. Positioning Spring
10. Column Assembly (W-Truss)

The complex main gear assemblies retracted into faired wing wells located inboard of the inboard engine pylons and nacelles.

The B-58's main gear bogies were complex, rugged assemblies mounting four wheels and tires and their associated braking systems on each of two hefty axles. The units were compact and small, but fully capable of handling the dynamics of supporting an eighty ton bomber during taxi, takeoff, and landing. Between each pair of tires can be seen the frangible wheel which was developed in response to the continuing B-58 problem of tire failure.

The B-58's main gear assemblies were extraordinarily strong structures with complex retraction sequences. Somewhat surprisingly, landing gear retraction or extension failures were very rare. However, strut, bogie, and axle assemblies were known to have broken, and on at least one occasion, a failure of this type led to the aircraft being written off permanently.

The drag chute housing was mounted inside the fuselage empennage section. The chute was ejected through two small doors which were mechanically opened immediately prior to chute deployment. Chute attachment was to the bulkhead at the forward end of the drag chute compartment.

The B-58A's Raytheon-developed search radar was an articulated Doppler unit with excellent range, good dependability, and high accuracy.

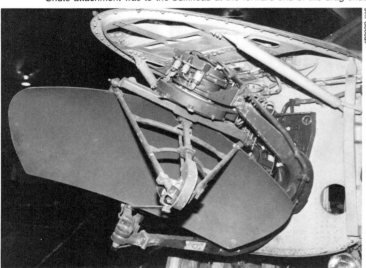

The search radar antenna dish was compact, but highly efficient. The entire unit rotated and turned while in its conventional search mode.

The inflight refueling receptacle and related plumbing were mounted just above the antenna-supporting forward fuselage bulkhead.

The B-58's resin-impregnated fiberglass radome was fairly conventional. Noteworthy is the fact that it contained no internal support structure.

The Autonetics-manufactured gyro platform for the B-58's navigation/bombing system sat on top of the primary computer unit just ahead of the second station.

G.D.

The six-dish Doppler radar system which provided data for the precise calcula-
tion of aircraft altitude and velocity was mounted in the empennage section of
the fuselage near the wing trailing edge.

Jay Miller/Aerofax, Inc.

Location of the Doppler unit was under the two plexiglass panels, shown. The
small, faired trailing edge pods were the aft receiving antennas for the
radar track breaking unit (T4).

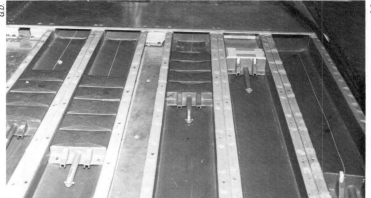

G.D.

The radar track breaking unit (T4) was interconnected with antennas covering
both the front and rear quadrants. The power amplifier, driver amplifier, and
receiver locked oscillator are shown.

Jim Goodall

From inboard working outward, a radar track breaker transmitting antenna,
radar track breaker receiving antenna, and radar warning
forward antenna are shown.

A chaff dispensing system was mounted in each upper main gear fairing. Chaff
was ejected through mechanically actuated slots in the tops of each wing
main gear fairing.

G.D.

The turreted tail gun assembly for the B-58 was aerodynamically faired to
conform to the rest of the aircraft empennage section. Spent
ammo shells were ejected through a ventral door.

Chuck Hansen collection

The radar for the tail gun was located in the bullet fairing above the tail cone.
Data from the radar was fed to a computer mounted behind the gun
and then relayed electromechanically to the gun itself.

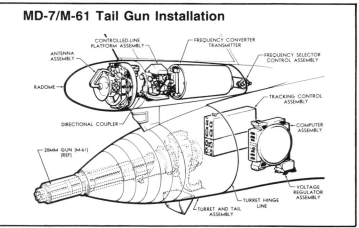

MD-7/M-61 Tail Gun Installation

CONTROLLED-LINE
PLATFORM ASSEMBLY

FREQUENCY CONVERTER
TRANSMITTER

ANTENNA
ASSEMBLY

FREQUENCY SELECTOR
CONTROL ASSEMBLY

RADOME

TRACKING CONTROL
ASSEMBLY

DIRECTIONAL COUPLER

COMPUTER
ASSEMBLY

20MM GUN (M-61)
(REF)

VOLTAGE
REGULATOR
ASSEMBLY

TURRET AND TAIL
ASSEMBLY

TURRET HINGE
LINE

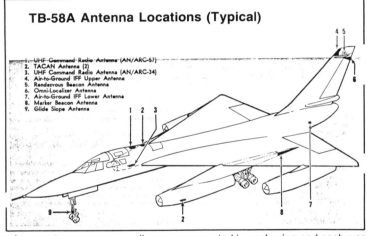

Chuck Hansen collection

The articulated tailcone was made up of tapered, concentric aluminum rings which were spring-loaded against each other to form a strong, but flexible aerodynamic shell.

Communications and Electronic Equipment

TYPE		DESIGNATION	USE	OPERATOR	RANGE (APPROX)	LOCATION OF CONTROLS
A/G IFF		AN/APX-47	IDENTIFICATION TO GROUND STATION	DSO	LINE OF SIGHT	DSO'S STATION
PI BEACON		AN/APN-136	INTER-AIRCRAFT POSITION INDICATION	NAVIGATOR	200 MILES	NAVIGATOR'S STATION
RV BEACON		AN/APN-135	TRANSMIT RANGE, BEARING, AND IDENTITY INFORMATION FOR RENDEZVOUS OPERATIONS	NAVIGATOR	200 MILES	NAVIGATOR'S STATION
INTERPHONE		AN/ARC-57	CREW COMMUNICATION	ALL CREW MEMBERS		EACH CREW STATION
UHF COMMAND RADIO			PLANE-TO-PLANE OR PLANE-TO-GROUND COMMUNICATION	ALL CREW MEMBERS	200 MILES AT 20,000 FEET OR LINE OF SIGHT	PILOT'S AND DSO'S STATION
UHF COMMAND RADIO		AN/ARC-34	PLANE-TO-PLANE OR PLANE-TO-GROUND COMMUNICATION	ALL CREW MEMBERS	200 MILES AT 20,000 FEET OR LINE OF SIGHT	DSO'S STATION
EMERGENCY COMMUNICATION SYSTEM		AN/ARC-74	PLANE-TO-PLANE OR PLANE-TO-GROUND COMMUNICATION IN EVENT OF COMMAND RADIO FAILURE	PILOT	200 MILES AT 20,000 FEET OR LINE OF SIGHT	PILOT'S STATION
LONG RANGE COMMUNICATION SYSTEM		AN/ARC-110	PLANE-TO-PLANE OR PLANE-TO-GROUND LONG RANGE COMMUNICATION	DSO	5000 MILES	DSO'S STATION
TACAN OR INSTRUMENT LANDING SYSTEM (ILS)	TACAN	AN/ARN-65	UHF NAVIGATION	PILOT AND NAVIGATOR	195 MILES	PILOT'S AND NAVIGATOR'S STATION
	LOCALIZER	AN/ARN-69	INSTRUMENT APPROACH	PILOT	45 MILES	PILOT'S STATION
	MARKER BEACON		LOCATION OF MARKER SIGNAL ON NAVIGATION BEAM	PILOT	LOCAL	PILOT'S STATION
	GLIDE SLOPE		GLIDE ANGLE INFORMATION FOR INSTRUMENT APPROACH	PILOT	25 MILES	PILOT'S STATION
AIR NAVIGATION RECORDING SYSTEM		AN/ASH-17	RECORDS NAVIGATION DATA	NAVIGATOR		NAVIGATOR'S STATION
BOMB DAMAGE EVALUATION SYSTEM		AN/ASH-15	BOMB DAMAGE EVALUATION	NAVIGATOR		NAVIGATOR'S STATION

B-58A Antenna Locations (Typical)

1. Long Range Communications Antenna
2. Search Radar Antenna
3. Radar Track Breaker (Right T2) Transmitting Antenna (3)
4. Radar Track Breaker (Right T2) Receiving Antenna (3)
5. UHF Command Radio Antenna (AN/ARC-57)
6. UHF Command Antenna (AN/ARC-34)
7. Radar Track Breaker (Left T4) Transmitting Antenna (2)
8. TACAN Antenna (2)
9. Radar Warning Forward Antenna (2)
10. Radio Altimeter Antenna
11. Radar Track Breaker (Aft T4) Receiving Antenna (2)
12. Radar Warning Aft Antenna
13. Air-to-Ground IFF Upper Antenna
14. Rendezvous Beacon Antenna
15. Position Indicating Beacon Antenna
16. Radar Track Breaker (Aft T4) Transmitting Antenna
17. Localizer Receiving Antenna
18. Radar Fire Control Antenna
19. Air-to-Ground IFF Lower Antenna
20. Doppler Transmitting Antenna
21. Doppler Receiving Antenna
22. Marker Beacon Antenna
23. Radar Track Breaker (Left T4) Receiving Antenna
24. Glide Slope Antenna

TB-58A Antenna Locations (Typical)

1. UHF Command Radio Antenna (AN/ARC-57)
2. TACAN Antenna (2)
3. UHF Command Radio Antenna (AN/ARC-34)
4. Air-to-Ground IFF Upper Antenna
5. Rendezvous Beacon Antenna
6. Omni-Localizer Antenna
7. Air-to-Ground IFF Lower Antenna
8. Marker Beacon Antenna
9. Glide Slope Antenna

fluid coolers, two cooler bypass valves, a reservoir bypass valve, two accumulators, two pressure switches, a pressure indicator, a quantity indicator, a spring-loaded surge damper, and two hydraulic shut-off valves. In addition, the utility system included landing gear, tail turret, and PCLA filters, a brake accumulator, and a brake hand pump. A 3,000 psi (2,500 psi normal) pneumatic system was provided to permit emergency landing gear extension and emergency braking.

Radar and Defensive Systems: Under the weapon system management concept pioneered by the B-58, Convair was responsible for the procurement and development of the defensive subsystems. Subsystem design had been initiated during the early stages of the development of the B-58 configuration. As each new configuration was evolved, studies were conducted to determine the feasibility and desirability of individual subsystems which might satisfy specific weapon system requirements. During these early stages, it soon became apparent that the desired operational characteristics of the aircraft imposed a completely new set of problems on subsystem design.

The Sylvania electronic countermeasures system was designed around the concept of deceptive techniques. These techniques were made available through special development of high power, wide band, receiving and transmitting tubes. In this subsystem it was further necessary to provide advanced electronic system techniques to take full advantage of the power and frequency coverage of the special tubes.

The defensive electronic countermeasures (DECM) system provided an early warning of the presence of other radar systems and was used to deceive, confuse, and jam them. The system consisted of the AN/ALR-12 radar warning equipment, the chaff dispensing system, and the AN/ALQ-16 radar track breaker equipment (this was the first production use of track-breaking where the range gate of the tracking radar was captured and led away from the attacker). The controls for these were located in the DSO's station.

The AN/ALR-12 radar warning equipment provided visual and aural warning while also automatically dispensing trackbreaking chaff upon receipt of a tracking radar signal. The systems consisted of a radar receiver composed of a decision circuit, a four channel video amplifier and four quadrant preamplifiers, four receiving antennas, one for each horizontal quadrant of antenna coverage, and necessary controls and indicators. It automatically received signals of any polarization on frequencies in the D, E, F, G, H, I, and J bands (1.0 to 12.50 gigahertz).

The AN/ALE-16 chaff dispensing system cluttered and confused enemy search and track radars. Various types of chaff could be dispensed either manually or automatically in varying amounts, sequences, and at various rates. System equipment consisted of a chaff dispenser controller, a chaff dispenser control panel, a sequencing control unit, an auxiliary chaff control panel, and ten chaff dispensers. There were five dispensers mounted in each wing and each was independently operated. Chaff packages were hydraulically forced into the dispensers and pneumatically dispensed through openings in the upper wing surfaces.

The AN/ALQ-16 radar track breaker was a repeater type jammer that generated deceptive radar jamming signals as a function of RF energy received from enemy tracking radars. When tracking radar signals were received the track breaker generated and transmitted deceptive angle and range information. The enemy range gate was captured by the transmitted signal at a minimum time delay with response to the true return echo. After range gate capture, angle and range deception information was then added to the transmitted signal. The angle deception information thus caused the tracking radar servo system to generate false antenna positioning information which in turn caused the tracking radar computer to compute false range information. The equipment for each track breaker system consisted of receiver-type antennas, transmitter type antennas, a receiver-locked oscillator, a driver amplifier, a power amplifier, and a solenoid power supply.

One of the most distinctive features of the B-58 was its tail gun system. This unit, born upon Convair's signing of an initial go-ahead contract on December 2, 1952, called for the development of a system to provide " . . . .lethal gunfire in the tail cone".

In June, 1953, the WADC approved General Electric's proposal for a defensive armament system but later had difficulty in satisfying GE's contract terms. Convair then agreed to seek new contractors while breaking the complete defensive system into its passive and lethal elements and acquiring each separately. Within a short time, Emerson had received a contract for a 30mm lethal unit.

By the end of 1953, the AF had decided also to study the possibility of using the A-3, or a jet-vane-controlled guided rocket developed as an independent missile task under Project MX-1601 (an integrated bomber defense study program calling for a rearward firing North American *Nasty* lightweight air-to-air missile that could change course by as much as 90° after launch), as an alternate. MX-1601 would later be cancelled with heavy emphasis once again being placed on the proposed Emerson gun system.

Early in 1954, the ARDC decided initially that the B-58 gun system proposed would use twin 30mm units (either T-182's or Navy Mk.4's), but this decision was rescinded in May, and because of weight and space limitations, a final choice of one T-171E2 (later, T-171E3) 20mm rotary cannon was made. Emerson completed a first-phase study of the B-58 system in September, 1954, and the first test system, less the turret, was assembled by April, 1955.

The program went through numerous evolutionary processes following prototyping and many firsts for an aircraft defensive gun system were eventually claimed. Among these were:

(1) First fully automatic fire control system with a tunable Ku band radar for production aircraft.
(2) First to use the *Black Warrior* automatic fire control concept in a bomber defense system. (This system was pioneered by C. S. Draper, Ph.D. of the MIT instrumentation laboratory. It contained a 3-axis inertially stabilized platform which formed a dummy gun line as a command signal for the T-171 cannon equipped turret.)
(3) First rearward firing system to include a solution to the anti-air fire control problem when mounted on a supersonic platform (the problem was that the muzzle velocity of the T-171 was lower than the forward motion of the aircraft at Mach 2—therefore the trajectory of the bullet was somewhat of a mystery due to the fact that it would, relative to the ground, be moving backwards as it departed the aircraft!).
(4) First system to include an integrally designed environmental control system for all packages including the ammunition storage container.
(5) First to use a declutching feeder concept to protect against high temperature cook off.
(6) First to use a solid state analog fire control computer for an airborne fire control system.
(7) First to use a hinged turret arrangement for ease of maintenance.

The total Emerson-built system consisted of an electronically directed and hydraulically driven tail turret and the MD-7 radar fire control system with controls at the DSO's station. The system was designed primarily for defense against gun and rocket-firing fighters flying aerodynamic lead pursuit courses. The radar was a Ku band, tunable unit with coverage in search of +/-50° azimuth, +42° and -48° elevation.

The tail turret was equipped with a General Electric manufactured T-171E-3 six-barrel 20mm rotary gun which was capable of firing up to 4,000 rounds per minute. The gun was aimed remotely by the fire control system and fired by means of a firing button. Ammunition, which was drawn from a box in the fuselage just forward of the turret, was pushed through a flexible chute to the gun by a booster motor. Tracing rates of this unit were ¼° to 60° per second. The firing zone was +/-30° azimuth and elevation and the lethal range was

1,500 yards. Total system weight was 1,852 lbs. including ammunition. A total of 1,200 rounds could be carried, this allowing a total of 30 seconds firing time at maximum rates.

The Emerson MD-7 radar fire control system consisted of a group of electronic packages which searched, acquired, and tracked targets (at ranges from 250 to 7,500 yards), computed lead and windage, and aimed the gun at the selected target. The radar antenna was located in a tail package located just above the turret at the vertical stabilizer root. A radar (automatic) fire control panel and a manual fire control panel were located in the DSO's station. Mach number and relative air density information were automatically supplied to the fire control system by the air data computer.

Navigation/Bomb Systems: The supersonic speed and high altitude capabilities of the B-58 precluded the use of conventional methods of navigation and bombing. Further complication was introduced by the resultant long trajectories of the bomb pod after release and the initial requirement for launching an air-to-surface missile. To provide adequate sighting resolution and the sighting range necessary because of the high speed of the aircraft and long bomb pod trajectories, a special purpose high frequency Ku band (16-17 kilo-megacycles) search radar was designed by Raytheon Corporation. The desirability of the high frequency for the search radar was proven in early 1955 through installation of prototype equipment in a B-36 (see Chapt. 6). The available signal/noise ratio from a Doppler radar at high altitude was proven in mid-1956 through special tests conducted at high altitude with prototype Doppler radar equipment. The resulting system provided an inherent overall accuracy on the order of ten times greater than that of previous navigation/bomb systems.

Other system features included a daytime-nighttime KS-39 astro-tracker (a device which automatically tracks a pre-set celestial body through employment of a photoelectric cell mounted in a telescope and so designed that an electric field is created which holds the observed body in the center of the telescopic field of view) designed by Kollsman Instruments to provide accurate heading information, and a completely integrated computing system which tied together the various elements of the over-all weapon system.

The navigation/bombing system was an integrated unit built by Sperry Gyroscope Corporation and designated AN/ASQ-42. In consisted of six major subsystems as follows:

Vertical Subsystem—contained the inertial elements, the aft fuselage mounted AN/APN-113 Doppler radar, and various computing elements; it provided the space references for the system and determined the ground velocity of the aircraft; it also calculated airspeed and wind;
Heading Subsystem—contained the astro-tracker, remote compass transmitter, and various computing elements; it determined the true heading of the aircraft, the angular relationship between the various coordinate systems used in the primary navigation system, and converted various signals from one set of coordinates to another; it also computed the direction and distance to the destination or target and supplied guidance signals to the autopilot;
Navigation Subsystem—contained electro-mechanical integrators and various other computing elements; it continuously computed the latitude and longitude of the aircraft in both true and transverse coordinates, and it generated data for other subsystems;
Sighting Subsystem—contained the nose-mounted search radar, radio altimeter, and various computing elements; it established the position of the aircraft relative to

a point on the earth and generated data for use in other subsystems;
Indicator Subsystem—contained controls and indicators used by the second station operator and the pilot in the operation of the primary navigation system; and it generated the pod release signal and performed various computing functions for other subsystems;
Malfunction Subsystem—contained various switches, testing equipment, and some substitute computing elements; it provided a means for detecting a malfunction in the primary navigation system, while also providing alternate methods for the successful completion of a mission. Integrated into this system was the stable table which was a gyro platform on which was mounted a pair of accelerometers, a doppler radar for input information, and a doppler-inertial mixer assembly.

The complete system could guide the aircraft over a great circle course to any desired destination without visual reference and with a minimum of radio-radar transmissions. The navigation mode was used during the entire mission except while on the actual bomb run. Automatic radar photography could be accomplished whenever the system search radar was not being used for navigator checks.

The primary navigation set (civil navigation aids were provided by Bendix; military navigation aids were provided by Motorola) was basically a Doppler inertial system, using the astro-tracker for a standard heading reference. The position of the aircraft, together with destination and intermediate fix points, was cranked into visual counters in terms of specific latitude and longitude. While the aircraft was enroute, the course and position were continuously computed by a precise dead reckoning operation. Periodic search radar sightings could be made over known fixes to check the accuracy of the dead reckoning computations, thus allowing for enroute adjustments. The aircraft attitude was sensed by the inertial elements while the altitude was obtained by a radio altimeter. All radiating equipment could be operated intermittent, if desired, or kept off for as long as five hours without seriously degrading system accuracy. Transverse coordinate operation was provided for accurate polar navigation, and a map comparator screen, located adjacent to the search radar scope, displayed radar map pictures for inflight comparison.

Another unique system was provided the navigator/bombardier in the form of an automatic data-handling system which recorded pertinent flight information for inflight reference and post-flight evaluation. Known as the inflight printer and designed by MelPar Corporation, this system received data from various sources throughout the aircraft and recorded the information on a paper tape. Such information such as time, present latitude and longitude, ground track and speed, and ''D'' values (differences between barometric and radar altitudes) were automatically recorded as often as once a minute or upon demand.

Miscellaneous Systems:

A Hamilton-Standard dual air-conditioning system supplied conditioned air for crew compartment heating, crew compartment cooling, crew compartment pressurization, pod heating, pod cooling, pod pressurization, electronic equipment cooling, landing gear tire cooling, windshield defogging, rain removal, inflation of the crew's canopy pressure seals, and fuel tank pressurization.

A small, eight-pound unit developed by Northrop and called a voice warning system was installed in the B-58 mid-way through its operational career. Mounted in the instrument panel of the third crew station, it contained a tape player (with 50' of magnetic tape) and related amplifiers and a series

Early MA-1 and MB-1 Options

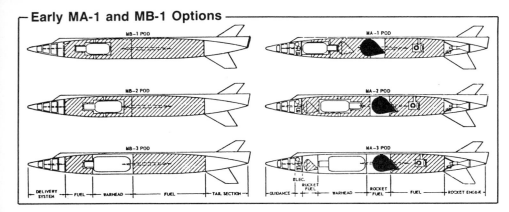

The first of many pod configurations completed for the B-58 program was the MA-1. This was a liquid-fuel, rocket-propelled unit equipped with a folding ventral fin, a pop-up dorsal fin, a fixed main wing surface, and a pitch-controlling movable canard.

The first pod drop took place in June, 1957, near Holloman AFB, NM, using this MB-1 free-fall bomb pod. The MB-1 was basically a finned, aerodynamic shell for a pair of fuel tanks and a variable yield thermonuclear bomb.

Two early test MB-1 pods are seen under construction in Convair's Ft. Worth, TX, facility. Most of the early pods were instrumented for trajectory and aerodynamic studies with the space normally occupied by a nuclear weapon filled with ballast.

of memory and logic circuits. A female voice (found through research to attract male attention more quickly than a male voice) would, in an emergency, inform the crew that an emergency situation was in progress. Every major event from engine fires to hydraulic system failures was included and a total of 20 emergencies could be programmed into the system from 50 inputs.

Two complete pitot-static systems, a primary and a secondary, supplied the pitot and static pressures necessary to operate various instruments and system components. An air data system provided aerodynamic intelligence to various control systems. It consisted basically of an electromechanical air data computer which processed raw data from the pitot-static probe and a temperature sensor probe located on the left side of the fuselage above the nose wheel well. This data was then fed to various flight control systems, the autopilot, the spike positioning units, the air conditioning system, the TACAN system, the pilot's Mach indicator, the primary navigation system, the bombing system, the air navigation data recorder, the fire control system, and the landing gear warning system.

The air conditioning system utilized bleed air from the 17th stage compressor discharge of the inboard engines. This air serviced the needs of the crew compartments, the electronic equipment, heating, pressurization, ventilation, windshield rain removal, defogging, and fuel tank pressurization. In a related system, bleed air from each engine served to accomplish anti-icing requirements on the engine inlet and inlet spike.

The Magnavox communication system provided a means of crew intercommunication, plus normal and emergency air-to-air and air-to-ground communication. The complete system was composed of an interphone and a UHF command radio system (AN/ARC-57), a secondary UHF command radio system (AN/ARC-34), an emergency communication system (AN/ARC-74), and a long range communication system (LRC). The communication system was equipped with ''mayday'' capability which provided a means of expediting communication in the event of an emergency.

An air-to-ground AN/APX-47 IFF (Identification Friend or Foe) system provided the aircraft with an automatic means of selective identification to ground, shipboard, or airborne IFF recognition installations operating in the L-band frequency range.

Other electronic element designators included an AN/ARN-69 TACAN; a AN/ARN-50 VHF nav. system; and AN/APN-136 PI beacon; and an AN/APN-135 RV beacon.

Aircraft lighting equipment was divided into two groups: exterior lighting and interior lighting. The exterior group included landing lights, taxi lights, navigation lights, anti-collision lights, air refueling slipway lights, and a light for ground refueling. The interior group consisted of various instrument, panel, flood, and tunnel area lights necessary to provide adequate lighting for the crew compartments.

Each crew station was provided with food storage compartments, a portable 1½ quart relief container, ash trays, and thermal curtains. The latter were silver coated and silicon treated.

The AN/ASH-15 IBDA (Indirect Bomb Damage Assessment) system was used for the free-fall bomb pod to provide continuous pod position data to the aircraft after pod release. This data was recorded on an inflight recorder in the aircraft. At the time of warhead detonation, a bhang-meter (photoelectric cell) and a camera in the aircraft would record the light intensity of the burst and the burst location. From the data recorded it would have been possible to determine yield, pressure altitude of the burst, pod-to-aircraft range at the time of the burst, and azimuth from aircraft to ground zero.

Pods and Bombs: Many different pod configurations were conceived for the B-58 during the course of its test and production life, though only a few actually reached the hardware stage. What follows is a listing of all known pods, pod configurations, and pod studies:

MA-1C—This was one of the 4 original pod configurations studied for the B-58 and it was known initially as the controlled bomb pod. It was to be a rocket-propelled version of the MB-1, permitting the B-58 standoff launch capability. Expected range of the 27,108 lb. unit was approximately 160 miles. For the three warheads studied for the pod, maximum altitude during the flight to target was expected to be up to 108,000' at a speed of Mach 4. A Sperry guidance system was to control the pod during its flight to target. Before launching, the guidance system determined the pod's present position and computed the desired heading. After launching, it controlled the operation of the pod's 15,000 lb. th. JP-4 and RFNA (red fuming nitric acid) fueled Bell Aerospace LR81-BA-1 rocket engine. It also ordered the pitch angle for the climb and glide and dive angles to the target.

Total powered flight time was 65 seconds. The pod was designed to climb at a 20° angle, glide at 7°, and dive to the target at 70°. Throughout the flight the guidance system corrected the heading to keep the pod on course. The control system commanded the pod's maneuvers and provided stability.

Pod power came from a self contained PGU (power generating unit) which was located in a compartment just ahead of the warhead compartment. It provided electrical, hydraulic, and pneumatic power to the pod after inflight launching. Power was obtained from a chemically driven gas turbine that operated a 5 KVA, 400-cycle alternator to power the electronic equipment, a hydraulic pump to operate the control surfaces, and a blower to cool the pod components after pod launching.

The pod guidance and control system mission options included: variable launch altitude (35,000' to 60,000'); variable release radius (10 to 160 miles); variable off-course release (as much as 30°); variable warhead size; jam proof guidance (a self-contained inertial guidance unit); and invulnerability to known countermeasures and intercept techniques.

MB-1C—This was the standard free-falling unit utilized by the B-58 throughout its early flight test program and during its first few years of operational service. It was 57' long with a diameter of approximately 5'. Empty weight was 2,500 lbs. without the standard W39Y1-1 warhead or ballast (the latter was required in place of the warhead in order to meet B-58 inflight and static ground condition cg requirements), and 8,550 lbs. with. Maximum weight when fully fueled and with a warhead was 36,087 lbs.

The pod was attached to the aircraft by three pneumatically actuated hooks (one forward and two aft) which were mounted to the pod. The pod consisted of an equipment bay, a forward fuel tank and munitions bay, an aft fuel tank, a tail cone and fins, and a pylon. The fins were mounted at 45° from the horizontal center line of the pod and were slightly offset to give the pod a slow rotation during its trajectory. The pod incorporated a 28-volt nicad battery and four barometric switches for arming and fuzing the warhead. A pitot tube served as

A test MB-1 pod, painted red, black, and white for photographic reference and visual documentation purposes, is hooked to B-58A, 55-663, during pod drop tests at Kirtland AFB, NM. Most of the early test pods contained transmitters for relaying data back to monitoring stations.

A special ground transport trailer was developed specifically for the MB-1 pod. This unit was relatively easy to maneuver underneath a B-58 and was provided with independent steering and hydraulic pod lifting systems.

With the Mk.43 nuclear weapon pylons in place under the B-58's wing root sections, MB-1 pod fin tip clearances were marginal. This problem was eliminated with the introduction of the TCP.

Rare photograph of the virtually unknown MC-1 dedicated photo reconnaissance pod. This pod was cancelled before the first could be flown.

Optical sensor payloads of the MC-1 pod were variable, depending on mission requirements. This model of the MC-1 camera compartment (the rest of the pod was occupied by fuel) illustrates one configuration providing cameras with focal lengths up to 36''.

107

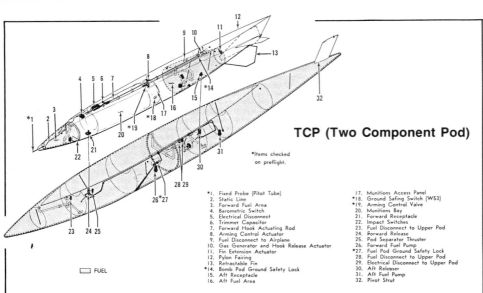

TCP (Two Component Pod)

*Items checked on preflight.

*1. Fixed Probe (Pitot Tube)
2. Static Line
3. Forward Fuel Area
4. Barometric Switch
5. Electrical Disconnect
6. Trimmer Capacitor
7. Forward Hook Actuating Rod
8. Arming Control Actuator
9. Fuel Disconnect to Airplane
10. Gas Generator and Hook Release Actuator
11. Fin Extension Actuator
12. Pylon Fairing
13. Retractable Fin
*14. Bomb Pod Ground Safety Lock
15. Aft Receptacle
16. Aft Fuel Area
17. Munitions Access Panel
*18. Ground Safing Switch (W53)
*19. Arming Control Valve
20. Munitions Bay
21. Forward Receptacle
22. Impact Switches
23. Fuel Disconnect to Upper Pod
24. Forward Release
25. Pod Separator Thruster
26. Forward Fuel Pump
*27. Fuel Pod Ground Safety Lock
28. Fuel Disconnect to Upper Pod
29. Electrical Disconnect to Upper Pod
30. Aft Releaser
31. Aft Fuel Pump
32. Pivot Strut

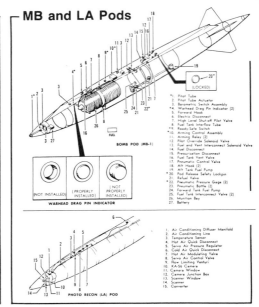

MB and LA Pods

BOMB POD (MB-1)

WARHEAD DRAG PIN INDICATOR

[NOT INSTALLED] [PROPERLY INSTALLED] [NOT PROPERLY INSTALLED]

1. Pitot Tube
2. Pitot Tube Actuator
3. Barometric Switch Assembly
*4. Warhead Drag Pin Indicator (2)
5. Forward Hook
6. Electric Disconnect
7. High Level Shut-off Pilot Valve
8. Fuel Line Interflow Tube
*9. Ready-Safe Switch
*10. Arming Control Assembly
11. Arming Relay (2)
12. Pilot Override Solenoid Valve
13. Fuel and Vent Interconnect Solenoid Valve
14. Fuel Disconnect
15. Pressurization Disconnect
16. Fuel Tank Vent Valve
17. Pneumatic Control Valve
18. Aft Hook (2)
19. Aft Tank Fuel Pump
*20. Pod Release Safety Lockpin
21. Refuel Valve
*22. Pneumatic Pressure Gage (2)
23. Pneumatic Bottle (2)
24. Forward Tank Fuel Pump
25. Fuel Tank Interconnect Valve (2)
26. Munition Bay
27. Battery

PHOTO RECON (LA) POD

1. Air Conditioning Diffuser Manifold
2. Air Conditioning Line
3. Temperature Sensor
4. Hot Air Quick Disconnect
5. Servo Air Pressure Regulator
6. Cold Air Quick Disconnect
7. Hot Air Modulating Valve
8. Servo Air Control Valve
9. Flow Limiting Venturi
10. KA-56 Camera
11. Camera Window
12. Camera Junction Box
13. Scanner Window
14. Scanner
15. Converter

The TCP consisted of a small bomb/fuel pod (shown) fitted into a larger fuel-only pod. The latter could be jettisoned when its fuel was depleted, thus lowering the B-58's weight and aerodynamic drag.

The upper component of the TCP had a retractable ventral fin which was deployed automatically upon pod release. The nuclear warhead was carried in a bay just ahead of the large black vertical stripe.

"Super Sue", B-58A, 58-1007, is seen with both standard pod types carried by the "Hustler"—the TCP (in the foreground), and the MB-1 (attached to the aircraft). Both pods remained in the active inventory until the end of the B-58 program, though the TCP, due to its several advantages, was much the preferred pod to carry. The MA-1, however, was capable of accommodating a significantly larger warhead.

An advanced TCP was built but apparently never flown. This unit, thought to have been developed for the still-borne B-58B, was several feet longer than its production predecessor, thus accommodating more fuel.

The lower component of the little-known stretched TCP. The test specimen shown was manufactured using parts from a stock test TCP that was not used during the TCP drop program.

In order to assure the clean release of the lower component of the TCP, a kicker was attached to the top of the single vertical fin. This served as a fulcrom point for the pod as it fell from the aircraft.

The upper component of the TCP faired cleanly into the lower component. The small fins of the upper component had ample clearance without being modified to accommodate lower component dimensional requirements.

A stagnant flow problem occurred between the Mk.43 nuclear weapon pylons and the fuselage, requiring vortex generators to be added.

The Mk.43 nuclear weapon pylons were mounted at the wing root/fuselage interface point. Aerodynamically clean and having little frontal area, they created only a modest drag problem throughout the B-58's performance envelope. The addition of the Mk.43's, however, did increase drag considerably.

a pressure source for the arming and fuzing switches and could be extended before pod release by means of a switch on the weapon lock and arm panel. Fuel and fuel pressurization disconnnects engaged matching components on the aircraft when the pod was attached. All disconnects released and closed instantly when the pod was released.

As noted in Chapt. 7, a number of MB-1 pods were modified to incorporate a Fairchild KA-56 camera and associated systems in a forward compartment for use as low-altitude, high-resolution reconnaissance systems. When so modified, the MB-1 was redesignated LA-1. The system consisted of the camera and magazine, a scanner and converter, a pod camera control panel, and an air conditioning and electrical system. The KA-56 was a panoramic type camera capable of horizon-to-horizon scanning with automatic exposure control and image motion compensation. The camera magazine was automatically driven by the camera drive mechanism. The magazine held up to 1,000' of film and could be removed from the pod for loading. The scanner and converter furnished data to the camera for image motion control. The pod camera control panel was located at the navigator's station and replaced the weapon monitor and release panel when the photo recon pod was installed.

Another little-known MB-1C pod modification was undertaken in 1961 when pod B-127 was modified by Convair for special downward ejection seat tests. These tests explored the capabilities of both the B-58 and North American XB-70 encapsulated ejection seats. Nicknamed the *Guppy Pod*, the unit had a completely reconfigured weapon bay that had the accouterments necessary to accommodate the test ejection seats. There was also a special ventral fairing around the ventral opening which protruded down some 18'' from the pod. This unit was eventually delivered to Edwards AFB, CA where in mid-June, 1961, it was successfully utilized in the first of many ejection seat tests.

One of the lesser known reasons the MB-1 pod had a relatively short operational service career was a long term and apparently incurable problem with fuel leakage into the weapon bay. Lead tape used to line the weapon bay and protect the warhead from fuel leaks proved ineffective in its role. Several years of unsuccessful tape application and damage to several warheads helped hurry the introduction of the TCP.

A versatile positioning trailer was developed for the

MB-1 and later used in slightly modified form for the TCP. This unit had four-wheel steering, a rail system for pod positioning, and a hydraulic lift, pitch, yaw, roll, forward and aft, and lateral movement system.

TCP—The "two component pod", or TCP, maintained the same general profile of the older MB pod, and utilized the same attachment points, but was capable of retaining the warhead unit while discarding the lower fuel cell unit when it was empty. The TCP was actually two pods, with one nestled in the other. The upper component, or BLU 2/B-1 bomb pod, contained two fuel tanks, one forward and one aft of the warhead cavity, a munitions bay, a tail cone, a parachute retardation system, a pylon, and three fins. Two of the fins were mounted to the sides of the pod at 30° to and above the pod horizontal centerline. The third (lower) fin was located on the pod lower vertical centerline and was retracted within the upper pod when the lower pod was attached. Overall length of the upper component was 35' and maximum diameter was 3'6''. Gross weight with maximum fuel and a Mk.53 warhead was 11,970 lbs. Without fuel, the dry weight, including a Mk.53 warhead or ballast, was 7,700 lbs.

The lower component, or BLU 2/B-2 fuel pod, was also divided into two tanks separated by a common bulkhead. The forward fuel tanks in the upper and lower components were connected by an intervent line and a quick disconnect coupling which allowed them to operate as a single tank. When either or both the forward and aft tanks were selected open during aerial refueling, the selected tank or tanks would fill automatically to the high level shutoff.

The fuel pod was carried beneath the upper pod by one forward and one aft releaser. A pivot strut was mounted on the aft end of the pod to facilitate proper separation between lower pod and upper. Lower pod dimensions included an over-all length of 54'0'' and a maximum diameter of 5'0''. Gross weight in fully loaded condition was 26,000 lbs. Empty weight was 1,900 lbs.

The fuel pod was expendable and was released during flight after all fuel in both the upper and lower components was consumed. The bomb pod remained with the aircraft for release during the delivery run.

During the delivery run to the target, there were several major functions of separation performed by gas pressure generated from explosive cartridges. The first separation was that of the lower component from the upper. Under

certain flight attitudes and conditions, the lower component would continue to fly because of the negative pressure between it and the upper component. Provisions were included that would gently but firmly push the lower component downward and away from the upper component. A "pogo stick" (connecting strut) was also provided the lower pod for preventing a backward or upward lurch until it was completely free of the aircraft.

The second separation was the release of the bomb pod. This was accomplished without throwing the pod into an undesirable separation attitude, thereby resulting in greater target-hitting accuracy. The third separation occurred after the upper component bomb pod became a free body approaching its target. At the precise moment and requiring less than a 60th of a second to accomplish, it cut itself in half and discarded everything that was no longer needed.

MC-1—Fairchild Camera and Instrument Company received a letter contract on May 27, 1953, to do Phase I studies on a dedicated photo reconnaissance pod for the B-58. Fairchild studied both airborne equipment (cameras, mounts, control systems, control panels, view finders, etc.) and ground processing equipment. Fairchild, in turn, let contracts to Aeroflex for mounts, Nordon for the viewfinder, Boston University for the optics studies, Columbia University for the computer techniques, and Kodak for the ground processing equipment.

The Phase I studies were completed in March, 1954, and a system specification was submitted by Convair to the AF for approval. The AF requested certain revisions to the specification on July 20, 1954. After subsequent revisions, the AF gave approval to the photo recon system spec on December 3, 1954. Phase I studies determined that the necessary time indexing film plus the weight and space limitation prohibited utilization of standard AF cameras and controls. In the process of repackaging and modification to make compatible with the overall weapon system considerable weight saving and some overall improvement over then extant AF equipment was accomplished. The weight of B-58 recce system cameras, for instance, was 65% that of comparable AF cameras.

Utilization of the standard MB-1C pod was determined to be feasible and the only actual airframe modification required was the removal of a package and bomb system panel section in the second crew station and its replace-

Mk.43 Thermonuclear Weapon

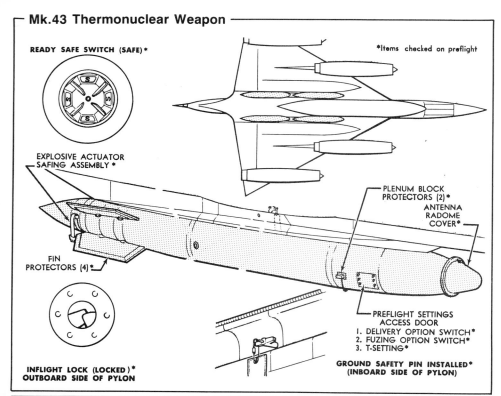

READY SAFE SWITCH (SAFE) *

*Items checked on preflight

EXPLOSIVE ACTUATOR SAFING ASSEMBLY *

PLENUM BLOCK PROTECTORS (2) *

ANTENNA RADOME COVER *

FIN PROTECTORS (4) *

PREFLIGHT SETTINGS ACCESS DOOR
1. DELIVERY OPTION SWITCH *
2. FUZING OPTION SWITCH *
3. T-SETTING *

INFLIGHT LOCK (LOCKED) *
OUTBOARD SIDE OF PYLON

GROUND SAFETY PIN INSTALLED *
(INBOARD SIDE OF PYLON)

G.D.

Four practice Mk.43 thermonuclear weapons are seen suspended from wing pylons under 59-2456 during a test flight out of Carswell AFB. The aircraft is also carrying a TCP. Few problems were encountered while dropping the Mk.43 weapons throughout the B-58's speed envelope.

G.D.

The Mk.43's fit snugly under the wing root of the B-58 and were essentially parallel to the wing chord centerline. The Mk.43 was a variable, or adjustable yield weapon. Its burst characteristics could be controlled to accommodate the destructive force required to eliminate any given target.

ment with the appropriate photo navigation package and panel.

The MC-1 pod recce equipment package consisted of the following: a multi-camera system consisting of three 36'' focal length 9'' x 18'' format cameras (vertical and side obliques) mounted in a stabilized mount; a tri-camera system consisting of three 6'' focal length 9'' x 9'' format cameras with the vertical in a stabilized mount and the side obliques in non-stabilized mounts; one 3'' focal length 2¼'' x 2¼'' format forward oblique camera in an isolation-adapter mounting; a camera control system; a nose-mounted television view finder; an operator's control unit; a fan of five 3'' focal length cameras; a Melpar recording system; a Sperry navigation system; and a Raytheon search radar scope camera. Total sensor system weight was 998 lbs.

This equipment could be carried in either of two configurations: a high-low altitude configuration consisting of the first 3 listed camera groups, or a low-altitude configuration having the six 3'' focal length cameras, the 6'' vertical camera, the control system, the view finder, and the operator's panel.

The time index recording system worked in conjunction with the aircraft central recording system. This unit made it possible to print all correlation data on each negative. This included speed, altitude, earth coordinates, weather conditions, and a time index.

Complementing the recce pod and its associated optical sensors were various ground processing units, several printers, and an automatic print chopper—all available to handle the various film formats.

In early July, 1955, because of funding limitations, the reconnaissance pod and its various systems were cancelled. The program was reinstated in September, 1955, however, when funding was again appropriated, but it eventually died a permanent death in early 1958, following the completion of a single pod. The pod was never flown under a B-58, though aircraft 55-671 had been scheduled as the testbed aircraft.

MD-1—Convair, in early 1952, at the request and with the funding support of the AF, moved ahead with a program to design and build an electronic reconnaissance pod. This unit, which utilized many of the shell components of the standard MB-1 free-fall bomb pod, was equipped with electromagnetic energy sensors developed by Melpar that covered a wide selection of frequencies and bandwidths and could record gathered information for later detailed examination.

The basic pod mission was to analyze and record the nature, direction, and time of intercept of all enemy radar signals reaching the aircraft. A photographic system permitted reference imagery to be made of all questionable radar pulses to prevent the recording of erroneous data.

At the time of each analysis, a recorder which was also located in the pod recorded navigational and weather data and Greenwich time. The recorder also printed a log of navigational data that could be used by the crew for manual navigation if the primary navigation system failed.

After an ELINT mission a ground system was expected to rapidly process the gathered data and present it in printed form ready for use.

Only one pod was eventually completed to fulfill the requirements of this contract, but it was never flight tested. Economic constraints and the fact that the ELINT mission was being adequately accommodated by ERB-47H's and a variety of other ELINT aircraft, killed the project before program execution.

CW (Chemical Warefare) Pod—Information concerning this unit remains virtually non-existant, but it is thought to have been a dedicated chemical warfare pod configuration. This unit would have carried a poisonous gas container in place of the more conventional nuclear warhead configuration.

Mk.43 Thermonuclear Weapon—As related in Chapt. 6, the B-58 was configured, mid-way through its operational career, to carry four conventional thermonuclear weapons on external pylons which were mounted under the wing between the fuselage and the main landing gear. Two weapons were carried on either side of the fuselage in tandem. Each weapon was attached to a rack by cartridge actuated hooks (one forward and one aft) which latched on lugs attached to the top of the weapon. The racks contained the release mechanism and electrical disconnects for weapon monitoring and were enclosed in the streamlined pylons.

The main components of the Mk.43 were a jettisonable nose cone which covered the contact spike, a center section subassembly which housed the warhead, and a tail section which housed the retardation parachute and supported the four tail fins. An inspection window located on the lower right side of the center section allowed visual check of the ready safe switch. The Mk.43 weighed approximately 2,100 lbs., had a length of 12', a maximum diameter of 1.5', and a variable yield of up to 1 megaton.

"Quick Check"—See Chapt. 8
AN/APQ-69—See Chapt. 8
ALBM—See Chapt. 8

B-58A/TB-58A Specifications:

Overall wingspan	56'9.90''
Overall length	96'9.383''
Overall height	
(at vertical fin tip)	29'11.061''
Wing root chord	651.073''
Wing tip chord	0'' change
Wing mean aerodynamic chord	434.049''
Wing airfoil section designation	
Root	NACA 0003.46-64.069
Span station 56.5	NACA 0004.08-63
Tip	0
Wing angle of incidence	3°
Wing angle of sweepback	
Leading edge	60°
Trailing edge	-10°
Wing angle of dihedral	
(outboard of station 56.5)	2° 13 min. 46 sec.
Wing aspect ratio	2.096
Wing area (less elevons)	1,364.69 sq.'
Elevon area (total)	177.84 sq.'
Elevon span	15'
Vertical fin height	14'6''
Vertical fin chord (max. at root)	200''
Vertical fin tip chord	64.828''
Vertical fin airfoil section	NACA 005-64
Vertical fin angle of	
sweepback(l.e.)	52°
Vertical fin angle of	
sweepback(t.e.)	63° 17 min. 36 sec.
Vertical fin area (less rudder)	120 sq.'
Rudder tip chord	2'8''
Rudder root chord	4'11''
Rudder area (total)	40 sq.'
Fuselage maximum width	
(F.S. 378.50)	64.21''
Fuselage maximum height	
(F.S. 345.46)	77.76''
Fuselage overall length	91'8.19''
Outboard engine nacelle	
center to fuselage centerline	21'7''
Inboard engine nacelle	
center to fuselage centerline	12'1''
Main gear track	40'8''
Main gear tread	13'4''
Height of pilot's canopy	
above ground	13'9''
Height of navigator/bombardier	
canopy above ground	13'3''
Height of DSO canopy	
above ground	13'2''
Pilot's canopy width	42.08''
Pilot's canopy length	63.97''
Nav/Bomb canopy width	43.13''
Nav/Bomb canopy length	46.927''
DSO canopy width	42.16''
DSO canopy length	44.16''
B-58A Empty weight (w/o pod)	55,560 lbs.
B-58A Basic weight (w/o pod)	57,916 lbs.
TB-58A Empty weight (w/o pod)	52,400 lbs.
B-58A Empty weight (w/MB-1C)	64,115 lbs.
B-58A Basic weight (w/MB-1C)	66,471 lbs.
B-58A Maximum taxi weight	164,000 lbs.
TB-58A Maximum taxi weight	147,000 lbs.
B-58A Maximum gross weight	
(in flight)	176,890 lbs.
TB-58A Maximum gross weight	
(in flight)	158,000 lbs.
B-58A landing weight	63,100 lbs.

B-58A Performance:

Maximum speed below 25,000'	Mach .91
Maximum speed @ 40,000'	Mach 2
	(or 600 knots IAS)
Structural limit speed	Mach 2.2
(momentary operation only)	(650/660 knots)
Cruise speed	531 knots
Landing ground roll	2,615' (2,525'
(@ 63,100 lbs.)	w/drag chute)
Takeoff ground run at SL	
(@ 160,000 lbs.)	7,850'
Max. rate of climb at SL	38,650' per min.
Time to 30,000'	11.2 min.
Normal cruise altitude	38,450'
Target area altitude	55,900'
Combat ceiling	63,400'
Ferry range	4,100 n. mi.

G.D.

A special hydraulic lift attachment was developed to accommodate the height requirements for mounting a Mk.43 weapon under a B-58. Weighing just over a ton, the Mk.43 was not an easy weapon to move.

G.D.

Special camera pods were used to photograph everything from landing gear dynamics during landing and takeoff, to pod drops and ejection seat tests. Camera pod structural requirements were extraordinary due to their environment and the speed capabilities of the B-58.

G.D.

Various types of cameras could be accommodated internally. The majority of the B-58 tests dictated the need for high-speed motion picture photography, but periodically, still cameras were utilized to capture specific items. The camera pods were most often seen mounted on the engine nacelles.

For high altitude test work and prior to the introduction of the encapsulated ejection seat, the MC-2/3 high altitude suit was worn by crews for protection in the low pressure, minimal oxygen environment.

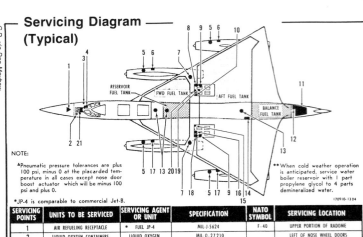

Servicing Diagram (Typical)

NOTE:

▲Pneumatic pressure tolerances are plus 100 psi, minus 0 at the placarded temperature in all cases except nose door boost actuator which will be minus 100 psi and plus 0.

*JP-4 is comparable to commercial Jet-B.

**When cold weather operation is anticipated, service water boiler reservoir with 1 part propylene glycol to 4 parts demineralized water.

170910-1304

SERVICING POINTS	UNITS TO BE SERVICED	SERVICING AGENT OR UNIT	SPECIFICATION	NATO SYMBOL	SERVICING LOCATION
1	AIR REFUELING RECEPTACLE	＊ FUEL JP-4	MIL-J-5624	F-40	UPPER PORTION OF RADOME
2	LIQUID OXYGEN CONTAINERS	LIQUID OXYGEN	MIL-O-27210		LEFT OF NOSE WHEEL DOORS
3	IFR ACCUMULATOR	▲ DRY NITROGEN	MIL-N-6011, GRADE A, TYPE I OR II		NOSE WHEEL WELL
4	FUEL TANKS (SINGLE-POINT GROUND REFUELING)	＊ FUEL JP-4	MIL-J-5624	F-40	NOSE WHEEL WELL
5	ENGINE OIL TANKS (4)	SYNTHETIC OIL	MIL-L-7808	O-148	RIGHT SIDE NACELLE (EA ENG)
6	PRIMARY HYDRAULIC SYSTEM AND RESERVOIR	HYDRAULIC FLUID	MIL-H-8446		RIGHT SIDE NACELLE NO. 3 OR NO. 4 ENGINE
7	AIR CONDITIONING TURBINE SUMP (2)	SYNTHETIC OIL	MIL-L-7808 FILTERED TO 10 MICRONS OR LESS	O-148	LOWER WING SURFACE, INBOARD OF EACH INBOARD PYLON
8	PRIMARY HYDRAULIC RESERVOIR	HYDRAULIC FLUID	MIL-H-8446		RIGHT MAIN WHEEL WELL
9	WATER BOILER RESERVOIR (2)	**DEMINERALIZED WATER	MIL-D-4024		MAIN WHEEL WELLS
10	CANOPY PNEUMATIC RESERVOIR	▲ DRY NITROGEN	MIL-N-6011, GRADE A, TYPE I OR II		RIGHT MAIN WHEEL WELL
11	DRAG CHUTE COMPARTMENT	DRAG CHUTE PACK	CONVAIR SPEC FZC-4-355		BOTTOM AFT FUSELAGE
12	DRAG CHUTE PNEUMATIC RESERVOIR	▲ DRY NITROGEN	MIL-N-6011, GRADE A, TYPE I OR II		FORWARD OF DRAG CHUTE COMPARTMENT
13	FUEL TANKS (INDIVIDUAL TANK GRAVITY REFUELING (3))	＊ FUEL JP-4	MIL-J-5624	F-40	TOP FUSELAGE
14	FLIGHT CONTROL ACCUMULATOR (4)	▲ DRY NITROGEN	MIL-N-6011, GRADE A, TYPE I OR II		LOWER AFT FUSELAGE, LEFT SIDE
15	CHAFF DISPENSER ACCUMULATOR	▲ DRY NITROGEN	MIL-N-6011, GRADE A, TYPE I OR II		LEFT MAIN WHEEL WELL
16	BRAKE ACCUMULATOR EMERGENCY BRAKE & GEAR PNEUMATIC RESERVOIRS	▲ DRY NITROGEN	MIL-N-6011, GRADE A, TYPE I OR II		LEFT MAIN WHEEL WELL
17	UTILITY HYDRAULIC SYSTEM AND RESERVOIR	HYDRAULIC FLUID	MIL-H-8446		RIGHT SIDE NACELLE NO. 1 OR NO. 2 ENGINE
18	UTILITY HYDRAULIC RESERVOIR	HYDRAULIC FLUID	MIL-H-8446		LEFT MAIN WHEEL WELL
19	PRIMARY HYDRAULIC SYSTEM ACCUMULATOR	▲ DRY NITROGEN	MIL-N-6011, GRADE A, TYPE I OR II		RIGHT MAIN WHEEL WELL
20	ESCAPE CAPSULE EMERGENCY PRESSURIZATION SYSTEM	MC-1A AIR COMPRESSOR	COMPRESSED DRY AIR		RIGHT MAIN WHEEL WELL
21	NOSE DOOR BOOST ACTUATOR	▲ DRY NITROGEN	MIL-N-6011, GRADE A, TYPE I OR II		NOSE WHEEL DOORS

Flight test crews wore conventional flying gear and a back-pack type parachute. The SACseat was designed to accommodate this chute and to function based on its semi-manual actuation.

Generally, crews found the B-58's accommodations slightly confining, but comfortable. The SACseat was designed for maximum comfort during long missions.

Chapt. 10:
Powerplants, Fuel Systems, and Fuels

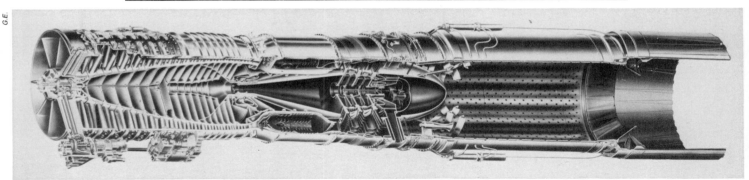

The General Electric J79-GE-5 turbojet engine was one of the world's most advanced and powerful production jet engines at the time of its debut as the powerplant for the production B-58A. Nominally rated at 15,600 lbs. th. at sea level, it eventually proved highly reliable and very much the ideal powerplant for Convair's awesome "Hustler".

Propulsion studies to define the powerplant characteristics best suited to airframe configuration and mission requirements were undertaken by Convair early in the B-58 program. Engines in both operational and developmental status were examined. As none of the engines examined appeared capable of meeting the basic performance parameters outlined for the new bomber, General Electric agreed to create an engine using the company's new and advanced J73 as a basis. The resulting engine, the J73-X24A, was eventually redesignated J79 and declared the primary propulsion unit for the B-58. Innovations brought together for the first time in one engine with the J79 included variable stators, modulated afterburner, and a variable ejector nozzle.

Following selection of the engine by Convair, an intensive development program was initiated to assure meeting the design objectives. Wind tunnel testing of the inlet and nozzle configuration was performed. General Electric ran tests on all engine components before releasing the designs for manufacture. General Electric then conducted complete engine development tests at its Evendale facility to refine the design. The major tests to assure proper design and operation in flight were conducted at the Arnold Engineering Development Center in Tullahoma, TN, and at the NACA Lewis Flight Propulsion Laboratory in Cleveland, OH. A complete nacelle, incorporating an early J79 and inlet control system, was tested supersonically by the NACA. Further cowled tests were run at AEDC to check the complete flight spectrum and all engine subsystems. These tests saved many hours of flight time and assured proper matching of the engine and installation.

The first eight B-58's completed and delivered were equipped with first-generation General Electric YJ79-GE-1 engines nominally rated at 14,350 lbs. th. in maximum afterburner, and 9,300 lbs. th. at Military power. These were basically experimental engines and were not capable of sustained operations with any regularity. Major modifications were required to permit continuation of the B-58 flight test program, and it was not until the arrival of the J79-GE-5 that the engine could be depended upon to perform as promised.

In its operational form, the B-58A and TB-58A were both powered by four General Electric J79-GE-5A or J79-GE-5B engines. The approximate thrust rating for each engine at standard sea level static conditions was 15,600 lbs. at 7,460 rpm with maximum afterburner, 10,300 lbs. at 7,460 rpm at Military power, and 9,700 lbs. at 7,460 rpm at normal power.

The J79-GE-5A/5B was an axial-flow, afterburner-equipped turbojet engine consisting of a 17-stage compressor, 10 can-annular-type combustion chambers, a three-stage turbine, an afterburner, and a variable exhaust nozzle. Air entering the compressor section of the engine was automatically controlled by variable positioning inlet guide vanes which acted as an inlet air metering device.

The first six stages of the 4 piece, steel case compressor were equipped with six rows of variable positioning steel stator vanes which were positioned so that at a particular engine speed and compressor inlet temperature the inlet air struck the vanes at the most effective angle of attack. There were 11 rows of fixed steel blades. The inlet guide vanes and variable stator vanes were connected externally and rotated in unison to control compressor pressure ratio and maintain an adequate stall margin under all operating conditions.

The rotor comprised 17 discs of Timken alloy steel, with steel blades, bolted to flanged stub shafts. The compressor and turbine, which were splined together, were supported by three bearings and rotated as a single unit. The compressor section pressure ratio was approximately 12 to 1 and the air mass flow was 180 lbs./sec. at 7,460 rpm.

The cannular combustors were two-piece units with a steel outer shell and ten interconnected flame tubes of Incoloy "T" alloy. There were ten duplex type fuel burners around the diffuser section, with downstream injection.

The turbine was of the 3-stage axial flow type. It had a two-piece steel casing with hollow nozzle vanes and solid stator blades. The turbine wheels had solid blades, and were flange-bolted to the conical drive shaft.

The afterburner was of the integral close-coupled type. The fuel spray bars were at the front end, with downstream injection. The fully variable exhaust nozzle had 24 sectional shutters and 4 hydraulic actuators.

The fuel pump was a single Pesco dual fuel unit with an 850 psi Hamilton Standard or Woodward main flow control.

The exhaust nozzle functioned as a variable restriction through which gases leaving the engine were accelerated to convert as much as possible of their pressure and temperature to velocity for thrust.

Each engine was provided with a fuel control system (which consisted of two separate systems—one for engine fuel control and one for afterburner fuel control; these regulated engine speed by supplying and controlling fuel flow; the system also positioned the inlet guide and variable stator vanes of the compressor section and initiated afterburner operation), a main ignition system (of which there were two—one main, and one afterburner; the main ignition system was a single-type, low-tension, capacitor discharge system; the afterburner system was a continuous

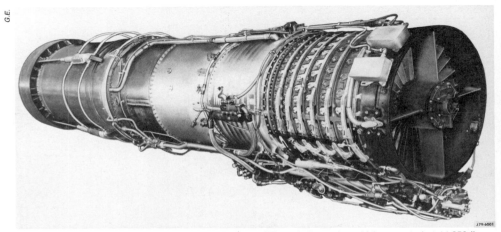

Early pre-production B-58's were powered by the YJ79-GE-1 turbojet engine which was rated at 14,350 lbs. th. at sea level. This engine had a very limited TBO (time between overhauls) and numerous teething problems. It was, however, the first Mach 2-capable production turbojet engine in its class.

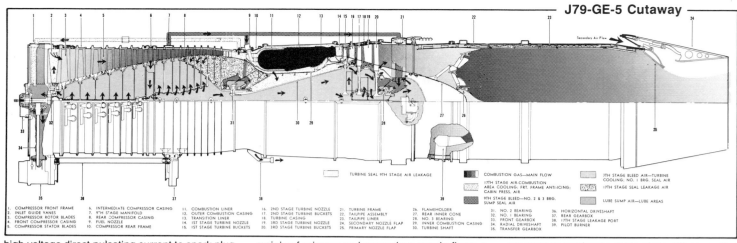

TURBINE SEAL 9TH STAGE AIR LEAKAGE

COMBUSTION GAS—MAIN FLOW

7TH STAGE BLEED AIR—TURBINE COOLING; NO. 1 BRG. SEAL AIR

17TH STAGE AIR-COMBUSTION AREA COOLING; FRT. FRAME ANTI-ICING; CABIN PRESS. AIR

17TH STAGE SEAL LEAKAGE AIR

9TH STAGE BLEED—NO. 2 & 3 BRG. SUMP SEAL AIR

LUBE SUMP AIR—LUBE AREAS

1. COMPRESSOR FRONT FRAME
2. INLET GUIDE VANES
3. COMPRESSOR ROTOR BLADES
4. FRONT COMPRESSOR CASING
5. COMPRESSOR STATOR BLADES
6. INTERMEDIATE COMPRESSOR CASING
7. 9TH STAGE MANIFOLD
8. REAR COMPRESSOR CASING
9. FUEL NOZZLE
10. COMPRESSOR REAR FRAME
11. COMBUSTION LINER
12. OUTER COMBUSTION CASING
13. TRANSITION LINER
14. 1ST STAGE TURBINE NOZZLE
15. 1ST STAGE TURBINE BUCKETS
16. 2ND STAGE TURBINE NOZZLE
17. 2ND STAGE TURBINE BUCKETS
18. TURBINE CASING
19. 3RD STAGE TURBINE NOZZLE
20. 3RD STAGE TURBINE BUCKETS
21. TURBINE FRAME
22. TAILPIPE ASSEMBLY
23. TAILPIPE LINER
24. SECONDARY NOZZLE FLAP
25. PRIMARY NOZZLE FLAP
26. FLAMEHOLDER
27. REAR INNER CONE
28. NO. 1 BEARING
29. INNER COMBUSTION CASING
30. TURBINE SHAFT
31. NO. 2 BEARING
32. NO. 1 BEARING
33. FRONT GEARBOX
34. RADIAL DRIVESHAFT
35. TRANSFER GEARBOX
36. HORIZONTAL DRIVESHAFT
37. REAR GEARBOX
38. 17TH STAGE LEAKAGE PORT
39. PILOT BURNER

high-voltage direct pulsating current to spark plug type), and a starter system.

Movement of the MIL-L-7808 spec. synthetic engine lubricating oil was provided by a Bendix-Utica 60 psi oil supply system. The oil supply tank of each engine was installed around the upper right quadrant of the engine in the region of the front compressor case. The oil tank had a capacity of 4½ gallons. The oil tank supplied oil to the engine, variable exhaust nozzle system, and constant speed drive unit on a priority basis. From the oil tank, oil flowed to the constant-speed drive and to the two pressure elements of the gear-type oil pump. One element of the pump supplied oil to the variable exhaust nozzle system; the other element supplied pressurized oil for lubrication and cooling to the three main engine bearings, the transfer gear case, and the rear gear case. After the oil passed through the engine bearings and gear cases and the exhaust nozzle system, it was scavenged by three pumps and returned to the oil tanks through the main scavenge filter and two oil coolers. The oil supplied to the constant-speed drive was scavenged by its pump, filtered, and also returned to the oil tank. Oil system pressure was generally from 3 to 4.5 psi.

Frontal areas of the engines were anti-iced by air from the anti-icing system, which derived its hot air from engine compressor air.

The variable exhaust nozzle system controlled the exhaust area to provide optimum thrust and specific fuel consumption for varying engine operating conditions. It also served to protect the engine from overheating. The system consisted mainly of primary and secondary nozzle flaps, a primary nozzle control unit, primary and secondary nozzle pumps and actuators, thermocouples, a temperature amplifier, a control alternator, and a secondary nozzle control valve. The primary and secondary nozzle pumps, using oil from the oil supply system, supplied hydraulic pressure for nozzle actuation. Each primary nozzle control unit and respective engine throttle was mechanically interconnected and synchronized so that throttle movement would automatically result in proper actuation of the primary nozzle. The secondary nozzle flaps were used to provide maximum thrust and reduce drag during the cruise and military operating ranges. These were opened during idle and afterburner engine operation, and closed for operation in the cruise and military ranges.

The engines were mounted in individual air cooled (secondary air for inflight nacelle cooling was provided by using part of the engine ram air; ram air entered two scoops, located in the air inlet of each nacelle, and passed through bypass flaps and the hydraulic oil cooler and aft between the engine and nacelle to be expelled into the engine exhaust gases) nacelles suspended beneath the wing and were numbered from left to right with the left outboard engine being No. 1. Engine changes into and out of these nacelles could be made in under 3 hours.

Each nacelle was equipped with a variable positioning spike which was used to maintain an efficient airflow to the engine throughout the speed range of the aircraft. At supersonic speeds, shock waves formed at the engine air inlets. If the shock waves were not kept outside of the diffuser so that the air in the diffuser was subsonic, airflow to the engine would be greatly reduced. The inlet spike system prevented this from occurring by maintaining a constant ratio between two control pressures—a static pressure measured on the inner surface of the inlet lip and a total pressure measured on the spike lip.

Movement of the spike was forward and aft. During normal operation, control of this movement was completely automatic. The spike remained in the aft or retracted position until an airspeed of Mach 1.42 was reached. At this speed, a switch in the air data computer closed and supplied a 28-volt direct current signal to the control unit, activating the system. The transducer received the control pressures, computed their ratio, and produced an electrical error signal when the computed ratio was incorrect. The amplifier received the error signal from the transducer, amplified it, and closed a relay which supplied 200-volt AC power to the actuator. The actuator drove the spike in the proper direction.

Four throttles, one for each engine, were located in a quadrant on the left side of the pilot's station. The throttles were mechanically linked to the control units of their respective engine and controlled engine speed, fuel flow, primary and secondary nozzle area, variable inlet guide and stator blade positioning, and afterburner operation. A throttle torque booster, installed on the input shaft side of the engine fuel control, aided in moving the throttle. Fuel pressures from zero to 900 psi were taken from the discharge side of the main fuel pump and routed to the torque booster.

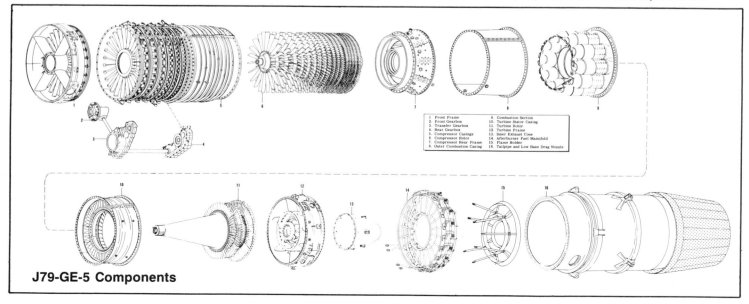

1 Front Frame
2 Front Gearbox
3 Transfer Gearbox
4 Rear Gearbox
5 Compressor Casings
6 Compressor Rotor
7 Compressor Rear Frame
8 Outer Combustion Casing
9 Combustion Section
10 Turbine Stator Casing
11 Turbine Rotor
12 Turbine Frame
13 Inner Exhaust Cone
14 Afterburner Fuel Mainifold
15 Flame Holder
16 Tailpipe and Low Base Drag Nozzle

J79-GE-5 Components

Engine Specifications

Military Designation	YJ79-GE-1	YJ79-GE-5	J79-GE-5A	J79-GE-5B
Weight	3,150 lbs.	3,443 lbs.	3,570 lbs.	3,635 lbs.
SLS air flow (lbs./sec.)	161	163	162.5	162.5
Compression ratio	12:1	12.2:1	12.15:1	12.15:1
Augmentation	sector a/b	sector a/b	sector a/b	sector a/b
Compressor inlet dia.	30.37''	30.37''	30.37''	30.37''
Compressor inlet area	650 sq.''	654 sq.''	654 sq.''	654 sq.''
Max. accessory rad.	25.05''	25.6''	?	?
Lube oil consumption	2 lbs./hr.	1 lb./hr.	1 lb./hr.	1 lb./hr.
Exhaust pipe dia.	34''	34''	34''	34''
Nozzle envelope dia.	37.57''	38''	38''	38''
Max. dia.	38.25''	38''	38''	38''
Length	207.17''	202.04''	202.17''	202.17''
Limit Mach @ s.l.	1.0	1.0	1.0	1.0
Limit Mach @ 35,000'	2.0	2.0	2.0	2.0
Max. thrust @ s.l.	14,500 lbs. /7,460 rpm	15,600 lbs. /7,460 rpm	15,600 lbs. /7,460 rpm	15,600 lbs. /7,460 rpm
Mil. thrust @ s.l.	9,800 lbs. /7,460 rpm	10,000 lbs. /7,460 rpm	10,000 lbs. /7,460 rpm	10,000 lbs. /7,460 rpm
Cont. thrust @ s.l.	8,900 lbs. /7,460 rpm	9,370 lbs. /7,460 rpm	9,700 lbs. /7,460 rpm	9,700 lbs. /7,460 rpm
Steady state exhaust gas temperature/C.	?	596° + /-11°	596° + /-	596° + /-
Max. exhaust gas temperature/C.	?	760°	760°	760°

The J79-GE-5 featured variable stator blades and a modulated afterburner—two items that were significant milestones in the history of turbojet engine development.

The B-58/J79 fuel system was, in its day, the most complex and sophisticated ever installed in an operational aircraft. The MIL-F-5624B spec. JP-4 fuel was stored in four major tanks broken down into forward, aft, reservoir, and balance units. Two more tanks were located in the MB-1 pod. The forward portion of both wings and the fuselage between bulkheads 5.0 and 6.0 comprised the forward tank; the aft portion of both wings and the fuselage between bulkheads 9.0 and 12.0 comprised the aft tank; the fuselage section between bulkheads 6.0 and 8.0 comprised the reservoir tank; and the fuselage section between bulkheads 12.0 and 19.0 comprised the balance tank. Fuel tank corrosion inhibitors were also provided. The aircraft fuel system could operate with or without the pod fuel tank system attached.

During normal engine operation, fuel was routed to the engines through manifolds which were attached to the booster pumps within the forward and aft tanks. The aft fuel tank delivered fuel to the supply manifolds through four booster pumps located in the tank. Each pump delivered fuel to its entire output to one supply manifold; two pumps delivered fuel to the left supply manifold and two pumps delivered fuel to the right supply manifold. The forward tank incorporated the same features of booster pump operation and engine supply manifold arrangement as the aft tank. However, there were only two booster pumps in the forward tank. The aft wing tank pumps were rated at 35,000 pph; the forward wing tank pumps were rated at 42,000 pph; and the pod tank pumps were rated at 42,000 pph.

The reservoir tank acted as an accumulator tank by utilizing an autotransfer system which maintained a specified tank level until the other tank fuel supplies had been depleted. Each booster pump in the reservoir tank was arranged so that half of each pump supply fed into the left supply manifold and half fed into the right supply manifold. The balance tank was not utilized for direct engine supply; however, fuel could be transferred from the balance tank to the forward tank when needed. The center-of-gravity control system maintained the selected cg position of the aircraft either automatically or manually by transferring fuel between the forward, aft, and balance tanks.

Ground refueling could be accomplished by either of two systems: a single-point refueling system or a gravity refueling system. Single-point refueling was accomplished through the refueling adapter located in the nose wheel well. Fuel flowed from the adapter through a dual check valve; then it flowed through the reservoir tank refuel valves located in the reservoir tank. After the reservoir tank was filled, the remaining tanks were filled by routing fuel as selected. Pressure above 5 psi was vented overboard through the tank vent control valve.

Gravity refueling was accomplished through three gravity fillers located on the top centerline of the aircraft; one each for the forward, aft, and reservoir tanks. The balance tank could not be filled using gravity filling. Fuel had to be transferred to the balance tank.

The B-58 was equipped with an air refueling system capable of receiving fuel from a KC-135A. The system, consisting of a flying boom receptacle, a slipway door, hydraulic valves and actuators, a hydraulic pressure transfer cylinder, and a signal amplifier, was mounted in the upper portion of the nose radome some 45'' ahead of the pilot's windscreen (the prototype system, tested on several of the early pre-production B-58's, was mounted 89'' ahead of the pilot's windscreen). When the slipway door was opened, it formed a guide for the flying boom. The door was normally flush with the contour of the radome when closed. A lamp, equipped with two bulbs, was located in the receptacle slipway to aid the tanker boom

operator during night refueling. The maximum air refueling speed at 29,100' or above while taking fuel from a KC-135A equipped with a high speed boom and ruddervators was Mach .90. Below 29,100' the speed dropped to Mach .85.

The B-58 was equipped with a fuel dump system which provided an emergency means of reducing the gross weight of the aircraft in flight. The system included a control solenoid valve and a dump probe assembly. When it was necessary to jettison fuel, the control valve was opened by means of a guarded dump switch on the fuel control panel. The dump switch opened a control solenoid valve which allowed engine supply manifold pressure to disengage the probe latch, to extend the probe and to open the dump valve. The probe extended approximately two feet outward from the left side of the balance tank just aft of the wing trailing edge. As the probe extended, it ruptured a thin cover over the dump probe port. The maximum extension speed for the fuel dump probe was 300 knots TAS and the maximum fuel dump speed was approximately Mach .45.

The YJ79-GE-1 engine was used to power the prototype B-58, 55-660, and the seven pre-production aircraft that followed. Difficulties with this engine were eventually overcome, though the first flight of 55-661 was delayed for several months while rotor tolerance problems were corrected.

One of the least heralded yet technologically most important aspects of the B-58 propulsion program was the successful development of the nacelle-mounted supersonic intake and its articulated spike.

The variable-area exhaust nozzle developed for the J79 was a significant, but relatively unknown propulsion system advance. It was a major factor in determining the size of the B-58's performance envelope.

Significant wind tunnel time was spent in optimizing the B-58's engine nacelle configuration. Each of the nacelles was a strong but complex tube fitted with several internal bypass tunnels.

Though both inboard nacelles were obviously pylon mounted, the outboard nacelles were actually attached to the wing via a very abbreviated stub pylon serving only as a support structure.

The inflight refueling receptacle was mounted behind a triangular door on the upper surface of the nose, just behind the nose radome. It was hydraulically actuated from the pilot's cockpit.

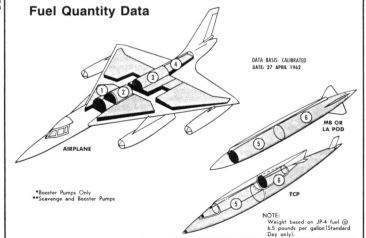

Fuel Quantity Data

DATA BASIS: CALIBRATED
DATE: 27 APRIL 1962

AIRPLANE

MB OR LA POD

TCP

*Booster Pumps Only
**Scavenge and Booster Pumps

NOTE:
Weight based on JP-4 fuel @ 6.5 pounds per gallon (Standard Day only).

	TANKS	GROUND-SERVICED				AIR-REFUELED			
		FULLY SERVICED IN GROUND ATTITUDE (2.3° Nose Down)		USABLE FUEL IN NORMAL FLIGHT ATTITUDE (2.5° Nose Up)		FULLY SERVICED AIR REFUELING ATTITUDE (6.5° Nose Up)		USABLE FUEL IN NORMAL FLIGHT ATTITUDE (2.5° Nose Up)	
		U.S. GALLONS	POUNDS	U.S. GALLONS	POUNDS	U.S. GALLONS	POUNDS	U.S. GALLONS	POUNDS
	FUEL LINES	103	672	32	211	120	781	32	211
AIRPLANE	1 FWD	3,202	20,811	*3,172 / **3,195	20,619 / 20,770	3,177	20,648	*3,147 / **3,170	20,456 / 20,607
AIRPLANE	2 RES	610	3,963	607	3,945	640	4,163	638	4,145
AIRPLANE	3 AFT	5,893	38,306	*5,816 / **5,884	38,000 / 38,245	6,122	39,794	*6,075 / **6,113	39,488 / 39,733
AIRPLANE	4 BAL	1,219	7,925	1,206	7,839	1,261	8,195	1,248	8,109
MB OR LA POD	5 FWD	1,922	12,496	1,912	12,426	2,008	13,055	1,998	12,985
MB OR LA POD	6 AFT	2,250	14,625	2,244	14,585	2,306	14,991	2,300	14,951
TCP	5 FWD	1,844	11,988	1,837	11,941	1,870	12,154	1,863	12,107
TCP	6 AFT	2,041	13,266	2,031	13,204	2,092	13,601	2,083	13,539

A. Individual B-58 histories by designator/USAF serial number/airframe number (pod data implies only that the aircraft was seen at one time or another with the pod noted—pods were interchangeable in most instances and were not assigned to only one particular airframe):

USAF via Jim Goodall

▲ **XB-58/(YB/RB-58)/55-660/1**—ff. 11/11/56; eventually logged a total of 150 flights (totaling 257 hrs. 30 min. including 28 hrs. 23 min. at supersonic speeds); first B-58 Mach 1 and Mach 2 flights; used for fuel line surge tests during late 1959; used as ALBM transport in 1959/60; delivered to Kelly AFB, TX on 3/15/60; eventually scrapped at Kelly AFB, TX following use as B-58 ground maintenance trainer; carried pod B-142, nicknamed *Old Grandpappy*.

G.D.

▲ **YB/RB-58/(later TB-58A)/55-661/2**—made ff. w/pod on 2/16/57; used during Phase II testing initiated 9/18/57; transferred from Convair to 6592nd TS on 8/8/58; made first inflight refueling on 6/11/58; used during low level ejection seat tests at Edwards AFB, CA; made 1st airborne human ejection on 2/28/62; converted to TB-58A and served with 305th BW; nicknamed *Mach-In-Boid*; disposed at MASDC (arrived 1/9/70; inventory #BQ063) by Southwestern Alloys, Tucson, AZ, on 7/13/77.

G.D.

▲ **YB/RB-58/(later TB-58A)/55-662/3**—ff. 5/6/57; used during Doppler radar and radar altimeter tests; first pod drop on 6/5/57; used for development testing of autopilot and primary nav/bomb system components; first aircraft to complete test program on 4/25/59; first aircraft to blow all tires during landing on 8/30/58; used for frangible wheel tests at Edwards AFB, CA, on 1/20/61; used for YJ93 testbed and redesignated NB-58A; converted to TB-58A; used for XB-70A chase at Edwards AFB, CA; eventually assigned to 305th BW; while with 305th, set record by flying 256 sorties without a late or missed takeoff; disposed at MASDC (arrived 1/16/70; inventory #BQ083) by Southwestern Alloys, Tucson, AZ, on 7/21/77.

G.D. via Walter Alling

▲ **YB/RB-58/(later TB-58A)/55-663/4**—ff. 8/12/57; used in pod drop program and made first supersonic pod drop on 9/30/57 and first Mach 2 pod drop on 12/20/57; made first flight above 60,000' on 12/20/57; made first low level TCP drop on 11/19/60; made first supersonic upper TCP drop on 12/11/60; used by NASA for SST sonic boom test in 1962; converted to TB-58A and served with 305th BW; grounded in 1969 following fire caused by oxygen leak and electrical spark in cockpit area; statically displayed at Grissom AFB, IN.

G.D.

▲ **YB/RB-58/(no. ser. – allocated)/4A**—on 3/12/57 carried by Convair B-36 to Wright-Patterson AFB, OH and used for static testing.

G.D.

▲ **YB/RB-58/55-664/5**—ff. 11/30/57; airloads data test aircraft; had large #5 marked on empennage section; used during inflight refueling trials; first mission profiles flown for operational use from 6/27/58 to 3/17/59; carried pod B-122; destroyed on 11/7/59.

Aerofax, Inc. collection

▲ **YB/RB-58/55-665/6**—ff. 9/28/57; first test aircraft to AF on 2/15/58; used during B-58 Phase IV testing in 1958; first delivered to Edwards AFB, CA on 2/14/58; assigned initially to the ARDC; beginning on 2/15/59, modified to test AN/ASG-18 radar system and associated GAR-9/AIM-47 missile for F-108 and later, YF-12A programs; presently located on Edwards AFB photo test range.

Anthony Olheiser

▲ **YB/RB-58-55-666/7**—ff. 3/20/58; used as GE J79-GE-5 engine/airframe interface test aircraft; failed to complete *Mission 7-Up-2* range test on 8/29/58; on 11/18/58 flew 32 minutes at sustained design speed of Mach 2 w/YJ79-GE-5's; used during follow-up *Seven-Up* tests at Holloman AFB, NM in 1959; made longest early test program flight of 11 hr. 15 min. on 8/16/62; used for series of subsonic, low-level flights to measure B-58's response to atmospheric turbulence; carried pod B-134; statically displayed at Chanute AFB, IL wearing 61-2059 serial number.

Emerson Electric via Bart Cusick

▲ **YB/RB-58/55-667/8**—ff. 12/14/57; fire control system testbed (tests lasted ten months and were conducted at Eglin AFB, FL in 1959; target was Lockheed F-104A; no actual ammunition was fired; camera was used instead); carried pods B-1-1, B-2-1; destroyed on 6/4/60.

G.D.

▲ **YB/RB-58/(later TB-58A)/55-668/9**—ff. 5/13/58; flown with nav/bomb system installed; eventually used as special projects testbed including Hughes AN/APQ-69 SLAR, Goodyear AN/APS-73, and advanced nav/bomb systems; originally scheduled to become the first aircraft equipped with GE J79-GE-9 engines for B-58B; converted to TB-58A and became last B-58 assigned to the 43rd BW; nicknamed *Wild Child II* and later, *Peeping Tom* during AN/APQ-69 program; initially stored at MASDC (arrived 1/16/70; inventory #BQ084), but saved for transport by C-5A to Southwest Aerospace Museum, Fort Worth, TX where it is now displayed.

G.D. via Don Mayhew

(Photo Unavailable)

▲ **YB/RB-58A/55-669/10**—ff. 5/3/58; used for T-4 and C-2 passive ECM systems tests; used for engine performance tests; used for autopilot evaluation flights; scheduled for conversion to TB-58A; destroyed on 10/27/59.

G.D.

▲ **YB/RB-58A/(later TB-58A)/55-670/11**—ff. 6/26/58; placed in climatic chamber at Eglin AFB on 7/8/58 and removed 9/58; delivered to 43rd BW on 8/13/60 following conversion to TB-58A beginning on 10/5/59; ff. as TB-58A prototype took place on 5/10/60; carried pod B-178; disposed at MASDC (arrived 12/11/69; inventory #BQ020) by Southwestern Alloys, Tucson, AZ, on 8/16/77.

▲ **YB/RB-58A/58-1009/16**—ff. 12/15/58; had large #16 painted on fuselage just under aft panel of windscreen; assigned to the 6592nd TS at Edwards AFB as of 5/25/59; fourth aircraft to be modernized for SAC service under production conversion program; used for evaluation of nav/bomb and production fuel systems; carried pod B-136; nicknamed *Sweet Sixteen*, *El Toro de Moron*, and *Bonanza*; disposed at MASDC (arrived 12/12/69; inventory #BQ023) by Southwestern Alloys, Tucson, AZ, on 6/9/77.

USAF via Jim Goodall

▲ **YB/RB-58A/(later TB-58A)/55-671/12**—ff. 10/24/58; used during range demonstration flights on 6/27/58; made 18 hr. 10 min. flight on 3/22-23/60; accepted by the 6592nd TS for pod drop and suitability testing on 10/58; on 4/9/60 became last aircraft accepted from *Junior Flash-Up* program; became 4th TB-58A; logged record 179 flying hours during 58 day test period; nicknamed *Mary Ann* and *All Day All Night . . .*; assigned to the 43rd BW; disposed at MASDC (arrived 1/12/70; inventory #BQ067) by Southwestern Alloys, Tucson, AZ, on 7/11/77.

G.D. via Ed Yingst

▲ **YB/RB-58A/58-1010/17**—delivered to the AF on 3/59 and used during Category II testing; second aircraft to be modernized for SAC service under production conversion program; assigned to the 43rd BW; nicknamed *Hot Stuff*; disposed at MASDC (arrived 12/16/69; inventory #BQ029) by Southwestern Alloys, Tucson, AZ, on 7/11/77.

G.D. via Don Dupre

▲ **YB/RB-58A/(later TB-58A)/55-672/13**—ff. 10/7/58; accepted by the AF on 9/30/58; used during pod drop program at Kirtland AFB, NM and modified to incorporate a large data link antenna on the right side of the fuselage; during Kirtland AFB tests, had *Q Twice* on right side of fuselage and *Clean Sweep* on left; became second TB-58A; nicknamed *Lucky 13* and *Sweet Sadness*; carried pods B-179 and B-13; disposed at MASDC (arrived 1/15/70; inventory #BQ080) by Southwestern Alloys, Tucson, AZ, on 8/3/77.

G.D. via Douglas Robinson

▲ **YB/RB-58A/58-1011/18**—ff. 1/30/59; first pod drop with functional nav/bomb system on 2/12/60; fifth aircraft to be modernized for SAC service under production conversion program; first aicraft delivered to the 43rd at Little Rock AFB, AR on 8/64; nicknamed *Wicked Witch*, *Trailblazer*, and *Pulaski Hustler* (this was the first aircraft with this name; upon its arrival at LRAFB, a sub-title was added, *. . . . The Polish Prostitute*; 59-2429 was also given the nickname *Pulaski Hustler* at a later date); disposed at MASDC (arrived 12/11/69; inventory #BQ021) by Southwestern Alloys, Tucson, AZ, on 6/6/77.

(Photo Unavailable)

G.D.

▲ **58-1012/19**—ff. 2/60; nav/bomb test aircraft used during Category II testing; destroyed on 5/14/59.

(Photo Unavailable)

▲ **YB/RB-58A/(later TB-58A) 58-1007/14**—ff. 11/8/58; used for functional development of the nav/bomb system; had #14 painted on left fuselage side, front and rear; became third TB-58A following removal from production conversion program; as TB-58A, assigned to 43rd BW; nicknamed *Super Sue* and *Boomerang*; disposed at MASDC (arrived 1/15/70; inventory #BQ081) by Southwestern Alloys, Tucson, AZ, on 8/5/77.

▲ **YB/RB-58A/58-1013/20**—ff. 2/60; first aircraft to enter *Junior Flash-Up* program and first to complete same; sixth aircraft to go through production conversion program; delivered to 43rd BW, LRAFB, AR; disposed at MASDC (arrived 12/29/69; inventory #BQ043) by Southwestern Alloys, Tucson, AZ, on 7/25/77.

G.D.

▲ **YB/RB-58A/58-1008/15**—accepted by and delivered to the 6592nd TS for pod and suitability testing on 10/58; destroyed on 12/16/58.

Aviation News via Chris Pocock

▲ **YB/RB-58A/58-1014/21**—seventh aircraft to be modernized for SAC service under production conversion program; delivered to 43rd BW, LRAFB, AR; disposed at MASDC (arrived 1/7/70; inventory #BQ055) by Southwestern Alloys, Tucson, AZ, on 6/29/77.

Bill Mann

USAF

▲ **YB/RB-58A/58-1015/22**—ff. 3/19/59; used during pod drop program and high gross weight tests 3/59 through 12/59; flew low level (550') mission from Ft. Worth to Edwards AFB via El Paso, TX, Phoenix, AZ, and Bakersfield, CA at an average speed of 610 knots on 9/18/59; made first sustained long range Mach 2 flight on 10/15/59 during 70 minute flight from Seattle, WA to Dallas, TX; seriously damaged at Edwards AFB, CA on 4/13/60 when right main gear tires failed during takeoff; last aircraft to go through production conversion program; accepted by the AF on 10/23/62 and delivered to 43rd BW, Carswell AFB, TX on 10/25/62; carried pod B-1-7; nicknamed *Little Joe* and *Ginger*; disposed at MASDC (arrived 12/22/69; inventory #BQ040) by Southwestern Alloys, Tucson, AZ, on 8/9/77.

G.D.

▲ **YB/RB-58A/58-1021/28**—first aircraft to enter production conversion program; delivered to Carswell AFB on 12/30/60; assigned to 43rd BW; as of 10/65 had highest number of B-58 flight hours (1,078); had large red 2 on vertical fin; disposed at MASDC (arrived 12/15/69; inventory #BQ027) by Southwestern Alloys, Tucson, AZ, on 6/27/77.

▲ **YB/RB-58A/58-1016/23**—third aircraft to go through production conversion program; assigned to the 43rd BW; destroyed on 5/20/65.

G.D.

G.D.

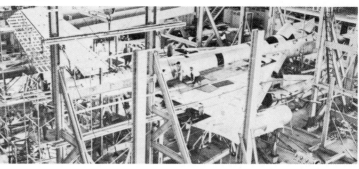

▲ **YB/RB-58A/58-1017/24**—assigned to the 43rd BW; destroyed on 9/16/59.

▲ **YB/RB-58A/58-1022/29**—on 3/60 became fatigue test aircraft and used for cyclic loading tests through 1/61; aircraft was completed some two months before conversion to fatigue test program; destroyed during fatigue test program some five years after program begun.

Bill Mann

G.D.

▲ **YB/RB-58A/58-1018/25**—ff. 4/29/59; delivered to the AF on 4/30/59; used during ECM system test program; eighth aircraft to go through production conversion program; assigned to the 43rd BW; nicknamed *Reddy Kilowatt* and *Omega*; successful emergency landing at Edwards AFB following left landing gear failure during takeoff; disposed at MASDC (arrived 12/15/69; inventory #BQ026) by Southwestern Alloys, Tucson, AZ, on 6/24/77.

▲ **YB/RB-58A/58-1023/30**—ff. 7/24/59; nav/bomb test aircraft and first production standard aircraft; destroyed on 4/22/60.

George Bracken

USAF via Craig Kaston

▲ **YB/RB-58A/58-1019/26**—ninth aircraft to go through production conversion program; assigned to the 43rd BW; nicknamed *Black Dragon* and *Beech-nut Kid*; disposed at MASDC (arrived 1/5/70; inventory #BQ045) by Southwestern Alloys, Tucson, AZ, on 7/28/77.

▲ **B-58A/59-2428/31**—first B-58 to incorporate an operationally configured tail gun installation; used in Project *White Horse* cold weather tests at Ellsworth AFB, SD in 1/60 (3 sorties flown and 20 hours logged); on 11/30/59 became first tactical inventory aircraft accepted by the 6592nd TS; delivered to Carswell AFB, TX on 12/1/59; on 1/18/63 became first aircraft to complete Phase I of the *Hustle Up* program; also became first aircraft received by Convair for Phase II of *Hustle Up*; assigned to the 43rd BW; carried pod B-196; disposed at MASDC (arrived 1/8/70; inventory #BQ057) by Southwestern Alloys, Tucson, AZ, on 7/6/77.

G.D.

Pete Bulban

▲ **YB/RB-58A/58-1020/27**—tenth aircraft to go through production conversion program; assigned to the 43rd BW; destroyed 12/27/61.

▲ **B-58A/59-2429/32**—first aircraft assigned to the 1960 SAC bombing competition at Bergstrom AFB, TX; on 4/15/60 became the first aircraft to enter the *Flash-Up* program; later became the first aircraft to enter *Flash-Up Cycle II*; assigned to the 43rd BW; second aircraft to be nicknamed *The Pulaski Hustler*—first was 58-1011; disposed at MASDC (arrived 12/18/69; inventory #BQ034) by Southwestern Alloys, Tucson, AZ, on 8/2/77.

Pete Bulban

G.D.

▲ **B-58A/59-2430/33**—accepted by the AF on 1/28/60 and delivered on 2/10/60; second aircraft assigned to the 1960 SAC bombing competition at Bergstrom AFB, TX; eventually assigned to the 305th BW; disposed at MASDC (arrived 1/13/70; inventory #BQ069) by Southwestern Alloys, Tucson, AZ, on 8/10/77.

▲ **B-58A/59-2436/39**—on 8/1/60 became first aircraft delivered to AF with complete tactical systems installed; assigned to the 43rd BW; disposed at MASDC (arrived 1/9/70; inventory #BQ061) by Southwestern Alloys, Tucson, AZ, on 7/5/77.

Doug Slowiak

USAF via Richard Boicer

▲ **B-58A/59-2431/34**—made 78 minute Mach 2 flight while assigned to the 6592nd TS; later assigned to the 43rd BW; disposed at MASDC (arrived 12/8/69; inventory #BQ012) by Southwestern Alloys, Tucson, AZ, on 6/29/77.

▲ **B-58A/59-2437/40**—assigned to the 43rd BW; nicknamed *Firefly II* (59-2451 was nicknamed *The Firefly*) and *Rigley's Baby* (the latter following the permanent grounding of the aircraft after an accident at Little Rock AFB, AR); airframe remains were visible at Little Rock AFB for many years, though it is reported that these have now been moved to the SAC museum at Barksdale AFB, LA.

Bill Mann

G.D.

▲ **B-58A/59-2432/35**—assigned to the 43rd BW; nicknamed *Regal Beagle*; disposed at MASDC (arrived 12/19/69; inventory #BQ037) by Southwestern Alloys, Tucson, AZ, on 8/1/77.

▲ **B-58A/59-2438/41**—assigned to the 43rd BW; occasionally seen carrying an LA-1 recce pod; disposed at MASDC (arrived 12/19/69; inventory #BQ038) by Southwestern Alloys, Tucson, AZ, on 5/25/77.

Bill Mann

Bill Mann

▲ **B-58A/59-2433/36**—assigned to the 43rd BW; nicknamed *Now or Never*; carried pod B-177; disposed at MASDC (arrived 1/7/70; inventory #BQ051) by Southwestern Alloys, Tucson, AZ, on 7/20/77.

▲ **B-58A/59-2439/42**—used in ground suspended vibration tests and flutter analysis; assigned to the 43rd BW; disposed at MASDC (arrived 1/12/70; inventory #BQ064) by Southwestern Alloys, Tucson, AZ, on 8/1/77.

Aviation News via Chris Pocock

Aerofax, Inc. collection

▲ **B-58A/59-2434/37**—first aircraft to enter *Flash-Up* program; assigned to the 43rd BW; nicknamed *Cannonball*; disposed at MASDC (arrived 12/17/69; inventory #BQ032) by Southwestern Alloys, Tucson, AZ, on 6/24/77.

▲ **B-58A/59-2440/43**—last aircraft to complete *Flash-Up Cycle II*; thought to be last aircraft to visit the US when on 5/69, it was seen at RAF Mildenhall during Armed Forces Day; assigned to the 43rd BW; disposed at MASDC (arrived 1/8/70; inventory #BQ056) by Southwestern Alloys, Tucson, AZ, on 7/6/77.

G.D.

(Photo Unavailable)

▲ **B-58A/59-2435/38**—used during pod drop program; had 17 small component pod symbols, 11 big component pod symbols, and 40 bomb symbols painted on nose during stay at Kirtland AFB, NM; made 1st Mach 2 upper pod drop 2/10/61; made first Mach 2 lower pod drop 8/8/61; made first multiple weapon drop; conducted first over water pod drops off the coast of Florida near Ft. Walton—tested fusing and aiming on water impact; assigned to the 43rd BW; nicknamed *Shackbuster*; carried pods B-1-11 and B-2-16; disposed at MASDC (arrived 1/7/70; inventory #BQ052) by Southwestern Alloys, Tucson, AZ, on 6/27/77.

▲ **B-58A/59-2441/44**—along with 59-2442, participated in *Operation Quick Step* and on 1/14/61, set high speed course records (6 altogether) including 1,284.73 mph avg. speed while carrying payload; crew received Thompson Trophy; assigned to the 43rd BW; nicknamed *Road Runner*; disposed at MASDC (arrived 1/5/70; inventory #BQ044) by Southwestern Alloys, Tucson, AZ, on 8/4/77.

Left margin credits (top to bottom): USAF; Theodore Van Geffen, Jr.; Aviation News via Chris Pocock; Aerofax, Inc. collection; Jay Miller/Aerofax, Inc.; Aerofax, Inc. collection

Right margin credits: Norm Taylor via Rick Pavek; Dennie Darnell; Bill Mann; Aviation News via Chris Pocock; Bill Mann

▲ **B-58A/59-2442/45**—along with 59-2441, participated in *Operation Quick Step* and set three world records for class including 2,000 km closed course flight averaging 1,061.80 mph carrying payload; assigned to the 43rd BW; seen carrying LA-1 recce pod on occasion; in 11/12/69, became last aircraft to leave Little Rock AFB; disposed at MASDC (arrived 11/12/69; inventory #BQ003) by Southwestern Alloys, Tucson, AZ, on 8/9/77.

▲ **B-58A/59-2448/51**—assigned to the 43rd BW; disposed at MASDC (arrived 11/20/69; inventory #BQ009) by Southwestern Alloys, Tucson, AZ, on 5/27/77.

▲ **B-58A/59-2443/46**—assigned to the 43rd BW; nicknamed *Bye Bye Birdie*; destroyed 6/15/65.

▲ **B-58A/59-2449/52**—on 10/30/62, became first aircraft to enter *Hustle-Up* program; assigned to the 43rd BW; nicknamed *Hobo 49*; disposed at MASDC (arrived 1/13/70; inventory #BQ068) by Southwestern Alloys, Tucson, AZ, on 7/12/77.

▲ **B-58A/59-2444/47**—assigned to the 43rd BW; nicknamed *Lucky Lady V*; disposed at MASDC (arrived 12/10/69; inventory #BQ017) by Southwestern Alloys, Tucson, AZ, on 5/27/77.

▲ **B-58A/59-2450/53**—assigned to the 43rd BW; disposed at MASDC (arrived 1/15/70; inventory #BQ078) by Southwestern Alloys, Tucson, AZ, on 6/16/77.

▲ **B-58A/59-2445/48**—assigned to the 43rd BW; nicknamed *Sno White*; disposed at MASDC (arrived 12/17/69; inventory #BQ031) by Southwestern Alloys, Tucson, AZ, on 6/28/77.

▲ **B-58A/59-2451/54**—used on 5/10/61 to set the world speed records over 669.438 mile closed course (avg. speed 1,302.048 mph); on 5/26/61 set New York to Paris speed record of 3 hrs. 19 min. 51 sec. at an average speed of 1,089.36 mph; crew awarded Mackay Trophy on 5/13/62; nicknamed *The Firefly*; destroyed on 6/3/61.

▲ **B-58A/59-2446/49**—assigned to the 43rd BW; disposed at MASDC (arrived 11/3/69; inventory #BQ001) by Southwestern Alloys, Tucson, AZ, on 7/19/77.

▲ **B-58A/59-2447/50**—assigned to the 43rd BW; nicknamed *Rapid Rabbit*; destroyed 2/15/62.

▲ **B-58A/59-2452/55**—assigned to the 43rd BW; carried pod B-1105; disposed at MASDC (arrived 1/9/70; inventory #BQ059) by Southwestern Alloys, Tucson, AZ, on 5/27/77.

▲ **B-58A/59-2453/56**—assigned to the 43rd BW; nicknamed *Top Cat*; disposed at MASDC (arrived 1/5/70; inventory #BQ046) by Southwestern Alloys, Tucson, AZ, on 8/22/77.

George Bracken

▲ **B-58A/59-2459/62**—assigned to the 43rd BW; destroyed 3/5/62.

▲ **B-58A/59-2460/63**—assigned to the 43rd BW; displayed for Pres. John Kennedy during firepower display at Eglin AFB, FL; disposed at MASDC (arrived 11/18/69; inventory #BQ007) by Southwestern Alloys, Tucson, AZ, on 6/6/77.

(Photo Unavailable)

▲ **B-58A/59-2454/57**—assigned to the 43rd BW; suffered from fuselage break during service requiring major repairs; nicknamed *Wild Child* and *Patches*; disposed at MASDC (arrived 1/14/70; inventory #BQ073) by Southwestern Alloys, Tucson, AZ, on 8/23/77.

(Photo Unavailable)

▲ **B-58A/59-2461/64**—initially assigned to the 43rd BW; on 5/11/61 became first aircraft assigned to the 305th BW; later painted temporarily to look like *The Firefly* (59-2451) so that a film concerning the real *Firefly* (which had been destroyed) could be completed; disposed at MASDC (arrived 1/14/70; inventory #BQ074) by Southwestern Alloys, Tucson, AZ, on 8/19/77.

Chuck Mayer

▲ **B-58A/59-2455/58**—assigned to the 43rd BW; carried pod B-1108; disposed at MASDC (arrived 1/15/70; inventory #BQ077) by Southwestern Alloys, Tucson, AZ, on 6/30/77.

(Photo Unavailable)

▲ **B-58A/59-2462/65**—assigned to the 305th BW; destroyed 4/12/62.

USAF

▲ **B-58A/59-2456/59**—used for sonic boom studies at Edwards AFB, CA from 9/1/61 through 3/1/62; became AFSC aircraft; had *Q* on left side of nose only; used to set 85,360.84' altitude record while carrying 11,023 lb. payload; used for Phase I multi-weapon capability tests while on bail to Convair; used for takeoff and landing engine out tests at Edwards; assigned to the 43rd BW; carried pods B-170, B-3-6, B-2-4, B-3-1, and B-2-15; disposed at MASDC (arrived 12/9/69; inventory #BQ015) by Southwestern Alloys, Tucson, AZ, on 6/1/77.

Jay Miller/Aerofax, Inc.

▲ **B-58A/59-2463/66**—on 8/9/62 became last aircraft to be accepted from the *Flash-Up* program; delivered to the 43rd BW; carried pod BQ-002; nicknamed *The Heart of Dixie*; disposed at MASDC (arrived 11/7/69; inventory #BQ002) by Southwestern Alloys, Tucson, AZ, on 6/10/77.

Bill Mann

▲ **B-58A/59-2457/60**—assigned to the 43rd BW; disposed at MASDC (arrived 1/8/70; inventory #BQ058) by Southwestern Alloys, Tucson, AZ, on 6/27/77.

Aerofax, Inc. collection

USAF via NASM

▲ **B-58A/59-2458/61**—assigned to the 43rd BW; won Bendix and Bleriot Trophies; nicknamed *Cowtown Hustler*; statically displayed at the USAF Museum, Wright-Patterson AFB, Dayton, OH.

▲ **B-58A/60-1110/67**—accepted by the AF on 6/8/61 and assigned to the 305th BW on 6/14/61; was originally scheduled to serve as the production prototype B-58B and as such would have been modified to accept GE J79-GE-9 engines; nicknamed *City of Peru* though at one time, a horizontal bar was painted in between the first two 1's to make the word ''Ohio''; disposed at MASDC (arrived 12/18/69; inventory #BQ035) by Southwestern Alloys, Tucson, AZ, on 8/18/77.

Hobert Esposito

B-58A/60-1111/68—accepted by the AF on 6/8/61 and assigned to the 305th BW on 6/12/61; nicknamed *Four Aces*; disposed at MASDC (arrived 12/8/69; inventory #BQ013) by Southwestern Alloys, Tucson, AZ, on 6/8/77.

History Office, Kelly AFB

Carl Porter

B-58A/60-1112/69—assigned to the 305th BW; disposed at MASDC (arrived 1/5/70; inventory #BQ047) by Southwestern Alloys, Tucson, AZ, on 7/15/77.

B-58A/60-1116/73—assigned to the 305th BW; destroyed 12/8/64.

USAF

Aviation News via Chris Pocock

B-58A/60-1113/70—assigned to the 305th BW; disposed at MASDC (arrived 12/16/69; inventory #BQ030) by Southwestern Alloys, Tucson, AZ, on 6/28/77.

B-58A/60-1117/74—assigned to the 305th BW; disposed at MASDC (arrived 1/14/70; inventory #BQ076) by Southwestern Alloys, Tucson, AZ, on 8/2/77.

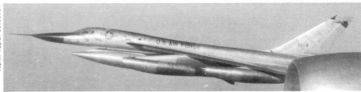

Norm Taylor collection

B-58A/60-1118/75—assigned to the 305th BW; carried pod B-182; disposed at MASDC (arrived 12/15/69; inventory #BQ028) by Southwestern Alloys, Tucson, AZ, on 6/27/77.

Jay Miller/Aerofax, Inc.

Paul Stevens

B-58A/60-1114/71—assigned to the 305th BW; during flight test at Convair, had state of Texas painted on nose; disposed at MASDC (arrived 11/17/69; inventory #BQ006) by Southwestern Alloys, Tucson, AZ, on 6/8/77.

B-58A/60-1119/76—one of the first aircraft modified for iron bomb (etc.) capability during short TDY assignment to 43rd BW; aircraft assigned to the 305th BW; nicknamed *Pink Panther* and *City of Kokomo*; destroyed 12/12/66.

L. A. Babbitt

Doug Slowiak

B-58A/60-1115/72—assigned to the 305th BW; disposed at MASDC (arrived 1/13/70; inventory #BQ071) by Southwestern Alloys, Tucson, AZ, on 7/21/77.

B-58A/60-1120/77—assigned to the 305th BW; disposed at MASDC (arrived 12/12/69; inventory #BQ025) by Southwestern Alloys, Tucson, AZ, on 6/14/77.

USAF via Jim Goodall

▲ **B-58A/60-1121/78**—assigned to the 305th BW; nicknamed *Can Do*; disposed at MASDC (arrived 12/22/69; inventory #BQ041) by Southwestern Alloys, Tucson, AZ, on 8/11/77.

Leroy Nielson via Paul Minert via Marty Isham

▲ **B-58A/60-1122/79**—assigned to the 43rd BW; disposed at MASDC (arrived 11/19/69; inventory #BQ008) by Southwestern Alloys, Tucson, AZ, on 6/3/77.

Paul Stevens via Doug Slowiak

▲ **B-58A/60-1123/80**—assigned to the 305th BW; disposed at MASDC (arrived 1/5/70; inventory #BQ048) by Southwestern Alloys, Tucson, AZ, on 8/4/77.

USAF via Douglas Robinson

▲ **B-58A/60-1124/81**—assigned to the 305th BW; disposed at MASDC (arrived 12/11/69; inventory #BQ022) by Southwestern Alloys, Tucson, AZ, on 6/14/77.

Jay Miller/Aerofax, Inc.

▲ **B-58A/60-1125/82**—assigned to the 305th BW; disposed at MASDC (arrived 12/8/69; inventory #BQ014) by Southwestern Alloys, Tucson, AZ, on 6/3/77.

▲ **B-58A/60-1126/83**—assigned to the 305th BW; disposed at MASDC (arrived 1/7/70; inventory #BQ054) by Southwestern Alloys, Tucson, AZ, on 7/13/77.

(Photo Unavailable)

▲ **B-58A/60-1127/84**—assigned to the 305th BW; disposed at MASDC (arrived 12/18/69; inventory #BQ036) by Southwestern Alloys, Tucson, AZ, on 8/12/77.

(Photo Unavailable)

▲ **B-58A/60-1128/85**—assigned to the 305th BW; destroyed on 7/22/65.

(Photo Unavailable)

▲ **B-58A/60-1129/86**—assigned to the 305th BW; disposed at MASDC (arrived 1/9/70; inventory #BQ062) by Southwestern Alloys, Tucson, AZ, on 8/15/77.

▲ **B-58A/61-2051/87**—by the AF on 12/1/61 and assigned to the 305th BW on 12/4/61; later assigned to the 43rd BW; disposed at MASDC (arrived 11/14/69; inventory #BQ005) by Southwestern Alloys, Tucson, AZ, on 6/13/77.

▲ **B-58A/61-2052/88**—assigned to the 305th BW; disposed at MASDC (arrived 1/13/70; inventory #BQ070) by Southwestern Alloys, Tucson, AZ, on 8/8/77.

▲ **B-58A/61-2053/89**—assigned to the 305th BW; disposed at MASDC (arrived 1/6/70; inventory #BQ049) by Southwestern Alloys, Tucson, AZ, on 7/28/77.

Aviation News via Chris Pocock

▲ **B-58A/61-2054/90**—assigned to the 305th BW; disposed at MASDC (arrived 11/13/69; inventory #BQ004) by Southwestern Alloys, Tucson, AZ, on 6/9/77.

USAF via Jim Goodall

▲ **B-58A/61-2055/91**—assigned to the 305th BW; disposed at MASDC (arrived 12/22/69; inventory #BQ042) by Southwestern Alloys, Tucson, AZ, on 7/22/77.

USAF via Morton Higgs

▲ **B-58A/61-2056/92**—assigned to the 305th BW; destroyed on 4/18/69.

(Photo Unavailable)

▲ **B-58A/61-2057/93**—assigned to the 305th BW; destroyed on 9/14/62.

Robert Esposito

▲ **B-58A/61-2058/94**—assigned to the 305th BW; disposed at MASDC (arrived 11/21/69; inventory #BQ010) by Southwestern Alloys, Tucson, AZ, on 6/1/77.

Aerofax, Inc. collection

▲ **B-58A/61-2059/95**—assigned to the 305th BW; flew 8,028 n. mile mission from Tokyo to London, non-stop at an average speed of 938 mph; nicknamed *Can Do* and *Greased Lightning*; statically displayed at the Strategic Aerospace Museum, Offutt AFB, Belleville, NE.

Aerofax, Inc. collection

▲ **B-58A/61-2060/96**—assigned to the 305th BW; disposed at MASDC (arrived 12/17/69; inventory #BQ033) by Southwestern Alloys, Tucson, AZ, on 8/2/77.

Aerofax, Inc. collection

▲ **B-58A/61-2061/97**—assigned to the 305th BW; destroyed 6/14/67.

(Photo Unavailable)

▲ **B-58A/61-2062/98**—assigned to the 305th BW; first B-58 to be equipped with encapsulated ejection system (ff. w/mod 3/2/62); destroyed on 4/18/68.

(Photo Unavailable)

▲ **B-58A/61-2063/99**—assigned to the 305th BW; destroyed on 8/26/63.

Robert Lawson

▲ **B-58A/61-2064/100**—assigned to the 305th BW; disposed at MASDC (arrived 1/14/70; inventory #BQ075) by Southwestern Alloys, Tucson, AZ, on 7/5/77.

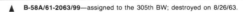

(Photo Unavailable)

▲ **B-58A/61-2065/101**—assigned to the 305th BW; destroyed 11/13/67.

USAF via Bart Cusick

▲ **B-58A/61-2066/102**—initially bailed to Convair for test work following completion; assigned to the 43rd BW; disposed at MASDC (arrived 1/7/70; inventory #BQ053) by Southwestern Alloys, Tucson, AZ, on 6/13/77.

(Photo Unavailable)

▲ **B-58A/61-2072/108**—assigned to the 305th BW; disposed at MASDC (arrived 12/12/69; inventory #BQ024) by Southwestern Alloys, Tucson, AZ, on 7/26/77.

Aerofax, Inc. collection

▲ **B-58A/61-2067/103**—assigned to the 305th BW; disposed at MASDC (arrived 1/9/70; inventory #BQ060) by Southwestern Alloys, Tucson, AZ, on 6/30/77.

Ed Yingst collection

▲ **B-58A/61-2073/109**—assigned to the 305th BW; destroyed on 4/3/69.

Doug Slowiak

▲ **B-58A/61-2068/104**—assigned to the 305th BW; nicknamed *Deputy Dog*; disposed at MASDC (arrived 12/10/69; inventory #BQ018) by Southwestern Alloys, Tucson, AZ, on 6/9/77.

Ken Buchanan collection

▲ **B-58A/61-2074/110**—assigned to the 305th BW; disposed at MASDC (arrived 11/24/69; inventory #BQ011) by Southwestern Alloys, Tucson, AZ, on 5/23/77.

Aviation News via Chris Pocock

▲ **B-58A/61-2069/105**—assigned to the 305th BW; disposed at MASDC (arrived 12/9/69; inventory #BQ016) by Southwestern Alloys, Tucson, AZ, on 5/24/77.

John Cree collection

▲ **B-58A/61-2075/111**—assigned to the 305th BW; disposed at MASDC (arrived 1/12/70; inventory #BQ066) by Southwestern Alloys, Tucson, AZ, on 7/15/77.

Robert Esposito

▲ **B-58A/61-2070/106**—assigned to the 305th BW; disposed at MASDC (arrived 1/12/70; inventory #BQ065) by Southwestern Alloys, Tucson, AZ, on 8/17/77.

Lan Lambert

▲ **B-58A/61-2076/112**—assigned to the 305th BW; disposed at MASDC (arrived 1/13/70; inventory #BQ072) by Southwestern Alloys, Tucson, AZ, on 6/16/77.

Jerry Geer via Jim Goodall

▲ **B-58A/61-2071/107**—assigned to the 305th BW; disposed at MASDC (arrived 1/15/70; inventory #BQ079) by Southwestern Alloys, Tucson, AZ, on 7/19/77.

Aviation News via Chris Pocock

▲ **B-58A/61-2077/113**—assigned to the 305th BW; disposed at MASDC (arrived 12/10/69; inventory #BQ019) by Southwestern Alloys, Tucson, AZ, on 7/26/77.

▲ B-58A/61-2078/114—accepted by the AF on 10/25/62 and delivered to 43rd BW on 10/26/62; nicknamed *Top Dawg*; disposed at MASDC (arrived 1/16/70; inventory #BQ082) by Southwestern Alloys, Tucson, AZ, on 8/5/77.

▲ B-58A/61-2079/115—accepted by the AF on 10/25/62 and delivered to the 305th BW on 10/26/62; nicknamed *The Thumper*; disposed at MASDC (arrived 12/19/69; inventory #BQ039) by Southwestern Alloys, Tucson, AZ, on 5/25/77.

▲ B-58A/61-2080/116—ff. 10/23/62; last B-58 built; accepted by the AF and delivered on 10/26/62; assigned to the 305th BW; assigned MASDC inventory #BQ050 (arrived 1/6/70) prior to being placed on static display at the Pima County Aerospace Museum, Tucson, AZ.

A note concerning the disposition of B-58's at Davis-Monthan AFB. Sealed bidding for ''B-58 aircraft carcasses'' was opened on 10/13/76 at 9:00 a.m. by the DoD Defense Supply Agency. The aircraft were sold in 8 lots of approximately 10 aircraft each. The final sale price averaged less than 2 cents per pound per airframe.

B. B-58 ACCIDENTS

The B-58's accident record was perhaps its most serious failing. Out of 116 aircraft built some 26 were destroyed before the type was removed from the active AF inventory. In addition, several aircraft, such as 55-663, were damaged seriously enough to prevent their being returned to flightworthy status.

Accident causes varied greatly. The majority occurred during the B-58's flight test and operational evaluation period, with a more reasonable attrition rate being attained late in its operational career. Many of the accidents did not need to happen, and many were not attributable to the aircraft; others were the result of mechanical or systems failures that were basically the end product of the quantum leap forward the B-58 represented.

What follows is a complete listing of all major B-58 accidents:

12/16/58, 58-1008; 38 n. miles north, northeast (Deaf Smith County) of Canon AFB, NM; accident cause was loss of control during normal flight when autotrim and ratio changer were rendered inoperative due to an electrical system malfunction; AF pilot was Maj. Richard D. Smith (fatal); AF nav/bombardier was Lt. Col. George A. Gradel (survived); AF DSO was Capt. Daniel J. Holland (survived).

5/14/59, 58-1012; at Carswell AFB, Convair facility; accident cause was fuel leak and accidental ignition; two Convair ground support people were killed.

9/16/59, 58-1017; at Carswell AFB, TX; accident cause was tire failure during takeoff roll and associated unsuccessful aborted takeoff; AF pilot was Maj. Kenneth K. Lewis (survived); AF nav/bombardier was Maj. Willis A. Edgcomb (fatal); AF DSO was Capt. Lee N. Barnett (fatal).

10/27/59, 55-669; 7 n. miles west of Hattiesburg, Larmar County, MS; accident cause was loss of control during normal flight; Convair pilot was Everett L. Wheeler (survived); Convair flight engineer was Michael F. Keller (survived); and Convair flight engineer was Harry N. Blosser (fatal).

11/7/59, 55-664; 25 n. miles southeast of Lawton, OK; accident cause was never absolutely established, but the official accident report noted ''design deficiency in that the directional restoring moments on the aircraft were not adequate for the test conditions''; Convair pilot was Raymond Fitzgerald (fatal); Convair flight engineer was Donald A. Siedhof (fatal); there was no third crew member as the aft compartment was utilized for test instrumentation.

4/22/60, 58-1023; 29 n. miles northwest of Ogden, Weber County, UT; accident cause was loss of control during normal flight due to Mach/airspeed/air data system failure; Convair pilot was Ray E. Tenhoff (fatal); Convair flight test engineer was Walter Simon (fatal); Convair flight test engineer was Kenneth G. Timpson (survived).

6/4/60, 55-667; 26 n. miles east, southeast of Lubbock, Lubbock County, TX; accident cause was loss of control in normal flight due to atmospheric conditions and subsequent abandonment of aircraft in supersonic flight regime; Convair pilot was Jack L. Baldridge (fatal); Convair flight engineer was Hugh D. Coleman (fatal); Convair flight engineer was Charles T. Jones (fatal).

6/3/61, 59-2451; 5 n. miles east, northeast of LeBourget Airport, Paris, France; accident cause was attempted low-altitude aerobatic flight; AF pilot was Maj. Elmer E. Murphy (fatal); AF nav/bombardier was Maj. Eugene F. Moses (fatal); AF DSO was 1st Lt. David F. Dickerson (fatal).

12/27/61, 58-1020; 4.3 n. miles northeast of Cole Camp, MO; accident cause was engine flameout due to ruptured fuel manifold during normal flight; AF pilot was Capt. Clarence L. Montgomery (survived); AF nav/bombardier was Capt. Louis N. Hughes (survived); AF DSO was Capt. John M. Roddy (survived).

2/15/62, 59-2447; 38 n. miles east of Lawton, OK; accident cause was loss of aircraft control due to Mach and airspeed system malfunction during normal flight; AF pilot was Maj. John C. Irving (survived); AF nav/bombardier was Capt. John C. Fuller (survived); AF DSO was Capt. Donald J. Avallon (survived).

3/5/62, 59-2459; at Carswell AFB, TX; accident cause was mechanical failure of the flight control system; AF pilot was Capt. Robert E. Harter (fatal); AF nav/bombardier was Capt. Jack D. V. Jones (fatal); AF DSO was 1st Lt. James T. McKenzie (fatal).

4/12/62, 59-2462; near Bunker Hill AFB, IN; accident cause was control system failure shortly after takeoff; AF pilot was Capt. William E. Hale (survived); AF nav/bombardier was Capt. Duane D. Dickey, Jr. (fatal); AF DSO was 1st Lt. George P. O'Connor (survived).

9/14/62, 61-2057; 2 n. miles northeast of Butlerville, Jennings County, IN; accident cause was structural break-up caused by control system failure during normal flight; AF pilot was Lt. Col. John J. Trevisani (fatal); nav/bombardier was Capt. Arthur I. Freed (fatal); AF DSO was Capt. Reinardo P. Moure (fatal).

8/26/63, 61-2063; near Bunker Hill AFB, IN; accident cause was a hard landing; AF pilot was Maj. William E. Brandt (survived); AF nav/bombardier was Maj. William L. Berry (fatal); AF DSO was Capt. William M. Bergdoll (fatal).

The charred remains of B-58A, 59-2451, shortly after its catastrophic accident during the Paris Airshow on June 3, 1961. All three crew members were fatally injured.

Barely four years after the demise of 59-3451, 59-2443 met a similar fate at the Paris Airshow when it was totally destroyed during a landing attempt. Miraculously two of its crew members survived.

12/8/64, 60-1116; near Bunker Hill AFB, IN; accident cause was collapse of landing gear during taxi; AF pilot was Capt. Leary J. Johnson (survived); AF nav/bombardier was Capt. Manual Cervantes, Jr. (fatal); AF DSO was Capt. Roger L. Hall (survived).

5/20/65, 58-1016; near Little Rock AFB, AR; accident cause was a hard landing; AF pilot was Capt. Ralph L. Semann (survived); AF nav/bombardier was Capt. Steve Kichler, Jr. (fatal); AF DSO was 1st Lt. Ronald T. Smetek (survived).

6/15/65, 59-2443; at LeBourget Airport, Paris, France; accident cause was undershooting during final approach to the runway; AF pilot was Lt. Col. Charles D. Tubbs (fatal); AF nav/bombardier was Maj. Harold M. Covington (survived); AF DSO was Maj. Vincent S. Karaba (survived).

7/22/65, 60-1128; at Bunker Hill AFB, IN; accident cause was departure of aircraft from runway during landing roll; AF pilot was Capt. John P. Noonan (survived); AF nav/bombardier was Capt. Lawrence C. Arundel (survived); AF DSO was 1st Lt. Kenneth Leatherbarrow (survived).

12/12/66, 60-1119; 1.3 n. miles west of McKinney, Lincoln County, KY; accident cause was collision with the ground during a low level bomb run; AF pilot was Maj. Richard F. Blakeslee (fatal); AF nav/bombardier was Capt. Floyd E. Acker (fatal); AF DSO was Capt. Clarence D. Lunt (fatal).

2/23/67, 59-2454; at Little Rock AFB, AR; accident cause was structural failure of the aircraft forward fuselage section while taxiing; AF pilot was Lt. Col. Bruce A. Ellis (survived); AF nav/bombardier was Capt. Robert A. Hendrickson (survived); AF DSO was Capt. Arlen W. Rohl (survived). This aircraft was eventually repaired and returned to service.

6/14/67, 61-2061; 6 n. miles south, southwest of Darrozett, Lipscombe County, TX; accident cause was abandonment of aircraft in flight due to minor weather damage and pilot ejection seat anomaly; AF pilot was Maj. Clinton R. Brisendine (survived); AF nav/bombardier was Capt. William R. Bennett (fatal); AF DSO was Capt. Gary M. Cecchett (survived).

11/13/67, 61-2065; 3 n. miles southwest of Bunker Hill AFB, IN; accident cause was loss of control during initial climb after takeoff; AF pilot was Maj. Galen A. Dultmeier (fatal); AF nav/bombardier was Capt. Ronald E. Schmidt (fatal); AF DSO was Capt. Leroy J. Hanson (fatal).

4/18/68, 61-2062; at Bunker Hill AFB, IN; accident cause was loss of control due to mechanical failure shortly after takeoff; AF pilot was Maj. Donald N. Close (fatal); AF nav/bombardier was Maj. Eugene R. Harrington (fatal); AF DSO was Capt. Johnny D. Banks (fatal).

7/16/68, 59-2437; at Little Rock AFB, AR; accident cause was materiel failure in that the righthand main landing gear outer cylinder failed catastrophically at, or near brake release prior to takeoff causing the gear to collapse during landing; AF pilot was Maj. George R. Tate (survived); AF nav/bombardier was Capt. Ray G. Walters (survived); AF DSO was Capt. Francis Mosson (survived).

4/3/69, 61-2073; ½ mile east of Rokeby, Lancaster County, NE; accident cause was systems failure during normal flight; AF pilot was Capt. Thomas G. Hogg (survived); AF nav/bombardier was Capt. James R. McElvain (survived); AF DSO was Capt. Richard R. Nauman (survived).

4/18/69, 61-2056; 7 n. miles north, northwest of Danville, Vamillion County, IL; accident cause was abandonment of aircraft following suspected system anomalies; AF pilot was Maj. Press McCallum, Jr. (survived); AF nav/bombardier was Capt. Robert A. Graf (survived); AF DSO was Maj. Victor I. Mayer (survived).

A main landing gear strut failure at Little Rock AFB, AR on July 16, 1968, led to the demise of 59-2437. Though the aircraft was not totally destroyed, it was permanently grounded.

The c.g. location of the B-58 was critical at all times, even when the aircraft was sitting statically. B-58A, 60-1118, demonstrates the end result of not considering fuel location with the pod removed.

Non-tire related landing gear problems were relatively rare with the B-58, but when they occurred, they were invariably serious. A bogie failure on the left main gear of B-58A, 58-1018, following takeoff, on September 19, 1961, caused this accident at Edwards AFB. Thanks to excellent piloting technique, this aircraft returned to earth with only minor damage and was quickly repaired to fly again another day.

C. SURVIVING B-58'S

There are a total of 8 B-58's extant as of this writing. These aircraft are:

▲ **55-663**—As TB-58A permanently displayed at the entrance to Grissom AFB, IN. Aircraft is mounted on concrete blocks.

▲ **59-2437**—As B-58A the standing remains of this aircraft have been sitting derelict at Little Rock AFB for some fifteen years. It has been rumored, however, that the airframe has been moved to Barkesdale AFB, LA for future restoration and eventual display in the new museum there.

▲ **55-665**—As B-58A last reported still to be sitting statically on the Edwards AFB, CA photo test range. Discussions have been conducted concerning the possibility of refurbishing this aircraft for permanent display in a proposed Edwards AFB history museum. Condition is extremely poor.

▲ **59-2458**—As B-58A permanently displayed at the United States Air Force Museum, Wright-Patterson AFB, OH. This aircraft has recently been completely refurbished for display and is now unquestionably the finest surviving *Hustler* specimen.

▲ **55-666**—As B-58A permanently displayed at the entrance to Chanute AFB, IL and last noted to be wearing a spurious serial number (61-2059).

▲ **61-2059**—As B-58A permanently displayed at the Strategic Aerospace Museum, Offutt AFB, NE.

▲ **55-668**—As TB-58A permanently displayed in the Southwest Aerospace Museum near the entrance to the General Dynamics Fort Worth, TX plant. Wings, landing gear, and empennage section had to be removed to permit this aircraft to be transported from Davis-Monthan AFB to Fort Worth via Lockheed C-5A. It has since been reassembled.

▲ **61-2080**—As B-58A permanently displayed at the Pima County Aerospace Museum, next to Davis-Monthan AFB, Tucson, AZ.

D. B-58 MARKINGS AND MODELS

With the exception of the prototypes, the B-58 was not a particularly colorful aircraft. Markings were fairly standard for the late-1950's and 1960 period, and all operational aircraft were bare metal with a black (sometimes gloss, sometimes flat) nose radome. More detailed markings data are shown in the accompanying drawings and elsewhere in this volume, but it is important to note all stenciling was done in red, yellow, orange-yellow, blue, white or black.

The question of the camouflaged B-58 program has been one that has been of major interest to this author for many years. Having now interviewed many pilots, program directors, SAC commanders, maintenance supervisors, line chiefs, and a large number of SAC and AF historians, the author has come to the firm conclusion that the closest the B-58A ever came to camouflage paint was the drawing in T.O. 1-1-4 (see accompanying illustration). All B-58A flight crews involved in tactical use of the aircraft (the ones scheduled for camouflage paint) have stated absolutely that no aircraft, to their knowledge was ever painted in camouflage paint of any kind.

There have been several B-58 models, in kit form, commercially available over the years. The following list is believed to include all kits manufactured to date:

Aurora	1/91 scale	Comet	1/91 scale	Monogram	1/121 scale
Aurora	1/175 scale	Heller	1/93 scale	Monogram	1/48 scale
Aurora	1/76 scale	Italaerei	1/72 scale	Revell	1/94 scale
Comet	1/175 scale	Lindbergh	1/64 scale	Testor	1/72 scale

The only known decal sheet to date is Microscale's 72-0470.

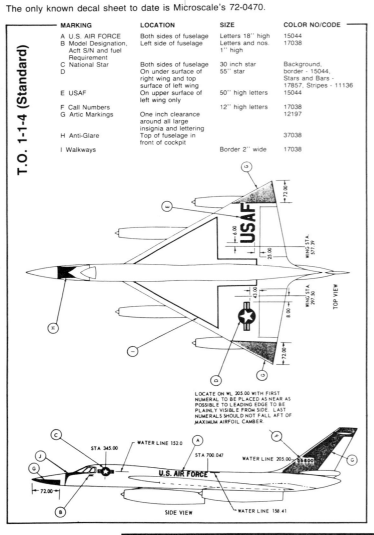

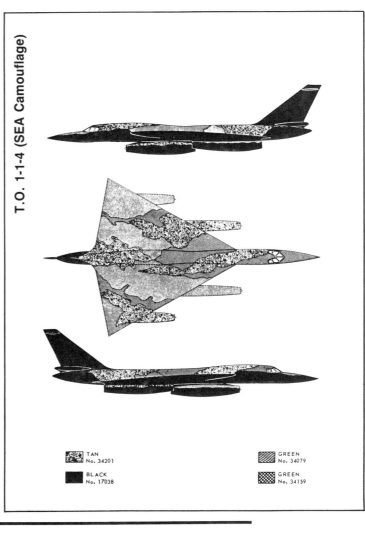

E. ABBREVIATIONS

AF—Air Force
AFB—Air Force Base
AFLC—Air Force Logistics Command
AFSC—Air Force Systems Command
AMC—Air Materiel Command
ARDC—Air Research and Development Command
ASD—Aeronautical Systems Division
ATC—Air Training Command
CCTS—Combat Crew Training School
CEP—Circular Error Probable
CFE—Contractor Furnished Equipment
CPFF—Cost Plus Fixed Fee
DoD—Department of Defense
DSO—Defensive Systems Operator

ECM—Electronic Countermeasures
EWO—Emergency War Order
FY—Fiscal Year
GEBO—General Bomber (Study)
GFE—Government Furnished Equipment
GOR—General Operational Requirement
GSE—Ground Support Equipment
ILS—Instrument Landing System
MAC—Military Airlift Command
MASDC—Military Aircraft Storage and Disposition Center
MITO—Minimum Interval Takeoff
NACA—National Advisory Committee for Aeronautics
NASA—National Aeronautics and Space Administration
n.m.—nautical miles

OT&E—Operational Test and Evaluation
R & D—Research and Development
RDT&E—Research, Development, Testing, and Evaluation
SAAMA—San Antonio Air Materiel Area
SOR—Specific Operational Requirement
SSB/HF—Single Side Band/High Frequency
TAC—Tactical Air Command
TACAN—Tactical Air Navigation
TCP—Two-Component Pod
WADC—Wright Air Development Center
WADD—Wright Air Development Division
WSO—Weapon System Operator/Officer
WSPO—Weapon System Project Office

F. Major Subcontractors

The following is a complete listing of all major subcontractors utilized by Convair during the course of the B-58 production program: Advance Industries; Air Technology Corp.; Bendix Pacific Division of Bendix Corp.; Bendix Radio Division of Bendix Corp.; Eclipse-Pioneer Division of Bendix Corp.; Emerson Electric Manufacturing Co.; Federal Telephone and Radio Co.; International Telephone and Telegraph, Industrial Products Division; Link Division of General Precision, Inc.; Magnavox Co.; Menasco Manufacturing Co.; Hamilton Standard Division of United Aircraft; Hughes Aircraft Co.; Melpar, Inc.; Minneapolis-Honeywell Regulator Co.; Motorola, Inc.; Raytheon Co.; Reflectone Electronics; Sperry Gyroscope Co.; Stanley Aviation, Corp.; Sylvania Electronics Systems; Westinghouse Electric Corp.

Bibliography: Please note that the bibliographical technique used by the author is not necessarily conventional; the arrangement and information are for the reader's convenience only.

Books (by author, title, publisher, publisher's location, publication date, and number of pages):

AFSC/ASD, **Development of Airborne Armament 1910-61, Vol. II, AFSC/ASD,** 1961, page length per volume varies.
Arkin, Cochran, and Hoenig, **Nuclear Weapons Databook, Vol. 1, U. S. Nuclear Forces and Capabilities,** Natural Resources Defense Council, Inc., 1984, 340p.
Blanchard, Chinnery, and Swann, **MASDC, Davis-Monthan AFB, Arizona,** Aviation Press, London, 1983, 256p.
Boyne, **Boeing B-52, A Documentary History,** Jane's Publishing Company, London, England, 1981, 160p.
deVries, **Taube, Dove of War,** Historical Aviation Album, Temple City, CA, 1978, 84p.
Convair, **B-58 Manufacturing Plan, Vol. 1, Project Concept,** Convair, 1/60, 46p.
Convair, **B-58 Manufacturing Plan, Vol. 3, Wing and Elevons,** Convair, 9/58, 62p.
Convair, **B-58 Manufacturing Plan, Vol. 4, Free Fall Bomb Pod,** 9/58, 56p.
Convair, **Contractual Technical Compliance Inspection TB-58A No. 1,** Convair, 1960, 37p.
Convair, **The Convair B-58 Airplane, Pilot Indoctrination,** Convair, 1956, 56p.
Convair, **TB-58A Cockpit Mock-Up Review,** Convair, 12/3/59, 28p.
Eastman, **Mach II, A Case Study of the J79 Engine,** OCAMA, USAF, 1961, 114p.
Ethell, **Komet, The Messerschmitt Me-163,** Sky Books Press, NY, 1978, 160p.
General Dynamics, **Dynamic America,** Doubleday & Company, NY, 1958, 426p.
General Electric, **J79 Flight Line Reference,** General Electric, Ohio, 1961, ?p.
Green, **The World's Fighting Planes,** Doubleday, NY, 1964, 216p.
Gunston, **Bombers of the West,** Charles Scribner's Sons, NY, 1973, 283p.
Hanniball, **Aircraft, Engines, and Airmen,** The Scarecrow Press, Inc., NJ, 1972, 825p.
Higham and Siddall, **Flying Combat Aircraft of the USAAF-USAF, Vol. 1,** Iowa State University Press, Ames, IA, 1978, 159p.
Horten and Selinger, **Nurflugel,** H. Weishaupt Verlag, Germany, 1983, 240.
Kens and Nowarra, **Die Deutschen Flugzeuge,** 1933-1945, J. F. Lehmanns Verlag, Germany, 1977, 1,081p.
Lasby, **Project Paperclip, German Scientists and the Cold War,** Atheneum, NY, 1971, 338p.
Lippisch, **Ein Dreieck Fliegt,** Motorbuch Verlag, Germany, 1976, 142p.
Mingos (editor), **The Aircraft Yearbook,** 1947, Lanciar Publishers, Inc., NY, 1947, 511p.
National Aeronautics Association, **World and United States Aviation and Space Records,** National Aeronautics Association, Washington, D.C., 1983, 369p.
Pace, **Valkyrie, North American XB-70A,** Aero Publishers, Inc., Fallbrook, CA, 1984, 104p.
Peacock, **Convair B-58 Hustler and Variants,** Aviation News, England, 1978, 18p.
Robinson, **The B-58 Hustler,** Arco Publishing, NY, 1967, 63p.
SAC Office of History, **Development of Strategic Air Command,** 1946-1976, ?, 1976, 186p.
San Antonio Air Logistics Office of History, **A Pictorial History of Kelly AFB, 1917-1980,** USGPO, 1984, 477p.
Shortal, **A New Dimension, Wallops Island Flight Test Range, The First Fifteen Years,** USGPO, Washington, D.C., 1978, 774p.
Swanborough and Bowers, **United States Military Aircraft Since 1908,** Putnam & Company, London, England, 1971, 675p.
Taylor (editor), **Jane's All the World's Aircraft** (various editions 1955-1970), Sampson Low/Jane's Publishing, London, England, page length per volume varies.
Thomas, **History of the Development of the B-58 Bomber, Vols. 1-6,** ASD/USAF, 1965, page length per volume varies.
USAF/Convair, **Electrical Systems, USAF B-58A and TB-58A Aircraft,** ?, 1960, ?p.
USAF/Convair, **Exterior Markings, B/TB-58A Aircraft,** T.O. 1B-58-8, ?, 1965, ?p.
USAF/Convair, **Flight Manual B-58A, USAF Series Aircraft,** T.O. 1B-58A-1, ?, 1965, ?p.
USAF/Convair, **Ground Handling, Servicing, and Lubrication USAF Series B-58A and TB-58A Aircraft,** T.O. 1B-58A-2-3, ?, 1963, ?p.
USAF/Convair, **Handbook Maintenance Instructions, Fuel System, USAF Series YB/RB-58A Aircraft,** USAF/Convair T.O., 1B-58A-2-7, ?, 1958, ?p.
USAF/Convair, **Interim Flight Manual, YB/RB-58A Aircraft,** FOIB Report GHB-15-1, ?, 1958, ?p.
USAF/Convair, **Partial Flight Manual TB-58A, USAF Series Aircraft,** T.O. 1B-58(T)A-1, ?, 1965, ?p.
USAF/Convair, **Pneudraulics, USAF Series YB/RB-58A Aircraft,** ?, 1958, ?p.
USAF/Convair, **Technical Manual General Airplane USAF Series B-58A and TB-58A Aircraft,** ?, 1962, ?p.
Wilkinson, **Aircraft Engines of the World,** 1959/60, Wilkinson, 1959, 320p.
Unknown, **43rd Bombardment Wing, Medium,** Carswell AFB, 1964, ?p.

Magazines (by date, article, author):

Aerospace Historian
6/73, ''The Hustler's Record'', Test
Air Enthusiast Quarterly
#2 issue, ''Convair's Delta Alpha'', Hallion
Air Force Magazine
2/64, ''Greased Lightning'', Smith
Air Progress
5-6/66, ''Faulty Nose Landing Gear....''
Air University Review
9-10/80, ''To Acquire Strategic Bombers, The Case of the B-58 Hustler'', Hall
11-12/81, '' The B-58 Bomber, Requiem For A Welterweight'', Hall
?, ''The B-58'', Hirsch

The Airman
10/61, ''Hustler'', Karten
American Aviation
7/14/58, ''Beer and Pretzels....CFAE and GFAE'', Oswald
7/29/57, ''B-58 Owes Performance to Materials, Design Breakthroughs'', Bentz
Aviation Week & Space Technology
4/11/49, ''Delta Wing Prototype Flies'', staff
4/16/56, ''Convair Gives First B-58 Engine Details'', staff
6/4/56, ''B-58 Foreshadows Mach 2 Powerplant'', Anderton
9/10/56, ''B-58 Hustler'', staff
9/24/56, ''Flight Characteristics Of B-58 Simulated With Modified F-94'', staff
11/5/56, ''Hustler May Make First Flight This Week'', staff
12/10/56, ''Small Tire For B-58 Supports Heavy Load'', staff
12/17/56, ''B-58 Hustler Packs A Big Punch In A Small Frame'', Anderton
12/31/56, ''How Hustler Handles Its Payload'', staff
1/7/57, ''B-58 On Takeoff'', staff
1/14/57, ''Principles of B-58 Inlet Control System Revealed'', Cushman
2/25/57, ''B-58's Versatile Pod Concept'', staff
5/20/57, ''B-58 Flights Taped By New Data System'', staff
5/27/57, ''B-58 Simulator Program Aided Development of Control System'', staff
6/24/57, ''Versatile System Cools B-58'', staff
7/15/57, ''Irvine Details B-58 Design Advances'', Lewis
7/29/57, ''B-58 Makes Extensive Use Of Honeycomb'', staff
8/17/57, ''Ejection From B-58 Tested'', staff
7/28/58, ''B-58 Hustler Drops Detachable Pod On New Mexico Range'', staff
8/4/58, ''B-58 To Be Tested Under New Program'', staff
9/15/58, ''Support Gear Taylored to B-58 Systems'', staff
12/15/58, ''First Details of B-58's Air Conditioner'', Tally
11/14/60, ''B-58A Proposed For Transport Research'', staff
12/28/64, ''Laurels for 1964'', Hotz
B-58 Hustler News
10/61, ''Non-Frangible Wheels'', Warynick
Combat Crew
6/60, ''The Hustling Hustler'', Johnson
11/63, ''First Impressions Of A Hustler Driver'', Soloman
11/64, ''Pilot Of The Month'', ?
12/64, ''How Slow And Still Go'', Potts
Flight/Flight International
9/30/55, ''The Area Rule'', Technical Editor
Interavia
2/60, ''US Missiles Latest Pictures'', ?
Journal Of The Royal Aeronautical Society
11/62, ''Flight Characteristics of the B-58 Mach 2 Bomber'', Erickson
Koku-Fan
11/61, Photo essay on Paris Airshow, ?
1/62, Photo essay on B-58, ?
The Navigator
Winter/58, ''Hyperhoming Hustler'', Bright
Winter/65, ''Recipe and Receipt'', Weeks
Winter-Spring/65, ''Tokyo to London 8 Hours 35 Minutes'', Barrett
?, ''Navigating The B-58'', Polhemus
Popular Science
8/61, ''World's Fastest Bomber'', Griswold
7/62, ''The Back-Seat Driver Of The B-58'', Griswold
Pri-Fly
#45?, ''Convair's Super Hustler'', Cully
Readers Digest
4/64, ''The Bomb Carrier Nobody Can Stop'', Drake
SETP Cockpit
7-8-9/76, ''Test Flight—The Arena Of Truth'', Tate
True
?, ''B-58 The Incredible Hustler'', Harvey

Newspapers (by date, newspaper, article, author):

11/12/56, Houston Chronicle, ''First US Supersonic Bomber Flies 38 Minutes'', staff
4/57, Wingspread, ''Hustler Hustled In Bomb Bay Of B-36'', staff
4/19/57, Houston Chronicle, ''Hot New Jet Bomber Allowing Cutbacks In B-52 Production'', staff
7/11/57, Houston Post, ''Supersonic B-58 Publicly Unveiled'', staff
11/29/57, Atomic Flyer, ''Hustler Arrives For Pod Drop Test'', staff
12/28/58, Houston Chronicle, ''US To Cut B-58 Production'', staff
9/17/59, Fort Worth Star-Telegram, ''Crash of Hustler Third Since Production Start'', staff
11/8/59, ?, ''B-58 Cracks Sound Barrier, Explodes; 2 Die'', staff
11/11/59, Fort Worth Star-Telegram, ''Go Little Joe'', staff
12/2/59, Houston Chronicle, ''First Operational B-58 Accepted By Air Force'', staff
12/20/59, Houston Chronicle, ''Pilots Group Blasts FAA For Jet Test'', staff
3/7/60, Wall Street Journal, ''Soviet Effort to Build Supersonic Transport Spurs Trial of B-58 As Passenger Craft'', Kraar

5/27/61, Houston Post, "NY-Paris Trip Takes 3 Hours 20 Min.", staff
10/11/60, Wall Street Journal, "Air Force Plans To Cut Back, End B-58 Program", staff
8/64, ?, "First Hustler Arrives", Blunk
10/9/64, Hughes News, "Unveiled. . .A New Public Defender", staff
10/12/67, Little Rock AFB Air Scoop, "What It Takes To Launch A TB-58", staff
11/14/67, ?, "B-58 Crew Presumed Dead", staff
11/30/67, Little Rock AFB Air Scoop, "CCTS Turns Above Average Airmen Into Mach 2 Masters", staff
1/23/69, ?, "Phaseout of B-58s Rescinded", staff
10/28/69, ?, "Bakalar Air Force Base To Be Closed; State To Lose B-58s, Fighters In Cutback", staff
10/28/69, ?, "Military Cut Affects Air Base And Arsenal", staff
10/30/69, ?, "Scrapping of Grissom B-58s Will Reduce Personnel, Cost", staff
11/1/69, ?, "Hustler Bows Out Without Act In Anger", staff
11/6/69, Fort Worth Star-Telegram, "Last B-58 Plane To Leave Plant Friday Under Phase-Out Plan", staff
11/6/69, Little Rock AFB Air Scoop, "First B-58 Withdraws From USAF Inventory," staff
1/16/70, Little Rock AFB Air Scoop, "43rd Bids Adieu To B-58, KC-135", staff
2/6/70, Little Rock AFB Air Scoop, "43rd To Be Reactivated", staff
?, ?, "Crew Safe After B-58 Emergency", staff
?, ?, "Ballinger-Sweetwater Line Due For B-58 Sonic Booming", staff
?, ?, "Entire Fleet of B-58 Planes To Be Scrapped", staff

Of special note is the old in-house Convair publication known as *Convairiety* (now called *GD World*); almost every issue examined by the author, covering the key B-58 years from 1955 through 1963, contained significant historical data. Though there are simply too many issues to list here, *Convairiety* is highly recommended for a more detailed account of many of the events noted in this book.

Miscellaneous References:

"Actual Weight And Balance Report For B-58A (Bomber Airplane)", Convair, 5/1/61.
"B-58 Capsule And Status Review", ?, 10/5/61.
"B-58 Human Factors And Crew Evaluation, Convair, ?.
"B-58 Major Flight Accidents", Air Force Inspection and Safety Center, Norton AFB, CA.
"B-58 Official World Records And Trophies", Convair, 2/3/69.
"B-58A Flight Crew Air Refueling Procedures With KC-135", USAF, 8/1/66.
"Bleriot Speed Trophy", Convair, ?.
"Brief Description of B-58 Manual Control System", Convair, ?.
"Characteristics Summary, Bomber (Intercontinental XB-58), USAF 10/29/53.
"Characteristics Summary, Bomber (Version I) MX-1626", 7/18/51.
"Characteristics Summary, Bomber (Version II) XB-58", USAF, 8/12/53.
"Chronology Of First Supersonic Bomber—B-58", Convair, 1965.
"Compte-Rendu d'Accident", Airport De Paris, 6/12/61.
"Compte-Rendu d'Accident Mortel Survenu Aun Avion Militaire De L'USAF", Airport De Paris, 6/29/61.
"Convair's B-58", Convair, 3/1/57, 109p.
"Design Features Of The B-58", Davis, Convair, 7/10/57.
"Escape Capsule", Convair, ?.
"Evaluation Of TB-58 Circling And Sidestep Maneuvers", Calloway and Parr, DOT/FAA, 10/64, 27p.
"Fuel System (B-58 and TB-58A), T.O. TB-58A-2-1", USAF, ?.
"Historical Data On Aircraft Developed But Not Produced, 1945-Present", USAF/AMC, 3/57.
"History of SAC Reconniassance", Jan.-June, 1965, SAC.
"History of Super Hustler", Convair.
"J79-5A and -5B Engine Operating Limits", ?.
"KC-135 Boom Operational Limits", ?.
"Mackay Trophy", Convair, ?.
"Main Landing Gear (B-58A and TB-58A), T.O. 1B-58A-2-8", ?.
"Nuclear Armament, Its Acquisition, Control, And Application To Manned Interceptors, 1951-1963", Ray/ADC, ?.
"Reasons And Background Leading Up To The Planning And Scheduling Of This Test On Airplane #5 (Investigation Item #7)", Convair 11/14/59.
"Request for Homologation World 'Class' Record FAI Closed Course New York/Paris, France", National Aeronautics Association, 5/26/61.
"Significant Dates In The B-58 Hustler Program", Convair, 11/11/69.
"Standard Aircraft Characteristics, B-58A", USAF, 11/64.
"Standard Aircraft Characteristics, XB-58", USAF, 10/29/53.
"Supplemental Flight Manual B-58A, T.O. 1B-58A-1A", USAF/Convair, 2/7/64.
"Table of General Limitations B/RB-58 Test Airplanes", Convair, 10/29/59.
"Transmittal Copy Of Ames Memorandum Regarding Proposed Tests Of An Advanced Version Of The B-58 In The Ames Unitary Tunnel", NACA, 5/3/57.
"The 43rd Bomb Wing", USAF, ?.
"The Quest For An Advanced Manned Strategic Bomber, USAF Plans And Policies, 1961-1966", USAF Historical Division, Liaison Office, Nalty, 8/66, 60p.
"The Thompson Trophy", Convair, ?.
"Trans Atlantic Speed Dash", Convair, ?.
"Two Component Pod", Convair, ?.
"Visit Of Ira H. Abbott To WADC In Connection With Performance Predictions For The B-58 Airplane", NACA, 3/2/55.
"Weapon System Management And The B-58", Esenwein, Convair, 7/10/57.

Videos and Films:

Video—A.R.P. Company's Video Research Division (Post Office Box 4617, North Hollywood, CA 91607) "B-58 Round-Up" (includes "Bendix Trophy", "Champion of Champions", "Tall Man Five-Five", "Low Altitude Bombing", and "Bleriot Trophy") covers most of the more important Convair public relations department B-58 films. A second volume entitled "B-58 Volume Two" (includes "B-58 First Flight", "Hustler Capabilities", "B-58 MITO", "First Trainer B-58", "B-58 Landing Study", "Escape and Survive", and "Kitty Hawk for the Escape Capsule") has also recently been released and covers many of the B-58's historically significant program milestones and developments. Both titles are available from ARP direct.

Film—"ALBM Report No. 1", Convair, 5/11/59
"ALBM Report No. 2", Convair, ?.

Interviews/Correspondence With:

David Anderton   Frank Davis   Charles Harrison
Russell Blair   Vinko Dolson   Victor Mayer
Churchill Boger, Jr.   Jim Eastham   Vincent Murone
Adolph Burstein   B. A. Erickson   Bill Reeter
Dick Campbell   Earl Guthrie   Dan Sweeney

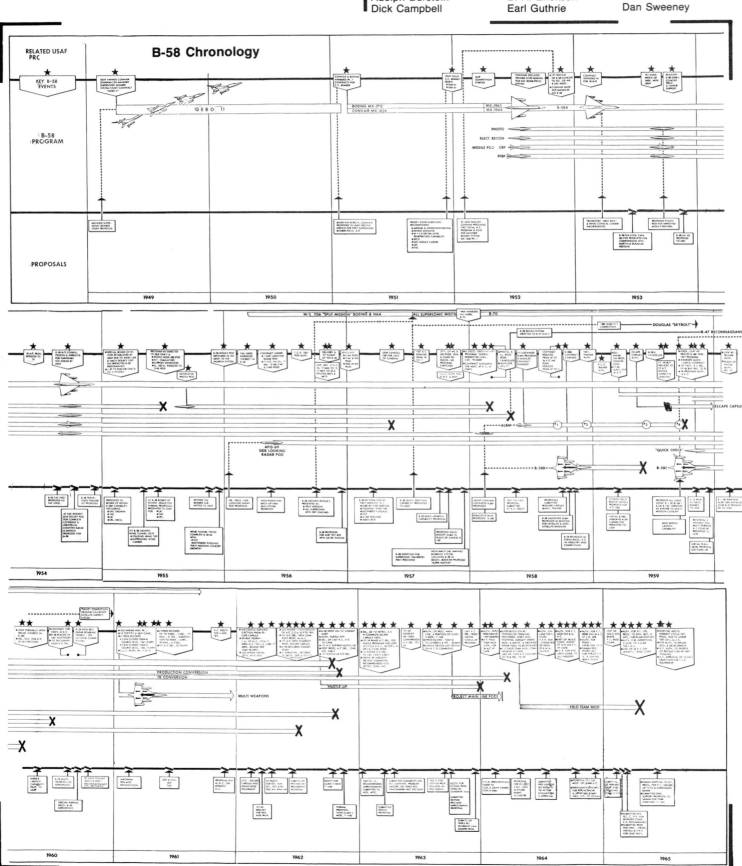

B-58 Chronology

Index